Praise for
For Social Betterment

'*For Social Betterment* explores, for the first time, both the foundations of social work education in Australia and the influences and influencers on social work as an emerging profession. The book is a compellingly written profile of how social work education moved beyond its voluntary framework, drawing on approaches from the UK and the US to develop policy and practice across health, education, criminal justice and public welfare to improve the lives of individuals and families. The book carefully documents the dissemination of social work ideas and values, and the contributions to social change that continue still. It is a remarkable history of the ideas and influences that shaped the emergence of social work education and practice in Australia.'

Rosemary Sheehan
Professor, Department of Social Work, Monash University

'What a generous tour de force of a book. Sixty years of social work history are collated, illustrated and analysed in a readable and accessible style. British and American influences were prominent in the early days, but the stories of social work pioneers in and from Australia are covered here by Jane Miller with sensitivity. Other nations, too, will have much to learn from this book in a sort of 'how to' build up their own profession's histories. And for those with an eye to the future, this book ends with a tantalising set of research questions for future historians to explore.'

Jill Manthorpe
Professor Emerita of Social Work, King's College London

'Richly detailed, broad in scope and eminently readable, Dr Miller's latest work provides a superb contribution to the history and development of professional social work practice and education in Australia. She presents a compelling account of the "fight for standards" in building a professional identity and the extent to which Australian social work was able to benefit by incorporating best practices drawn from American and British experience.'

Bill O'Reilly
Former President,
Columbia University School of Social Work Alumni

SOCIAL WORK
EDUCATION
IN AUSTRALIA

JANE MILLER

Published by Monash University Publishing
Matheson Library Annexe
40 Exhibition Walk
Monash University
Clayton, Victoria 3800, Australia
publishing.monash.edu

Monash University Publishing: the discussion starts here

Jane Miller © Copyright 2024
Jane Miller asserts her right to be known as the author of this work.

All rights reserved. Apart from any uses permitted by Australia's *Copyright Act 1968*, no part of this book may be reproduced by any process without prior written permission from the copyright owners. Enquiries should be directed to the publisher.

For Social Betterment: Social Work Education in Australia
ISBN: 9781922979438 (paperback)
ISBN: 9781922979445 (PDF)
ISBN: 9781922979452 (epub)

A catalogue record for this book is available from the National Library of Australia

Design by Les Thomas
Typesetting by Jo Mullins
Author photograph by Laurie Nichols

Cover image: Social worker in Fitzroy backyard 1963. Reproduced courtesy of the Brotherhood of St Laurence and the Fitzroy Local History Collection.

Printed in Australia by Griffin Press

All proceeds from the sale of this book will go to the Len Tierney Social Work Travelling Award of the School of Social Work, University of Melbourne

Contents

Foreword vii

Introduction: Social Work – A New Concept in 1929 Australia ... 1

1   The Emergence of Social Work in Britain and the US 15
2   Precursors of Social Work in Victoria 38
3   Australia's First Social Work Courses 57
4   Victoria's First General Social Work Course 73
5   International and National Opinion Leaders and Networks 93
6   Jocelyn Hyslop: A Public Intellectual 106
7   Consolidating the Course, 1945–1960 124
8   Winning and Losing: The Hoban Years 143
9   The Post-war Search for Overseas Expertise 164
10 A United Australian Profession 189
11 Changing Themes in Social Work 203

Appendices 213

    Appendix 1: Milestones in international social work 213
    Appendix 2: Milestones in Australian social work 223
    Appendix 3: The road to a unified profession in the US and the UK 240
    Appendix 4: Establishment of Australian social work education, 1929–1942 242
    Appendix 5: Georgina Sweet's letters regarding Town Hall meeting to establish general social work education, 25 April 1931 244
    Appendix 6: Guest list for official welcome to Jocelyn Hyslop, held at the Lyceum Club, Melbourne, 7 December 1934 247
    Appendix 7: Strengthening of Victoria's Board of Social Studies curriculum following commencement of Jocelyn Hyslop in 1934 248

Appendix 8: Snapshots of Victoria's Board of Social Studies over time, showing gradual change of composition 250

Appendix 9: Organisations represented on the Victorian Council for Social Training, 1937–1938 254

Appendix 10: Prospectus for the subject 'Modern political institutions', University of Melbourne, c. 1938 256

Appendix 11: Two-year Diploma of Social Studies, University of Melbourne, 1942 257

Appendix 12: Three-Year Diploma of Social Studies, University of Melbourne, 1947 258

Appendix 13: Diploma of Social Studies Courses A (Generic) and B (Personnel), 1960s 259

Appendix 14: Ruth Hoban – Research, publications and sabbatical leave reports 260

Appendix 15: Full-time staff of the social studies department, University of Melbourne, 1940–1960 263

Appendix 16: American Fulbright social work scholars who visited Australia, 1953–1963 264

Appendix 17: Australians holding the Mental Health Certificate from the London School of Economics and Political Science 267

Appendix 18: George Paton, vice-chancellor of the University of Melbourne, memorandum to staff regarding Communist allegations, 1 May 1962 268

Appendix 19: Three influential British social workers 269

Appendix 20: Founding executive of the Australian Association of Social Workers 271

Appendix 21: Name changes of women mentioned 275

Acknowledgements 277

Image Credits 281

Notes 283

Bibliography 323

Index 339

About the Author 355

Foreword

Social work emerged as a vocation in the nineteenth century. Social work emerged as a profession in the twentieth century, yet it did not cease to be a vocation. Jane Miller, in tracing the evolution of social work education in Australia from 1900 to 1960, describes clearly how those who taught the first generation of social work graduates were deeply motivated by their sense of vocation.

Based on her extensive doctoral research, Jane Miller's book challenges the orthodox assumption that social work education in Australia was a colonial clone of the British system, and presents a powerful case for the significance of North American influences. She analyses the development of social work as a profession in Australia in the context of the international networks that emerged before the advent of the welfare state, enabling the transmission of ideas across national boundaries in the search for new solutions to social problems. Jane is correct to claim that Australian social workers know more about the eminent American founding mothers of their profession, Jane Addams and Mary Richmond, than they do about the women, and some men, who forged the path for social work in this nation.

Bringing alive many of the long-forgotten early leaders of social work, Jane Miller introduces us to the highly talented Jocelyn Hyslop (1897–1974), the first head of social work at the University of Melbourne. Hyslop arrived in Melbourne in 1934, having completed a study tour in the United States en route from England. She was greatly impressed by what she witnessed in the US, and based the social work course she created on that of the renowned New York School of Social Work. Fieldwork comprised 50 per cent of the course, and theory was closely connected to practice, in contrast to Britain, where a chasm between social science and social work practice existed in courses such as that of the London School of Economics.

Hyslop developed a two-year generic social work course based on subjects such as psychology, economics, social history, political institutions, mental hygiene, child study, and hygiene and nutrition. Fieldwork was its core, as it continued to be in the three-year Diploma of Social Studies established in 1947. Hyslop was actively involved in the wider community, questioning ideas about poverty that still prevailed during the Great Depression. A gifted public speaker and eloquent writer, Hyslop regularly challenged her middle-class audiences, asking how many of them had ever been into a state school, a hospital outpatients department, a pawn shop, a sustenance office, a prison or a juvenile court.

But this is not a narrative based on individuals, as important as the principal figures are. Jane Miller draws on various historical sources to identify and demonstrate how an influential network of people and institutions, such as the Citizens Welfare Service (formerly the Charity Organisation Society) and the Red Cross, worked together to create the conditions for a social work course at the University of Melbourne, and strongly supported it in its formative years.

Although the book focuses on Melbourne in particular, it also provides an excellent overview of the early development of social work education at the University of Sydney – the home of Australia's first school of social work – and in other states. Close collaboration between the founders of social work education across Australia saw the development of a national curriculum. Jane Miller also outlines how collaboration by many of these same leaders, such as Norma Parker, led to the development of the professional body the Australian Association of Social Workers, in 1946, followed by the creation of a national journal in 1951.

This book shows us how the emergence of social work and social work education is deeply rooted in its social and historical contexts. The polio epidemic of the early 1930s, for example, led to the appointment of Isabel Hodge, the first social worker at the Royal Children's Hospital. We also learn how World War II created an urgent demand for industrial welfare supervisors in the munitions industry, and how, in the post-war period, psychiatric social workers were needed to help in the rehabilitation of service personnel. Similarly, non-government organisations such as the Red Cross and International Social Service urgently needed social workers to work with refugees.

With the expansion of federal government responsibilities during and after the war, social workers were increasingly in demand by government bodies, not only by hospitals and non-government organisations. Lyra Taylor (1894–1979) looms large as a leader of the profession in this period. The first woman law graduate admitted to the bar in New Zealand, Lyra then studied social work and, on her return from Canada in 1943, established a national social work service in the Federal Department of Social Services.

Reading this book made me yearn to have known women such as Lyra Taylor, who was still alive when I was a young social work graduate, but of whom I then knew nothing. It also made me reflect on my one chance encounter with an elderly woman with a warm smile and modest manner who introduced herself to me in a small suburban church hall after I had given a presentation. Little did I know that I was in the presence of Alison Player (1906–2005), who had led medical social work education and pioneered the deinstitutionalisation of child welfare in Victoria, as well as having been president of the Australian Association of Social Workers.

How is it that we know so little of our nation's early social workers? I think there are many reasons. The crowded curriculum of social work courses means that the history of our profession is rarely taught today. Also, in responding to pressing contemporary problems, perhaps we forget the value of understanding how our current institutions, policies and practices came into being, and were changed. And could it be that what we now perceive as the blind spots of our predecessors on matters such as gender and ethnicity inclines us to disregard the significance of their achievements, often under conditions that would seem insurmountable to us today?

Jane Miller's book brought home to me that social work educators must prepare students for challenges we cannot foresee. As young graduates in the 1970s, my peers and I grappled with 'new' problems such as child abuse, sexual assault, family violence and substance abuse, without specific preparation. In turn, some of my own newly graduated students in the 1980s grappled with phenomena such as problem gambling and the HIV/AIDS epidemic, for which I had not specifically prepared them. How do we best equip students with transferable knowledge and skills to adapt to new social circumstances and difficulties? And, perhaps more profoundly, how do we nurture the values of vocation, that foundation stone on which social work knowledge and skills are built?

The eminent American social work educator and practitioner Helen Harris Perlman wrote in her 1989 book *Looking Back to See Ahead* that 'if ... we look to the past as a way of seeing more clearly and penetratingly its meanings and uses for our immediate present and near-future, then it may serve us well'.

Jane Miller has served us very well indeed.

Professor Emeritus Dorothy Scott AM
Honorary Professorial Fellow, Social Work,
University of Melbourne
Adjunct Professor, Australian Centre for Child Protection,
University of South Australia

Introduction

Social Work – A New Concept in 1929 Australia

An understanding of social welfare history can add to social workers' understanding of themselves and of the why and how of the development of their profession. It can contribute to the forging of social workers' personal and professional identity, of their self-understanding and their social awareness.

Verl Lewis, 1977[1]

In the year 2029, Australian social work education will celebrate its centenary. But, as we approach this anniversary, it becomes clear that much of the history of the profession has been forgotten, or is merely a shadowy memory – more gossipy than factual. The only comprehensive history of the Australian social work profession is John Lawrence's 1965 volume, based on his doctoral thesis.[2] This was written when there were only four schools of social work in Australia: at the universities of Sydney, Melbourne, Adelaide and Queensland.[3] Social work education started almost thirty years later in Australia than in Europe, North and South America, and even Africa.[4] Over the past ninety years it has evolved from experimental courses run in Sydney and Melbourne, outside the walls of (but supported by) their local university, to a strong profession taught in thirty-one universities around Australia.[5] In 1929, when social work education commenced in this country, the cities of Sydney and Melbourne each had just one university.

Verl Lewis, social work educator and historian, was right when he said that understanding their own history is essential for social workers' self-understanding and self-awareness. Who are the social workers today, and where have they come from? Are they doctors' handmaidens, because of their origins in almoning, or do their connections to the settlement movement make them radical agents of change? Perhaps their origins in the Charity Organisation Society mean that they are agents of social control. Was it the influx of American academics in the 1970s that swayed Australian social workers to an American approach? There is some truth in all these assertions, but the story of Australian social work education is both more complex and more nuanced than this.

Australian social work education began in Sydney and Melbourne in 1929 and in Adelaide in 1936; these were the nation's only such courses until the University of Queensland course began in 1956. The core of this book is a case study of the founding years of social work in Melbourne. But it is not a story about Melbourne only: because the early social workers worked together and influenced each other, developments in the other states and the successful establishment of a national professional association after World War II are also part of this account.

When Australian social work commenced in 1929, Australia was a nation that we might find difficult to relate to today. The federation of colonies that we take for granted had only taken place in 1901, and the national parliament did not meet in Canberra until 1927, just two years before social work education started. Before that, it met in Melbourne. The Great Depression, which affected Australia very badly, was about to begin, the slow economic recovery eventually helped by another traumatic event, World War II. Before air travel and telephones became commonplace, many Australians felt isolated from the developed countries with which most of them identified. In 2023, Melbourne's population numbers more than five million,[6] of whom approximately one-third were born overseas, in any of a very large number of countries. In 1930, at the beginning of this story, Melbourne's population was just one million, most of whom traced their ancestry to Britain. Between 2011 and 2017, a survey of 140 cities found Melbourne to be 'the world's most liveable city', although in the most recent survey, in July 2023, it had dropped to third.[7] In the late 1950s Melbourne was a parochial city, still oriented to Britain and only just beginning to get over its isolation from what it perceived as 'the rest of the world' (namely, Britain, Europe and the US). When American movie star Ava Gardner was in Melbourne in 1959 to make *On the Beach*, a film about a post–nuclear holocaust world, it was reported that she had called Melbourne 'the perfect place to make a film about the end of the world'. Though the comment is probably apocryphal, it is likely to have gained currency because it reflected the opinion of many Australians at the time. Bright university graduates could not leave these shores quickly enough, travelling to England (not America) as soon as possible. Barry Humphries and Germaine Greer are two internationally known examples of clever young University of Melbourne alumni who fled overseas in the 1950s and 1960s.

Despite the different social environment and mores that prevailed eighty years ago, there are enduring themes in social work. Certainly the young social workers of the 1930s and 1940s were middle-class women, who wore hats and gloves for their regular home visits and addressed both colleagues and clients formally as Mr, Mrs or Miss (well before Ms had been dreamt up). Nevertheless, they are clearly recognisable as the forebears of today's social workers, struggling to support people who were marginalised, and attempting to change the systems that oppressed or excluded them. The same values are evident: in particular, empathy for their clients and a refusal to blame them for the circumstances in which they found themselves. The students were encouraged to be questioning and empathic. The attempt in the 1930s by Alison Player, a doctor's daughter who was very conscious of her privileged middle-class status, and a student colleague to live on 'sustenance' (the unemployment benefit) for a week is an example of the questioning by young students of the era. Player recalled years later that, following this experiment, 'we decided that no one could live on sustenance, nobody ever thought that people could live on nine shillings a week. But we thought we should just test it.'[8]

When I had finished writing this book, I realised that it is, more than anything, a story about a fight for standards – a fight for best practice in social work. In the 1930s the neophyte profession in New South Wales was torn apart by bitter differences over teaching standards, while in 1938 Victoria's Board of Social Studies had to vigorously defend its course from government criticism that standards were too high.[9] Against considerable odds, the early social workers in both jurisdictions still refused to compromise. Disagreement over standards has been a recurring issue in the ensuing ninety years. To these uncompromising forebears Australia owes the high standard of its social work education, and the fact that today there is a single, united, social work profession across the nation.

Social workers cannot afford to leave the writing of social work history to professional historians unfamiliar with the practice of social work, because historical researchers, like all researchers, have their own biases.[10] American social worker and historian Robert Fisher holds that the large amount of social welfare writing in the US is being carried out by historians 'most of whom know nothing about social work'.[11]

The situation in Australia is much the same. Scholar Shurlee Swain echoes Fisher's views, suggesting that Australian social historians are interested in charity, philanthropy or welfare as an entrée to wider debates about society and community, and tend to be more interested in the receiver of aid than in the giver.[12] Historians tend to overlook the distinction between untrained charity worker and social worker, which is important from a social worker's perspective. In Swain's view, social workers have usually seen history in terms of professional genealogy, with a 'subtext … being the attempt to establish a clear claim to professional status' and delineating a boundary between them and their frequently 'untrained and judgmental' predecessors. She talks of social work history leaving a 'trail into the future, a trail encompassing oppression and empowerment, abuse and care'.[13]

The split between the way in which the two professions approach the writing of welfare history makes it crucial for social workers to carry out their own studies. Of those who have written from the social work perspective, some conclude that Australia had both British and American influences, with the American being stronger.[14] One describes an entirely American influence.[15] Writers on medical social work have made particularly strong claims for British influence on Victorian social work,[16] while local writers have focused mainly on Australia.[17] Turning to Australian social historians, the majority ascribe Australian social work origins entirely to Britain.[18] Australian educational historians,[19] who researched the Australian child guidance movement (to which social workers were integral), found the child guidance outlook to be recently emerging from the shadow of British tradition.

This book, written from a social worker's perspective, documents the way in which social work education was established in Victoria. But Victoria's story could not be told without talking about New South Wales, whose first formal social work training was starting at exactly the same time (in 1929). The two states, and later their first universities, led the social work training movement in Australia. So this is also a story of how Australian social work training began, and how the profession was established nationally.

The dilemma facing the early social work proponents was this: how could they prepare young and inexperienced middle-class women to help poor and disadvantaged individuals and families change the course of their lives, using the skills of the new profession of social work? The social work course in Victoria attracted women university graduates who wanted a career other than teaching or librarianship; its first head, Jocelyn Hyslop, worked hard at promoting social work to students from private girls' schools. The early social work students were often the daughters of the advocates of the new training course, for whom the living conditions of Melbourne's poor came as quite a shock. For example, Jessie Brookes (later Jessie Clarke OAM) was the daughter of Mrs Herbert Brookes (née Ivy Deakin), so Jessie's grandfather was Australia's second prime minister, Alfred Deakin.[20] Ivy Brookes served on the Board of Social Studies in Victoria and was a substantial donor to the course. In 1972, another graduate of the late 1930s, Alison Player (later Mathew), the doctor's daughter mentioned earlier, reflected on the social distance between the students and their clients:

> I would say that there must have been a very small minority of social workers as a whole who had any political leanings other

than Conservative ... they came from the respectable middle-class groups, and I remember striving and striving at various stages to look out ways of bringing into the training people who came from different sorts of groups, from trade union backgrounds and so on.[21]

Finding adequate financial resources during the Great Depression, and recruiting trained teaching staff in a nation with no tradition of professional social work, were two hurdles that the new courses faced. Despite setbacks such as a bitter conflict with New South Wales' first head of social work in the 1930s (which was only resolved when the course was taken over by the University of Sydney), and unfounded but scandalous allegations in the 1950s of Communist infiltration at the University of Melbourne, the staff of these universities persevered and laid the foundations of today's Australian social work profession.

Because of the relatively late commencement of Australian social work education,[22] the Australians were able to compare developments in both Britain and the US as they pondered how they should run their training courses. By the mid-1940s, University of Melbourne social work educators were articulating clearly that they wanted to teach social casework on American lines and to develop a cadre of effective field teachers of the kind found in America, and not generally available in Britain. In other words, this was a quest for expertise.[23] During the 1930s, social workers in New South Wales had major disagreements on the core elements needed in a social work curriculum; those whose views coincided with the views of the Melbourne group won the day by 1940.

Beginning in the nineteenth century and finishing in 1960, this is not a neat story moving from difficult beginnings to ultimate success.

Introduction

It is a story of highs and lows, opportunities seized, and chances lost. It ends on a note that is more ambivalent than triumphant. The massive expansion of social work education that led to the demand for trained social workers finally being met did not commence until the 1970s, but the universities of Sydney, Melbourne and the smaller Adelaide had established national social work education standards and reached national agreement on the core competencies needed for social work practice that still underpin the profession in Australia.

This story starts with the question of the extent to which Victoria's original social work education followed United States models. My research uncovered Australian philanthropists searching out US know-how as far back as the nineteenth century, when Professor E.E. Morris, founder of Victoria's Charity Organisation Society (COS), visited the US and England, bringing back news from the National Conference of Charities and Correction. He concluded that Australia had more in common with the US than with Britain, because they were both 'young' countries with large geographic distances to be covered. The search for Amerian social work expertise continued through S. Greig Smith and his publishing of information from US journals in the COS journal, *The Other Half*; Dr Georgina Sweet and her international women's connections through her national presidency of the Australian Young Women's Christian Association (YWCA) and membership of the Pan-Pacific Women's Association; and Dr John Newman-Morris, who had been impressed with American social work education (which he had seen first-hand at the New York School of Social Work in 1930) and who as a doctor had been influenced by the work of Dr Richard Cabot, the father of US medical social work. On her first day in Melbourne, in December 1934, British-born Jocelyn Hyslop, the first head of the training course from which descended the current

University of Melbourne degree program, announced her intention of adopting American teaching methods and American curriculum, a decision from which she did not resile.

After World War II, the University of Melbourne continued to adopt American methods. From the start, the embrace of a generic training course reflected the American approach of the time. The 1940s and 1950s saw a determined effort to develop expertise in social casework and to improve professional supervision and fieldwork education – the hallmarks of American, not British, social work. The University of Melbourne attempted to attract Americans to work there, though not succeeding until 1959. However, the Fulbright scholars brought to Australia by the University of Sydney, the increasing number of local social workers who had undertaken the LSE's (American–designed and funded) Mental Health Certificate, and in 1955 the return from the New York School of Social Work of Len Tierney,[24] who was to become the long-term head of social work at Melbourne,[25] strengthened local expertise over this period.

While the dominant influence in Victoria was American, the role of British social work and social science cannot be overlooked. Three outstanding social workers – Edith Eckhard, Jean Robertson and Helen Rees – helped establish the course, and other British social workers taught in Australia: British almoners (medical social workers) Agnes Macintyre and Joan Brett, and later Audrey Rennison, who taught in the almoner course, all played leadership roles. Also important were ten British social workers recruited by the Australian Red Cross Society (ARCS) immediately after the war to strengthen supervision of practice, as they both helped deal with the problem of a lack of social workers to meet demand, and brought their own expertise as supervisors. Although the University of Melbourne did not look to British social work to guide it in teaching social work practice, in particular field supervision and casework, it did adopt British sociology, economics, social history and the concept of social biology.

Social work educators did not necessarily follow national lines in their views on social work. Helen Rees was British, yet went against the prevailing trend in Britain in her support of generic, not specialist, teaching. Edith Eckhard was at the centre of British social work, but had been exposed to American psychiatric social work ideas when visiting America courtesy of the Commonwealth Fund (established by the Harkness family, whose wealth derived from Standard Oil). After his study in America in the 1950s, the Australian Arthur Livingstone emphasised the way in which professional skills could be generalised from one society to another.

The real challenge for social work educators in Victoria, then as now, was to define the essence of social work expertise. Jocelyn Hyslop regularly reminded the Board of Social Studies (BSS) that its young graduates had to be fully educated in the practice of their profession, because they would be pioneers, working in agencies that were unfamiliar with what they had to offer. She had stated at the outset that the course should prioritise 'teaching for a profession'. The early social work educators were searching for expertise. They wanted to define social work expertise and find the best ways of imbuing it in their students.

***

In this book I have done my best to present a balanced view of the development of Australian social work education, but as a social worker with many years' experience, I must admit that I am biased towards the profession and the work of my fellow social workers. Sociologist and historian Ann Oakley has pointed out that 'complexity is inherent in the relationship between the person telling the story and both what the story is about and its purpose', saying: 'Truth-telling, which sounds such a noble enterprise, is itself the most complex of acts.'[26]

I have had to make choices about what material to include and what to leave out, so shaping my particular version of this story. Many of the small dramas have been omitted. There were nuanced arguments and minor disagreements, which were important in their day, but have had to be omitted from a linear overview of sixty years of development.

In her book *The Uses and Abuses of History*, Canadian historian Margaret Macmillan advocates that:

> We must do our best to raise the public awareness of the past in all its richness and complexity. We must contest the one-sided, even false, histories that are out there in the public domain. If we do not, we allow our leaders and opinion makers to use history to bolster false claims and justify bad and foolish policies.[27]

I have attempted to be equally honest about the successes and failures experienced along the way, without being either too adulatory or too blameful. I hope that the addition of this history, with its perspective that differs from the existing histories of social work in Australia, will provide balance. I have attempted to contest what I consider 'false claims' as mentioned by Margaret Macmillan, and hope that this particular historical account may help to inform contemporary social work education. Although the influence of American ideas and practices has been clear, social work in Victoria, and indeed Australia, has not followed the well-established American practice of celebrating its pioneers. Australian social work students will be familiar with the women who forged American social work, such as Jane Addams and Mary Richmond, because their stories appear in Australian textbooks. Australia's early and influential leaders, by way of contrast, are largely invisible in the contemporary literature. Yet Jocelyn Hyslop's ideas continue to be relevant today. They endured even after the Australian leadership baton was taken up in the post-war period by Sydney's Norma Parker, Hyslop having left Australia for good in 1946. In writing this Australian history of social work, I hope that stories of Australia's founding social workers will find their way into contemporary social work literature.

I should mention here that I use the term 'generic social work' with the British or Australian meaning: a single generalist course of training that covers all fields of practice (such as health, mental health, probation and parole, and family work, among others). For American readers, 'generic' is more likely to mean a course that teaches all the modes of intervention, including casework, group work, community work and so on. The focus of social work practice in Australia and internationally has changed as social attitudes have changed and new problems or needs have emerged. This is discussed briefly in Chapter 11.

In the past fifty years, Australia's relationship with the United States of America has changed. In the first part of the twentieth century, Australian universities were dismissive of US academia and looked to Britain for models of excellence. With this background it is even more surprising that Victorian (and Australian) social work relentlessly pursued American expertise, not British, but unsurprising that they found trouble navigating American social work networks.

During the period discussed in this book, Melbourne, Sydney and Adelaide each had just one university. In Melbourne the university was referred to as 'the University', or for insiders either 'the Uni' or 'the Shop'. Most of the work of establishing social work as a profession happened in the capital cities; in the post-war period, social workers sent to rural centres by Red Cross and the Commonwealth Department of Social Service were breaking new ground. However, to avoid confusion I have identified the courses by their state, not their capital city. This is especially important as the three founding courses were run outside their local university until they could demonstrate that they met appropriate academic standards.

1

The Emergence of Social Work in Britain and the US

What is needed, it seems to me, is some course of study where an intelligent young person can ... be taught the alphabet of charitable science.

Anna Dawes (US), 1893[1]

The time will come when no town will be without its training college for social workers.

Helen Bosanquet (England), 1893[2]

It is not possible to understand the origins of Australian social work education without knowing what had happened in Britain and the United States twenty years before any Australian courses commenced. Australians had been observing them, and both Victoria's and New South Wales' courses made a deliberate choice to follow America's approach, not Britain's. (Western Australia also looked to the US, while South Australia was more influenced by Britain.) American historian and social worker Katherine Kendall points out 'the amazing coincidence of the almost simultaneous appearance of schools of social work' in a number of American and British cities, as well as in Amsterdam and Berlin.[3] By 1923 social work had started in Chile, due to a chance meeting between the Belgian physician and pioneer of social medicine, Dr René Sand, and the founder of the International Conference of Social Work and a leader in public health and social welfare in South America, Dr Alejandro del Rio of Santiago. Social work courses commenced in South Africa (Cape Town and Transvaal, 1924) and China (University of Yenching, 1922) before Australia. India (Tata Institute, 1936) commenced its first social work education at around the same time as Australia.[4] Dr John Newman-Morris was the only Australian who attended the Second International Conference of Social Work, held in Hamburg in 1932, and would have been well aware of international social work initiatives. However, in deciding how to teach social work, Australia looked to the US and the UK, not to other countries.

Though social work education in the US and UK followed very similar paths at first, by 1912 they were developing significant differences, the results of which can be clearly seen today. In the US today, social work has been successfully established as a single unified profession, whereas in Britain it continues to struggle as a semi-profession, a 'bureau profession',[5] or, as some writers claim, not one profession but many social occupations.[6]

At three turning points, decisions were made that promoted unity in the US and set the scene for fragmentation in Britain. Because of the United State's strong consolidation of the profession and the priority given to teaching the skills that a neophyte social worker needed in the field, early Australian proponents were attracted to American social work. They were less impressed with British social work education because it taught social theory, with little emphasis on what the social worker actually did.

The origins of social work

Both the social sciences and social work trace their origins to philanthropically minded people and organisations who wished to use a scientific approach to understand and quantify the problems that arose in the overcrowded slums of the cities that sprang up following the Industrial Revolution. It was clear that haphazard charitable efforts were of very limited value and that there must be a better way. Charles Dickens' novel *Oliver Twist* accurately describes the depravity caused by the desperate living conditions of the London poor in the nineteenth century.

An occupation called 'social work' is a late nineteenth-century concept. Other names had been suggested for the young profession, such as the clumsy 'philanthropology'.[7] The idea that it was either possible or necessary to teach the skills and theory needed for what social workers now do was completely novel. When Anna Dawes raised this idea at the International Congress of Charities, Corrections and Philanthropy, which was held in conjunction with the Chicago World's Fair in 1893, she was the first person in the US to suggest this. In the same year, Helen Bosanquet, who was the Shoreditch (London) district secretary for the Charity Organisation Societies (COS), also forecast the development of social work training.[8]

The main nineteenth-century precursors of professional social work in Britain and the US were the settlement movement and the COS. Both originated in Britain, but were quickly picked up in the US, where, despite sharing a name and broad directions, they developed their own unique character. So what were these differences, and how did the settlement movement and the COS develop on opposite sides of the Atlantic?

The settlement movement

The British settlement movement started in 1884, when Octavia Hill, who had studied art under wealthy art critic and social reformer John Ruskin, agreed to undertake the humane management of the London slum properties that Ruskin had inherited, with a mission to improve the tenants' living standards. Katherine Kendall has pointed out that the principles behind Hill's work were closely related to what later became social work principles: Hill helped people to help themselves, and believed in the intrinsic value of each individual. A caring relationship was formed between Octavia Hill and her agents and the tenants.[9] In 1885 the first settlement house, Toynbee Hall, was established by Samuel Barnett, who had worked with Octavia Hill. Its goal was for educated young men (university students or graduates) to meet the poor on their own territory and involve them in intellectual and artistic pursuits, in order to promote friendships between the rich and the very poor. A little later, women also became involved in settlements.[10]

On the other side of the Atlantic, men's Settlement houses were established in New York in 1886 and Boston in 1891. In 1889 a group of college-educated women,[11] whom historian James Leiby describes as 'a type unheard of in England', opened College Settlement in New York.[12] Chicago's Hull House, also established in 1889 by Jane Addams and Ellen Gates Starr following their visit to Toynbee Hall, is the best-known American settlement.[13] By 1893 Hull House, which was in a locality inhabited mainly by recent immigrants,[14] had established forty clubs, a day nursery, gymnasium, dispensary and many other facilities.[15] Addams and the Hull House volunteers were active social reformers, whose achievements included countering municipal corruption, improving local sanitation (garbage collection, toilet facilities and clean water were priorities, especially to stem typhoid), stopping child labour, and helping to establish the first children's courts. Addams was involved in both the peace movement and the movement for equal rights for women in America.[16] She is the only social worker and the first American woman to receive a Nobel Peace Prize (shared with peace advocate and president of Columbia University, Nicolas Murray Butler), and was, in the opinion of Leiby, 'foremost among many "notables" in the settlement movement'.[17]

As well as pursuing social reform and working with individuals and groups, the American Settlement houses undertook social research (later taken over by university-based sociologists). Eventually the houses moved from an informal, unstructured model to become more structured organisations.[18]

The Charity Organisation Societies (COS)

Although settlements were involved in conceptualising and developing social work education (and hence the academic discipline of social work), particularly in America, it was the Charity Organisation Societies that played the most significant role. The London COS was established in 1869 to bring order to the chaotic philanthropic sector and solve the problems of pauperism.

The particular contribution of the COS was its 'scientific' approach, which Jane Lewis in her history of the London COS/Family Welfare Association sums up as 'meaning that they had to examine their practices carefully so that the Society did not become just one more relief society'.[19] A high priority for the COS was the coordination of the plethora of charitable organisations, in order to prevent duplication of effort by agencies and double-dipping by clients. While part of its mission was to eliminate fraud and indiscriminate begging as a way of life, its supporters also wanted to ensure that the finite funds were given to those in most need. Today's social workers are direct descendants of the COS investigators and friendly visitors.[20] Under the direction of C.S. Loch, secretary of the COS from 1875 to 1914, its activities to rationalise charity were not without critics at the time, and more recently.[21]

The first COS in the United States was established in Buffalo, New York, in 1877 by an Episcopalian clergyman, Stephen Humphries Gurteen, after a visit to England. Gurteen had emigrated from England to the US in 1863.[22] By 1882 there were twenty-two COS in the United States, and the commitment to 'scientific charity' had spread to charitable organisations beyond the COS.[23]

Social workers frequently portray the COS and the settlement movement as in opposition to each other. They varied over time and place so it is difficult to generalise. However, recent research has demonstrated the way in which they were able to work in close collaboration.[24]

Early social work education

In England the settlement movement had a direct link to the first social work education. Octavia Hill instituted formal training of staff in the 1880s, and by 1890 she and Margaret Sewell from the University Women's Settlement were running a one-year training program, which was eventually taken over by the London COS's Committee on Social Education.[25] The settlement house training in America was done by observation of other settlement house workers, rather than through a formal training program.[26]

In both countries the COS played an important role in initiating formal courses for training in social work. Following Anna Dawes and

Helen Bosanquet's calls for training, Mrs Dunn Gardner presented a paper to the governing council of the London COS in 1894 arguing for the establishment of 'Schools of True Charity'.[27] In the US, social work pioneer Mary Richmond gave a paper entitled 'The need of a training school in applied philanthropy' at the National Conference of Charities and Correction in 1897.[28] In 1903 the first independent, full-time school of social work in Britain, the London School of Sociology and Social Economics, was established by the London COS. The following year the New York COS expanded its summer school (established in 1897) to a full-time, one-year training program.[29] Over the next twenty years, social work education expanded and developed similar curricula in both countries. In 1908 social work was being taught in Liverpool and Birmingham as well as London, and by 1919 the US had seventeen schools of social work.[30]

The first turning point

The year 1912 marked a watershed in British social work teaching, and was the moment when it and American social work began to diverge. In that year, the COS reluctantly agreed to an offer from the London School of Economics and Political Science (LSE) to take over its course. The LSE had been started by Sydney and Beatrice Webb, who were both Fabian Socialists and social scientists. The Webbs were no friends of the COS, having strongly disagreed with it over the Royal Commission on the Poor Laws and Relief of Distress (1905–09) and seeing 'no reason for such persons [social workers] to exist'.[31] The debate about whether social reform would remove the necessity for social workers has cropped up in many places and eras. For example, the social work profession was well established in countries such as Estonia in the pre-Communist era but was eradicated during Communism, then re-established post-Communism. And it is interesting to see a large social work profession emerging in China today, where a social work course had commenced in 1922 at Yenching University but ceased under the Communist regime.[32]

The COS realised that its course, which was struggling financially, could not compete with the well-resourced LSE. The LSE course became the model for subsequent British university social work programs.[33] The original COS course, which had evolved from practice, placed a strong emphasis on skills, and included a specialised 'Department of Practical Instruction in Administration'.[34] Indeed, in 1906, C.S. Loch insisted that all the teachers should themselves have 'passed through the severe discipline of casework'.[35] The COS feared that the LSE's strong emphasis on social sciences would lead to the neglect of practical social work training. In the words of Marjorie Smith:

> With the transfer of what had begun as a professional education plan for social workers to an academic institution without clear understanding of the difference involved, only one result could obtain: the professional aspects would become less important and the academic and theoretical more important.[36]

E.J. Urwick, who had headed the COS course,[37] became head of the LSE's new department of social administration, and was able initially to protect the professional content of the educational program.[38] In 1924, aged fifty-nine, he moved to Canada, where he became a major figure in the development of Canadian social work.[39]

Ultimately, the COS's fears that training in the practical skills of social work would not continue in the LSE proved well founded. In the opinion of both Katherine Kendall and Marjorie Smith, the reason why a number of students took on the further year of almoner training in England was to gain the practical expertise not taught at the LSE but essential for their work.[40] When one LSE graduate from that period, who became a senior medical social worker, was asked what had been the connection between the academic and practical sides of her training, she replied: 'None whatsoever!'[41] Thus, an unintended consequence of British universities taking on social work education was the development of a range of training schemes outside universities.

In 1912, the very year in which the COS ceded its social work course to the LSE, one of the United States' founding social workers, Mary Richmond, stood firmly against a plan for the teaching of social work practice to be subsumed by social theorists. She confronted Edward Devine, director of the New York School of Philanthropy, over his plans to bring in 'university men' to teach social work students. Her argument was that social workers did not need a separate education of unrelated social science theory, but rather that social work theory had to be developed from its practice. Martha Morrison Dore of Columbia University has argued that it was the autonomous nature of the New York School of Philanthropy that enabled it to maintain an identity as a school for practitioners rather than theoreticians.[42]

This set American social work on the path to establishing a body of professional knowledge derived from practice for the academic discipline of social work. In 1909, Mary Richmond was recruited from Philadelphia by the newly established Russell Sage Foundation (founded by philanthropist Olivia Sage) to become its director of charity organisation,[43] and she moved to New York.[44] In 1917 her groundbreaking text *Social Diagnosis* was published. The book was based on extensive research into the social work records of a family agency and a hospital, in order to identify which methods worked, and which did not. Among other research strategies, Richmond arranged for an accredited group of teachers of casework to review some edited case records, which had been 'printed in full with all their sins upon their heads (bad work is almost as instructive as good)'.[45] Thus in the US the theory and practice of casework were painstakingly developed from research into the effectiveness of the efforts of social work practitioners, whereas in England social workers had largely handed over research to sociologists and social scientists.

The other difference between British and American social work was that the US continued a strong fieldwork component, and by 1915 field teaching was integrated into the social work curriculum. Following the presentation of papers at the National Conference of Charities and Correction by Zilpha Drew Smith (whose career had been in Associated Charities of Boston and later in the new Boston School of Social Work, and to whom Mary Richmond dedicated *Social Diagnosis*),[46] and by Edith Abbott of Hull House (who was later to become dean of the School of Social Service Administration at the University of Chicago), a pattern was established whereby 50 per cent of student time was spent in field training, in settings selected and closely supervised by the schools of social work.[47] This became integral to American social work education and is one of the critical factors in its development. This also was to be one of the first standards advocated by Jocelyn Hyslop and adopted by the Board of Social Studies in Victoria in 1934.

This was a moment in which social work education in Britain and in America could have gone in either direction. American social workers decided to emphasise field education and to develop theory from practice, while Britain, with the exception of the almoners (and the psychiatric social workers who came later), followed a broad social science curriculum, with less emphasis on practice education.

The second turning point

The next important historical development was the burgeoning of medical and psychiatric social work. The way in which the profession as a whole evolved was that a new field would emerge, social work activity would ensue, and training for it would develop soon after. So, the development of new domains and the broadening of the curriculum occurred in tandem.

The development of medical and psychiatric social work was not a single, dramatic turning point in the way that the decision to teach a largely practical or largely theoretical social work course had been. Medical social work was a strong field of social work from its inception in both countries. It was incorporated into general social work education in the US, and took its own separate educational path in Britain. Psychiatric social work, which emerged a little later, originated in the US and was taken to Britain almost thirty years later. While it had been enthusiastically incorporated into American social work education and strengthened the profession, it had a weaker influence in Britain, and widened existing divisions between fields of practice.

Medical social work, or 'almoning' as the British initially called it, started in Britain and the US at the turn of the twentieth century. In 1895, C.S. Loch of the COS established a system of hospital almoners in London hospitals to prevent outpatient clinics being abused as a source of free medical care by people who could afford to pay.[48] Initially almoners were trained by the COS, then from 1907 until 1971 they were trained by their own institute,[49] which took responsibility for training, setting standards and deciding who was eligible to practise. In 1971, it was wound up in the aftermath of the 1968 Seebohm (government) inquiry into the organisation and responsibilities of local authority personal social services in England and Wales, and following the establishment of the British Association of Social Workers.[50]

In the US in 1905, ten years after the COS had commenced almoner training in London, Dr Richard Cabot introduced medical social service at Massachusetts General Hospital.[51] Cabot's intention, in contrast to Loch's budget-driven approach, was humanitarian: to alleviate the desperate social conditions that prevented proper treatment and recovery of the hospital's patients. Ida M. Cannon, a graduate of the Boston School of Social Work, established medical social work in the US.[52] From the outset, American medical social work education was embedded in existing social work courses. The first was the Boston School of Social Work (1912), which later became Simmons College, followed closely by New York and Philadelphia.[53] There was communication between British and American medical social workers; for example, Ida Cannon was close friends with Cherry Morris and Anne Cummins of St Thomas's Hospital, London. Georgia Travis, the first American social worker to come to Australia on a Fulbright award, had met Cherry Morris in Chicago in 1931 and reconnected with her in London in 1954 after her Australian visit.[54]

The next large specialty, psychiatric social work, was to have a more dramatic effect on the profession and its sense of identity. The US and Britain followed the same pattern as they had with medical social work, in that the US included the new field of endeavour in its general social work education relatively early, whereas Britain established a separate training course, which continued for some time. The first psychiatric social work education in the US was a six-month course started in 1914 at the Boston Psychopathic Hospital, run by social worker Mary Jarrett and medical director Elmer E. Southard. By 1918 a school for psychiatric social work had been established at Smith College, also in Massachusetts. Subsequently schools of social work in New York, Chicago and Philadelphia all incorporated 'mental hygiene' (mental health) and psychiatric social work into their curricula.[55]

The child guidance movement, which started in the US in 1922, was a multidisciplinary movement that saw young offenders as victims needing social and psychological help, rather than as criminals to be incarcerated in adult prisons and dealt with in the adult legal system. It provided supportive intervention from a team usually comprising psychologists, psychiatrists and social workers. This movement, together with the Commonwealth Fund and the (American) National Committee for Mental Hygiene, which was set up to prevent juvenile delinquency, all influenced social work education profoundly. The Commonwealth Fund financed the child guidance movement, and was later to have an important influence on British social work.[56] In 1929, fifteen years after the first American psychiatric social work education commenced, the Commonwealth Fund negotiated the establishment of the LSE's Mental Health Certificate course. Its curriculum was developed on an American model and was financed by the Commonwealth Fund.[57] Two social workers from the Commonwealth Fund, Barry Smith and Muriel Scoville, monitored the British curriculum closely, visiting regularly.[58]

This was part of a broader strategy to promote the child guidance movement in Britain. The first generation of British psychiatric social work educators was taken to the US for intensive training. Edith Eckhard, head of the social work course at the LSE, had encouraged this, and herself spent between January and April 1928 in the US on a Commonwealth Fellowship.[59]

The LSE Mental Health Certificate was the only British psychiatric social work course until 1944.[60] By 1954, psychiatric social work courses were also being taught in Edinburgh, Manchester and Liverpool.

By 1964 the LSE had trained 73 per cent of British psychiatric social workers, almost everyone who held posts in the teaching of fieldwork, or in research, and 70 per cent of those who had become teachers in higher education.[61]

Turning back to the American story,[62] psychiatric social work radically changed the character of American social work, in a way that medical social work had not. While medical social work and general social work had a great deal in common (as Mary Richmond's research had shown), psychiatric social work introduced a dramatically new approach, fulfilling the profession's wish to find a scientific basis for its work. Furthermore, as social workers were mainly involved in family and individual work, psychological theories of human development were directly relevant. Porter Lee, head of the New York School of Social Work, articulated the value of this additional expertise in his presentation to the Fifth Annual Report of the Commonwealth Fund (1922–23): that the practices of social work, psychiatry and psychology closely overlapped each other.[63] Three years later, Edward D. Lynde, secretary of Associated Charities, told the National Conference of Social Work (the renamed National Conference of Charities and Correction) that 'whereas casework had been identified with problems of economic dependency in the past, it was in reality a helping device applicable to all classes and variety of need'.[64] Social workers moved away from the major emphasis on integrating and coordinating, towards human relationships skills or therapy familiar to today's social workers.[65] The introduction of psychiatric social work in Britain also had a dramatic effect. The Mental Health Course at the London School of Economics, which commenced in 1929, was the first course in a British university with what Jocelyn Hyslop later described as 'training for a profession' as its main aim.[66]

The psychiatric social work movement was not as strong in Britain as in the United States.[67] The case discussion that was integral to the practice of psychiatric social work challenged social work in Britain, where in some places case discussion had been frowned on because it would interfere with the social worker's 'inborn gifts'.[68] By 1930 Americans were seeing social work as a single profession, with generic training that could equip the student for a range of specialties. In Britain, training was offered separately for each of the many specialist social work occupations.

The third turning point

The third turning point in the US involved two connected initiatives, which together resulted in firm consolidation of the American social work profession by 1952. To this day, equivalent consolidation has not occurred in Britain.

The first of these American achievements resulted from the Milford Conference, where casework leaders from New York, Philadelphia and Boston met in 1923, 1924 and 1925 to define social casework. They drew out the fundamental principles and practice of social casework, which at that time was carried out in a range of settings (such as health, probation and education). The Milford Conference's report affirmed that 'its principles and methodologies cut across specialties and provided a common base for social casework as a major division of social work practice'.[69] Consensus on this definition was a necessary precondition for deciding how to teach social work and what the minimum requirements would be. Although casework is only one aspect of social work, this was an affirmation that social work was a single profession, with skills and knowledge that were transferable across fields of practice. This stance was consistent with Mary Richmond's earlier conclusions, which she had described in *Social Diagnosis*. American social work had defined its singular discipline; its next task was to defend the status of the Master of Social Work as the national entry-level qualification for practice.

The American Association of Social Workers had been formed in 1921.[70] In the late 1940s the National Association of Schools of Social Administration was established to represent the interests of undergraduate social work schools that had sprung up around the country – mainly in departments of sociology – in response to a national undersupply of social workers. These schools were graduating social workers with Bachelor of Social Work degrees.[71] But the original Master of Social Work programs saw this as a threat to their standards. Eventually the warring parties agreed on a study of 'the provision and distribution of educational facilities in relation to present ... demand for social service personnel'.[72] The Carnegie Corporation funded what came to be called the Hollis-Taylor inquiry, headed by educationist Ernest V. Hollis, assisted by social work practitioner and educator Alice Taylor, to establish principles for programs of social work education. The Hollis-Taylor report was published 'to a mixed reception' in 1951, the main outcome being the establishment in 1952 of the Council on Social Work Education, which took over responsibility for social work education through accreditation, consultation, research and publications.[73] This successfully prevented a split in social work education and so assisted with strengthening of the profession.[74] In 1955 the National Association of Social Workers was established, through the merging of seven social work associations.[75] In the US, the status of the Master of Social Work qualification is still successfully protected.[76] By 1955 US social work had achieved a single association to represent the profession as a whole, and another association to maintain teaching standards. This differs from Australia, where a single association, the Australian Association of Social Workers, represents the profession and also, through its role in accrediting courses to allow their graduates to become members of the Australian Association of Social Workers, plays an important part in setting minimum standards.

Although American social work was unified by 1955 (as indeed was Australian social work), British social work continued to follow divergent paths. Writing in her book on training for the social services in 1945, the British social worker Elizabeth Macadam, a strong advocate for social work education, described social work as 'a vague and elastic term which covers a large variety of occupations, some of which call for professional qualifications of different kinds'.[77] She compared the situation with the US, which 'With its youthful agility in seizing new ideas and translating them into action has out-distanced us in their recognition of social work as a profession and in their provision for its training'.[78]

British social work in the inter-war years has been characterised as a 'marginal occupation'. In addition to separate training for different fields of practice, British fragmentation was compounded by non-university-based training being offered as short courses, evening classes, and even a correspondence course for probation officers provided by the Home Office.[79] St Thomas's Hospital social worker Cherry Morris (coincidentally, the daughter of Professor E.E. Morris, founder of Melbourne's COS) edited a book entitled *Social Work in Great Britain*, published in 1954. Its 'Appendix: Facilities for Training' illustrates the fragmentation starkly, providing separate addresses for training in family casework, medical social work, psychiatric social work, probation work, moral welfare work and child care officers.[80] Britain's narrow specialisations inhibited 'freedom of transfer' of the social worker between fields of practice, in the way that was possible in the US and Australia at that time.[81]

In the 1950s there was an international trend towards general as opposed to specialist social work training. This had been endorsed by a 1951 meeting of the United Nations' Social Commission.[82] By this time, at least some British social workers were interested in bringing together all the strands of the profession.

The first concerted attempt to teach generic social work in Britain was the LSE's course in applied social studies, also known as the Carnegie Experiment. This new course was watched with interest by the heads of seven other courses who were considering following this model,[83] as at that time the LSE was graduating approximately half of Britain's new social workers.[84] The program was spearheaded by Dame Eileen Younghusband, whose interest in social work had started with work in the Settlement movement. A forceful woman in her own right and the daughter of famous British explorer Sir Francis Younghusband, she persuaded the Carnegie United Kingdom Trust, with which she had a close relationship, to provide four years of funding to establish a new, one-year, generic social work program at the LSE – and thus the applied social studies course commenced in 1954. Eileen Younghusband is remembered today for her role in chairing the Ministry of Health working party on social work training, which published the 'Younghusband report' (1959) that led to the establishment of the Council for Training in Social Work. She is still honoured by social workers internationally with the biennial Eileen Younghusband Memorial Lecture for the International Association of Schools of Social Work.

Younghusband invited American Charlotte Towle,[85] possibly best known for her text *Common Human Needs* and for creating a generic casework curriculum linking knowledge of human behaviour with administration in the public sphere, to come to the LSE on a Fulbright scholarship to establish the program.[86] But the appointment four years earlier in 1950 of the charismatic Richard Titmuss CBE, FBA, to head the LSE's department of social administration (where social work was located), a department that Ann Oakley believes 'really belonged to Eileen Younghusband',[87] undermined the chances of this program succeeding.

This was an opportunity to transform British social work education by introducing a single curriculum for all fields of practice, with a strong field education component. Instead, it brought to a head conflict between Younghusband and Titmuss. It should be said that not all British social workers supported this initiative – British social work academic and historian Malcolm Payne felt that many hesitated to support it as they saw the Carnegie Experiment as the introduction of 'American casework'.[88] But looking back to the early COS course, which had been embedded in practice, Katherine Kendall argued that the Carnegie course was a return to social work's roots.[89] The situation was complicated by the fact that the social work course in the LSE was already held in low regard in the institution; the almost entirely female staff were frequently on contracts and were paid less than the men in social administration, as they were not considered to be academic staff.[90] The treatment of Edith Eckhard illustrates the status of women and of the teachers of practice. Although Eckhard was regarded as 'the heart and soul'[91] of the social science department, her personal file in the LSE Archives makes for sad reading: in 1929, after ten years during which she carried a large teaching load and was de facto head of the department, the LSE continued to refuse to grant her permanency because of her lack of publications.[92] Meanwhile the male head of department simultaneously held the position of assistant editor of *The New Statesman*.[93]

When the Carnegie funding concluded in 1958, David Donnison attempted, at Titmuss' request, to embed the generic program at the LSE by combining two existing courses – the childcare program (child welfare), which was run by Clare Britton (better known as Clare Winnicott following her marriage to child psychiatrist Donald Winnicott), and the psychiatric social work course run by Kay McDougall – and placing McDougall in charge. This not only distressed Britton, but also led to the resignation of Younghusband, and of Kate Lewis, who had assisted in the Carnegie course.[94]

A great deal has been written about the bruising 'LSE Affair': Australian academic Alma Hartshorn wrote *Milestone in Education for Social Work* (1982); David Donnison describes his involvement in *Social Policy and Administration Revisited*,[95] and Kathleen Jones' biography of Younghusband also deals with it.[96] Titmuss' daughter, sociologist Ann Oakley, extends previous accounts with her frank analysis of the gender and class issues that fuelled the conflict. Her account is strengthened by her access to material that her mother had withheld from the LSE archives at the time of Richard Titmuss' death. Not only was generic social work not introduced to Britain at this time, but long-term damage was done. The celebrated British social worker Olive Stevenson recalled in her memoir that social work teaching and social administration continued to be uncomfortable bedfellows at the LSE. She described her experience at the LSE twenty years later (in the 1970s), mentioning the 'awkward boundary between social work and social policy academics where "the twain never met" (separate tables in the dining room were usual)'.[97] Sadly, the LSE, the first British university to teach social work, closed its course in 1997.[98]

Not until the early 1970s did British social work commit itself to generic education. When it did so, the British Association of Social Workers broke an earlier undertaking with medical and psychiatric social workers by deciding to grant full membership to social workers with two-year qualifications, resulting in what one social worker described as 'a particular sense of betrayal'.[99]

While in the US the Milford Conference and then the Hollis-Taylor report had defined the discipline of social work and protected the domain of the profession, even by the end of the period covered in this book an agreed definition of social work and protection of the domain of social workers had not been achieved in Britain. Appendix 3 summarises the early parallel developments in British and American social work and the earlier move to a single professional association and educational model in the US. Social work in the two countries parted ways; the US established its National Association of Social Workers fifteen years before Britain established the British Association of Social Workers (1970), and the US had control of educational standards twenty years before Britain did.

Up to this point I have given a snapshot of the progress of social work education in Britain and the US. But the development of American social work cannot be understood without understanding the generous philanthropy of the time, and the national communication mechanisms of which there was no British equivalent. American conferences and journals influenced Australia – and doubtless other countries.

In the US the National Conference of Charities and Correction, inaugurated in 1874, was a significant national forum for philosophical and policy discussion, attended by a range of professionals, including doctors, psychiatrists and lawyers, as well as by social workers and philanthropists. It met annually in different parts of the United States for a few days, and published its proceedings.[100] Its meetings were the catalyst for the first international social work conference, which was held in Paris in 1928. When he visited the US in 1889, the president of the Melbourne COS, Professor E.E. Morris, was impressed by the San Francisco conference and by the willingness of Americans to travel for days to reach it.[101]

From the late 1880s the US published journals that circulated nationally. Firstly there were *Lend-A-Hand* (Boston), *Charities Review* (New York COS) and *The Commons* (Chicago). By 1905 the amalgamated publication *Charities and the Commons* brought these readerships together, and in 1906 added *Jewish Charity* (New York). Eventually in 1909 the New York COS reorganised all these journals into *The Survey*, supported by the Russell Sage Foundation, with an initial readership of 10,000.[102] The Melbourne COS library held copies of *The Survey* from 1910 to 1940 (and its articles were frequently quoted by S. Greig Smith in *The Other Half*, the journal of the COS of Melbourne).

There was no comparable national conference in Britain, and until 1970 Britain's many small professional social work organisations produced separate journals or newsletters.[103] *Case Conference*, founded and edited by Kay McDougall of the LSE in 1954,[104] was an important contribution to generic social work thinking, but it was not until the establishment in 1970 of *The British Journal of Social Work* and *Social Work Today* after the Seebohm report (1968) that British social work achieved a generic national journal.

The National Conference of Charities and Correction and the various journals benefited from the remarkable phenomenon of early twentieth-century American philanthropy. Philanthropic trusts gave generously to social work in the United States.[105] These foundations were extraordinarily wealthy: in 1900 Andrew Carnegie's assets were

$350 million, John D. Rockefeller's $900 million, Stephen Harkness of Standard Oil's Commonwealth Fund $100 million, Russell Sage's $65 million.[106] The new foundations not only gave money on a grand scale but also supported a scientific approach. The Commonwealth Fund was responsible for starting the child guidance movement in the US and internationally, but the greatest direct contribution to American social work came from Olivia Sage. In 1907 a bequest of $10 million from the estate of railway executive and financier Russell Sage to his widow Olivia established the Russell Sage Foundation. It promoted social work and the development of the social sciences, funded *The Survey* to the tune of more than $355,000 over forty years, and contributed funds for social work training in Boston, St Louis, New York and Chicago.[107]

While in the US the traffic in ideas was greatly enriched by national conferences and journals, British social work was without national professional forums and received only a fraction of the philanthropic money available to America. Even in 1960 British social work was still fragmented, lacking a national definition of itself, and without effective communication for the profession as a whole. This problem continues into the present. Standards for entry to the profession in Britain vary but remain lower than in both the US and Australia. Some British social workers share this view: Jonathan Dickens, writing in 2011, found that 'Forty years after Seebohm, social work is in as much need as ever of clear leadership and a strong national voice; but the battles about who should provide it are as heated as ever.'[108] Ironically, the young Australian profession, which had only entered universities in 1940, already had a national professional association, the Australian Association of Social Workers, by 1946.

2

Precursors of Social Work in Victoria

There is no training ground for social work in Melbourne save that of stern experience.

S. Greig Smith, 1930[1]

Philanthropically minded people in Sydney and Melbourne were the leaders in calling for social work training in Australia, although each city trod a different path. This was an era when most travel between the continent's two largest cities was by train, and communication was by mail. Although Sydney and Melbourne were in contact, their mutual influence was far less than would be the case in the present era of electronic communications and air travel.

Why Melbourne needed a Charity Organisation Society

Following the Victorian gold rush of the 1850s, Melbourne, then Australia's largest city, and the capital of the colony of Victoria, was one of the wealthiest cities in the world, with well laid out streets, and grand parks, gardens and public buildings. Rich Melburnians lived in mansions on the tree-lined boulevards of St Kilda Road and Royal

Parade, or in the distinctive iron-lace terrace houses of the inner suburbs. But urban infrastructure had not kept up with population growth, and the open drains and cesspits that prevailed before the introduction of a sewerage system earned Melbourne the nickname of Smellbourne. Carlton, where the university was located, was divided from North Carlton by a stinking open sewer. When the university's first professor of law, Edward Jenks, arrived from England in 1889, he commented: 'We have foul water, no drains, hideous architecture, and bad roads, while over-crowding, prostitution, and disease are in many respects worse than anything except the vilest quarters in England.'[2]

Events that occurred during one of Melbourne's regular typhoid epidemics, when the resources of public hospitals were overstretched, led to the establishment of the COS. In January 1887 an unemployed former goldminer, fifty-year-old John Jackman, died of peritonitis in a cab at the door of the Melbourne Hospital.[3] The policeman who had rushed him to the hospital was not able to negotiate admission, as all beds were full; the Alfred Hospital (on the other side of the city) also refused admission.[4] Jackman's tragic and avoidable death caused a furore in Melbourne. *The Argus* newspaper covered the inquest extensively, expressing outrage and disgust.[5] Following heated correspondence from *Argus* readers, Professor E.E. Morris of the University of Melbourne wrote an article outlining 'the concept of charity organisation [on the English model] and proposing establishment of a COS in Melbourne'.[6] Morris's concern was that a major contributor to the death of Jackman was the disorganised way in which hospital admissions occurred, so that one man could die, while another – who may not have even been entitled to public hospital treatment – occupied a bed.[7] By June that year, following public meetings, the COS had been established in Melbourne. Morris was to play a leading role in the COS for the next fifteen years, until his death in 1902. From its establishment in 1887 until 1945, the Charity Organisation Society played an important part in developing and implementing policies to help the poorer residents of Victoria.

Australians today are accustomed to national government provision of a minimum income through a system of pensions and benefits that ensures that no one actually starves. In contrast, in the nineteenth-century colony of Victoria, there was no direct government provision for people without an income. Until 1901 Australia consisted of six separate, self-governing British colonies (Queensland, New South Wales, Victoria, South Australia, Western Australia and Tasmania). Following Federation in 1901, when the colonies became separate states of the Commonwealth of Australia, significant powers were handed to the Australian Parliament, which sat in Melbourne until 1927 before moving to the new national capital, Canberra.[8] The states, however, retained responsibility for health, housing, child welfare, and care of the destitute. The Australian Government played almost no role in providing pensions, aside from the means-tested age and invalid pensions,[9] and from 1912 a lump-sum maternity allowance. More generous provision commenced only after World War II.[10]

In Victoria in the 1890s, government funding went to institutions set up to house disadvantaged individuals and families, not to direct income support as would be the case in the second part of the twentieth century.[11] The 'indigent' were looked after by charities such as the Benevolent Asylum at North Melbourne and Dr Singleton's Night Shelters. Children in need were taken in by the Protestant and Catholic orphanages, while the colonial government's Neglected Children's Department took responsibility for children who were directed to it through the court system.[12] The Ladies' Benevolent Societies, which spanned the entire colony of Victoria, handed out subsistence provisions, as did other charities such as the Salvation Army and the St Vincent de Paul Society. The situation was chaotic: some beggars targeted the wealthy with begging letters and visits to the door, some begged from churches, some in the streets, and they also presented themselves to the plethora of charities.[13] Altruistic Melburnians gave to these charities and as subscribers had entitlements to their services (for example, to send for assistance someone with whom they were acquainted), but the distribution of donations was uneven. As the COS had done in the US and Britain, the Melbourne COS stepped in to bring order to this chaos, believing that, if equitably distributed, there would be enough money to go around.

As well as attempting to coordinate the provision of these various services, the COS also developed policy and advocated on behalf of the poor. It attempted to take a systemic approach to their situation, grappling with the issues of fair and responsible distribution of charitable funds and the problem of how to assist the destitute without creating permanent dependency (known then as 'pauperism'). Its paternalistic attitudes to the poor are at odds with present-day values but were not out of step with charitable thinking of the time. There was a widespread belief that 'helping the undeserving … only encouraged them in their aberrant lifestyle'.[14] The Melbourne COS drew on overseas expertise, particularly that of the COS in the US and UK.

To a large extent, today's social work roles have evolved from a combination of the inquiry officers and friendly visitors of the COS. As discussed earlier, social work also has origins in the Settlement movement, but the strongest influence in Melbourne was the COS. But these early workers were not social workers in the way we understand the term today. Later professional social workers railed against the 'policing and detective' work carried out by inquiry officers. In an interview with *The Argus* newspaper in 1944, the University of Melbourne's first social work director, Jocelyn Hyslop, argued that to many people social service 'smacks of patronage', and as a trained social worker she specifically rejected the nineteenth-century charitable approach whereby people in poverty were caught out in 'wrongdoing' and told how to manage their lives.[15] She emphasised clients' rights to make decisions about their own lives. The evolution of social work as a profession in Melbourne, as in the US and Britain, was intimately connected with the COS. But it was an evolutionary process, and the later professional social workers differed significantly from the earlier inquiry officers and friendly visitors.

The Melbourne COS was breaking new ground on the issue of making fair decisions about who should receive income support – an issue that remains a matter for debate today (although it should be noted that in 2020 the 'unprecedented' Covid-19 pandemic did see unusual government generosity in supporting individuals and businesses through the JobSeeker and JobKeeper programs). Today, the sorts of decisions made by the COS one hundred years ago are normally made through the Australian Government's pensions and benefits system. Although the terminology that the COS used, applying labels such as 'impostor' and 'cadger', is shocking to our ears, the organisation's aims were virtually identical to those of Australian Centrelink today. Like Centrelink, the COS wanted to encourage people without disabilities to find work rather than live on handouts. It also wanted to ensure that the limited charitable relief that was available went only to people who were truly in need, not to a minority of people in relatively comfortable circumstances who were making a good living from begging. The thorough identity checks and detailed income and assets tests administered by Centrelink today are an attempt to achieve exactly the same end as the COS's nosey investigations. But the COS's central register and occasional public unmasking of an 'impostor' were weak tools compared with Centrelink's national database. Today, impostors, known as 'dole cheats' or 'dole bludgers', who either deliberately or inadvertently claim Centrelink benefits to which they are not entitled, risk jail for up to ten years and fines, as well as public shaming. The harshness with which Centrelink treats twenty-first century recipients of welfare was illustrated in the 2020 'robodebt' scandal.[16]

In its long history, the Melbourne COS went through several changes. Its *raison d'être* disappeared after World War II, mainly because of increased prosperity and better provision of government financial benefits. It changed its name to the Citizens Welfare Service and its goals to a range of family counselling programs.[17] The two leaders of the COS were Professor E.E. Morris (1887–1902), and S. Greig Smith (1909–57). Their thorough investigation of charity and early social work in England and America over thirty years was an important factor in the eventual establishment of professional social work in Melbourne.

The Morris era (1887–1902)

Professor Edward Ellis Morris (1843–1902), founder and first president of the Melbourne COS, was born in India, graduated from Oxford University, was a committed Anglican, and came to Melbourne in 1875 to take up the position of headmaster of the Melbourne Church of England Grammar School (for boys).[18] In 1879 he married one of the daughters of George Higinbotham – journalist, lawyer, and later chief justice of Victoria. In January 1884 Morris was appointed to the chair of 'modern languages and literatures' at the University of Melbourne. He was known as 'the philanthropic professor'. While the

COS was his main philanthropic interest after 1887, he was also a member of the Visiting Committee for Industrial Schools and Jika Reformatory, and he regularly promoted his causes through local and overseas newspapers.[19] As a Charity Organisation Society, the Melbourne group adopted the same principles and methods as its London forebear. Mr William Grey, a member of the Central Council of the London COS, was present as a visitor at the Melbourne COS's inaugural meeting, when it was decided to ask the London COS to send papers on aspects of its work.[20]

The COS was closely linked to the Melbourne establishment. For its first fifty years, its annual general meetings were usually presided over by the governor of Victoria, the lord mayor of Melbourne, or, on occasion, the Anglican archbishop of Melbourne (never the Catholic one). It was doubtless of assistance that Sir Henry Brougham Loch, governor of Victoria at the time of establishment of the COS, was a relative of C.S. Loch of the London COS. Lady Loch was a supporter, and made donations as well as referring applicants.

The COS worked on micro and macro levels, its overall goal being to achieve systemic change while also opening its doors to individuals in need. At first it hoped to undertake only assessment, referral and coordination of relief-giving but quickly found that it could not avoid providing financial assistance as well. Paid inquiry officers were employed to investigate the circumstances of applicants. Professor Morris found that the middle-class, female, volunteer-friendly visitors, who complemented the inquiry officers with a more gentle and supportive approach (more like the later social workers) in the American and British COS, were difficult to find in late nineteenth-century Melbourne,[21] where such women were already fully occupied with the statewide network of Ladies' Benevolent Societies.[22]

An important goal of the COS was to discourage the work-shy from a life of begging, and to link the unemployed to work. In September 1887, three months after commencement, the COS decided to open a book for people available for casual work,[23] and by the early twentieth century an employment register was kept and regularly reported on (another role later taken on by the Australian Government, with the establishment of the Commonwealth Employment Service). From 1890, following Morris's visit to the US in 1889, the COS established a wood yard, where men requesting relief chopped wood to show their willingness to work for remuneration. During the economic depression of the 1890s, the COS was involved with questions of unemployment and work schemes in the working-class suburbs of Port Melbourne, Brunswick, Collingwood and Spotswood, and in establishing a labour colony in the country town of Leongatha.[24]

Coordination of services was another item on the COS agenda. In December 1889, just two years after its establishment, the COS was distributing a guide to charities, which it had developed to assist with coordination.[25] In November 1890 it held the First Australasian Conference on Charity, and a second one in 1891.[26] Proceedings of both were printed by the Victorian Government Printer.[27] As part of the COS's efforts to coordinate charitable work in the early twentieth century, its members worked on a central register, to which all charities would contribute names of clients in order to prevent duplication (or double-dipping).[28] These were both initiatives that Professor Morris had observed in the US.

The COS was regularly called upon to intervene in broad social issues, such as 'baby farming'[29] (the controversial practice whereby desperate single mothers boarded out their babies, often to be neglected or die)[30] and Melbourne's winter distress planning.[31] It was largely due to the work of the COS that the 1890 Royal Commission on Charitable Institutions was convened. Morris was a member of this commission, whose recommendations Paul Anderson considers 'embodied the concepts of charity organisation'.[32]

In 1889 Morris visited the US. His impressions are recorded in a paper he gave at a meeting of the COS council at the Melbourne Town Hall in March 1890, in which he spoke enthusiastically of what he had seen, including the Sixteenth National Conference of Charities and Correction, held in San Francisco in September 1889, shortly before his arrival.[33] This was the national conference series that had given American philanthropists and later social workers an opportunity to share and develop ideas. Morris opined that Americans, unlike the English, were 'not frightened by a trip of which the miles are counted by thousands, and which involves travel by day and night for the best part of a week'. The Boston COS impressed him with its thoroughness and the large number of friendly visitors. Morris also visited Brooklyn and Manhattan, where he was taken to the wood yards where men demonstrated their willingness to work so that 'work be rendered, and the relief not given to the able-bodied for nothing'. He was also enthused by the COS laundries, which served as both a work test and as a training school for women. He told his Melbourne audience about the New York COS's system of central registration, which used a card catalogue 'capable of indefinite expansion', and ended his talk with a quote from a 'brother president in New York':

> I shall expect to see this society finally secure a house which shall shelter as a kind of mother home all the other charities of the city, where they shall be in close and intimate relation with each other, comparing results, economising effort, and diffusing

charity; so that, while every deserving case will receive prompt attention, neither effort nor money will be wasted. As I read these words, I thought that is exactly what we want in Melbourne.[34]

Although the title of Morris's talk includes both England and the United States, the English COS, where he visited C.S. Loch, rated no more than a paragraph. Morris made his interest in the American approach very apparent at the Town Hall meeting, and it is clear that the COS saw this as an important lecture, as it was subsequently published as a pamphlet. Following Morris's American tour, the Melbourne COS adopted a number of American COS methods and programs, because Morris had concluded: 'in that our city is a new city we have, perhaps, more in common with the societies of the States than with the parent society, our prototype in London'.[35] Introduced shortly after Morris's return were the wood yard (1890) and two Australasian conferences (1890 and 1891), and when the COS eventually established Morris House in 1924, it took on the American 'mother home' role mentioned above. In short, Morris's tour to the US in 1889 marks the point at which the Melbourne philanthropists who became advocates for social work made their first serious links with America.

During the economic depression of the 1890s, the COS was forced to reconsider its firmly held beliefs about the individual's responsibility for his or her own poverty. Following a speculative land boom, Melbourne was one of the places worst affected by this depression: banks collapsed and an estimated one-third of breadwinners were out of work. The money from overseas that had funded the city's expansion dried up. Melbourne charities were flooded with working-class families who had never before needed charitable support. Morris wrote to the London *Times*, asking English people who drew income from Australia to make donations to the COS.[36] In the opinion of one historian, 'Morris possessed a gritty honesty, and in 1894, aware that the best efforts of the Society and Melbourne's charities had neither alleviated poverty nor reduced unemployment he turned homewards.'[37] But the agent-general, *The Argus* and the Victorian premier all attacked Morris for his negative portrayal of the colony, and from then on he was *persona non grata* with the government.[38] Sad to say, E.E. Morris died in England in 1902, at the age of fifty-eight.

The Smith era (1909–1957)

The COS continued its work in much the same way after Morris's death, firstly with T.C. Mackley, who had been secretary since 1889, in charge of day-to-day affairs.[39] But in 1909 Mackley became ill, and a 24-year-old Glaswegian, Stanley Greig Smith,[40] who had recently emigrated to Australia for health reasons, was appointed as secretary, at first temporarily, and then, after Mackley's death, permanently. He was appointed from a field of 115 applicants. Smith had experience with the British civil service in Whitehall and with the London County Council, and had also been a junior reporter for his father, the editor of the *Glasgow Weekly Herald*. He was to work as secretary of the COS for forty-eight years, retiring in 1957.[41]

Smith's role became more like that of a twenty-first century chief executive officer, who manages an organisation with the support of its executive, rather than that of a nineteenth-century secretary who does the bidding of the executive. In the words of Ruth Hoban, the second head of the University of Melbourne social studies department:

> for demographic, sociological and economic reasons, social problems had become more numerous, varied and complex than

ever before. Voluntary welfare societies had proliferated to meet ever-growing diverse and geographically scattered needs.[42]

Lobbying

During Smith's time at the COS, the organisation became more active in influencing government. It gave evidence to the Royal Commission on the Housing Conditions of the People (1914); the Committee of Inquiry into Feeblemindedness (1923); the Royal Commission on National Insurance (1926); the Royal Commission on Child Endowment (1927); the Slum Abolition Board (1938); and the Federal Select Committee on Social Security (1941).[43] Smith is remembered for his long campaign to pass the *Hospitals and Charities Act* in 1924, a legislative proposal that had been presented to parliament regularly since 1912,[44] and which was important because it instigated registration of charities and guarded against duplication of charitable effort. Of equal importance was his role, thirty years later, as chairman of the joint committee on the *Children's Welfare Act* (1954), whose recommendations were largely incorporated into the legislation when it was passed.

In his role as secretary of the COS, Smith involved himself in many local causes, ranging from being a foundation member of the Children's Welfare Association of Victoria (1913) and the Lord Mayor's Metropolitan Hospital Fund (1922), to honorary secretary of the Carlton Central and Local Repatriation Committee (1919), plus half-a-dozen other welfare and children's organisations. His contributions also included running the Patriotic Fund at the beginning of World War I at the request of the lord mayor of Melbourne, negotiating with the Australian Government over the harsh administration of the new invalid pension, and the welfare and protection of the newspaper boys who sold papers in dangerous conditions on Melbourne's streets.

Smith's articles and letters to the editor on social welfare appeared frequently in the daily press, church magazines and publications of social welfare societies.[45]

Networking and co-location

Smith placed a strong emphasis on communication. He travelled in country Victoria and interstate.[46] In Melbourne he promoted agency networking through conferences of relieving agencies on central registration (1914),[47] and in 1926 commenced a weekly conference of representatives of social agencies to discuss common problems and exchange ideas. The charities guide continued to be printed sporadically. The construction of Morris House, a purpose-built home for the COS, was an important achievement of Smith's era. This three-storey, art deco–style building on the corner of Exhibition and Little Collins streets in the heart of Melbourne was a practical expression of a coordinated approach and of friendly cooperation between charities. As had been anticipated by Morris in 1890, it also housed other charities, such as the Victorian Society for the Prevention of Cruelty to Children, and offered its library and meeting rooms for general use. The foundation stone was laid in July 1924, an event that was followed by afternoon tea at one of Melbourne's smartest hotels, the Oriental, situated at the 'Paris end' of Collins Street.[48] But in 1957, due to financial problems, Morris House was sold.[49] The building still stands and is now an up-market bar and restaurant, once again called Morris House. Ironically, in 1980 in the changed welfare environment of the late twentieth century, when the emphasis was less on small charitable groups (helping others) and more on small self-help groups (helping themselves), Ross House in nearby Flinders Lane was established to meet similar goals. It brought many small self-help groups together under one roof, resulting in the sort of synergy that Morris House once had.

American publications

COS ideas were also disseminated through its library, which was open to anyone working in the sector. Most of this library collection was American, with little Australian material.[50] By the 1920s *The Other Half* (published 1926–37), the COS journal that replaced *The Charity Review* (1900–16), was showing a strong American influence. Both these journals were important in working through and disseminating ideas – local and international – about social problems and the COS's goals. *The Charity Review* emulated *British Charity Review*, whereas Smith's *The Other Half* was in philosophy and style based on *Better Times* and *The Family*, both from New York.[51] Smith, as editor, frequently quoted from *The Survey*, which he described as 'probably the leading social welfare journal in the English-speaking world',[52] and often reprinted large excerpts from it. The journal's title, *The Other Half*, was probably inspired by a New York book of photojournalism published in 1890 by Jacob Riis,[53] which exposed the degraded living conditions of the poorer residents of New York. The second issue of *The Other Half* advised readers that they could borrow *The Survey* (New York), *The Family* (US), *Better Times* (New York), *Hospital Social Service* (New York), *Charity Organisation Quarterly* (London) and *Bulletin of Child Welfare League of America* from the COS library – all but one of these being American.

International knowledge transfer

Professor Morris was not the only COS supporter to travel overseas to investigate social work. The reformer and feminist Catherine Spence, who had taken an active role in the Melbourne COS's two national conferences, represented the COS of South Australia and Melbourne at the International Conference of Charities, Correction and Philanthropy held at the Chicago World's Fair in 1893. She gave a paper on the Adelaide program of boarding out children, which she had pioneered. This was the conference at which the first appeal for the training of social workers (mentioned in Chapter 1) was recorded,[54] but whether Spence reported back on this to the local COS is not known. The first International Conference of Social Work was held in Paris in 1928, and the only Australian attending was not in contact with the COS,[55] *The Other Half* of March 1936 advising that 'as far as is known, neither Australia nor New Zealand was represented'.[56] Dr John Newman-Morris of the Australian Red Cross Society, who worked closely with Smith in the Victorian Institute of Hospital Almoners (VIHA) and on the Board of Social Studies, attended the 1932 conference in Frankfurt, and Smith attended the 1936 London conference. Both brought back publications, and Smith wrote a comprehensive report for *The Other Half*.[57]

The COS also took advice from Australians returning from abroad. When Alice Henry, the Australian women's labour reformer,[58] and Edith Onians of the City Newsboys Society[59] returned from visits to the US, they updated the COS. *The Other Half* reviewed Onians' book *Men of Tomorrow*.

The COS and social work

Over many years, the COS actively helped pave the way for social work education in Melbourne. As early as January 1892, the secretary suggested that the COS take advantage of the University Extension Movement to organise a 'class of practical sociology' with lectures by Professor Morris.[60] In the *Charity Review* of 1910 Smith wrote: 'Probably in no city in the world could training in social work be found more necessary than in

Melbourne. Our motives are good; our methods chaos.'[61] In 1916 Smith gave a lecture for the Children's Welfare Association on 'Social work as a field for service'.[62] In *The Other Half* in 1933 he reminded readers of 'social work achievements', which had been suggested by the COS as far back as 1917. These included a call for social service departments in public hospitals, now achieved by the establishment of the almoners.[63] In 1930 Smith delivered 'an experimental course of lectures on social casework and social problems to a class including Presbyterian deaconess and YWCA trainees'.[64] After the establishment of *The Other Half* in 1926, social work training was frequently discussed in its pages.

In March 1929 the journal broke the news of the founding of New South Wales' Board of Social Study and Training, stating: 'Australia has been dilatory in recognising the need for special education for social work' and describing professional social work education in the US and Canada.[65] In December 1929, after the arrival of Agnes Macintyre to start the almoner department at the Melbourne Hospital, the journal carried a long article on almoner work.[66] Other articles followed in similar vein.[67] In December 1930 the lead article in *The Other Half* was about the need for general social work training, pointing out that society demanded qualified medical practitioners for physical ailments, and suitably trained workmen to build their houses, yet 'when it comes to the question of social maladies … they don't mind very much who does the ameliorative or constructive work that is necessary'.[68] Until its demise in 1938, *The Other Half* continued to discuss and promote social work training and the young social work profession.

From the 1920s onwards, the term 'social worker' started to appear in the minutes of COS meetings. Greig Smith did not hold a social work qualification, but, after the establishment of the first Victorian training course, he was accepted as a social worker by trained Australian social workers. His combination of experience and wide reading equipped him so well for this role that he was regularly called on to teach social work students, and was made an honorary life member of the Australian Association of Social Workers in 1965.

The COS also worked in hospitals. From as early as 1913 its Aesculapius Fund was regularly called upon by Melbourne hospitals,[69] and even by the Victorian Government's Children's Welfare Department for the supply of wheelchairs and prosthetic limbs.[70] The COS worked for the Dental Hospital and the Women's Hospital (after 1954 the Royal Women's Hospital),[71] and had a longstanding relationship with the Alfred Hospital. In 1923 it supplied an artificial leg for an Alfred Hospital patient, despite her being known as 'an impostor and a beggar',[72] demonstrating that, while COS staff might have held judgemental attitudes, this did not necessarily stand in the way of helping otherwise 'undeserving' people in circumstances when they met COS criteria. In an address to a country hospital in June 1929, Smith said: 'My own society, the COS, has been doing a good deal of this family welfare work for some hospitals for several years. The Alfred Hospital, for instance, regard us, quite openly and freely, as their almoner'.[73] But when the first British almoner arrived in Melbourne, Smith was welcoming and took up the position of honorary secretary of the Victorian Institute of Almoners (from 1933 named the Victorian Institute of Hospital Almoners), befriending the English almoners and lecturing to the almoner students.

As well as providing coordination of the welfare sector and policy advice on improvements, the COS played an important role in defining the need for social work education in Melbourne. It sought out examples of best practice in the charity sector overseas, being particularly impressed with the US.

The settlement movement in Australia

As discussed in Chapter 1, the settlement movement influenced early social work education in Britain, although its influence on social work education in the United States was less strong. Attempts to establish settlements in Victoria were unsuccessful. The 1933 BSS minutes reveal that Dr James Darling, headmaster of the prestigious Geelong Grammar School, was interested in Victoria's six 'public' schools (that is, the most exclusive private schools for boys) and their old boys' associations starting a settlement along the lines of Toynbee Hall. For some reason he warned that it was 'advisable to avoid the name settlement in Australia', encouraging various other names such as 'community centre'. Darling suggested that these community centres would include clubs for boys, girls and men, a juvenile unemployment centre, prison visiting and a library. The BSS hoped that a university settlement on the English model could also act as a centre for research into social problems, assist a social survey of Melbourne being undertaken by Smith, and provide some student field training.[74] Lydia Eady, a member of the 1941 cohort of social work students, described a student placement at the Port Melbourne settlement: 'a group of young men led by a philanthropist ... used to go down in the evening and entertained the big boys, taught them woodwork and played games ... After the war came it was more of a family welfare place.'[75] Despite support from Rotary, particularly Rotarian Angus Mitchell,[76] and the work of Englishman Graham Taylor, who had English settlement experience and had also enrolled in the social work course, this Port Melbourne settlement attempt did not survive long. Dr Georgina Sweet, one of the founders of Victoria's social work course, had backed earlier attempts to start a settlement in Bouverie Street, Carlton, near the University of Melbourne, along the lines of that which had been established in Sydney in 1891.[77] Its enduring legacy was a kindergarten. Any influence that the settlement movement had on early social work education in Victoria was theoretical, coming from the British experience of people such as Jean Anderson and Professor Alexander (Sandy) Boyce Gibson, and from the literature. The University of Sydney succeeded in establishing a settlement house, and as mentioned in the next chapter, it influenced the development of social work education.

The Australian Red Cross Society

On the other hand, the Australian Red Cross Society was crucial in the early development of professional social work training. Its Melbourne Hospital Auxiliary employed Agnes Macintyre, an almoner from St Thomas's Hospital in London, to establish the first almoner department in Victoria. Later Sir John Newman-Morris played a vital role in the Victorian Institute of Hospital Almoners (VIHA) and in the employment of social workers by the Australian Red Cross Society.

The COS had prepared the ground for social work education in Victoria, and the overseas examples that caught its interest were American. Thus, when social work education did eventually start in Melbourne, there was some knowledge of professional social work, particularly of developments in the US. Local networks could be used to provide student placements and part-time lecturers. These existing networks were the bedrock on which the advocates for social work education were able to build. Without this preliminary work and the COS networks, the difficulties that confronted Jocelyn Hyslop and the Board of Social Studies would have been far greater.

3

Australia's First Social Work Courses

A very small number of people carried the main burdens of the Australian training movement in its early years and some had a long association with it.

John Lawrence, 1965[1]

For two decades, Australia's three southeastern states supplied the country's only social work education. For entirely different reasons, New South Wales and Victoria each set up separate schools for general social work and specialist almoner training, despite the overriding interest in generic training on American lines. Both almoner courses were relatively short-lived, the Victorian course amalgamating with the generic course in 1947 and the New South Wales course joining the University of Sydney course in 1958. Thus, Australia elected to follow the unified educational model of the United States. When South Australia established its general training course in 1936, it replicated Sydney and Melbourne's organisational arrangements. The profession was very small, with just fifty-four social workers in New South Wales, fifty-three in Victoria, and twelve in South Australia in 1940.² Western Australia had not attempted to establish local social work training, but the Catholic Church made an important contribution when it sent three women graduates from Perth to train as social workers in the US.

Establishing social work in New South Wales

It was the National Council of Women that initiated Australia's first generic social work education, in Sydney in 1929,³ not, as in Melbourne, the COS. Isabel Fidler, daughter of a Wesleyan minister and the first tutor to women students at the University of Sydney, was involved with the university's settlement. As convener of the National Council of Women's Standing Committee on Education, she brought together senior members of the university's academic staff with representatives of the council to discuss establishing social work education. In each state where social work schools were established, the pattern was for a small group of influential people to push for training.⁴ By 1929 a group of opinion leaders from community organisations, as well as members of the university's academic staff, had established New South Wales' Board of Social Study and Training (BSST), which would run the course until 1951.⁵ In Sydney, Professor Tasman Lovell was the inaugural president of the BSST.⁶ Like Victoria's Greig Smith, Lovell had excellent networks, being president of the New South Wales Council of Social Service and chairman of the New South Wales Child Welfare Advisory Council.⁷ The second president, Harvey Sutton, professor of medicine, Rhodes scholar, member of the Sydney University settlement and a man with broad interests in health and welfare,⁸ steered the board through the unhappy times in 1937–40 to university acceptance.

The BSST's first director of training, Aileen Fitzpatrick, had neither qualifications nor experience in social work. She held a Bachelor of

Arts from the University of Sydney, and had taught classics in high schools. Nevertheless, as a member of the National Council of Women's Standing Committee on Education, she was appointed as director of training, on a voluntary basis from 1929, becoming salaried in 1932.[9] A controversial character, Fitzpatrick has been described as 'a large effusive person with an ability to win over those who mattered',[10] and is said to have 'coloured the whole of the pre-war Sydney period'.[11] She had the strong personality and drive needed for the role of change agent, but unfortunately lacked one crucial qualification for this job: expertise. She helped establish the organisational structures needed to put in place professional social work education,[12] but her complete inability to teach social work or develop an adequate curriculum resulted in a serious setback that would have ramifications for years to come. As a result, Victoria took the early lead in developing a social work curriculum in Australia (see Appendix 4).

Problems started to emerge after Fitzpatrick spent nine months of 1932 observing schools of social work in the United States, Canada, the United Kingdom and Europe, and then in 1935 took a group of her students on a tour of North American centres (both trips funded by the Carnegie Corporation). Fitzpatrick returned from abroad considering herself a qualified social worker, but in fact had little understanding of the requirements of a professional training course in the discipline.[13] New South Wales' social work leaders believed that she was making exaggerated claims about her qualifications, such as describing the New York School of Social Work as her 'own old school of social work'.[14] Claims that she was the person who invited Porter Lee, director of the New York School of Social Work, to visit Sydney in 1937 are also debatable.[15] In fact, Lee's visit was part of a tour instigated by the Carnegie Corporation's Frederick Keppel, who had already visited Australia and had a definite vision for what Lee might achieve by an Australian visit as part of a far-reaching tour of the 'Southern Dominions', including New Zealand and South Africa.[16]

The trained social work leaders who had growing concerns about Fitzpatrick's competence included English-trained Australian almoners Stella Davies and Kate Ogilvie, and Englishwoman Helen Rees, the former head of almoner training in Melbourne[17] as well as Norma Parker who had trained in the US. Fitzpatrick tried to characterise the argument as one between the American-trained (herself and Parker) and British-trained almoners, whom she scorned, but Norma Parker shared the professional concerns of the New South Wales almoners.[18] In frustration the New South Wales almoners decided that their only alternative was to set up independent professional training, establishing the New South Wales Institute of Hospital Almoners in 1936 and appointing Helen Rees as its first directress.[19] Speaking at a seminar in Melbourne fifty years after these events, Norma Parker could still vividly recall the bitterness of this conflict.[20]

Fitzpatrick's appointment had been a mistake,[21] and was eventually acknowledged as such: when social work education was subsumed into the University of Sydney in 1940 it was on the condition that Fitzpatrick not be reappointed.[22] So, although New South Wales had established the first generic social work education in Australia, the divisive behaviour of Aileen Fitzpatrick hampered early progress, and alienated the social workers of that state, with the temporary result of fragmentation of the social work education effort in New South Wales.

In 1940 a newly arrived Canadian tutor, 33-year-old Elizabeth Govan, was thrust into the role of first director of the social work course at the University of Sydney, initially in an acting capacity. Govan held a Canadian Diploma in Social Service and was a graduate of the universities of Oxford and Toronto. She was confirmed in her role after the war prevented the successful applicant – a male economics lecturer – from leaving England.[23] After Govan resigned in 1945 to return to Canada, J.A. Cardno, a British psychologist, was appointed as the next director of training. When he transferred to the psychology department in 1949,[24] Norma Parker acted as director until 1955, when Dr Morven Brown was appointed as reader. (The University of Sydney's course would not have a professionally qualified social worker at its helm again until 1978, when Stuart Rees was appointed professor of social work.)[25] Social work education in New South Wales returned to the model of one generic course in 1958, when medical social work was incorporated as a third-year specialty of the three-year diploma at the University of Sydney or in the final year of the four-year combined Bachelor of Arts/Diploma of Social Work, along similar lines to the University of Melbourne, in 1947.[26]

New South Wales, though it had started off strongly in training social workers, foundered because of the choice of the first director. The resultant tensions eroded social work's influence in the state in the pre-war period. The New South Wales almoners did continue to actively support social work as a generic profession, and Norma Parker – who was part of this dissident group – later worked on the academic staff of the University of Sydney as assistant to the director from 1942,[27] with several periods in charge, and in 1946 became the first president of the Australian Association of Social Workers.

The New South Wales Board of Social Studies and Training, comprising senior academics and diverse local opinion leaders, was the model adopted by Victoria and South Australia, the two other Australian jurisdictions that succeeded in establishing social work training before World War II.

Victorian beginnings

The first social work training provided in Victoria was almoner training, commencing in 1929. For at least a decade before this, the COS had been providing a quasi–social work service to hospitals, particularly the Alfred Hospital, and had an active interest in promoting professional social work. However, it was a hospital without particular COS connections, the Melbourne Hospital, that in 1929 employed Victoria's first trained almoner, Agnes S. Macintyre. Macintyre had been recruited from St Thomas's Hospital in London, and in 1929 became the directress of Victoria's first social work training course, run by the Victorian Institute of Almoners (VIA).

The evolution of the almoner department at the Melbourne Hospital can be traced back to the Melbourne Hospital Red Cross Auxiliary (Toorak and South Yarra branch), which commenced in November 1921.[28] This organisation donated linen, established a volunteer-run tearoom, and by 1924 had set up a social service bureau to help patients who had not completely recovered when they left hospital. It purchased a special ambulance car to transport patients as far as the outlying bayside suburbs of Frankston and Cheltenham.[29] The realisation that a skilled and paid worker was needed to organise the social service bureau was a natural progression from these early welfare initiatives.

Various individuals contributed to the introduction of professional medical social work into Victorian hospitals. Mrs Constance Hughes (a nurse before her marriage to Dr Wilfred Kent Hughes) played a role in establishing the social service bureau at the Melbourne Hospital.[30] Mr R.J. Love, the Victorian Government's inspector of charities, who was impressed by his observations of British almoners on a trip in 1927,[31] persuaded the Melbourne Hospital's volunteers to employ an almoner. Mrs Norman Brookes (later Dame Mabel Brookes), president of the Queen Victoria Hospital for Women and Children, in March 1929 convened the first meeting to discuss the desirability of a scheme to train almoners in Australia.[32]

Love's notes following his observations in America and England show that he had fully grasped the essentials of social work. He stressed the important role of almoners in ensuring that the social or living conditions of patients would not stand in the way of their following necessary medical treatment, the necessity of paid and trained staff, and the need to separate the role of medical almoner from 'detective' (assessing means to pay), to ensure that the almoner could have the full confidence of the people she was helping.[33] The COS immediately offered support, and it was in the COS boardroom that the VIA held its first meeting, in September 1929.[34] In 1931 Dr John Newman-Morris of the Melbourne Hospital and Red Cross was elected president of the VIA, taking over from Brookes and continuing in that role for the life of the VIA (which wound up in 1950).[35] Greig Smith, secretary of the COS, served as the VIA's honorary secretary for its entire twenty-one years.[36] Thus the two Victorian groups most interested in professional social work cooperated from the outset.

When Agnes Macintyre went back to England in 1931, British almoners took over: firstly Joan Brett (1931–33) and then Helen Rees (1933–35).[37] In 1935 Dorothy Bethune, following a year working in England, became the first Australian directress of almoner training.[38] In November 1930 Lynette Henderson and Mary Noall, after fifteen months of study, completed their training to become the first almoners to earn their qualifications in Victoria.[39]

The almoner training was formal and disciplined, covering practical tasks such as arranging convalescent care, assessing ability to pay for drugs or appliances, understanding hospital 'etiquette', and learning tolerance and acceptance of patients who came from a different social class.[40] Some flavour of the student experience was given by Joan Tuxen (later MBE), who is remembered particularly for her role as head of the Victorian Society for Crippled Children and Adults (1950–80).[41] She vividly recalled a field placement at the Royal Melbourne Hospital in 1939:

> ... the almoners were in charge of equipment and the means testing for equipment. I was sent to the ward to measure a woman for crutches and she had lost a leg and I threw back the blankets to measure her and of course I started to measure where the leg wasn't. The girl had hysterics because it was the first time she had seen that she didn't have a leg, so I had hysterics. The charge nurse had to come up and calm us both down, so that put me off ever working in hospitals.[42]

Home visiting was an essential part of the social work role. Again, Joan Tuxen recalled:

> If we went on home visits we were supposed to wear our hats and gloves and stockings and be little ladies. In the hospital we were dressed in the most awful student overalls – they were brown overalls that they wrap around, that tied on the side. We looked like the cleaning lady.[43]

There have been suggestions that the almoners divided on Catholic and Protestant lines, with the Catholics following American ideas and the Protestants British.[44] This view is not universally held,[45] and my own research found no evidence to support it.

For three years (1929–32) the VIA almoner course directed by Agnes Macintyre provided the only social work training available in Victoria. But from the very beginning it was recognised in many circles that a training course for general social work was needed more urgently than ever. In June 1931, on the initiative of Dr Georgina Sweet, the VIA, together with the Victorian Council for Mental Hygiene, the COS, the Central Council of Benevolent Societies, the YWCA, and the Victorian Government's director of education, convened a public meeting at the Melbourne Town Hall, at which it was unanimously agreed that a general social work training course was needed in Victoria.[46]

A general social work course commenced in 1933 under the aegis of a new Board of Social Studies (BSS), the main teachers being Greig Smith and Dorothy Bethune. In that year the Victorian Institute of Almoners changed its name to the Victorian Institute of Hospital Almoners. Nevertheless, the VIHA and BSS courses cooperated closely. In July 1933 the VIHA decided to make the two-year generic BSS diploma a prerequisite of the VIHA course, which then comprised eleven months of full-time practical work in hospitals.[47] In December 1940 the University of Melbourne took over the BSS course; all BSS staff and students transferred to the university, and the BSS held its first meeting as part of the university. In 1947, when the University of Melbourne's Diploma of Social Studies became a three-year qualification, medical social work was incorporated into its final year and the VIHA wound up its course (but not the organisation). It had trained 101 students between 1929 and 1947.[48] When the VIHA did eventually close in 1950, it said proudly: 'the Institute has been closely identified with all later developments down to the transfer of the training course to the University in 1941, and subsequently, through its representation on the University Board of Social Studies.[49] There was to be no misunderstanding: both courses were on the same mission.

From 1934, the presence of a handful of trained local almoners greatly assisted the BSS's new general course, because they could provide both field supervision and teaching, promote the profession generally, and on a practical level demonstrate the value of social work. But the role of the almoners in the 1930s differed from that of today's social worker. Their time was devoted almost entirely to meeting the practical and physical needs of hospital patients, including tasks such as helping those who needed special diets, and applying for modest weekly allowances in addition to their sustenance payments.[50] However, from 1934 Victoria's generic social work training under the direction of Jocelyn Hyslop brought a more psychological aspect to education, in line with the American casework approach. By the end of World War II, social workers had roles in family agencies, psychiatric social work, group work and community development.

The establishment of Victoria's first generic social work course is discussed more fully in Chapter 4. It is worth mentioning here, though, that when Jocelyn Hyslop arrived in Melbourne in 1934 as the first director of the BSS social work course, Helen Rees, directress of the VIHA, wrote her a warm letter of congratulations, and the two women maintained a trusting professional friendship thereafter. Victoria had been spared the internal professional conflict experienced by New South Wales.

South Australia

South Australia was the last Australian state to establish a social work course before World War II. In September 1935, as a result of the advocacy of Stella Pines (a World War I nurse who had spent time in North America, including a period in Ida Cannon's social service department at Massachusetts General Hospital), it was decided to establish social work training in Adelaide. A similar process to that which had led to setting up the Victorian and New South Wales courses was initiated, with the lord mayor presiding over a meeting at the Adelaide Town Hall, which resulted in the formation of a Board of Social Service and Training.[51] Those attending included opinion leaders from a wide range of community organisations, hospitals and the University of Adelaide. But Pines was unsuccessful in her bid to become the first director of social work training in South Australia;[52] instead, in 1936, Amy Wheaton was persuaded to return from London to take on the task, with a meagre honorarium of £100 per annum (compared with Hyslop's £400 in Melbourne). A gifted woman, who had an MA from the University of Adelaide and had studied at both the London School of Economics and Political Science and the Tavistock Institute, including taking some subjects in the Mental Health Certificate, Wheaton had been involved in local charitable efforts, but was not actually a qualified social worker. John Lawrence, who studied social work under her, described Wheaton as 'carrying the course almost single-handed and being underpaid for it'.[53] Wheaton herself recalled: 'I found that I had to build from bedrock, that the Board had no financial support, no premises, equipment or books, there were no trained social workers in the field, and the community had little or no understanding of their role.'[54]

The course was taken over by the University of Adelaide in 1942, following the provision of a dedicated grant by the South Australian Government. Wheaton was appointed as lecturer in charge, at the more appropriate salary of £400 per annum. Nevertheless, she was hampered by the same lack of trained field supervisors, and difficulties in recruiting qualified staff, that her counterparts in Sydney and Melbourne endured. Wheaton, who was not attracted to the Freudian ideas popular at the time among social workers such as Hyslop, had interests that were more sociological than psychological. Reflecting this standpoint, the students received a Diploma of Social Science.[55] The smaller University of Adelaide course worked closely with those in Sydney and Melbourne (which generously assisted with field placements), but played a less active role nationally.

Queensland and Western Australia

In this period there were also attempts to establish social work in Queensland and Western Australia. Between 1926 and 1928 a Catholic priest, Monsignor J.T. McMahon, who had become interested in social work while studying at the Catholic University of America in Washington, DC, spearheaded a move for the Catholic Church to train social workers. Three young Catholic university graduates – Norma Parker, Constance Moffitt and, a little later, Eileen Davidson – were sponsored by the church to study at the National Catholic School of Social Services in Washington.[56] McMahon's plan was for these three women to staff child guidance clinics being established by Dr Ethel Stoneman, a clinical psychologist who had also studied in the US.[57] But the onset of the Great Depression, and a change of state government, resulted in the shelving of plans for child guidance clinics. Unable to obtain work in Western Australia, these three social workers eventually moved east.

Western Australia also had an early interest in almoning, with the Royal Perth Hospital appointing Aimee Eakins, a nurse who later qualified with the VIHA, to establish a 'social service department', which she ran from 1927 to 1949.[58] It is difficult to know whether, as some have suggested, the late establishment of social work education in Western Australia was because most people there lived relatively frugally; the state had insufficient wealth for significant private philanthropy.[59] The small and newly established University of Western Australia may not have been ready to play the sort of role of the three longstanding eastern universities. Norma Parker recalled that when she was an undergraduate there in the 1920s the students numbered only 290.[60] Had the Western Australians galvanised a group of opinion leaders as the three eastern states had done, perhaps they might have been able to establish social work education there. Eventually Perth became the fifth Australian city to offer social work education, when a course was established at the University of Western Australia in 1964.

Nevertheless, Western Australia's three American-trained social workers made important contributions to the social work profession nationally: Norma Parker moved to Melbourne (1932–36), where she started the St Vincent's Hospital social work department; Moffitt followed her, gaining employment in the newly established Victorian Vocational and Child Guidance Clinic;[61] and in 1937 Eileen Davidson set up the almoner department at Lewisham Hospital in Sydney.[62]

After failing to gain the position of director of the South Australian course, Stella Pines made an unsuccessful attempt to establish social work education in Queensland.[63] Social work education did not commence there until 1956, under the leadership of its first lecturer in charge, Hazel Smith,[64] who was appointed after Melbourne's Len Tierney declined an offer to become its inaugural head.[65]

National curriculum, 1938

Cooperation between New South Wales, Victoria and South Australia began early. The Sydney Board of Social Study and Training (BSST) convened a meeting in May 1938 at which those running the generic social work courses of the three states agreed on a national curriculum and national minimum standards, and established an Australian Council of Schools of Social Work. The catalyst for this meeting was the visit to Australia by Gertrude Vaile,[66] a celebrated American social worker who had played an important role in establishing the (American) Association of Schools of Social Work, which eventually became the Council of Social Work Education. This was done in the belief that the only way to realise the full potential of social work education was for all the schools to work together in a unified way.

The May 1938 gathering was primarily a meeting of social work educators. Those present at all five sessions were Jocelyn Hyslop and Dorothy Bethune (Victoria), Amy Wheaton (South Australia), Aileen Fitzpatrick and M.C. Davis (New South Wales; Davis's role was an administrative one as she was not a social worker) as well as Gertrude Vaile. The absence of Helen Rees, then Sydney's director of almoner training, was regrettable, reflecting the bitter split between the New South Wales generic course and the almoners. Much was achieved at the meeting.[67] The standards espoused by the American Association of Schools of Social Work and the standards of Adelaide, Melbourne and Sydney schools were outlined and discussed. The participants agreed on a range of necessary personal qualifications for admission to the courses, that practical work should not be more than 50 per cent and not less than one-third of the work, and that practical work should be supplemented 'wherever possible by discussion with [a] trained supervisor', as well as holding class discussions of 'the principles lying behind the practice of casework'.⁶⁸ There was 'considerable uniformity of content between the curricula of the three Australian schools, the greatest diversity being in the training on health matters' (a polite reference to the Sydney rift with the almoners).⁶⁹ Starting salaries and strategies for government employment were also canvassed. In the fifth session of the conference, Harvey Sutton 'explained from the Chair' that forming an Australian Council of Schools of Social Work would facilitate approaches to the Federal Government for funding, and it could act as a national accrediting body which could award Australian diplomas.⁷⁰

In October 1938 Newman-Morris became the Australian Council of Schools of Social Work's first president, Sutton the first secretary, and Wheaton the first treasurer.⁷¹ In December the Victorian BSS decided that the Australian Council of Schools of Social Work should register with the International Committee of Schools of Social Work, and a vote of thanks was passed to Newman-Morris for his work in preparing the constitution.⁷²

In July 1938 a meeting of the Victorian Council for Social Training was held at the Melbourne Town Hall, to report on the national meeting held in Sydney. Afterwards Newman-Morris told *The Argus* that 'an effort would be made to "federalise" the activities of those directing the study of social work ... without unduly lessening their individuality ... they would be able to ensure common methods of training'.⁷³ He also pointed to the opportunity for international influence by a national body, as well as the value of establishing national standards to guard against the risk of lower standards, should 'social service training centres' be established by the smaller states. Incidentally, it is of note that during this meeting the name of the proposed body was changed from the Australian Council for Social Studies, which suggested an

English model, to the Australian Council of Schools of Social Work,[74] a direct replication of the name of the equivalent American body. Sad to say, the Australian Council of Schools of Social Work lapsed during World War II. An attempt in 1960 to re-establish a formal association of schools of social work was blocked at vice-chancellor level,[75] and even as I write (in 2023), there is no such organisation in Australia.

The model of a broadly representative board, comprising well-networked local opinion leaders and auspiced by the state's only university, which was established by New South Wales' founding social work course and adopted in both Victoria and South Australia, proved successful in establishing social work education. A particular strength of the managing boards of the courses was university support and strong academic membership, the high status in the community of its members and the strong networks that the members brought with them.

The networking between the states, at first informal and then formalised after the Sydney meeting with Gertrude Vaile in 1938 and the establishment of the Australian Council of Schools of Social Work, shows early evidence of American influence on all three courses. They all supported a generic approach, and a strong emphasis on fieldwork and the integration of practice and theory through discussion with a trained supervisor, as well as casework. There was a direct transfer of ideas from Vaile, about course content generally but particularly about the idea of establishing the national body for social work schools on similar lines to the American Association of Schools of Social Work.

Thus we see that Victoria did not develop its social work training in isolation; it both influenced and was influenced by the other states to varying degrees.

4

Victoria's First General Social Work Course

There was a unanimous agreement on the need for a [general] social work training course.

Victorian Institute of Hospital Almoners, 1950[1]

This University quite rightly does not stop to pick up any casual pedestrian who hails it. It has to be satisfied about credentials.

Alexander Boyce Gibson, 1945[2]

Although a number of Victorians had been interested in social work education, the news that New South Wales had started a general course of social work training in 1929 seems to have come as a surprise to them. As correspondence from Dr Georgina Sweet (national president of the YWCA) shows, various Melbourne people had been discussing establishing general social work training. It was Sweet who in 1931 brought together the interested parties to convene a meeting at the Melbourne Town Hall in order to start social work training. In a letter to Mrs Norman Brookes, president of the Almoners' Institute, Sweet advised that the New South Wales approach did not concur with the ideas of the Victorian proponents, but 'that did not necessarily mean that we were right and they were wrong, and therefore decided to wait a little and watch the results of the arrangements made in Sydney'. The Melbourne social work advocates had not judged Sydney's approach to be 'as satisfactory as could be wished'.³ Six organisations – the Almoners' Institute, the Victorian Education Department, the Central Council of Benevolent Societies, the COS, the Council of Mental Hygiene and the YWCA of Australia – then convened a meeting on 5 June 1931 at the Melbourne Town Hall. This well-attended meeting unanimously agreed to explore general social work training. The letter of invitation explained:

> Most countries with similar problems to Australia – e.g. Canada, U.S.A., Great Britain – have already well-established courses of this nature in connection with Universities. The Sydney University has already made a start in Australia itself to put this important, and seemingly permanent, demand for Social Service in all its aspects into the hands of workers who will approach this difficult part of the world's work with the scientific attitude which is based on reliable knowledge gathered up out of the combined experience and experiments of social workers throughout the world.⁴

Victoria commenced its social work course in 1933, under the direction of the Board of Social Studies (BSS). Seven years later, in 1940, having satisfied the university with its credentials, the BSS reached its goal of full entry into the University of Melbourne. The fact that Victoria had no tradition of professional social work, aside from its handful of newly graduated almoners, is a credit to the tenacity of the staff and the BSS.

The task was made more difficult by the Great Depression, which hit the university badly. Major budget cuts resulted in staff salaries being reduced by between 10 and 15 per cent in 1931,[5] although with the assistance of private endowments the university did continue a building program.[6] In 1933 Melbourne's population was approximately one million.[7] The University of Melbourne, Victoria's sole university, had a total enrolment of 3,333 students, of whom only 27 per cent were women, most being in the Arts Faculty.[8] When it attained full university status in 1940, the Diploma of Social Studies joined a number of small diploma courses, including public administration, journalism, ophthalmology, laryngology and otology, and gynaecology and obstetrics. At this time, when most women graduates went into the teaching profession,[9] the social work course offered women interesting and flexible careers.

Establishing education on American lines

The 1931 meeting at the Melbourne Town Hall had established some important principles for the social work course, the most important being unanimous agreement that establishing general social work training was even more important than the establishment of almoner training. This meeting inaugurated the Committee on Training for Social Work. *The Other Half* told its readers that, on 14 October 1932, this committee met with a subcommittee of the university's professorial board,[10] to discuss 'University co-operation in a two-years course of academical [sic] training for social work'.[11] This meeting agreed on the establishment of a board 'outside but officially linked' to the university. In 1933 this board, calling itself the Board of Social Studies

(BSS), distributed a document: 'Training for social workers. Board of Social Studies under the auspices of the Melbourne University', thus emphasising the close university relationship. Subjects were to be selected from the university curriculum as well as from those offered by the University Extension Board and the Workers' Educational Association.[12] The university itself was to supply the BSS with certificates for those who passed the examinations. The article concluded with the view that the recent conference would 'enable the proposed Board to carry on its work under University auspices, and justifies the hope of the ultimate inclusion of the course in the official programme of University work'.[13] G.L. (Gordon) Wood, associate professor of economics (in the Faculty of Commerce), was the first chairman of the BSS.[14] He involved himself actively in the establishment of the course, even travelling to America in 1934–35, where he observed social work education and joined the newly appointed director, Jocelyn Hyslop, in some of her American meetings. Wood was succeeded in August 1935 by professor of philosophy Alexander (Sandy) Boyce Gibson, who was chairman until 1941 and again from 1943 to 1947.[15]

At its first meeting, in 1933, the BSS drew up the curriculum of the proposed two-year course. It included lectures in economics, psychology, physiology, philosophy, public administration, commercial and industrial organisation, social legislation, and state social services (see Appendix 7). The practical work consisted of two half-days per week, either at the COS or visiting relevant institutions.[16] A significant decision for the future of Australian social work was made when, in July 1933, the Victorian Institute of Hospital Almoners (VIHA) offered to cooperate with the generic training course, thus avoiding the British problem of fragmentation between numerous specialist courses. The almoner course became an eleven-month program, taken after the generic training had been completed, with the student receiving a separate, additional certificate on completion.[17]

The first four general social work students – Misses Frances Penington, Muriel Watt, Marjorie Goodison and Lois Lethlean – started their training at the beginning of the 1933 academic year.[18] Until the arrival of Jocelyn Hyslop in December 1934, the directress of training of the VIHA (initially Joan Brett, then Helen Rees) and Greig Smith of the COS took charge of the training,[19] providing lectures and overseeing practical work. Their teaching was supplemented by sessional lecturers and university subjects. The BSS, initially comprising Associate Professor G.L. Wood, Professor J.A. (John) Gunn (economist, and director of the University Extension Board), Dr Georgina Sweet (zoology), H.F. Audley (possibly a public servant or philanthropist), Joan Brett and Greig Smith,[20] met fortnightly at Morris House and, as a management committee, was intimately involved with all operational decisions. It discussed minutiae such as a letter from Mr Ball[21] suggesting that 'modern political institutions' would be a more suitable university subject than political philosophy,[22] and an offer from Dr Scantlebury[23] of two tutorials 'without remuneration'.[24] The BSS members took a close interest in the selection of students, and discussed examination results and individual students' problems.[25] As would have been expected, there were teething problems. For example, in October 1933 the BSS noted a discussion with the students about their dissatisfaction with the practical work.[26] The students told Professor Wood that the work at the COS was 'too haphazard and undirected', and that they could not see clearly enough what lay ahead of them or which institutions might employ them in the future.[27] BSS members also took on broad promotional and fundraising roles.

The first director

The arrival of Jocelyn Hyslop in December 1934 heralded a new era in social work education in Victoria. Her salary had been funded by donations from Melbourne's business community.[28] After some discussion, the BSS had specifically rejected the New South Wales model of an untrained local director who could be trained in the job.[29] It is unclear exactly how the BSS found Hyslop, although it seems probable that the London School of Economics and Political Science's (LSE) Edith Eckhard, who knew her, may have been the link, as Eckhard had provided advice on developing the course.[30] A Miss Macintyre selected Hyslop from three candidates, whom she interviewed on behalf of the BSS in London.[31] Initially Hyslop had been hesitant, as she was 'very anxious not to spoil her future chances here … hopes soon to get a good post … however, she is tempted as she liked Melbourne' (which she had visited the previous year).[32] The BSS looked to America for advice and assistance, and was granted Carnegie Corporation funding to enable Hyslop to travel to Australia, via the US, to inquire into conditions in America while *en route*.[33] In addition the Commonwealth Fund played an active role in organising Hyslop's itinerary.

Right from the start, Jocelyn Hyslop put her stamp on the course. The day after her arrival in Melbourne she told *The Argus* that she thought American social work was 'avowedly professional' in comparison with English social work,[34] because American social workers were usually university graduates who had undertaken a further two years of field and theoretical study. On her first day in Melbourne Hyslop attended her first BSS meeting, where the chairman extended a 'hearty welcome'. This was followed by a tea party hosted by Georgina Sweet at the Lyceum Club,[35] a meeting place, then and now, for women graduates and artists. Approximately forty supporters of social work education attended.[36] Thirteen days later, at the next BSS meeting, Hyslop presented the board with a plan to radically reorganise the course in the light of her American observations. She offered the BSS a choice:

> To institute a purely professional training as was done in the US, where not much attention was paid to background, the work being largely post graduate and where fieldwork was used as a basis for theoretical teaching [or] To set up a school of social science more on English lines, where a great deal of attention was paid to theoretical background but where there was little connection between theory and fieldwork.[37]

Hyslop advocated for the American approach, because she believed that Australia should prepare social work students to graduate as effective practitioners, not merely set up schools of social science. This echoes the debate of Mary Richmond in 1912 and is the opposite of the LSE approach. For this reason Hyslop insisted that more attention should be paid to fieldwork, and that more time should be made available for it: she recommended doubling the fieldwork component to two full days per week throughout the course, rather than the previous two half-days per week. The BSS endorsed her recommendations in principle, appointing a subcommittee to consider the matter in detail. This group met in January 1935, during the university vacation, at the home of the professor of law, George Paton.[38]

At the first full BSS meeting after the long Australian summer holidays, the board accepted the subcommittee's recommendations in full. It also decided to change the name of the diploma from 'Social Science' to 'Social Service', to reflect that this was a course of professional training, not merely a study of the social sciences. Thus, by the end of Hyslop's third BSS meeting, the course had been radically overhauled and renamed.[39] Appendix 7 compares the curriculum in 1933 and 1935, and shows that following Hyslop's assumption of directorship the curriculum was academically stronger, contained more mental health and psychology content (on American lines), had a greater emphasis on casework, and better integrated practice with theory. The most outstanding change, however, was the change to 50 per cent fieldwork, based on the American model.

Lack of expertise

A particular challenge for Hyslop throughout her time as director of training was to devise a rigorous course of professional social work education using the inadequate resources available at the University of Melbourne. This required a kind of inventiveness and innovation unfamiliar to those starting qualifying social work courses today, where the profession is well established and the Australian Association of Social Workers (AASW) provides guidelines on minimum course requirements. In a circular letter to colleagues overseas in 1942, eight years into the job, Hyslop lamented: 'we have no chair of psychology, nor of sociology and we have to manage with philosophy and commerce'.[40] Hyslop's first achievement was having her radically changed curriculum approved by the BSS so quickly, but implementation was to be the next hurdle. Difficulties included finding suitable lecturers, field placements and field supervisors, as well as sheer economic survival. The dearth of suitable teachers – both at the university and in the field – was a constant matter of concern and discussion by the BSS in the 1930s.

Another major problem was the managing of workloads of both students and staff, and maintaining a delicate balance between the cost of university subjects and students' ability to pay. Over the first decade a range of sessional staff taught the students. Greig Smith from the COS and the directress of the VIHA were regular lecturers, and a range of others, including Dr Anita Muhl,[41] Mrs Eileen Edwards,[42] Dr Vera Scantlebury Brown and Dr Arthur Phillips.[43]

In order to provide a strong curriculum, on a tight budget, with very few teachers with social work training available, the BSS had to constantly finesse the course. The following litany gives some idea of the juggling involved. In March 1938, the director was given leave to refuse individual tutorials because of her workload; she also reported that in an 'effort to reduce the lecture load on staff and students' she and Gibson had arranged to shorten their courses in 'problems of society' and 'social philosophy'.[44] In 1938 Muhl agreed to take the 1939 mental hygiene lectures free of charge.[45] In 1940 the BSS agreed to run its own economics course (taken by future head of department Ruth Hoban), as the student workload with both psychology and economics was too onerous.[46] In 1941 the BSS considered running some subjects, such as social history, and physiology and nutrition, every second year,[47] and in September 1941 it decided that Hyslop would teach social history the following year, so as not to increase the course's financial deficit by sending students to the lectures offered by the university's history department. The idea of prerequisite subjects, raised by Gertrude Vaile during her 1938 visit to Melbourne, was discussed as another way of managing the heavy subject requirements.[48] Throughout the first decade there was a constant struggle to find suitable lecturers and identify appropriate university subjects.

An equally difficult problem was that of locating fieldwork supervisors. There was no pool of trained social workers, except for the handful of newly trained almoners and, as time went by, the BSS's own Diploma of Social Service graduates. As the course emphasised fieldwork training supervised by a qualified social worker, this was a constant headache, for which various cures were attempted over the years. For example, most of the pre-war students had a field placement at the COS, which had no trained social workers on staff. Alison Player remembered hers: 'I had some fieldwork there and I spent my time there filing records and paying the occasional visit. I can quite see really that I was so timid that they probably could hardly find a client they dare expose me to.'[49] Joan Tuxen described being 'more or less thrown to the wolves with fieldwork placements', but she was slightly more confident than Alison Player had been:

> Well, it was my first fieldwork placement with the COS … Greig Smith sent me to this address in North Melbourne … at that time North Melbourne was very slummy, there were good wide streets with Victorian houses but off the side lanes were very, very bad housing. So this address I had was off a very nice main street, down a lane, and a lane off the lane … I think it must have been a converted garage because it had an earthenware floor and no beds, but just dirty old rags which they would lie on the floor and pull the rags up over themselves for extra warmth.
>
> They cooked outside on a little kerosene flame … most of the people just had that because they couldn't afford electricity or gas.[50]

Tuxen was visiting homes in Preston, then a new suburb, for her final placement at the Children's Hospital (where she would have been supervised by a qualified social worker) during the infamous Black Friday bushfires (13 January 1939):

> ... the whole of Melbourne was covered with smoke because the Dandenongs, Mt Macedon, the You Yangs were all ablaze, and the temperature was 104 degrees. I, fortunately, wasn't dressed in what we usually were expected to wear, hats and gloves and stockings. I had three homes to visit in the Preston area. So I set off on foot because there wasn't very much linking transport, I got to a certain point and had to walk between the various houses. I was just so hot. I can remember all the details of the clothes I wore. I had on a beige frock with brown spots, a little brown collar, and then a straw hat with a bow under my chin to keep the hat on in the searing north wind that was blowing. And of course, Preston was just bare, no trees, so I staggered from milk bar to milk bar to try and get a little cool drink to keep me going. Of course, social workers those days didn't have cars and social work students were not paid their fares for visiting so I had to keep going.[51]

Field placements varied greatly; Tuxen had an interesting experience in her second placement, at Travancore Child Guidance Development Centre (the residential unit had started earlier but the clinic opened in 1938), although once again she did not have a social worker supervising her:

> I was there the day it opened. There was Dr Johnson, the psychiatrist, Dr Bachelor, the psychologist, a nurse, a psychology student and me as a social work student. We were the team, so we had to work out how the whole thing was going to function. I borrowed a book from the library on the Boston Child Guidance Clinic and used their application forms, so that became the basis

of the beginning for Travancore Centre. But I also had to do home visits to all the families of children who were in the Travancore Residential Centre for Mentally Defective Children. I just got rejected everywhere I went because they thought they'd placed their children and that was the end of it.[52]

In her director's report in June 1935, Hyslop advised that she was 'daily more conscious of the inadequacy of the course' and suggested that there was an 'immediate need' for the BSS to develop its own training in the community, with extra staff.[53] Between September and November 1937 the fieldwork situation was further complicated by an infantile paralysis (polio) epidemic; placements were restricted on medical advice, meaning social work students could not visit hospitals or the homes of clients.[54] (Home visiting was a far more important part of the social work role than it is today.) Just as with the curriculum problems, there was no ready solution to the fieldwork problem.

Hyslop discussed this with Porter Lee, head of the New York School of Social Work, during his Australian visit in 1937. Lee advised establishing a project, 'preferably in family welfare work, run by a staff member of the board, absorbing a fair number of students, and demonstrating to the community good methods of work, and co-ordination of relief and charitable efforts'. He felt that while it was not really the function of a school of social work to carry projects in the community, at this stage a certain opportunism was justified. As a result a subcommittee was established to explore the possibility of implementing Lee's idea with the COS.[55] In November the BSS explored the possibility of new fieldwork opportunities with the Ladies' Benevolent Societies and Singleton Clinic, but 'nothing constructive eventuated'.[56] In December 1937 the BSS decided to develop a student waiting list, purely because of the shortage of field placements.[57] Eventually in October 1938 the BSS decided, on the advice of another visiting American expert, Gertrude Vaile, to appoint an assistant to act as fieldwork tutor. Hyslop wrote to England, 'asking them to advertise such a post'.[58] This appointment would strengthen both the academic teaching and the fieldwork, and also provide some much-needed support to Hyslop. The subcommittee dealing with this matter recommended appointing Miss Jean Robertson (MA, Diploma of Social Science, Glasgow) of Rugby, England, from a field of twenty applicants, only one of whom was Australian, on condition that she spend five or six weeks with the London COS before leaving England.[59] Unfortunately, the outbreak of World War II disrupted these plans. Robertson spent only fifteen months teaching social work in Melbourne, after which she was seconded to the Australian Government's Department of Supply, and then to the Industrial Welfare Division of the Department of Labour and National Service, to assist in the development of industrial welfare work to support women working in factories on essential war industries.[60] In her place the BSS appointed Kate (Kit) Jacobs, a local graduate of the almoner and social work courses, who had headed the social work department at the Women's Hospital in Melbourne, and had recently returned from nine months at the New York School of Social Work, partially funded by the Carnegie Corporation.[61]

Kit Jacobs' tenure was even shorter than Robertson's: just eight months, due to her 'acceptance of a proposal of marriage from the USA'.[62] Hyslop was understandably irritated by this second defection. She attempted, unsuccessfully, to get the university registrar to intervene, pointing out what an 'inopportune moment' this was, as the social work department was 'in the middle of this extra work for the government' as part of the war effort.[63] The university's next tactic was to recall Robertson, who refused to return to her position, both because she was 'developing a new branch of social work' and also because the university salary was 'very much less than the one I am receiving'.[64] Eventually, in December 1941, the far less experienced Ruth Hoban, who had been teaching economics in the course since March 1940,[65] was appointed to the position of fieldwork tutor.[66] She was eventually to take over as director.

These examples of the many staffing vicissitudes serve to illustrate the difficulties that Jocelyn Hyslop and the BSS faced in achieving the quality of teaching to which they aspired.

Budget problems

The most serious problem that beset the BSS was, however, its financial situation, which remained precarious for the entire period of 1933 to 1940. The base funding for the course was student fees. The BSS relied on donations of money, and even gifts of basic items such as chairs and tables, from individuals including BSS members and philanthropically inclined Melburnians and trusts. It also depended on personal guarantees from BSS members, bank overdrafts, and fundraising card parties and other social events.[67]

The tenuous financial situation had repercussions for both staff and students. The cost of university subjects had to be taken into account when deciding whether to put them on the curriculum, in an effort to keep student fees at an affordable level. In March 1936 Hyslop advised the BSS: 'it is becoming increasingly difficult to continue in the present rooms ... there is no cloakroom or lavatory accommodation for students and they have nowhere to read'.[68] In March 1937 the course had an alarming projected deficit of £400 (the equivalent of Hyslop's annual salary).[69] Attempts to obtain funding from the Carnegie Corporation and the Victorian Government were unsuccessful. Although a deputation in March 1938 to the premier of Victoria, Mr Albert Dunstan of the conservative Country Party, requesting a grant of £1,000, was reported to the BSS as having been 'extremely cordial ... and promised sympathetic consideration',[70] still no government funding materialised. Matters were so serious that in December 1939 Hyslop offered to sacrifice half of her previous month's salary, an offer that the BSS refused. Instead, Dr John Newman-Morris personally guaranteed a £200 overdraft, for the second time.[71]

These financial problems were only resolved when the University of Melbourne took over the course in 1940.[72] But even as late as 1943, Hyslop described social studies in a letter to the vice-chancellor as a 'beggar department as regards class-rooms ... dependent on the charity of Arts and Commerce (neither very willing to be charitable!)'.[73]

Research

Despite the many pressures, Hyslop was determined not to confine the course to the teaching of social work skills, but to develop research capacity as well. She had attempted in this Victorian course to 'give a more equal emphasis' (than either Britain or the US had done) to social science and individual work.[74] She lectured in sociology, which she had studied at the LSE, and she and the staff conducted social surveys on the projected demands on two kindergartens,[75] and made recommendations on the Brotherhood of St Laurence's Carrum Downs rehousing settlement[76] and on the National Fitness Council and the Children's Court.[77] In 1940 Hyslop led a group of social workers and students surveying and assessing the suitability of foster homes for wartime refugee children, working solidly for three weeks including weekends, and visiting 1,600 homes.[78] Hyslop and

Jean Robertson published the results of this survey in *The Australian Quarterly*, where they predicted: 'we are assisting in a social experiment which should have far-reaching effects'.[79] Hyslop also contributed social work expertise to training the interview team for the Melbourne Social Survey of Household Living Conditions, which was carried out by economist Wilfred Prest to assist with post-war reconstruction.[80] Ruth Hoban conducted a well-received social services survey for the municipality of South Melbourne in 1942–43 (discussed further in Chapter 7).

High academic standards were another matter on which Hyslop and the BSS remained resolute, and it was due to these high standards that the course was accepted into the university in 1940. The BSS minutes of 1938 note: 'Dr. Morris reported that the Board's high standard was criticised by two members of the Charities Board.'[81] Members felt that this criticism was 'unjustifiable', and agreed to send a letter to the Charities Board, 'together with some new literature'.[82] In May 1941 Hyslop pointed out to the BSS that the standard of the Melbourne course was 'already higher than in some other states, and that Melbourne did not offer any one year courses, as did some other states'.[83] In his farewell speech to Hyslop in March 1946, Gibson summed up her contribution to academic standards:

> Right from the jump she announced the policy of training from which she has never swerved: fifty percent academic work and fifty percent fieldwork. This formula marks us off from any other training schemes in Australia. It keeps our numbers down and our standards up, and it gets us into trouble with the advocates of mass production. But it ensures a supply of workers who know both what they are doing and how to do it. That is Miss Hyslop's

contribution to social work in Victoria. Could there be a higher recommendation?[84]

University entry

From the end of 1936, the focus of the BSS was to have the University of Melbourne take over the course. On 28 September 1936, Gibson, Hyslop, Paton, Gunn, Newman-Morris and Bethune met with the university's professorial board to discuss the matter. The BSS believed that its academic standing would not be an issue, as the university had congratulated it on the 'soundness' of the course.[85] The fact that the diploma was a two-year course was a problem, as the university normally required diploma courses to take three years. It was, however, the BSS's precarious financial position that was thought to be the main barrier to university entry.[86]

BSS members believed that the course could be financially viable if social work became a university department.[87] In 1940 the BSS made one more call on the goodwill of its donors and guarantors to enable it to balance its books; in October that year the minutes recorded that there were 'sufficient gifts and guarantees obtained to allow the course to be self-supporting'.[88] Donations ranged from £1 to £100, coming from individuals (including BSS members) and various organisations.[89] The other potential barrier to university acceptance was the BSS's insistence on a minimum age of twenty, and the right to reject students considered unsuitable. The BSS successfully used the fact that the University of Sydney had already agreed to such a policy to convince the University of Melbourne to agree to this.[90]

In October 1940 Professor Gibson as BSS chairman read a letter from the registrar advising of final acceptance by the university council. All those present 'warmly agreed' to a vote of thanks to Gibson 'for the way in which he had negotiated this approach'.[91] All BSS staff, including secretarial staff, became university employees; currently enrolled students continued their education as full students of the university, receiving university diplomas on completion of their studies. On 13 December 1940 the BSS held its final meeting as an independent body outside the university. The members of the last non-university BSS were Professor Alexander Boyce Gibson (chair), Miss Dorothy Bethune (VIHA), Dr Georgina Sweet (academic and philanthropist), Mr Badger (Colin Badger, director of the University Extension Board),[92] Mr Menzies, Miss Kate Jacobs (tutor), Mr Greig Smith (COS), Professor Max Crawford (history), Dr Vera Scantlebury Brown (director of Victoria's Maternal and Child Health Service), Mrs Eileen Edwards (psychologist, part-time lecturer), Professor Peter McCallum (pathology) and Miss Jocelyn Hyslop (director).[93] Gibson predicted that the university had shown such goodwill that the social work staff would be 'moving among friends' in their new home.[94] The course officially commenced in the University of Melbourne when its first BSS meeting was held in the professorial boardroom on 19 December 1940.[95] This, not the usually cited date of 1941, is the correct date for the incorporation of social work education into the University of Melbourne.

In 1941 the staff moved into 'three contiguous rooms in the Old Chemistry Building which it is hoped will be put in order by the university'.[96]

In May 1939 the BSS had made a second change to the name of the diploma, now calling it the 'Diploma in Social Studies of the Victorian Council for Social Training'. The reason for this change is unknown, but it may have been to achieve uniformity with other states. After discussion, the words 'of the Victorian Council for Social

Training' were added, to continue to emphasise the professional nature of the qualification,[97] which had been so important in Hyslop's initial negotiations with the BSS.

By 1942 Hyslop had firmed up her ideas on the minimum requirements for training social workers. She summarised her thoughts in a memo in late 1942, recommending extension of the course to three years:

> In the past, two-year courses in Great Britain have produced social scientists, and the emphasis was upon social problems and their remedy. In the USA the emphasis was upon practice as a caseworker in an attempt to help the individual help himself.
>
> In Australia attempts have been made to give a more equal emphasis. But social work is so much in its beginnings here that the practical training must be emphasised, because the young worker is rarely able to learn from an experienced person ... The Director has always felt that in a new country where training opportunities are less good than overseas, and where the young worker often has to start a pioneer job, three years training is needed for all work, not only almoners. The third year should, like the last two years of the medical course, be largely practical in character, with a minimum of time given to lectures.[98]

The recommendations of this memo were adopted and sent to the professorial board. Because of the intervening world war, it was not until 1947 that the diploma actually became a three-year course.

Jocelyn Hyslop had arrived in Melbourne in December 1934. Just six years later, in December 1940, and despite enormous obstacles, the BSS had reached its goal of university status. Hyslop's contribution was remarkable, but her success would not have been possible without the extensive networks of the BSS members.

5

International and National Opinion Leaders and Networks

Is it merely the isolation of Australia that interferes with the attendance of Australians at such educational and inspiring international gatherings [International Conference of Social Work, held in London in 1936] ... Is not our social work – and especially our social work with families – on a comparatively low plane of efficiency just because we do not inform ourselves as we should of methods and progress in other big world centres?

The Other Half, 1936[1]

The speed with which a course of social work education was developed in Victoria was remarkable, but this is not a simple linear story of the systematic implementation of a popular plan. We need to understand the way in which ideas about social work teaching and curriculum were transferred, over more than a decade (1930 onwards), from the US to Australia. Such means of transferral included face-to-face contact, with Australians travelling to the US, and Americans to Australia. These new ideas were then disseminated locally, through an exhausting schedule of speeches, writing and membership of numerous committees.

In Victoria, such efforts were far more than one full-time staff member and a handful of sessional staff could possibly have achieved. Social work education in this state owed a great deal to a broad network of organisations that supported social work, and to a group of opinion leaders who had worked together for years. After the course had been established it was promoted and supported by these well-networked members of the Victorian Council for Social Training and the BSS. They, as well as the new social work educators, used their circles of influence, which rippled out across Victoria and Australia, through organisations, newspapers and radio programs. Each of these Melbourne leaders was connected to different networks, which they brought together at the BSS and the Victorian Council for Social Training.

Face-to-face international transfer of ideas

When the Committee for Social Training was formed at the Town Hall meeting in 1931, it had consciously joined an international social work profession. These local social work advocates were keen to continue to draw on expertise from their counterparts overseas. This had been the rationale for sending Jocelyn Hyslop to study American social work education en route to Australia. John Newman-Morris had also been in the US, investigating the teaching and practice of social work in 1930, and in 1932 he had attended the Second International Conference of Social Work in Frankfurt. In 1936 Greig Smith attended the Third International Conference of Social Work in London. Georgina Sweet was involved in the 1930 Pan-Pacific Women's Conference, where she would have met social work leaders, including Jane Addams, who was the honorary chair of its first conference.[2] Professor Gordon Wood had visited the New York School of Social Work with Jocelyn Hyslop in 1933.

Although travel overseas in the 1930s was beyond the reach of most Australians, America came to Australia, mainly through the Carnegie Corporation. Frederick Keppel (president of the Carnegie Corporation),[3] Porter Lee (head of the New York School of Social Work) and Gertrude Vaile (associate director of the department of social work at Minnesota University), all of whom Hyslop had met in the US, travelled to Australia where, as previously discussed, influential consultations were held. Keppel and Lee both came as representatives of the Carnegie Corporation. Following Keppel's Australian visit in 1935 he had asked Lee to 'visit the Southern Dominions to study social welfare groups in the main centers',[4] which Lee did in late 1936. Encouraged by the generous funding that the University of Sydney had received, in Melbourne the BSS had applied unsuccessfully to Keppel for a grant of £10,000.[5] This may explain why it was made clear when Lee visited Australia that 'Mr. Lee goes as a professional student of Australasian and African conditions, not with a view to stimulate a series of applications to the Corporation in a field it has no present intention of entering.'[6] However, over the next twenty years, the Carnegie Corporation was to make a number of small grants for University of Melbourne social work staff, including Kate Jacobs (1940),[7] Arthur Livingstone (1950)[8] and Ruth Hoban (1951).[9]

Tragically, a heart attack in Sydney cut short Lee's 1936 visit.[10] He managed some consultations there, despite frail health, but because his planned visit to Melbourne had to be abandoned Hyslop travelled to Sydney to consult with him.[11] He suggested that the BSS improve the prospectus to emphasise the professional aspect, discontinue 'popular teaching' in the community, and explore training of institutional social workers. He also made suggestions about the field placement shortage.[12]

It is of note that during this period there was only one English social work visitor to Melbourne: Miss Ferrard. In 1936 the BSS granted permission for her to give some honorary tutorials.[13] Unlike the social work leaders from America, this Englishwoman was a relatively junior social worker, a friend of Hyslop's who had been a fellow student in the Mental Health Certificate course at the LSE, and with whom Hyslop had at one time shared a house.

The opinion leaders of the Board of Social Studies

The BSS created a great deal of synergy. Its inaugural members represented the six diverse organisations that had called the 1931 Melbourne Town Hall meeting.[14] They were the chair, Associate Professor G.L. Wood (commerce); Professor J.A. Gunn (adult education); Dr Georgina Sweet (zoologist and philanthropist); Dr (Sir) Henry Carr Maudsley; Miss Joan Brett (second directress of training, VIHA); Miss Mary Gutteridge (Free Kindergarten Union and Kindergarten Training College);[15] Mr Stanley Greig Smith (COS); and Professor Leslie Wrigley (educationist).[16] It held its first meeting at Morris House on 22 February 1933.[17] By July 1933, Dr John Newman-Morris, who was chief spokesman for the VIHA and its president for most of its existence,[18] had become an ex-officio member of the BSS.[19] Later, the slum clearance advocate and urban reformer Oswald Barnett joined as treasurer (1936),[20] and the founder of Victoria's Maternal and Child Health Service, Dr Vera Scantlebury Brown, had joined by the late 1930s.[21] Until the 1950s the BSS comprised diverse and highly influential people who had strong networks locally and internationally. Four members will be discussed here as opinion leaders, because of the length of their service on the BSS, the significance of the role each one played, and the extensive networks to which each was connected. They are Greig Smith, Dr (later Sir) John Newman-Morris, Dr Georgina Sweet and Professor Alexander (Sandy) Boyce Gibson. The successive directresses of training of the VIHA each played an important role, both because of the social work expertise they contributed and because their presence made it clear that in Victoria social work was to be a single, unified profession. But they are not discussed here, because each of their terms on the BSS was relatively short (two years). All four of the opinion leaders to be discussed have entries in Australia's self-described 'pre-eminent dictionary of National Biography',[22] the *Australian Dictionary of Biography*, and all but Gibson received British Imperial Honours.[23]

Stanley Greig Smith

Stanley Greig Smith MBE, JP, FCIS (1884–1970) brought outstanding leadership to his employer (the Melbourne COS) and to the members of the extensive networks that he had established in the Victorian and Australian charitable sector. Chapter 2 discussed Smith's role in the 1920s in paving the way for social work education by disseminating information through conferences and *The Other Half*. Here I discuss his direct contribution to the Melbourne social work course.

Smith was on the VIHA executive (honorary secretary), the Victorian Council for Social Training (honorary treasurer) and the BSS from 1933 to 1959;[24] thus he was involved in all three bodies concerned with Victorian social work education. His membership of both the general social work and the almoner training bodies contributed to integration of the two training initiatives.

Smith's ability to bring together people of divergent views was an important asset in the establishment of social work training.

In describing Smith after his death, Ruth Hoban said that 'All he did was greatly aided by his warmth of personality, tolerance of ideas which differed from his own.'[25] The respect in which the local profession held him is illustrated by the fact that the Australian Association of Social Workers, which was created in 1946, made him a life member in 1965 after his retirement from work and from the BSS.[26] His combination of experience and wide reading equipped him so well for imparting information about the young profession that he was regularly called on to teach social work (including almoner) students.[27] Before Jocelyn Hyslop arrived in Australia in late 1934, it was Smith and Helen Rees (directress of training, VIHA) who took on the major responsibility for teaching the social work students.[28] It was also Smith who convened the meeting in 1935 that established the Victorian Association of Social Workers.[29] He was a man who won respect:

> for his wise counsel, unfailing good humour, and acute and far-sighted vision for the future of social welfare in Australia. He strove constantly for a better integration between voluntary welfare services in Victoria, and their closer co-operation with statutory effort; for a better standard of performance in individual societies, including his own, for a more effective and protective framework of social welfare legislation in Victoria, especially for children.[30]

Like many of the BSS members, Smith gave personal support to Jocelyn Hyslop – who was not always an easy person.[31] Apart from making a great intellectual contribution, Smith was an invaluable opinion leader on the BSS because he was at the hub of a network of local charitable organisations with which he was in regular, direct contact, as well as exerting influence as the editor of *The Other Half*.

In Ruth Hoban's tribute to Smith, written in 1971, she recalled something of his private life, including his close-knit family (his English wife, Frances, and their children: Ivan, Greig and Dearcy). He was active in the parents' association of Camberwell Boys' Grammar School, which the boys attended. He also wrote poetry and short stories, and was a member of the Camberwell Literary and Debating Society and the Australian Institute of Arts and Literature.[32]

Georgina Sweet

Dr Georgina Sweet OBE (1875–1946), a zoologist, was the 'most successful woman academic' of her time, according to University of Melbourne historian R.J.W. Selleck, and the first woman to be granted a Doctor of Science degree in Australia (in 1904, for her study of marsupial moles).[33] She was an adventurous traveller, including extensive travel in China and in 1922 a journey from Cape Town to Cairo with her friend the historian Jessie Webb. She was an inaugural member of the BSS, resigning in December 1945 only shortly before her death in January 1946. On her resignation, the BSS formally recorded its appreciation of her fifteen years of support, and after her death held a minute's silence in her memory.[34] She was 'moderately wealthy' after the death of her father, George Sweet, a Methodist lay preacher and accomplished amateur geologist who ran the Brunswick Brick, Tile & Pottery Company.[35]

Georgina Sweet bequeathed several scholarships in her name, including a bursary that still continues in the department of social work at the University of Melbourne.[36] Among her philanthropic gifts were stained-glass windows depicting Australian flora and fauna in a church in inner Melbourne (subsequently demolished as part of the Housing Commission's slum clearances in the 1960s).[37] In 1919 she became Australia's first female acting professor, but, despite 'enthusiastic support from academics at home and abroad', she was not appointed as professor on the retirement of her head of department, Professor Baldwin Spencer, although in 1920 she did become the university's first woman associate professor.[38]

Sweet was a Methodist and the first woman member of the council of the Student Christian Union.[39] She had many wider connections, particularly in women's organisations. She was a member of the Catalysts Club, a women's society (founded 1910) and of the Lyceum Club (founded 1912). She chaired the provisional committee for the founding of Women's College,[40] and was the first female member of the university's council (1936).[41] Her leadership roles in the Australian YWCA and the Pan-Pacific Women's Association gave her international links. The YWCA, which commenced in London in 1855 to protect working-class rural women from exploitation, and in Sydney in 1880 with the specific goal of protecting immigrant women in occupations such as servant and shop-hand, played an important welfare role that differed from its more limited role today. Sweet was its Australian president (1927–34) during the period when social work training was being established, and a vice-president of the world YWCA from 1934.[42] The Pan-Pacific Women's Association, whose members came from Pacific Rim countries (including Australia, New Zealand, the US, Japan, China and the Philippines), is based in Honolulu and was founded in the late 1920s. It held a number of conferences from 1928 onwards, and Sweet was its first international president. Historian Fiona Paisley describes it:

> Through turbulent years of Depression, world war, decolonization, and cold war, its delegates met to practice a new way of being

in the world, one combining social reform with an anti-racist politics built upon ideals of cross-cultural exchange and interracial harmony ... providing a specific venue for and by women internationalists in the region.[43]

To the BSS, Georgina Sweet brought status at the university and among the wider Melbourne community, particularly its women's organisations, and an extensive personal and professional women's network in Australia and abroad. Her ability to lead and to promote ideas can be seen in her initiative to call the inaugural Town Hall meeting, and ensure attendance from local interest groups. The degree of her commitment to the social work lecturers is caught rather touchingly in the BSS minutes in 1942: 'Dr. Sweet expressed her concern at the tremendous burden of work brought upon the director and her staff by war conditions and expressed a hope that the next six months would be less arduous.'[44] This was not the only occasion on which she had shown this kind of concern. Not only was Sweet a strong opinion leader over many decades, but her local, national and international networks, particularly among women's groups, were remarkable. It is a great shame that no biography has been written of this outstanding leader.

John Newman-Morris

Dr (later Sir) John Newman-Morris (1879–1957) was an opinion leader in both health and welfare circles, and provided a link between the two. His lifelong concerns about the social and psychological effects of illness (which led to his leadership of the Australian Red Cross Society during and after World War II) made him an early leader in public health. He was president of the Victorian Institute of Hospital Almoners for most of its existence (1931–50), an ex-officio BSS member, and president of the Victorian Council for Social Training (1933–43), the committee to which the BSS reported. Thus, like Smith, he was on all three bodies responsible for social work education. He was a surgeon, and in 1927–28 was president of the British Medical Association.[45]

Newman-Morris was appointed to the Victorian Charities Board (to which both hospitals and charities were accountable) in 1929 and became chairman of the Queen's Memorial Infectious Diseases Hospital at Fairfield. He was a member of the University of Melbourne's standing committee of convocation, and was significantly involved with both the Australian Red Cross Society and the Victorian Council for Crippled Children (which played an important role in rehabilitating children after the polio outbreaks that occurred regularly in Australia until the introduction of a vaccine in 1956).[46] In 1930 he published a monograph, *Social Work in Hospitals: Some American Investigations*.[47] This covered the history of medical social work in the US, with detailed descriptions of the work of the medical social workers, including their recording methods, how they related to other staff, their remuneration, examples of the problems with which they worked, and how this improved medical practice and the functioning of hospitals. He observed at first-hand Antoinette Canon of the New York School of Social Work teaching a Saturday morning casework class. He spoke with heads of hospitals and of hospital social service departments. His monograph spends some time on the views of Dr Richard Cabot. It also describes the role of the American Association of Hospital Social Workers and concludes with a recommendation that Australia follow the American model of starting hospital social service departments with one social worker and building up 'as the need arose for extension'.[48] Given that Newman-Morris had just become a member of the first executive committee of the Victorian Institute of Hospital Almoners, and joined a subcommittee, along with Mrs Norman Brookes, Dr Ethel Osborne, Miss Agnes Macintyre and Mr Greig Smith, 'to draw up a curriculum of theoretical studies',[49] it is not surprising that this monograph reads like a guide to constructing an almoner course.

Newman-Morris, like Smith, fostered strong collaboration between the medical social work specialty and general social work. He also brought influence in medical and hospital circles, and in the 1940s played a crucial role from his position as chairman of Australian Red Cross. This included sending a small cohort of Australian social workers to Britain in 1944 to study psychiatric social work at the LSE (discussed later).

Alexander (Sandy) Boyce Gibson

The university connection brought another set of opinion leaders with important networks in both the university and the local community. Upon the resignation of the first chairman of the BSS, economist G.L. Wood, Alexander (Sandy) Boyce Gibson (1900–1972) was appointed as chairman in August 1935.[50] Between 1923 and 1935 he had lectured at the universities of Glasgow, Oxford and Birmingham (where he had been associated with their social studies course and the settlement movement) and at the Workers' Educational Association in Staffordshire, before succeeding his father (William Ralph Boyce Gibson) as professor of philosophy at the University of Melbourne.[51]

Gibson was educated at Melbourne Church of England Grammar School, the University of Melbourne and Balliol College Oxford. During his thirty-one-year tenure (1935–66) the department of philosophy at Melbourne attained 'an international reputation for philosophical originality and liveliness'.[52] His position as dean of the Faculty of Arts between 1939 and 1941, while also chairman of the

BSS, positioned him well for his negotiations with the professorial board in 1940 to have social work training finally brought under university auspice. Having an opinion leader of Gibson's status was of great importance in ensuring that the new course was welcomed into the university. He not only offered support to Jocelyn Hyslop, but as chairman of the BSS also saw it as his duty to be well informed about social work literature.

Other opinion leaders

These were just four of the members of the BSS. There were many other extraordinarily well-connected members over the first decade: Vera Scantlebury Brown, Oswald Barnett and Mary Gutteridge, to name just three. The BSS was ever conscious of the importance of spreading its influence widely, as illustrated in the discussions in 1938 when it was decided that a vacancy be filled by a Catholic. The appointment of Mrs Woinarski of the Ladies' Benevolent Society[53] drew in two interest groups through one member: the powerful statewide Ladies' Benevolent Society network and the Catholic Church.

Spreading the word

BSS members, particularly Smith, Newman-Morris and Sweet, had networks through which to promote the value of social work education. From its inception, the BSS sought out publicity opportunities in local papers, magazines and on radio. *The Argus* newspaper's columnist known as 'Vesta' (New Zealand–born Stella May Allan), who was trusted by the BSS, wrote a number of articles in her 'Woman to Woman' column.[54] Vesta was 'a household word for authoritative information and advice' on matters such as women's affairs, children's interests and community welfare. Like Sweet, she was both a member of the Lyceum Club and a delegate to the Pan-Pacific Women's Association Forum of 1930 in Hawaii.[55] All the Melbourne newspapers carried stories on the BSS, but *The Argus* gave regular coverage, including the full interviews with Hyslop on her day of arrival and at her point of retirement.[56]

In its first year, 1933, the new national magazine *The Australian Women's Weekly* carried articles about the BSS.[57] Hyslop and other BSS members also gave radio talks, on both the national broadcaster, the ABC (Australian Broadcasting Commission, now Corporation), and commercial radio.[58] From 1926 onwards *The Other Half* regularly discussed and promoted social work training. This was a small, readable newsletter directly targeted at those working in, or interested in, welfare. *The Other Half* also advertised the books and journals available from the COS library; in the isolated Australia of the 1930s, this collection was a very influential source of information about the latest developments overseas.

The intersecting networks of the main opinion leaders ensured that information about the young profession spread quickly in Victoria.

6

Jocelyn Hyslop:
A Public Intellectual

... she fought both in season and, most fortunately, also out of season for the claims of the trained social worker, and she has stayed long enough to achieve a revolution.
Alexander Boyce Gibson, Melbourne, 1945[1]

The most brilliant person social work has had in Australia.
Kate Ogilvie, Sydney, 1958–59[2]

From the moment Jocelyn Hyslop disembarked from luxury American ocean liner the *Monterey* shortly before Christmas 1934, Melbourne embraced her enthusiastically. Thirty-seven years old, stylishly dressed, with an upper-class English accent and a string of qualifications, Hyslop was just what Melbourne's social work circles had been hoping for – and more. She immediately gave a taste of her leadership style, telling the reporter from *The Argus*, one of Melbourne's leading newspapers, that Australia should follow American social work methods, not English.[3] Within two months she had overseen a major revision of the curriculum, and changed the name of the BSS diploma to reflect her views on the professional nature of the course. The BSS had paved the way, and continued to provide crucial support, but it was Hyslop who ensured that, by 1940, social work education had been placed on a sound footing at the University of Melbourne. She was the change agent Melbourne needed. When she resigned in September 1944,[4] senior university staff acknowledged her achievements. Vice-chancellor John Medley wrote: 'I and all members of the University Council and staff will miss you very greatly. You have made the department into a real factor in the University and the community and the work which you have done reflects the highest credit upon your ability and enthusiasm.'[5] Boyce Gibson said in his farewell speech:

> … the place occupied by the professional social worker in Victoria and the standards which the professional social worker is now expected to achieve, are the result of Miss Hyslop's own personal achievement. Miss Hyslop came to Melbourne in 1934, at a time when the pioneers in voluntary social work had reached that point of success at which the results of their practical experience had to be welded into a theory, and supported by a study of the social sciences. It was at this moment that Miss Hyslop arrived, and she seized it, as she seizes all moments, with both hands.[6]

The essential elements that Hyslop put in place in the 1930s remained the basis of social work education at the University of Melbourne, and in Australia generally, for the next thirty years. Indeed, her influence can still be felt today. The Melbourne course was imbued with her ideas, which had been strongly influenced by American social work.

Leading the way

Jocelyn Hyslop proved to be an outstanding appointment. Of the three heads of social work courses in Australia in the 1930s, she was the only one with both academic social work qualifications and practical experience in the field. She was also the only one with previous tertiary teaching experience. Perhaps it was her immersion in the complexities of actually doing social work in the slums of London as a young graduate that made her so conscious of the need for new graduates to be thoroughly schooled in what some British writers called 'technique' and Americans called 'social casework': the practical knowledge of what to do when faced with a client and a problem.

In her interview with *The Argus*, Hyslop outlined her views on how Australian social work training should proceed. This was her manifesto. She said that the course for both men and women would establish training in 'child welfare work, relief work, family welfare, work among juvenile and adult delinquents, medical social work, organisation for community needs (such as recreation, adult education and social research)'.[7] She looked forward to a compromise between British and American methods of training, saying that in America 'the great majority of students are graduates ... and in no school can the qualification be obtained in less than two years of fieldwork and theoretical study'.[8]

Hyslop contrasted the English approach, by which 'social science is taught and practical experience is arranged in the field', with the American method, which integrated theory and practice in the classroom:

> ... in the United States, the practice of social work in individual cases is taught and much of the classroom material is presented

by the students from their day-to-day experience in the field. Thus the practice of social casework has become a technique essential to all workers in the field of social relationships, and this technique is constantly considered, weighed, tested, and its usefulness measured in varying situations.

She went on to say that 'the English student, who is usually not a graduate, is given a wide background of knowledge – the historical development of society to its present structure, and the philosophies underlying social change. He is given much less help in his work handling the problems of individuals.'[9] She described the American training as 'avowedly professional', though going on to speculate: 'Perhaps a better form of teaching than either may yet be evolved in Australia.' Here she articulated her platform: a course for both men and women; a minimum two years of training (already being implemented by the BSS); a single training course for many fields of practice (on the American model); medical social work included in the general training; a decided preference for this to be a postgraduate course; a strong emphasis on integration of practice and theory, with 50 per cent fieldwork and 50 per cent academic work; development of skills in casework as a priority; and a scientific approach (referring to both social research and the weighing and testing of the usefulness of social casework in varying situations).

The first seven points are a direct transfer of American ideas. The last point, social research, may have referred more to Britain than America, as Hyslop was less familiar with American sociology and looked to Britain for that expertise. Nevertheless, 'the weighing and testing of usefulness' is a clear echo of the work of Mary Richmond in New York.

In her decade in Australia, Hyslop did not diverge significantly from these views. She regularly reiterated her vision as she attempted to bring it to reality in this far-flung country with its ignorance of professional social work.

Family background and education

Jocelyn Hyslop was born in Britain in 1897, where her parents' families had roots in northern England and Scotland, although both her mother and father had colonial childhoods. Her father, Canon Archibald Hyslop, was born in India, educated at St Paul's School and King's College, Cambridge, taught at Harrow, and after ordination in 1901 became the warden of Glenalmond School, Scotland.[10] Her mother, Alice Sophie, was the daughter of Dr Maynard of Rangoon, Burma (now Yangon, Myanmar).[11] Alice died aged thirty-six, shortly after the birth of Jocelyn's younger brother, when Jocelyn was just three years old. A year later, Canon Hyslop married Miss Bushell, a vicar's daughter. Apart from this, nothing is known of Hyslop's early life until, at the age of thirteen, she became a boarder at St Leonards, a girls' school in St Andrews, Scotland, which had been founded by noted suffragist Dame Louisa Lumsden to give girls an education equal to that of their brothers.[12] The 1915 *St Leonards Gazette* records Hyslop as being head of school and captain of games for her house, her best sport being cricket. She received a school scholarship, given to those intending to go on to higher studies.[13] After a year working as games and form mistress at Wycombe Abbey, a girls' school in Buckinghamshire,[14] Hyslop enrolled at the LSE.

Between 1918 and 1932 Hyslop had three periods of study at the LSE, interspersed with employment. The leadership qualities that she had demonstrated at school continued to be evident at the LSE, where the student union paper, *The Clare Market Review*, records her as a committee member of the Student Christian Union between 1918 and 1920, including terms as secretary and treasurer.[15] She was also, according to one source, 'a popular figure in the school'.[16]

Hyslop was awarded several scholarships,[17] and after completing the Social Science Certificate (the social work qualification) with distinction in 1919, and Diploma of Sociology in 1920,[18] she worked for three years as a social worker for the London County Council, then moving to a teaching position at Avery Hill, the London County Council's training college for teachers. Avery was a non-denominational college that emphasised practical placements in play centres, settlement houses, and baby welfare, in London's slums.[19] In 1927 she earned a Bachelor of Science (Economics) with second-class honours, with special subject sociology.[20] To these traditional British social work qualifications she added the newly established Mental Health Certificate (with distinction) in 1932.[21] This was to be highly significant for Australian social work, as the certificate was the fully American social work qualification that had been transplanted in Britain, and the first course in professional social work training in any British university.[22] In the American style it had 'an emphasis on a close interconnection of fieldwork and academic study on a concurrent basis, so that the week was divided into days spent in study at the School and in supervised work in mental hospitals and child guidance clinics'.[23] Hyslop was then accepted for a doctorate, but was unable to afford the fees.[24] Her last position before coming to Australia was as the first psychiatric social worker for the Leeds Babies' Welcome Society (1934), where she organised mental health work in nursery schools (preschool and childcare, for impoverished families).[25] Hyslop had chosen difficult areas of work in the slums of London and England's poverty-stricken north. An eyewitness description of the harsh life in London's East

End in 1933 speaks of 'warren-like streets, squalid alleyways and dank courtyards festooned with lines of washing'.[26]

When Hyslop travelled through America on her way to Australia she was already familiar with American social work ideas. Although it was the Carnegie Corporation that had funded her American visit, much of her program was arranged by the Commonwealth Fund. Mildred Scoville, a social worker employed by the Commonwealth Fund and who had established close friendships with many British social workers through her frequent visits, set up a range of interviews for her. She welcomed Hyslop into the Commonwealth Fund's educational program, writing to Miss Dawley of the Philadelphia Child Guidance Clinic:

> She was one of our fellowship students in the Mental Health Course at the London School of Economics, and has come to me for assistance in working out a worthwhile program during her brief stay here ... I think she will be interested in learning about all aspects of the Clinic's work and will probably have a great many pertinent questions to ask as she is a very intelligent person and seems to know in advance just the type of information she wants to obtain.[27]

In a letter to Miss Tracy, director of the course in psychiatric social work at Western Reserve University, Cleveland, Scoville advised:

> Although she personally is interested in all things psychiatric, her special interest in this country happens to be much broader, as she will, of course, have to set up all types of social work training, of which for some time there will be very little that is psychiatric. I think the only real training already started in

Melbourne is that for medical social workers, but she will have to develop other aspects of the work in the face of such tremendous difficulties as having practically no trained social workers in the organisations in Melbourne.[28]

Scoville saw to it that Hyslop visited child guidance clinics and social agencies, as well as meeting leaders in social work education. She wrote a personal letter of introduction to Chicago's Charlotte Towle, the social worker who twenty years later would play a significant role in introducing American generic social work to the LSE as part of the Carnegie Experiment (discussed in Chapter 1).[29] Hyslop was able to draw on Scoville's experience in establishing a new course of social work in England as she planned for her future role in Australia.

Hyslop summarised her impressions of American social work education in a letter to Frederick Keppel in 1934.[30] She singled out the New York School of Social Work[31] and the Pennsylvania school as 'the most useful'. She was impressed with the fact that the New York School was 'arriving at a generic training which will make the worker such that he or she can do a social casework job, in whatever agency may hire him or her'. She felt that Pennsylvania was 'probably training its workers on more psychiatric lines, but would appear to be working more closely with the agencies' than the New York School.[32] She also commented on Cleveland (too beholden to the local community), Chicago (high standards but too many students) and Minnesota (insufficient professional training). She was impressed that field teachers were appointed and paid by the university. The American study tour helped Hyslop refine her ideas, giving her an opportunity to see generic education in action in New York and observe examples of high academic standards and sound field education.

Philosophy of the individual in society

In Melbourne Jocelyn Hyslop did much more than inaugurate professional social work education; she promoted social work ideas and values to the community at large. She held a consistent underlying set of beliefs about the role of the social worker as encompassing the individual and their situation in society (what social workers now refer to as 'person in environment'). She was as interested in the causes of social dysfunction as in its remedies. Two articles published in 1938 explain her philosophy. *The Australian Quarterly* published a version of a speech that Hyslop had given for Women's College at the University of Melbourne, which had opened the previous year, entitled 'A philosophy of social progress'.[33] This article is a plea for greater involvement of the citizenry in planning for welfare, and for greater understanding of the disadvantaged in society. It criticises inaccessible government institutions and members of society who move only in their own confined circles, ignorant and uncaring about others. She talks about the concern of the social worker 'with the achievement of social welfare, on different levels, psychological, physical, material and in different spheres, governmental or voluntary'. She speaks of 'social invalids' who must 'be helped to a readjustment within which the burdens of life can be effectively resumed'. She challenges her audience to think about questions such as whether, if the unemployed are victims of the economic system, they should be entitled to the 'same kind of consideration as is received by the returned soldier'. She criticises the prevailing social order, and people's complacency: 'we see every day the results of our social order in sustenance strikes ... the cripple whose parents are unwilling for him to learn a trade lest he lose his pension'. She suggests that, because of the way society was organised into narrow interests, further complicated by the complexities of Australia's dual state and federal systems, 'we cannot participate in government even by criticism ... Canberra is too far away, State functions are too centralised.[34] We do not have controversial periodicals ... Things which are really well done, such as Baby Health organization, kindergarten work, parks and gardens ... are functions in which local interest and local participation are both possible and actual.' She challenges the audience: 'How many people have been into a State School, a hospital out-patients department, a pawn-shop, a sustenance office, a prison or a juvenile court?' and concludes:

> Thus I would say that ultimately it is one's attitude that counts – the way in which we interpret people's behaviour, the degree to which we are prepared to respect the personality of a fellow-citizen, and the view we take of the capacity of social good of our social institutions and organizations. Have we any right to condemn the sustenance road workers for idleness, while we forget the months of underfeeding, the blistered hands, and the lack of incentive in a 'rationed' task? It is the right of every one to expect such consideration, and it is the duty of all to attempt to give it. Such reciprocity will give us social justice – the only possible condition of social progress.[35]

The *Hospital Magazine* of August 1938 ran a typically feisty article by Hyslop: 'Training Council's Director Urges Expert Attack on Problems' Real Causes: Aid for Re-adjustment in the Families'.[36] In this article, aimed at a medical and nursing audience, Hyslop focuses on promoting the role of the thoroughly modern social worker. She seeks to lay to rest any connection between her social work course and old-fashioned charity work. She is scathing about the English tradition, which has 'laid too much upon "service" – doing something for people rather than providing the conditions with which people can do things for themselves', blaming this on 'an aristocratic tradition tempered by religious and humanitarian influence', alluding to nineteenth-century governments that 'confused poverty with vice'.[37] She shows how the emphasis on preventive medicine in the twentieth century affected the way social problems were viewed: 'research showed that sweated labour led to malnutrition and truancy among school children far more often than parental neglect'. She looks to the new and scientific future, pointing out that the Great War had brought a 'spectacular development in the field of psychology with … realisation of the importance of personality, types and patterns'. She applauds the US, where this new knowledge was applied in the field of social service, as 'it was realised that social planning was likely to be inappropriate unless it were related to the needs of the individual and his ability to co-operate'.[38] She looks to a psychological approach in the future, where children will not be admitted to institutions, but the social worker can find out 'why there are difficulties and help the parents themselves to make such a readjustment that the child can remain at home'. She goes on to stress that social workers have gone beyond the idea of 'doing' or 'giving', to 'finding out' and suspending judgement until the facts are known, the most important thing being 'the problem as the client sees it – for after all, it is his problem'. The social workers she is training will be equipped to:

> attack the problems of society with understanding and knowledge – knowledge of social history, economics, political theory, social philosophy, psychology, physiology – and practical acquaintance with social legislation … It [the Victorian Council for Social

Training] believes that much social service is only palliative, and theoretical studies are integrated for the student in actual social work practice on which half the two-year course is spent.[39]

Hyslop regularly juxtaposed the bad old methods of charity against a new approach that refused to blame people for their predicaments. Her analytical and scientific approach looked to a future where many of these problems would be prevented.

Hyslop was in demand as a public speaker. The wide span of her interests can be seen in reports of some of her many public engagements, where her views reached a general audience. In 1936 she addressed the Legal Women's Association on the subject of children's courts, advocating for a single children's court backed up by treatment facilities, rather than the eighteen courts then operating:

> The very term Children's Court is a contradiction ... The word child normally implies freedom from responsibility; the word court, on the other hand, implies responsibility to the community ... [In Victoria] a child is tried and convicted under the same procedure as an adult. In England the Court ascertains and finds guilty without actually convicting.[40]

In 1938, under the heading 'Social Work Criticised', *The Argus* reported Hyslop's speech to the Rotary Club, in which she criticised 'chaotic conditions in voluntary and State social welfare work', and asked: 'who receives any good at all from the deplorable and scandalous scramble among organisations to raise money for our hospitals?' She concluded: 'a little clearer thinking might help us all'.[41] During her time in Australia she managed a heavy speaking and lecturing load, gave radio talks, and involved herself in organisations as diverse as the Slum Abolition League, the Playgrounds Association, and the Commonwealth Nutrition Enquiry.[42] Her busy schedule was facilitated by the provision of a car by one of her philanthropic supporters.

In October 1944, on the announcement of her impending retirement as director of the BSS, Hyslop gave a frank interview to *The Argus*: 'To many people the term social service smacks of patronage – but I think these people are wrong. I believe that in all our schemes for social betterment, State or voluntary, we need the social service worker and the contribution she can make.'[43] The article goes on to discuss Hyslop's views on what the social service worker's contribution is *not*:

> It is not giving charity – soup, flannel, and groceries – as in the good old days in England; neither is it giving good advice, telling people how to bring up their children, how they should spend their money; nor is it inspection – hoping to catch people out in wrongdoing or with their houses untidy. What the social worker does is to try to help people to help themselves.[44]

Hyslop's ideas circulated well beyond social work circles; indeed, she has been identified as one of the early influences in social science in Melbourne.[45] And her words were not merely theoretical rhetoric. Hyslop knew exactly how to bring about change at the local level, as a letter she wrote to a former student, Edna Mendelsohn (née Smale), in May 1946, advising her on establishing an association to develop local preschools, shows:

> I think you want to aim at a Council, and two or three reps. from pre-school groups; (there may be complications when you come

to Baptists in Ivanhoe v Baptists in Fairfield. I think they should count as one.) This gives a good representation which they feel is satisfactory – and then aim at series of c'ttees. Some ad hoc e.g. when a new KG is to be built, with a permanent Executive. Probably your present shd be a constituent body, sending its 3 reps unless they decide a particular member should have more. Your Executive wd. need to be very strong and good. Probably you will want Reps of Health Dept, K.G. Union, N.S. Edu. Bd and L. City Council on your Council and any other body from time to time as seems helpful ... a meeting be called to which all interested be asked including the Reputable and disreputable, and the local Edu Dept Inspector so that the black sheep and white may have the chance to come in.[46]

She finished off with advice about promotional strategies, including letting the press know they were conducting a survey on facilitation of coordinating preschool activities, as a prelude to advertising the public meeting.

Social workers in the twenty-first century are interested in whether forceful leaders such as Hyslop thought of themselves as feminists. While today it would be assumed that Hyslop was a feminist, she worked in the period between the two waves of feminism. Although she attended a boarding school founded by a suffragist and was an outspoken leader, acutely aware of society's role in causing individual disadvantage, issues of women's rights do not appear anywhere in Hyslop's writing. Ann Oakley's recent biography of herself and her famous father, Richard Titmuss, head of social administration at the LSE from 1950, throws some light on the gender politics in universities between the two waves of feminism. She describes in some detail 'the injustices of gender' in the department of social administration at the LSE, where the social work staff was entirely female in this mainly male environment.[47] This had been Hyslop's training ground – and indeed, the career of her mentor Edith Eckhard is an example of the exploitation of a hard-working woman in a sexist environment. Eileen Younghusband (roughly a contemporary of Hyslop's) reflected in an interview that it had never occurred to her that she was being 'kept down because she was a woman', but that she had grown up with 'the whole attitude that women were inferior to men. It was never said, it was just part of the atmosphere.'[48] Being a woman of the same era and similar background, Hyslop is likely to have shared Younghusband's unquestioning acceptance of the inevitability of the lower status of women. Her confident actions speak of feminism, just as Younghusband's did, but she was not the only strong woman living between the first and second wave of women's movements who did not have a raised consciousness about the discrimination that resulted from her gender.

To round out the picture it should be noted here that the charming and brilliant Hyslop was also deeply troubled. Melbourne's Professor Gibson described her as 'controversial, highest qualifications, any amount of go, enterprise. High standards, intolerant of incompetence, enlightened and intelligent'.[49] She was a 'grand planner', but had a 'cutting tongue [and] trod on people's toes'. He also remarked on her 'instability'.[50] Patricia Duxbury (née Holmes) (whose role in developing psychiatric social work is discussed in the next chapter) recalled: 'her tutorials could be disconcerting … you never knew if you were a "goodie" or a "baddie"'.[51]

Advice on future directions

After her resignation, Jocelyn Hyslop wrote a number of papers about the future of social work education in Melbourne. She strongly advocated extending the course to three years,[52] because 'the young worker often has to start a pioneer job', and argued that three years' training was needed for all workers, not only almoners. She recommended a model close to the LSE, with a male sociologist in charge and a 'very good woman' to run social work training.[53] She made recommendations of suitable British sociologists, to 'ensure sound sociological thinking, related to community and individual needs', and advised that 'a keen young man, e.g. A.D.K. Owen,[54] might be got as director and to develop the department towards a status meriting the establishment of a Chair of Sociology or Social Science'.[55]

It is surprising to us today to find this advocate of professional training looking to place social work under a male sociologist, although Hyslop did argue that the disciplines would be a stimulus for each other. She may well have felt that the future of social work in the University of Melbourne would be better protected if it were to be located in a traditional department with its own professor to look out for its interests, rather than the unusual Melbourne situation in which social studies was a small, stand-alone course directed by the BSS, which had a non–social worker chairman. Ultimately, the lack of integration of the social work course into university structures and hierarchies was one of the causes of the difficulties it would face in the 1950s.

Postscript

After leaving Australia in 1946, Jocelyn Hyslop moved to South Africa and lost contact with her Australian colleagues.[56] There she became a novice in an Anglican order in Grahamstown, the Community of the Resurrection of Our Lord, and was professed in 1957.[57] (In 1943, following a severe bout of depression during which she had a life-changing spiritual revelation, she had returned to the Anglican faith which she had previously rejected.[58][59]) She used her old skills: teaching at training college, lecturing in divinity and psychology. She also did considerable work with children, 'outreach work', and undertook broadcasting and television responsibilities as well as editing *The Crozier*, the order's newsletter. After her death at the age of eighty, her memorial book records that she had 'an original mind and ... a wonderful gift for making contacts with every type of person – young and old, rich and poor, sick and well ... in her counselling there were never "cases" but persons for whom Christ died.' The skills and values of the social worker Miss Jocelyn Hyslop continued in Sister Jocelyn's religious life. Perhaps most significantly, this woman who had lost her own mother in infancy retained her lifelong commitment to, and empathy with, children. Many members of the Anglican Church were courageous in their opposition to Apartheid; it would be interesting to know how Hyslop responded to this situation in the last stage of her life.[60]

Jocelyn Hyslop stood for a new kind of social work, one that was scientifically based and allied with the disciplines of sociology and psychology, including psychoanalysis. She was dedicated first and foremost to high academic standards and to preparing students to be immediately effective in the workforce. As someone with a sophisticated understanding of the new fields of sociology and psychology, she played a role similar to that of a public intellectual in the twenty-first century, and was a popular and controversial speaker on a wide range of social issues. She looked to America for best practice in social work education; nevertheless, consistent with her view that perhaps Australia could achieve something better than England or America had done, she also continued to look at British sociology and the British model of locating social work in social science departments. Hyslop brought a high intellect, a commitment to social justice, practice wisdom, a fearless approach to promoting her ideas, and complete dedication to her work as the University of Melbourne's first social work training director. Melbourne's social work course was the product of Hyslop's vision and drive. Her work contributed significantly to providing a platform for social work education not only in Victoria but for the emerging Australian profession. Her influence continued well after she left Australia.

The next Australian social work leader of Jocelyn Hyslop's calibre was not in Melbourne but in Sydney: the American-trained Western Australian Norma Parker.

7

Consolidating the Course, 1945–1960

The American schools have long realised the importance of avoiding the growth of fields of Social Work mainly as specialisations, and consequently have constantly stated the generic aspect of social work. Through changes, particularly in our final year, we have tried to follow the American lead here.

Ruth Hoban to Carnegie Corporation, 1953[1]

In 1947 the University of Melbourne social work course became the first three-year generic social work course in Australia, fulfilling a long-term ambition of Jocelyn Hyslop and the BSS. In 1944 Ruth Hoban had been appointed director, without advertisement, but Hyslop remained actively involved until she left Australia in 1946. The main emphasis of the BSS continued to be on implementing Hyslop's vision of a rigorous, generic, three-year diploma with a strongly integrated fieldwork component

World War II had provided a strong impetus to Australian social work. It brought gratifying governmental recognition of the profession, but also placed enormous pressure on the new course and on Victoria's handful of qualified social workers. Despite a substantial increase in the number of students (in 1941 there were twenty-five full-time students in total; by 1946 there were forty enrolled in first year alone),[2] the rapidly expanding employment opportunities meant that supply could not keep up with demand.

Teaching for specialist fields of practice

One of the important questions to be settled by the BSS was how to offer generic training in such a way that it equipped social workers to work in the main fields: psychiatric social work, medical social work, and family casework.

From the very beginning the Melbourne (not yet University of Melbourne) social work course aimed to provide specialist streams in one generic course. By 1947 the main specialties were medical social work, psychiatric social work, group work, youth work, and industrial welfare/personnel.[3] Medical social work was the leading early specialty. Fortunately, the VIHA decided not to compete with the general social work training, the VIHA certificate immediately becoming an optional qualification to be taken after the two-year Diploma of Social Service as soon as it was established. Nevertheless, integrating medical social work into the Diploma of Social Service required sensitive handling. The VIHA had hoped to maintain its direct control over medical social work teaching, but by April 1945, after difficult discussions, the BSS resolved that the training of medical social workers in the final year of a three-year Diploma of Social Studies[4] should be controlled by a university committee consisting of representatives of the BSS and of the relevant external bodies.[5] With this decision, Victoria's only established specialist social work education was firmly incorporated into the generic course. Alison Player, the last head of the VIHA and the second national president of the AASW, performed a crucial leadership role here.[6] Player had completed the almoner training in 1936, but after reading American journals of social work she 'realized there was much more to social work than this ... and the one thing I had to do was to pack myself, as soon as I could get there, to America to learn about what social work was all about.'[7] Her first visit to the US in 1939 had convinced her of the importance of family social work, and it was in this arena at Turana (a Victorian Government children's home and reception centre) and at Kildonnan Presbyterian children's home that she eventually made her major contribution to social work, with an innovative and compassionate approach to children in care and their parents that was radical at the time.[8]

Jocelyn Hyslop, who had been strongly influenced by her own mental health education at the LSE, was keen to introduce psychiatric social work to the Melbourne course. She and later Hoban made every effort to strengthen education for psychiatric social work. Dr Arthur Phillips of Travancore (a Victorian Government child psychiatric centre, now part of the Royal Children's Hospital), who taught in the social work course from 1941 until his death in 1954 and was also on the BSS, offered fieldwork placements.[9] For instance, Joan Tuxen extended her student placement in the late 1930s to finish helping Travancore develop its new assessment protocol,[10] and Hyslop was keen to see that her graduates pioneered psychiatric social work at the Royal Park Psychiatric Hospital. (Her unsuccessful efforts to persuade the young Lydia Eady to take on the first social work position there are mentioned in the previous chapter.) During World War II the Australian Red Cross Society boosted the psychiatric social work effort nationally. Under the direction of Dr John Newman-Morris,

Red Cross urgently needed psychiatric social workers, to prepare for the influx of returned servicemen and women, particularly returning prisoners of war. After considerable discussion from 1943 onwards,[11] Red Cross awarded four scholarships for Australian social workers to undertake the LSE Mental Health Certificate. Three Melbourne graduates (Margaret Grutzner, Mernie Yeomans and Helen Clarke) travelled to Britain in 1944, with Sydney's Margaret Whale following in 1946.[12] Their contributions on return were not, however, only to Melbourne and Sydney, as they were dispersed around Australia's six states and played a leading role in teaching and supervising social workers and students nationally.

Nevertheless, the shortage of psychiatric social workers continued, and in May 1950 Phillips suggested introducing a special psychiatric social work course, where the problem of supervision could be overcome if 'a suitable graduate were sent abroad for training and subsequently appointed to train others in psychiatric social work'.[13] This was such a high priority that it was the Victorian state cabinet that decided to send Patricia Holmes to London to undertake the LSE Mental Health Certificate.[14] As so often happened with the clever young female social workers, Holmes did not make the anticipated contribution to psychiatric social work, leaving the workforce when she married Alan Duxbury in 1952 and subsequently having four children. Eventually she did contribute to the profession, working in the newly established Social Welfare Department of the late 1950s, as one of the pioneering social workers managing its transition from case management by clerks to professional social workers.

With the passage of time, social workers were increasingly employed in the psychiatric system, including several holding the LSE Mental Health Certificate. By the late 1950s Dr Alan Jeffrey's lectures on psychopathology provided a grounding in Freudian theory, as well as in psychosis and neurosis and their treatments. Students gained practical experience by attending Jeffrey's outpatient psychiatric clinic at the Royal Melbourne Hospital (a similar approach to the LSE Mental Health Certificate).[15]

Melbourne had never intended to develop a separate course of psychiatric social work education as had been done by the LSE. But when from 1960 the BSS employed LSE Mental Health Certificate graduate Lorna Hay (later Leckie) part-time while she also provided field supervision at the Children's Hospital and the Royal Melbourne Hospital, her teaching, combined with the psychopathology course, enabled students to gain a grounding in the basics for psychiatric social work in the generic diploma (see Appendix 11). In 1960 I was fortunate enough to have a placement with Miss Hay in Ward One North, the locked psychiatric ward at the Royal Melbourne Hospital, where I met patients diagnosed with psychosis. However, the social worker's role did not involve working directly with the patients; instead, they worked with the patients' families, negotiating a smooth transition for the patient back with the family and into the wider community upon discharge. Nevertheless, this experience did help me when, in my first job, at the Brotherhood of St Laurence, I encountered a seriously mentally ill patient: a truck driver who was suffering from paranoia and alarming delusions that included a fox sitting at the family breakfast table.

Group work appeared on the curriculum from 1947 onwards. It suffered from both lack of definition and lack of leadership. Initially 'youth work' and 'group work' were used interchangeably. In 1940s thinking in Melbourne, group work, community work and the settlement movement were interrelated,[16] and were seen as the preventive aspect of social work. The BSS ran short courses between 1943 and

1948,[17] when it closed them, as these efforts were distracting it from its main work of training social workers.[18] It decided instead to focus on the Diploma of Social Studies, and group work became one of the third-year specialties.[19] It was a pity that the BSS had not taken Porter Lee's advice in 1937 to focus on core professional training, rather than dissipating its limited resources on short courses, but it seemed unable to resist chasing funding opportunities.

The final specialist area with which the BSS concerned itself was industrial welfare education, which commenced in 1943 in response to a request from the Australian Government. Industrial social work, later called personnel work, consumed considerable time and resources, and also deflected the BSS from its main purpose. However, it did have the benefit of raising the profile of social work nationally. In providing industrial welfare training, the social work departments of the universities of Sydney and Melbourne played an important and hitherto unacknowledged role in the war effort, and in post-war reconstruction. As discussed in Chapter Three, when Jean Robertson gave up her university post in 1940 to develop industrial welfare in the newly created Commonwealth Department of Labour and National Service, she believed that a new field of social work was opening up. To assist the war effort, the BSS ran five industrial welfare courses, which were taken by university graduates but did not give them a social work qualification.[20] Then, as part of the post-war reconstruction effort, from 1944 the BSS agreed – despite its misgivings about the quality of such training, the syphoning-off of potential social work students and the strain on overworked staff – to run industrial welfare courses for ex-servicemen and women,[21] to 'give them a chance to adjust to civilian life'.[22] The University of Sydney social work course undertook similar work. In August 1945 the BSS had decided that industrial welfare training should be a third-year specialty in the diploma.[23] The industrial welfare/personnel specialty continued, but with declining enrolments. It was not core social work education, and was abandoned in 1974 when the Bachelor of Social Work was introduced at the University of Melbourne.[24]

Sydney and Melbourne's social work courses had made contributions of national importance during the war, though at the expense of their own mission to train professional social workers. The related initiative in 1943, when the Australian Government invited social worker Lyra Taylor to return from Canada to establish a social work section in its Department of Social Services (established 1939), was almost certainly a beneficiary of the national reputation of social work achieved by the industrial welfare courses.[25]

Settling on core curriculum

The commencement of Melbourne's three-year course in 1947 was a major achievement, finally removing the problem of overcrowding of the academic program, and allowing for additional background subjects as well as specialties in the generic course. It put an end to the constant changes of curriculum, and brought medical social work under its umbrella. By now the course was covering the American 'Basic Eight', which had been developed by the Association of Training Schools for Professional Social Work, the body that set minimum standards in the US. Meanwhile, the personnel course, known as 'Course B', had become more clearly separate. Students of both streams were encouraged to combine the Diploma of Social Studies with a Bachelor of Arts or Commerce. The British term 'almoner' was replaced by the American 'medical social worker'. Most importantly, Victoria had now put an end to the possibility of the development of many social work occupations, the situation that still prevailed in Britain. Like Hyslop,

Hoban saw clearly just why generic teaching mattered, as she explained in an article published in *Forum* in 1950:

> The training institution should stress more and more particularly in the final year, the generic aspects of social work. Artificial divisions in the field have tended in the past to lay stress on differences to the neglect of similarities in the practice of social work in its various settings. Students are rightly surprised, puzzled and confused by this. It is a dangerous tendency and can but weaken the profession of social work reducing it to the status of handyman to related professions ... The offer of specialisations in a third year should be accompanied by the offer of studies and discussion groups in social work which are common to all students in this year. The difference is one of social work setting rather than specialisation.[26]

While direct transfer of American methods for the core social work education increased until 1960, some background subjects were influenced by both Britain and the United States, and some others were purely Australian. The term 'social biology' was British, but a course with similar content appeared in American curricula (with names such as 'human behaviour and social environment'). Lectures in physiology, hygiene, and nutrition had appeared in Melbourne's course from its inception in 1933. In 1945, following advice from professor of physiology and BSS member Roy Douglas ('Pansy') Wright, it was agreed to replace these with social biology, which Wright advised would 'develop a knowledge of biology as a basis for sociology'.[27] Wright had probably been aware of the LSE's abortive attempt to establish a new discipline, 'social biology', which would span 'the borderland between science and social science',[28] and, as Wright assured the BSS, it would ensure that the student 'will appreciate human and social behaviour in the context of social or oecological relationships of other representative biological systems'.[29] In 1946, medical practitioners Dr Lena Thomas and Dr Elizabeth Wilmot were appointed to teach social biology,[30] which was first offered as a complete subject in 1947. In the 1960s, social biology would cover human physiology, anatomy and nutrition, with practical work including dissections in the medical laboratories. This provided a good grounding for those going into medical social work. The students were also introduced to the concept of ecology, situating humans in the natural world (amplified by a field visit to the Mornington Peninsula), but no social science was included. Social biology was discontinued with the introduction of the Bachelor of Social Work in 1974. It is an example of the way in which some British ideas were incorporated into the Melbourne course, particularly in the background subjects.

Social history was another subject included from the outset. To consolidate social history, a grant from the Australian Red Cross Society in August 1945 was used to send a young arts graduate, Laurie Douglas, to the LSE for twelve months,[31] to prepare her to take on this subject (which she taught until her retirement in 1989). Unfortunately, this course contained almost no American or Australian content.[32]

Psychology was one of the most important background subjects, because of its direct link to the practice of casework (and group work). As Hyslop mentioned in her 1942 circular letter, the University of Melbourne's lack of a psychology department hampered the teaching of the social work course. The subject had been taught by a series of part-time lecturers, and sometimes by Hyslop herself. In 1943 the BSS joined with others to lobby the professorial board to establish a psychology department, on the grounds that it was 'absolutely necessary

1. The first International Conference of Social Work was held in Paris in 1928, a year before Australian social work training began. Porter Lee, head of the New York School of Philanthropy who gave a paper at this conference, is thought to be the man on the right of the speaker.

2. Ida M. Cannon (r), the head of the first U.S.A. Medical Social Work Department, established in Massachusetts General Hospital, talking to a young social worker, under a portrait of Dr Richard Cabot, the founder of American Medical Social Work, in the hospital's Treadwell Library. Undated.

3. Porter Lee, the head of the New York School of Social Work (now Columbia University School of Social Work), visited Australia at the request of the Carnegie Corporation New York to advise the Sydney and Melbourne courses.

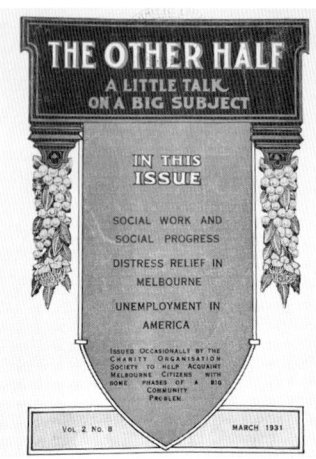

4. Stanley Greig Smith, head of Melbourne's Charity Organisation Society (COS), pictured in 1938 with dictaphone, was always keen to demonstrate his organisation's efficient and modern approach to philanthropy.

5. *The Other Half*, the American-influenced COS magazine (1926–37), was a forum for discussion of welfare issues.

6. Morris House was built in 1924 to house the Charity Organisation Society and related organisations. Today, it is a stylish pub and rooftop bar.

7. Edith Eckhard, who taught social work students at the London School of Economics from 1919 to 1952, corresponded regularly with the Melbourne Board of Social Studies.

8. Anne Cummins of St Thomas's Hospital London on a visit to her friend Ida Cannon in Cambridge Massachusetts (1924).

9. Melbourne's first Director of Training, Jocelyn Hyslop (r), pictured with her successor, Ruth Hoban (l), on the announcement of Hyslop's resignation in 1944. The picture demonstrates their scientific approach as they examine the card index system, which was as important for social research then as a computer is today.

10. Aileen Fitzpatrick headed the first social work course in Sydney (1929–40). Here in 1952, as Director of the Australian Council of Social Service, she presents Professor S.H. Roberts, vice-chancellor of the University of Sydney, with an ancient pottery vase from Cyprus, donated by Miss Helen Hall of the Henry St. Settlement in New York.

11. London-trained Sydneysider Kate Ogilvie MBE was appointed the first almoner (medical social worker) at Sydney's Rachel Forster Hospital in 1931. She taught medical social work at the University of Sydney from 1955 to 1964.

12. Elizabeth Govan, a graduate of the universities of Toronto and Oxford with Canadian social work training, was the first head of the University of Sydney's social work course (1940–45).

13. The English Helen Rees pictured at The Sydney Hospital, 1941, shortly before returning to Britain after serving as the head of Sydney's first almoner course.

14. J.A. (Jim) Cardno, British psychologist, who became the second director of the social work course at the University of Sydney (1946–49).

15. Norma Parker in 1931, aged twenty-five, in her hometown of Perth, Western Australia, on return from the Catholic University of America (Washington DC) where she had qualified as a social worker, becoming the first generically trained Australian social worker.

16. *Portrait of Norma Parker* by Marie Mansfield (oil on linen, 46x36cm, 2023) was painted from photographs and hangs in St Vincent's Hospital, Sydney, in recognition of her role as founder of its social work department.

17. Dr John Newman-Morris (later knighted) – president of the Victorian Institute of Almoners from 1931 until its dissolution in 1950. He was also a member of the Melbourne Board of Social Studies.

18. Dr Georgina Sweet OBE, pictured here in 1937, was a leading scientist and philanthropist and organised the public meeting in 1931 that inaugurated Melbourne's first general social work course.

19. Agnes Mcintyre from St Thomas's Hospital London was the first Directress of Almoner Training in Melbourne (1929–31) and thus the first trained Melbourne social work educator.

20. Isabel Hodge was in the first group of Agnes Mcintyre's almoner students and opened the Melbourne Children's Hospital Almoner Department in 1931. She is pictured here in the early 1930s with children recovering from polio during one of Melbourne's polio epidemics, which occurred in 1931, 1934 and 1937.

21. Isabel Hodge in her car, approximately 1932. Home visiting was an essential part of social work practice.

22. Amy Wheaton MBE, the inaugural head of the University of Adelaide social work course, is pictured with Dr H.V. Evatt (Australian Labor Party leader and High Court judge) and Dr G.V. (Jerry) Portus, academic and ABC broadcaster. The University of South Australia has named a building in her honour.

23. Hazel Smith (1966) the first head of department of the course in Social Studies at the University of Queensland, which enrolled its first students in 1956.

24. The Scottish Jean Robertson CBE, second trained social worker to be appointed to the University of Melbourne (1940). She later taught in New Zealand and Singapore and held the first Chair of Social Work at Hong Kong University.

25. American-trained Lyra Taylor OBE (1940), born in New Zealand, was the founding vice-president of the Australian Association of Social Workers. In 1944, Taylor was recruited to the Commonwealth Department of Social Services to start its social work and social research unit.

26. Ruth Hoban (l) head of the University of Melbourne's general social work course and Alison Player (r) head of the Melbourne almoner training course in Adelaide (1945) for a conference of heads of social work courses to discuss student supervision.

27. Alma Hartshorn OAM with University of Melbourne student Dana Zilinskas, a post-war immigrant from Lithuania, in 1953. Hartshorn, a Sydney social work graduate authored *Milestone in Education for Social Work: The Carnegie Experiment 1954–1958*. She finished her career at the University of Queensland, retiring in 1978.

28. Following mental health training at the LSE, Mernie Yeomans became the psychiatric social worker in the Red Cross Convalescent Home in Kew (Melbourne) and later supervised psychiatric social work students for the university.

29. Virginia Leigh, from 1943–44, worked with the Australian Red Cross Field Force New Guinea, then the UK Prisoner of War Reception Centre, and by 1945 was at the Singapore Prisoner of War Reception Centre. In 1948, she started the social work service in the Commonwealth Department of Labour and National Service.

30. Joan Tuxen, MBE Life Member AASW, is best remembered for her role as head of the Victorian Society for Crippled Children and Adults.

31. Betty Dow, who qualified as a social worker in Melbourne in 1937, worked for the Australian Red Cross Field Force in New Guinea 1942–45. Here she is pictured with a Chinese refugee from Batavia (Jakarta) at the Australian General Hospital in Lae. She later had a long career as the head of social work at the Royal Melbourne Hospital.

PAGE 18—THE SUN—Thursday, August 7, 1947

Should Welcome D.P.s Here, U.N.R.R.A. Worker Says

MISS NANCY FANCOURT, who has returned to Melbourne after two years as a U.N.R.R.A. welfare officer in the Augsburg area, southern Bavaria, believes many of the displaced persons in Germany would make worthwhile Australian citizens.

"They are intelligent, hard-working people, with ideas akin to our own, and I am sure they would have something to give Australia," she said.

In Augsburg and two adjacent Jewish camps, 29,000 displaced persons were still looking to other countries for acceptance, said Miss Fancourt.

Chief Almoner at the Queen Victoria Hospital before joining U.N.R.R.A., Miss Fancourt resigned this position some months ago.

"I promised the people in my care at Augsburg before I left that I would help them to come out here if at all possible," she said. "I would like to take an immigration post."

An assistant welfare officer when she commenced work at Augsburg, Miss Fancourt was soon appointed area welfare officer to the six camps in the district.

Food, clothing and accommodation were the main problems, she said. Rations had averaged 1500 calories per person per day; clothing, particularly footwear, was always in short supply, and living quarters (with 30 people in one barracks-room, and several families in a three-roomed apartment) were extremely cramped.

Schools in the camps were excellent, however, and kindergartens had been established on English and American lines.

The repatriation of Poles had been a big part of U.N.R.R.A.'s programme, said Miss Fancourt. Every encouragement was given them to return to their own country (the U.S. Army issued each person with 60 days' rations on arrival in Poland) and in the summer of 1946, the Augsburg team alone had repatriated 10,000 Poles.

Of the other nationalities, one group had gone to Brazil, 20,000 to Belgium, where employment was found for them in the mines, and a "trickle" to the United States.

Fresh from the poverty of Europe, Miss Fancourt sees Australia as a land of milk and honey.

"It is extraordinary to find cities with rooftops and no rubble," she said.—ELVA BREEN.

Miss Nancy Fancourt

32. Nancy Fancourt's 1947 interview with *The Sun* (Melbourne) gives a flavour of the confronting work young Australian social workers undertook in post-war Europe.

33. Melbourne graduate Margaret Grutzner on return home after LSE mental health training. Grutzner taught for many years at the University of Sydney.

34. In 1953, Georgia Travis was one of the first two American social workers to visit Australia on Fulbright scholarships, under the leadership of Norma Parker at the University of Sydney.

35. The second national conference of the AASW was held in Melbourne in 1949. Pictured L–R: Alma Hartshorn then working for Red Cross in Queensland, Margaret Whale (NSW) who had studied the Mental Health Certificate at the London School of Economics on a Red Cross scholarship, Mrs Paton from Tasmania, Miss A. Fox from Western Australia and Miss D. Pearce from South Australia.

36. Alison Player, second president of the Australian Association of Social Workers, pictured with Mr Basri, one of the twelve Columbo Plan students who attended the fifth biennial conference of the AASW in 1955.

37. A Melbourne hospital outpatient department (1950s) with white-coated social worker.

in the University and for the work of this Board'.[33] This department was founded in 1946, and psychology took an increasingly strong place on the curriculum. The BSS introduced intelligence tests to supplement the course selection interviews, but rejected the idea of Rorschach tests.[34] By 1951, the professor of psychology, South African Oscar A. Oeser, was chair of the BSS,[35] and he used this opportunity to promote the interests of his own department at the expense of social work, including undertaking paid research in areas that had been the preserve of social work.[36] By the 1950s the psychology department was actively poaching honours-level social work students. Geoff Sharp said that 'social work was still a low prestige activity. Some in the Psychology Department slandered it. The Professor told outstanding students they were wasting their time doing social work and the cream were skimmed off.'[37] I know from my own experience that the psychology department would send letters to social work students who obtained honours in Psychology 1, inviting them to transfer to a psychology degree.[38]

Appendices 10–13 demonstrate the way in which the course evolved into a generic model. Specialties were still clear in 1947, but by 1960 the main social work course (Course A) had become completely generic; the various specialties were dealt with in field placements and seminar series. By 1947 the economics, philosophy and politics subjects were rolled into Social Organisation A and B (see Appendix 12), which had predominantly Australian content, covering topics such as Australian social security, government, economics and, in the second year, a substantial sociology course.

Although I include research under this discussion of subjects, research was not seen as a separate subject, but as integral to professional education and to the department's work. The research on practice and outcomes that is regarded as necessary today did not figure in Australia in this earlier period, the focus being demographic and social survey work. These social workers were still endeavouring to define the domain of social work practice and establish where social need lay. Social studies department staff, particularly those at the universities of Melbourne and Adelaide, were among Australia's first social science researchers, but these courses were ignored when departments such as politics started to teach social science, or sociology departments were formally established.[39] Ann Oakley points to their common origins in social reform, referring to them as 'the socials'.[40] In Melbourne, the social work department undertook a survey in 1948 for the Victorian Society for Crippled Children and Adults and the City of Camberwell;[41] in 1952 alumna Jean Norman (née McGregor, later Downing) and her husband, Arthur Norman, funded a study of foster-home placement.[42] Hoban's first sabbatical leave report (1948) emphasised the need for more research.[43] In 1960 Hoban told the BSS that:

> investigations carried out in the Department of Social Studies during the year have mainly followed the survey method. The subjects of enquiry have been largely determined by outside social welfare organisations who have asked that particular studies be made and in most cases have contributed substantially to their costs.[44]

In short, the department was actively carrying out social research on behalf of agencies.

Refining the approach to fieldwork

Efforts to allocate 50 per cent of social work students' time to fieldwork (what we now call field education) on American lines continued throughout this twenty-year period, but were bedevilled by the struggle to find enough qualified supervisors. In February 1944, after explaining the essential emphasis on the 'practical side', the BSS noted:

> Students have practical experience in social work agencies for two full days weekly in the four long terms (amounts to about four months during the two years), two continuous months in the first long vacation and three continuous months after the second-year examinations. A total of about nine months practical work in the two years. Six to eight half-day visits of observation are made each year (court, prison, housing estate, factory, etc.).[45]

By the mid-1940s the assessment of fieldwork was becoming more rigorous. In the 1930s, fieldwork reports had been no more than five lines,[46] but by 1946 supervisors were filling out detailed reports. The 1946 first-year report pro forma, after identifying the agency, student and supervisor, covered the approximate amount and kind of work given to the student; general demeanour, personal appearance, punctuality and reliability; adaptation to agency routine and practice; degree of cooperation with staff and supervisor; attitude to type of work done in the agency; ability with people (contacts, obtaining information, interpretation, planning, recording); letters and telephoning; suggestions as to how the next supervisor could help; and, finally, general comments, including comparison with others at the same stage.

The second-year fieldwork report added some more rigorous questions, such as 'ability to use criticism in discussion with supervisor; capacity for self-criticism; detachment; securing movement in situations'.[47]

The department made major efforts to raise the standard of fieldwork supervision. In 1946 it offered three conferences on supervision, with presentations from Alison Player (the last directress of the VIHA and second president of the national AASW), Lyra Taylor (head of social work in the Commonwealth Department of Social Services) and Ruth Hoban (director of the department of social studies, University of Melbourne).[48] In 1947, while in the throes of exploring the capacity of the Citizens Welfare Service (previously COS) as a centre for casework training,[49] Hoban developed a detailed questionnaire that reveals her thinking about supervision at that time. It covered such matters as the need for the entire agency to demonstrate the right attitude to clients, that is, 'warmth and service'. It should not be 'merely used as a clearing house for other agencies', and the main aim should be 'the positive one of proving eligibility rather than the negative one of disproving eligibility ... the student should be able to make careful case studies and take part in this casework service which is the real reason for the existence of a family agency'. The supervisor's role was also to help the student integrate theory and practice, to direct the student to reading, and to conduct regular planned supervision.[50]

Fay Marles gives a frank account of a placement with a supervisor who, 'like many others, had not herself done the course ... I catalogued everything she did and said that was contrary to what we were being taught about being a good social worker', thus showing the reality of some field placements.[51] Marles complained to the director of the course in the regular monthly student interview; as a result, 'the agency did not have any further students'. Such were the dilemmas that the shortage of placements posed for the director. Nevertheless, Marles recalled that 'By the time I had completed my course, I had worked for at least a month each at the Royal Melbourne Hospital, Red Cross, Travancore Developmental Centre, Crippled Children's Society, Commonwealth Social Services Department and Children's Court Clinic' (all of which had trained social workers on staff).[52]

Red Cross continued to strongly support social work education, and donated money to the BSS, as well as to its counterparts in Sydney and Adelaide. With these funds Melbourne tried unsuccessfully to recruit British supervisors.[53] But it did manage to organise two-year joint staff appointments from 1945 to 1947 at the Playgrounds Association, the Citizens Welfare Service (where Joyce Sambell was appointed for two years to support family casework teaching), the Royal Melbourne Hospital for medical social work, and at the Exhibition Youth Centre and the Fishermen's Bend Community Centre for the group work specialty. The minutes note: 'Personnel Practice to be determined.'[54]

In August 1948 Hoban was invited to join the (management) committee of the Citizens Welfare Service.[55] In 1958 she noted the support of the former COS and Greig Smith for social work research, saying 'the appointment of Mr. Tierney as Director of Casework and Research was a direct result of this policy.'[56] This was the beginning of Len Tierney's substantial contribution to social work research and practice at the University of Melbourne.[57] After Hoban's 1951–52 sabbatical leave, she talked of the need for 'a stronger and closer relationship with fieldwork agencies', even suggesting payment to agencies – a practice she had observed in Britain and the US – and particularly lauding the American supervisors' conferences and handbooks.[58]

In 1954 the department produced a supervisors' handbook, entitled 'Supervision of Students in Fieldwork',[59] which specified the levels of expertise expected of students, set out the calendar of placements, and included a strong bibliography. It was modelled on handbooks that Hoban had seen in the US. The visit in 1963 of Ella Dye, Fulbright professor from Connecticut, resulted in a number of fieldwork training workshops, which Dye ran with Joyce Grant, head of psychiatric social work at the Royal Children's Hospital.[60]

Field supervision improved, but the problem of lack of placements continued, thus restricting the number of students the course could accommodate.

The lack of academic pathways for social workers

Another barrier to developing the young profession was the lack of academic pathways, as the University of Melbourne offered no higher degrees in social work until 1974. Hyslop had admired the American system, whereby most social work students were already graduates and undertook master's-level social work education, but in Melbourne this idea lay fallow.

In her autobiography, Fay Marles, whose distinguished career included being Victoria's first commissioner for equal opportunity and the first female chancellor of the University of Melbourne, illustrates the frustrations of the academically able student of social work in the 1940s. Having achieved high marks in both philosophy and history as part of her combined arts/social work course, Marles decided to ignore BSS rules that did not permit social work students to undertake honours on the grounds that the large fieldwork commitment made the honours load too onerous. She enrolled in honours in modern European history; after two months she was summonsed to a full BSS meeting to explain herself. After this 'sobering experience':

> ... I received a letter telling me that the board had considered my knowingly having flouted the rules but had taken into account Mr. Manning Clark's assessment that I should do honours. In the circumstances I would be permitted to continue the social work course, but only if I gave a written undertaking not to enrol in any honours subjects for its duration ... that was a moment

of truth. I knew an academic career was impossible without an MA. I also knew that there were only two other careers that I could pursue with an arts degree – teaching and librarianship – neither or which had any appeal.[61]

In September 1955 the University of Melbourne established a Master of Arts in Social Studies in the history department, for social workers who already held a bachelor degree in arts or commerce. Because the social work qualification was at a sub-bachelor's level, the master's could not be part of the social studies department. The first enrolment is recorded in 1956.[62] This scheme had little success; at least two of the early candidates (Lois Hobson and Barbara Beatty),[63] both talented students who went on to have outstanding careers in academia and government policy respectively, did not complete.[64] Although first mooted in 1963,[65] not until 1974 did the University of Melbourne establish a four-year degree: the Bachelor of Social Work. The University of Sydney was still offering a two-year diploma as late as 1955, but by 1965 had introduced a degree in social work.[66]

The lack of postgraduate education meant no succession planning in the academy. A new generation of Australian social work educators had not been developed – the few Australians who undertook higher degrees in social work usually did so overseas or in other disciplines such as sociology. This failure to build capacity meant that, when social work education expanded rapidly in the 1970s, Australia had to look once again to America and Britain for qualified teaching staff.

The impossibility of keeping up with demand

By the outbreak of World War II, demand for social workers in Melbourne had well outstripped supply. In addition to the needs of the

Department of Labour and National Service under wartime manpower planning laws for industrial social work education, the Australian Red Cross Society urgently needed social workers. In 1943 it approached the BSS, stating that it 'needed sixteen social workers immediately, two for Victoria and some with psychiatric training'.[67] Red Cross instituted a scheme of social work scholarships, but in May 1944 the BSS was worried that if this scheme continued, it would absorb half of its fifteen students, 'with resultant shortages elsewhere'.[68] By 1945 Red Cross had provided scholarships for the training of forty-eight students (nationwide) in various 'phases' of social work, including medical, general, and psychiatric social work.[69] This scheme concluded in 1947.[70]

Dr John Newman-Morris, one of social work's long-term advocates, was by now in a powerful position as chairman of the Australian Red Cross Society, and used his influence to strengthen the social work education project in Victoria and nationally. Red Cross attempted to strengthen the capacity of the profession generally, making grants to the universities to improve their academic and fieldwork staffing. For instance, in 1947 the Melbourne BSS received £3,000, plus an additional £846 for travel.[71] This grant made it possible to appoint fieldwork supervisors based in agencies, carrying a caseload for teaching purposes; provide a short course in social biology; and appoint additional tutors.[72] Red Cross's final contribution was to support the workforce during 1945 and 1946 by recruiting experienced British and American social workers, who could assist with the shortage of field supervisors.

Despite such help from outside agencies, the BSS seemed unable to think laterally about the supervision problem, and remained wedded to its existing model, even as the shortage worsened further after World War II with the expansion and professionalisation of Victoria's health and welfare sectors. Giving lack of field placements as the reason, in 1947 the BSS accepted only twenty-five students, rejecting twenty-two who were otherwise deemed suitable.[73] In May 1950 Hoban reported to the BSS that all the 1949 graduates had been employed, and that demand exceeded supply.[74] In 1952 the reforming British psychiatrist Dr Eric Cunningham Dax was brought to Australia to lead Victoria's newly created Mental Hygiene Authority. In July 1959 Dax advised the BSS that he would need 'many more social workers because of the early discharges from mental hospitals'.[75] Children's welfare services were also being professionalised. The director of the Victorian Government's newly created Social Welfare Department, A.R. (Alec) Whatmore, created (on the advice of Len Tierney) numerous social work positions to replace the workforce of clerks. Again, this was a mixed blessing for the BSS, and in 1959 it discussed the threat to professional social work posed by its inability to meet the 'imminent demand for social workers' from this new government agency. The BSS was concerned that, because of the social worker shortage, the Public Service Board would have 'no choice but to start short courses',[76] a prediction that would prove correct. The BSS considered that 'within a short period the State Government will probably become the main employer of social workers, expansion will be rapid'.[77]

Both the Mental Hygiene Authority in 1952 and the Social Welfare Department in 1960 created generous scholarships,[78] which included payment of fees and living allowances or full salaries, in order to secure staff for their departments. The Cancer Institute in 1950, and the Hospitals and Charities Commission in 1955, offered scholarships to attract medical social workers.[79]

In 1963 Hoban carried out a study of social studies courses in Australian universities. At that time, there were 1,500 voluntary welfare agencies, many of which employed social workers. By then social workers were also widely employed by the Commonwealth and state governments. In addition, there were social workers employed in nineteen city and rural hospitals in Victoria (which were still considered part of the voluntary sector). Hoban estimated that 40 per cent of Victorian social workers were employed in the voluntary sector, of which she was able to count only the hospitals.[80] Out of an establishment of 195 permanent positions, Hoban found there were forty-one vacancies. That is, more than 20 per cent of positions could not be filled. The actual number of permanent vacancies would have been higher, because non-government organisations were not included in Hoban's calculations. In 1956, enrolment in the three-year diploma totalled just sixty-two students, showing that capacity had not increased greatly since the early 1940s, when total enrolment in the two-year course ranged from fifty to eighty students. But by 1960 the total had more than doubled, to 127.[81]

The BSS lacked a strategy for meeting demand. The task was complicated by regular attrition of this predominantly female workforce. In talking with John Lawrence, Professor Gibson had commented on the great 'casualty rate', both among the students and in the workforce. Another of Lawrence's interviewees quipped that 'the output did not even keep pace with deaths, trips overseas and marriage'.[82] The BSS battled on with its only strategy: to attempt to increase the number of supervisors and to support and educate them.

Social work had been established as a needed occupation, but it was not until the establishment of additional university courses in the 1970s that the supply of graduates would begin to meet workforce demand.[83]

8

Winning and Losing: The Hoban Years

Miss Hoban, who is one of the most attractive of our lady visitors and seems to be an extremely competent person, arrived in New York today. She will plan to spend most of the first term making a thorough study of the New York School of Social Work.

Stephen Stackpole, Carnegie Corporation,
after lunch at the Harvard Club, September 1951[1]

Ruth's rift with the field was long-standing. In her speech she spoke of 'you' and 'we'. The majority in the field thought she did not really understand what social work was.

Alison Mathew, 1959[2]

Ruth Hoban was thrust into the position of director of training for the University of Melbourne's Board of Social Studies at a time when it was on the crest of a wave. A strong academic curriculum had been established, and the course was a national leader, enthusiastically embraced by the university. Unfortunately, this period, which began so positively, ended with the department being caught up in Cold War intrigues, and struggling to maintain its status in the university, leaving a trail of problems that would haunt it for decades. Though only intermittently head of the social work department at the University of Sydney, Norma Parker had a long tenure there, and her expertise in the practice of social casework, her expansive vision, and her role in the Australian Association of Social Workers led to her becoming the most important national leader in this period.

The changing role of the Board of Social Studies

During the 1940s the role of the BSS as a panel of experts who advised the University of Melbourne's professorial board on matters ranging from management of the course to broad policy on curriculum, as well as advocating for the course in many forums, continued. But by the 1950s the influence of the four original BSS leaders was waning. Georgina Sweet died at the beginning of 1946, and in 1948 Professor Sandy Boyce Gibson stepped down as chairman, handing over to professor of history Max Crawford. By this time, John Newman-Morris was heavily involved internationally with Red Cross, resigning from the BSS in 1956.[3] Only Greig Smith, who was near to retirement, continued his strong involvement, until his resignation in July 1959.[4] The frequency of meetings decreased to quarterly, and the discussions became more reactive and procedural. University members of the BSS were no longer familiar with social work literature,[5] and, as one senior staff member recalled: 'the Board of late years had become just a rubber stamp, but Ruth Hoban's relationship with the chairman [Professor Max Crawford] had been going for about ten years. Because of this she insisted upon referring on [to the BSS] practically everything and this annoyed the staff.[6] In 1957, following the death of Crawford's wife, he and Hoban married.

The BSS continued to report to the university's professorial board, was not part of a faculty, and was represented at professorial board meetings by its non-social worker chairman. This arrangement had been advantageous in the development stage of the course,[7] but by the 1950s left social work marginalised in the robust political environment of the university. The BSS ceased to plan actively for social work's future in the energetic way it had done in its first decade, neither pursuing Hyslop's idea of a social science faculty, nor developing a bachelor's degree.

Staff expansion

Attracting and retaining qualified teaching staff remained a problem, and compromises were frequently necessary, such as the appointment of non-social work staff or staff with less than the required qualifications.[8] Between 1940 and 1960, fourteen people were appointed as full-time teaching staff (see Appendix 15). Nevertheless, some of these compromise appointments worked out well. Arthur Livingstone, a University of Melbourne philosophy honours graduate with youth work experience, who in 1944 was appointed as temporary part-time tutor in both the youth leaders' training course and the industrial welfare course,[9] became lecturer and supervisor of group work, and lectured in social organisation.[10] He acted as head of department during Ruth Hoban's first sabbatical leave (1951–52). Livingstone later studied social work at the New York School of Social Work, and left Melbourne for good in 1954,[11] working for the United Nations in Pakistan, where he became the first head of the social work department at the University of

Panjab.[12] He then founded the University of Manchester's prestigious Institute for Development Policy and Management.[13] His departure from Melbourne, probably caused by tensions with Hoban, was a serious loss for the struggling department.

Many part-time staff members made a long-term contribution, including Mrs Eileen Edwards (child study), Dr A.R. Phillips (psychiatry), Alice Barber and Alison Player (case study), Hamish McKenzie, Dr Lena Thomas, Dr Elizabeth Wilmot and Dr Kate MacKay (social biology and its precursors), Lyra Taylor (social work III), and towards the end of the period Cynthia Turner (née Green), Delys Sargeant, Margaret Kelso and Beryl Thomas. Part-timers sometimes became full-time, as in the case of Catherine Brockenhsire (social work I) and Leonard Tierney (social work III), both of whom would spend their entire careers in the department. In 1960 Teresa Wardell joined as fieldwork administrator.

Wide advertising overseas in 1946 for lecturers in casework/field supervision and group work resulted in the highly satisfactory appointment of Audrey Rennison as casework lecturer in 1947. A Cambridge alumna with social work qualifications from the LSE and the Institute of Almoners,[14] she was described as 'a really strong candidate for the post'.[15] She later published widely on social work and sociology. The shortage of suitable applicants meant that the BSS had to compromise on the second position, appointing Alice Hyde (Diploma of Social Studies, Liverpool),[16] despite her not being recommended by the selection panel,[17] because of the desperate need for a group work demonstrator. Hyde had a long tenure at the university, but failed to make group work a strength in the Diploma of Social Studies.

When the diploma became a three-year course in 1947, the BSS faced the same problems as it had in the previous year in finding a lecturer for the third-year family casework course. The position was occupied temporarily by Alison Player.[18] After two unsuccessful rounds of advertising in Britain,[19] Hamish McKenzie of the Victorian Association for Advancement for the Blind was filling the role.[20] Not until 1951 was an Australian, Alma Hartshorn, appointed, remaining until 1955 when she resigned to work in Burma (Myanmar).[21] She later taught at the University of Queensland, published widely about health social work issues, and wrote a book on the Carnegie Experiment.[22] Her awards included a Fulbright scholarship and a Medal of the Order of Australia.[23]

In 1954 Geoff Sharp, an honours psychology graduate, transferred from the psychology department to take over Livingstone's research and sociology responsibilities. Ray Brown, a Fulbright scholar who held a Master of Social Work from Bryn Mawr (US) and a doctorate in history from Birmingham (England), joined the staff in 1957, leaving in 1960 to become head of social work at the University of Adelaide.

Len Tierney, a Melbourne arts and social work graduate who held a Master of Science (in social work) from the New York School of Social Work, had a joint appointment with the Citizens Welfare Service and the university. He became a full-time staff member in 1960 and played a leading role in the following decades. The LSE-educated psychiatric social worker Lorna Hay also joined the staff full-time in 1960.

The department relied heavily on the expertise of casual and part-time staff, particularly for teaching practice subjects. The two decades from 1940 to 1960 were a saga of appointments at below the desired standard, and of retaining well-qualified staff for only relatively short periods. However, the major influence during this entire time was Ruth Hoban.

The search for direct transfer of American expertise

Although the overseas staff employed after World War II were British, Melbourne's interest in American social work had not abated. In late 1948 the university invited Florence Hollis of the New York School of Social Work to take up a short-term lectureship in association with the Australian Red Cross Society.[24] This approach seems to have come out of the blue,[25] its background unclear, although Hollis's career was then peaking: she was teaching in the New York School of Social Work, with summers at the Smith College School for Social Work, and in 1949 would publish her book *Women in Marital Conflict* (and, incidentally, would undergo a radical mastectomy for cancer).[26] To interrupt her career for a year in Australia (on lower pay) must have been unthinkable. She was certainly admired in Australia: Norma Parker named her as 'one of the main figures in social casework development', along with Gordon Hamilton, Charlotte Towle and Bertha Reynolds.[27] Hollis declined graciously, but suggested some alternative candidates: Jeanette Hanford (Chicago), Mildred Frank (New York), Mildred Kilinski (Washington, DC), or Mary Hester (St Louis – the George Warren Brown School of Social Work). The university followed her advice in extending invitations, but without success.[28]

Another tried-and-true way of importing American methods and ideas was for Australian social workers to go to the US for training. Aileen Fitzpatrick from Sydney, and Kate Jacobs and Alison Player of Melbourne, had all spent time in the US in the 1930s, as had Jocelyn Hyslop. In 1948 Arthur Livingstone, by now a senior staff member, spent fifteen months there after attending the International Youth Conference in London as an Australian delegate.[29] Once back in Melbourne, he wrote to the Carnegie Corporation, which had partially funded his American visit: 'There is no question in my mind that a great part of the body of knowledge and practice in American Social Work has relevance and considerable importance for the needs of men in other countries.'[30] Some of what Livingstone learnt was disseminated to Australian social workers in his keynote speech on group work at the Third National Conference of the AASW in Adelaide in 1951.[31]

In 1951–53 Len Tierney undertook a Master of Science in social work at the New York School of Social Work, Columbia University; spent eighteen months observing British social work in Liverpool, Leeds and London; and undertook research. On his return to Melbourne he became director of the Citizens Welfare Service (formerly COS) and lectured part-time in the Diploma of Social Studies, having full responsibility for the final-year (social work III) program. Tierney was, therefore, the first American-qualified social worker to lecture at the University of Melbourne. His entire career was to be spent at the university and he subsequently facilitated American and Australian professional social work interchange.[32] The importance with which he viewed American social work is symbolised by his bequest: the Len Tierney Social Work Travelling Award enables a University of Melbourne social work graduate to study at Columbia University.[33] But Tierney's influence did not really begin to be felt until after the period covered in this book – following his appointment as supervisor of social work studies in 1961.[34]

The first American to actually lecture in social work at the University of Melbourne was Associate Professor J. Benjamin Beyrer of the University of Connecticut, who spent his 1960 sabbatical leave teaching subjects that had been left without lecturers during Hoban's second sabbatical leave.[35] In 1963 Ella Dye, Connecticut's coordinator of fieldwork, visited Melbourne on a Fulbright scholarship, to 'advise in the development of fieldwork training and methods of fieldwork supervision'.³⁶ This was the beginning of a continuing relationship with the University of Connecticut, particularly through Len Tierney and Catherine James, who in a later era regarded Carel Germain from Connecticut as a close professional friend.

Leadership style

From 1946 to 1960 Ruth Hoban was the dominant influence on social work at the University of Melbourne. Eileen Ruth Hoban (1908–96) was the daughter of a leading Methodist minister, the Reverend S.J. Hoban, superintendent of the Methodist Central Mission and Melbourne's Wesley Church in Lonsdale Street, in the heart of the central business district, and a man well known in Melbourne as a social reformer.³⁷ Ruth attended the Methodist Ladies' Colleges in Sydney and Melbourne. She gained a Bachelor of Commerce, Bachelor of Arts, and Diploma of Education at the University of Melbourne, as a pass student without a particularly distinguished record.³⁸ She taught in private Melbourne girls' schools from 1932 to 1937, then travelled to the LSE to undertake the Social Science Certificate (1938–39).³⁹ On returning home she was employed as a social worker for the International Refugees Council and the Victorian Housing Commission (1940–42). Her correspondence with John Lawrence puts an ordinary academic career in the best possible light.⁴⁰ She also glosses over her brief social work experience, which amounted to no more than three years, telling him:

> I had been a social worker with the Victorian Refugee Emergency Council and also with the Victorian State Housing Commission. My academic qualifications are B.Com, BA, Dip Ed, all from Melbourne and Cert of Social Science and Administration

(London). My basic course was really in commerce where I was one of the earliest inhabitants, i.e. when the Faculty was only a few years old. It ... began, I think about 1925 – when I took my degree there was no honours degree, though we could take honours in individual subjects provided they were being lectured in. Some subjects were given in alternate years but one could always take a subject without lectures and have a paper set at the end of the year. I later completed my Arts degree primarily for teaching purposes. After teaching in two Melbourne schools for, I think, five years, I spent a year in library work and economics research with the Victorian State Electricity Commission; then having saved enough money I set out for LSE to train as a social worker. I did my practical work in the field of family welfare and housing. And there you have the story as far as the Melbourne Directors are concerned.[41]

However well she could present her qualifications to Lawrence, local social workers were not impressed with Hoban's social work expertise. Not only had her professional experience been brief, but her qualification from the LSE was the sort of short and mainly theoretical course that Hyslop and the University of Melbourne BSS had specifically rejected, because it failed to provide the practical education that was the Melbourne course's hallmark. Nevertheless, Hoban did very well when standing in during Hyslop's illness in the early 1940s, and her South Melbourne survey, which was printed and widely circulated, had been a major success.[42] In 1944 – at a time when it was virtually impossible to find social work teaching staff – she was appointed to the position of director without advertisement. She continued to implement Hyslop's vision for the course and in 1947 was justifiably proud to be presiding over the first three-year social work course in Australia, arguing in the national journal that 'The products of the three year course can reach a much higher level of performance than graduates of the old two-year course.'[43]

Unfortunately, in a profession struggling to establish itself, it eventually became clear that Hoban had been promoted beyond her capabilities and, unlike some of her peers such as Norma Parker and Alison Player and the younger Len Tierney, all of whom continued seeking out new avenues for learning throughout their careers, Hoban seems to have become defensive of her status, and did not look for opportunities for her own growth and professional development.

Hoban's first sabbatical leave (1951–52), though exhausting, was a missed opportunity to make long-term academic friendships and immerse herself in further education. Possibly she saw her career in terms of being a university lecturer rather than a social worker. The trip was funded by the Carnegie Corporation, and it strengthened her interest in developing the course on American lines. Her second sabbatical report (1959) mainly confirms these general directions. The goal for the first sabbatical leave was 'to study developments in training for social work within universities'. In North America she studied teaching methods by attending lectures and seminars at Columbia University. She also focused on fieldwork, which continued to be a major concern in Melbourne, visiting a range of agencies and concluding that British and Australian social work educators could learn from the close relationships developed between training school and fieldwork agencies.[44] She applauded the handbooks on supervision that the schools distributed to fieldwork supervisors to allow them to 'see the place of fieldwork in the total curriculum and to understand the standard of work which students should be able to reach at each stage of training'. As mentioned previously, she created a similar handbook on return home, as well as starting supervisors' conferences, an idea that had also impressed her.[45]

Hoban familiarised herself with the Hollis Taylor report, and with the role of the Association of Training Schools for Professional Social Work in setting minimum standards – in particular its 'Basic Eight' requirements, which were largely present in the University of Melbourne's social work course by 1947 and locked in by 1960. At the Children's Bureau in Washington she met with Dr Helen Witmer, social worker in charge of research – another of Hoban's interests.

To the extent that Hoban brought back American ideas on fieldwork education, and that the generic Diploma of Social Studies increasingly embraced the 'Basic Eight' requirements, it seems clear that this American visit continued the transfer of American social work approaches that had commenced with Hyslop. Hoban was impressed with the degree of generic education, saying: 'Their argument which I feel is sound is that anyone with a good basic training in social work should be able successfully to apply social work method in any social work setting.'[46]

After her time in North America, Hoban went to England, where she was based in the LSE's department of social science and administration. She also travelled extensively and attended a British Association of Social Workers conference. She was at the LSE when Richard Titmuss had just been appointed head and Edith Eckhard was still responsible for social work education,[47] although by now Eileen Younghusband was the acknowledged social work leader. The question of the core education needed for social work was being actively debated at the LSE, which was at that time running six specialist courses leading to employment as a social worker.[48] The American Marjorie Smith had just completed her Fulbright study, 'Professional education for social work in Britain', in which Titmuss' introduction stated that 'social work education needs re-thinking in terms of fundamental principles'.[49] Eileen Younghusband was 'moving towards a view of social work as a single profession'.[50] Though still a radical view in Britain, this was the view to which the Melbourne BSS and staff had come years earlier. It was shortly after this that Younghusband started work on the Carnegie Experiment. Hoban's report does not enumerate the debates at the LSE, but does describe the variations and inconsistencies in British social work education, and characterises the relationship between fieldwork agencies and departments of social science as being 'on the whole rather loose'.[51] She felt that, unlike in Australia and the US, in Britain 'there is little or no teaching in social work method within Universities',[52] and she set out the differences in British training from that in the US and Canada.[53]

In 1953 Hoban wrote to Stephen Stackpole at the Carnegie Corporation, telling him that some of the changes she had implemented as a result of her first sabbatical included closer links with field agencies, a training scheme for fieldwork supervisors, and a system of fieldwork advisers (university staff), adding, 'we have reconstructed the content of our social work teaching in the final year of the Course', and going on to laud the American schools' generic approach. She also mentioned a move to a less formal method of teaching, which 'lends itself admirably to the presentation and discussion of social casework and social group work material'.[54] She shared her ideas in a paper at the AASW Conference in Adelaide in 1957.[55]

Ruth Hoban's commitment to American social work strengthened even further following her second sabbatical of 1958–59, which she took with her new husband, Max Crawford, who was on a Fulbright scholarship. In her report on this visit, she referred to the completion of 'a major social work curriculum study in North America for the North American Council of Schools of Social Work'.[56] This was probably the first volume of Werner Boehm's 1959 *Objectives for the Social Work Curriculum of the Future*, published by the Council on Social Work Education.[57] Hoban then discussed her time at the LSE, where 'Professor R. M. Titmuss [and] all members of his staff in the Department of Social Science and Administration gave me a very kind welcome'. During this visit, the battle between specialist and generalist social work was raging at the LSE, but Hoban did not mention it. She did refer to the 1959 Younghusband report on social workers in local authority health and welfare services,[58] and the Third International Survey of Training for Social Work,[59] prepared for the United Nations by Younghusband, commenting blandly that 'The British Universities I visited were paying considerable attention to both the reports recently prepared by Miss Younghusband.'[60]

Finally, a report dated December 1963, 'The Future Development of Social Studies Courses in the Australian Universities', written for the Australian Universities Commission, gives a flavour of Hoban's ideas towards the end of her time as director of social studies. Here she describes the current situation in Australia, where Queensland had by this time joined Sydney, Melbourne and Adelaide in offering social work education:

> Each student pursues his studies along three main channels – the physical and psychological development of man [sic], the study of society, and the theory of social work; the latter requiring him to undertake a considerable period of supervised practical work in approved welfare agencies ... Teaching in the methods

courses in social work is centered mainly around social casework and social group work, with often only superficial consideration being given to the methods of community development and social administration.[61]

This broadly describes the University of Melbourne social work curriculum in 1960. In this report Hoban was far more critical than in her first sabbatical report of the fragmentation in teaching in Britain, and of its lack of commitment to generic education.[62] Though criticising the US for its lack of training in personnel/industrial welfare social work, and suggesting (as she had done in 1951) that the minimum course standards in 'a small minority of cases' resulted in monotony and mediocrity and hampered experimentation, she went on to praise the American system overall:

> However, as far as the general training of social workers is concerned, the detailed and careful consideration which social work educators in the United States have given to the developments of their programmes of study is now being reflected in the offer of courses more appropriate, both academically and professionally, because of their wider scope and greater depth of study. And this policy has, in turn, contributed much to the development of education for social work in both Great Britain and Australia, and indeed, in many European and Asian countries as well.[63]

She made fifteen detailed recommendations,[64] the eight most significant being the introduction of a four-year degree course as a first qualification in social studies; offering a fifth year of study leading to the degree of Master of Social Studies, Social Work or Social Science; discontinuing the present undergraduate diploma courses in social studies; establishing chairs of social studies; expanding the number of field placements; building improved courses in community development and social administration through additional staff appointments; promoting teacher exchange schemes between departments of social studies in Australia and overseas; and special visits of social work practitioners who have achieved considerable stature in their fields.

Thus by 1960 Hoban was still articulating the American model of social work education as described, for example, by David Austin in his *History of Social Work Education*.[65] She had become increasingly critical of Britain's approaches, the problems of which had become more evident.

Difficulties with colleagues

By 1958 Hoban, as an associate professor, held the highest appointment of any Australian academic social worker, and social work seemed securely established at the University of Melbourne, despite student numbers remaining low. She appeared to have had a very successful fourteen years, and was about to take her second sabbatical leave, this time with Max Crawford, whom she had just married.[66]

But things were about to unravel. Relationships between Hoban and many of Victoria's most influential social workers in the field, as well as with her own staff, were tense. For instance, she had unwisely alienated a number of medical social workers, on whose support the school relied.[67] This was confirmed by both Alison Player and Beryl Thomas, two of Melbourne's most senior medical social workers, both of whom had taught in the course. Player described 'tension between Ruth Hoban at the university and the field generally'.[68] The University of Sydney–trained Beryl Thomas, then head of social work at the

Alfred Hospital, felt that the school was prejudiced against medical social work.[69] These strained relationships extended to other areas: according to Len Tierney, Ruth Hoban and David Scott 'were not on speaking terms'.[70] Scott held a senior position at the Brotherhood of St Laurence, a family welfare agency which played a strong role in training and employing social workers. Tierney described him as 'fighting for the use of trained social workers all over the place'. Scott was an attractive man, who was very well liked locally and should have been a strategic ally. In the central office of the Department of Social Services, an important national employer of social workers, Hoban 'had a row' (over student supervision) with its director and founder Lyra Taylor (another frequent sessional teacher in the course).[71]

Hoban's lack of practical social work experience combined with an air of superiority also counted against her in the field. Both Kathleen Crisp (Lyra Taylor's deputy) and Marion Urquhart (formerly head of social work at the Australian Red Cross Society and by then working in the Victorian Government's Maternal and Child Health Service) felt that Hoban lacked practical experience. Urquhart told Lawrence: 'Ruth Hoban was without practice experience. The present picture would have been different if Kit Jacobs [later Kit Cane] or Helen Eggleston [later Clarke] had remained on the University's staff. Both had left to be married.'[72]

The problem of Hoban's poor relationships with peers was summed up bluntly by former staff member Audrey Rennison: 'Ruth Hoban gave the social workers in the field the impression that she considered them inferior ... they thought she was a "two-faced bitch".'[73]

It was not only in the field that Hoban had personality clashes. She was also at loggerheads with the majority of the staff in her small department. Kate Ogilvie, one of Sydney's social work leaders, recalled:

'Ruth Hoban ... was on Hyslop's academic bandwagon, but did not have much feeling for individuals.'[74] In Geoff Sharp's opinion:

> Ruth Hoban had collected academic ornaments around her to upgrade her course, but had not been able to use their talents and they had become dissatisfied. She accused them of intrigue and being disloyal ... Arthur Livingstone and Audrey Rennison had been blocked by Ruth Hoban when they applied for further positions. Livingstone was virtually exiled.[75]

In this era when social work expertise was so hard to find, the loss of people of the calibre of Arthur Livingstone and Audrey Rennison was regrettable.

These problems were common knowledge in the tight-knit world of Australian social work. When in 1960 Hoban invited John Lawrence to apply for the assistant director post in social studies at the university, his memoir records: 'I did not know if I would emerge unscathed working so close to and under the direction of Ruth Hoban, but that would be a chance I would have to take.'[76] Norma Parker then drew Lawrence's attention to 'the number of fine people who no longer had any contact with the Melbourne University Department. She [Parker] asked me to keep these comments to myself but urged me to think long and hard before buying into the department.'[77] Lawrence decided not to apply; ultimately Jean Robertson was appointed, but withdrew in 1961.[78]

Before their marriage in 1957, the chairman of the BSS, Professor Max Crawford (whose wife was an invalid) and Hoban were known to be close. As Crawford's biographer, Fay Anderson, put it: 'Crawford was often seen in the presence of Ruth Hoban.'[79] Staff had been frustrated for some time, as Hoban did not allow free discussion in staff meetings, and passed any difficult decisions to the BSS and thus to Crawford as its chairman.[80]

Crawford was chair of the BSS for a decade, handing over to Professor Richard Downing (economics) in 1957,[81] the year in which he and Hoban married. When Hoban appointed Geoff Sharp as acting director for the period of her sabbatical leave,[82] he was hesitant to take on the role, and queried why it had not been offered to Ray Brown, who (unlike Sharp) was a social worker and held a PhD. Hoban indicated that she believed Brown to be psychologically unfit for this responsibility. Nevertheless, she was also ambivalent towards Sharp, as shown by the fact that she did not allow him to move in to her large office, arranging for a student to use it.[83] Sharp immediately found himself faced with some urgent administrative decisions, as the department was short-staffed and about to be evicted from its long-term home on campus.

In December the BSS was 'perturbed to learn that half the present full time staff members will be absent from the department in 1959'.[84] In a department of only six full-time academic staff members, Laurie O'Brien had been allowed sabbatical leave at the same time as Hoban. When Ray Brown unexpectedly accepted the position of head of the social work course at the University of Adelaide, the BSS was left very short-staffed.[85] To make matters worse, no plans had been made to re-house the social studies department, whose building was scheduled to be demolished in 1959 to make way for the new North Building (now known as the Redmond Barry Building). After unsuccessful attempts to find accommodation on campus,[86] the department was somewhat ignominiously moved off the main campus to 75 Royal Parade, where a busy avenue now separated it from the university. There were promises of supplementary accommodation in Morrah Street around the corner. The director had left the country without making plans for either accommodation or staffing.

Tensions between Hoban and Sharp were heightened in the director's absence.[87] Fay Anderson has examined the situation that arose on Hoban's return from leave, when the 'simmering tensions' came to a head. During Hoban's absence Sharp had called frequent staff meetings, 'often without a formal agenda but always with Minutes taken',[88] and decisions were reached by consensus. On return, 'Hoban believed she had lost authority because of the changes made by Sharp and the regular staff meetings were immediately discontinued.'[89] The situation reached an impasse, and 'Hoban became convinced her influence was being deliberately undermined because of Sharp's political affiliation with the Communist Party', an allegiance that was both perfectly legal at the time and that Sharp had never attempted to hide. Sir George Paton, the vice-chancellor, proved ineffective at resolving the situation. By the end of 1959 there was a suggestion that 'Hoban wanted one or more of her staff sacked from the Department if not from the university.'[90]

To understand what happened next it is necessary to know something of Cold War politics in Australia. In 1951 the conservative Menzies government had unsuccessfully attempted to outlaw the Communist Party, and in 1954 the politically inspired Petrov Inquiry had inflamed fears about Communism in Australia.[91] Fay Anderson, having examined Australian Security Intelligence Organisation (ASIO) files, argues that Crawford had attracted the attention of ASIO many years earlier, because of his left-wing views and his defence of academic freedom. In April 1961 Crawford surprised colleagues and friends by writing an uncharacteristic letter to *The Bulletin*, a right-wing journal, alleging Communist tactics in 'two small departments' in the university.[92]

Later that month a sensational and detailed article, 'Melbourne University Communists at work', appeared in *The Bulletin*.[93] It was clear that the main reference was to the social studies department. ASIO had been running what are known as 'spoiling operations' in the media. In Anderson's opinion, one of the most serious of these operations was directed at some of the social studies staff.[94] The unhappiness in the department had left it open to an attack of this sort, which was part of a larger ASIO strategy to discredit academics and universities. Ultimately, no evidence of a Communist plot was ever discovered, and an internal university inquiry found the accusations to be baseless. Apparently attempting to put an end to the malicious gossip, Vice-Chancellor Sir George Paton issued a statement to university staff on 1 May 1962 (see Appendix 18) reporting on the findings of an advisory committee that the university council had set up, with Mr Justice Adam as chairman:

> the committee decided that there was no evidence of a 'Communist Plot', and no evidence of anything which could be described as 'misconduct' (academic or otherwise) on the part of any member of staff ... it is only fair to the members of staff concerned to emphasise that these findings were accepted by the Council of the University ... the Council has dealt with these issues by a proper machinery, and the verdict of the umpire should be respected.[95]

But the damage had been done. Crawford never recovered his status, and he became 'a virtual ghost in his beloved department'.[96] After this, his research, a study of Victorian philanthropy, was conducted in collaboration with Hoban.[97] The reputations of all the social studies staff involved in this scandal were damaged, and it resulted in bitter staff divisions for years to come.

In 1961 Hoban moved out of the social studies department offices, though retaining her title of associate professor and her salary.[98] Jean Robertson, who was then working at the University of Singapore, had been appointed as assistant director in Melbourne, but later withdrew.[99] The 1960s began with the young Len Tierney being appointed to a newly created post of supervisor of social work studies.[100] This was the impasse that the social studies department had reached in 1960 when this history concludes. The results of the 'Communist plot' debacle affected the development of social studies at the University of Melbourne in the ensuing years. The ill-feeling among staff continued for decades and formed the uneasy backdrop to the period in which Len Tierney led the department.[101]

Unfortunately, this period, which had started so encouragingly, ended with the department drifting, located off campus, not having achieved a social work bachelor's degree or higher degrees, managed by a BSS that was by now anachronistic. Finally, the trumped-up claims of Communism caused a serious blow to the reputation of the department and dramatically set back its progress. However, Ruth Hoban continued to have personal supporters in Melbourne, as evidenced by the fact that she was granted life membership of the Victorian Council of Social Service in 1967, by which time she was mainly engaged in historical study which was never completed.[102] When Ruth Hoban died, in a nursing home in the eastern Melbourne suburb of Canterbury on 12 March 1996, she had been largely forgotten by the University of Melbourne and by the social work profession. A request from a niece in Queensland for the social work department to write an obituary was not followed up.[103]

9

The Post-war Search for Overseas Expertise

The worst Iron Curtain is the Cultural Iron Curtain around America – nobody knows what she is really like.
          Australian social worker to Fulbrighter Georgia Travis, 1953[1]

Although Ruth Hoban's time at the University of Melbourne ended disappointingly, she had succeeded in establishing Australia's first three-year undergraduate social work course, held the department together in the latter part of World War II and the immediate post-war period, and embedded a curriculum based largely on American ideas. After the war, various chains of choices and circumstances opened new channels of communication with American social work, and support from Britain continued.

American philanthropy: the Carnegie Corporation and the Commonwealth Fund

At the beginning of this book I described the way in which American philanthropy had underpinned Australian social work's beginnings. The

Carnegie Corporation and the Commonwealth Fund (of the Harkness Family) directly influenced Australian social work. Carnegie funded Aileen Fitzpatrick's two tours of the US, Jocelyn Hyslop's three-month study tour, and shorter visits by Arthur Livingstone, Kate Jacobs and Ruth Hoban. In the 1930s Frederick Keppel and Porter Lee both visited Australia on behalf of the Carnegie Corporation.

The Commonwealth Fund also contributed to Jocelyn Hyslop's American study tour. It had been entirely responsible for the introduction of the Mental Health Certificate at the LSE, completed by twelve Australians (see Appendix 17). The fund's Muriel Scoville took a special interest in Jocelyn Hyslop's American study tour and planned her itinerary, noting that she was one of 'our' alumni of the LSE Mental Health Certificate. And in 1944 Scoville responded to a special appeal to support Norma Parker in a twelve-month study of psychiatric social work in the US.[2]

Individual leadership was also critical; for more than two decades the American-trained Norma Parker and Lyra Taylor influenced the directions of Australian social work. They were part of the small group who in 1946 founded the Australian Association of Social Workers (AASW, discussed further in the next chapter) and became its inaugural national president and vice-president, respectively. Both of these women had completed postgraduate social work education in America in the 1920s. Parker's work at the University of Sydney and through the Fulbright program, and Taylor's work as founding director of the Commonwealth Social Services social work program, gave them unique opportunities to shape the direction of Australian social work.

Norma Parker

In a memorial tribute, John Lawrence described Norma Parker CBE (1906–2004) as 'Australia's most outstanding pioneer of professional social work, and a wonderful person to know'.[3] In 1969 the AASW established the Norma Parker Lecture, which is presented by the AASW national president at the biennial national conference.

Parker was the eldest of five children, growing up in Perth, Western Australia, where her father was an accountant.[4] She attended Sacred Heart High School, Perth, and won a State Government Exhibition to the University of Western Australia. She was one of the three young Western Australian arts graduates sent to the US in 1928 by the Catholic Church to study social work at the Catholic University of America (Washington, DC) in preparation for working in child guidance. On return, following the onset of the Depression, she was unable to find work in Perth; after a brief period working in Melbourne (1932–36), where she established the St Vincent's Hospital almoner department, she moved to Sydney, where she was to spend most of her life.[5] Norma Parker had been one of the group of Sydney social work leaders who had opposed Aileen Fitzpatrick's approach in the 1930s because of concerns that Fitzpatrick was not qualified to teach social work. In 1957 Parker married Clarence 'Mont' Brown, a survivor of the notorious Thai–Burma railway, but he died in 1964.

For fifty years Parker played a crucial leadership role in Australian social work. Her particular practice expertise, like that of Jocelyn Hyslop, was as a psychiatric social worker. Her interest lay in social casework; looking back in 1970 she reflected that 'the time belonged to social casework' and that the years of the Depression and those following World War II were 'hard years for many, many Australians. Social workers were pressured by this general community burden of need. We did what was close at hand and calling out to be done (social casework).' She acknowledged that group work and community organisation were 'taught and practised but they were secondary'.[6] Between 1941 and 1965 she worked at the University of Sydney, on more than one occasion acting as director of social work there. In 1965 she became associate professor and head of the department of social work in the school of sociology at the University of New South Wales.

Most of Parker's contribution was beyond the academic sphere, making her a major force in the establishment of professional social work in Australia. She not only wrote widely and insightfully on social work, but she also taught social casework skills – both to her students and to practitioners. Parker presented the first two papers at the casework refresher course held at the University of Melbourne under the auspices of the AASW in 1949. From 1940 to 1944 she was president of the Social Workers' Association of New South Wales,[7] and, as mentioned, became the first national AASW president. She helped to build the profession by generously mentoring and supporting her peers; for example, when she stepped down from the presidency, she saw to it that her successor, the Victorian Alison Player, had an opportunity to attend the international social work conference held in Toronto in 1954 by organising for all the branches to contribute to her fare.[8]

Parker became what Rebecca Hegar refers to as a 'cultural interpreter' between the United States and Australia,[9] moving easily between social work in the US and Australia. Her discussion of preparations for the 1949 national AASW casework refresher course to be held in Melbourne is an example of the way she understood the nuances of both cultures. Parker wrote that she had gathered from discussion as she visited the various states that members were keen to learn more about social casework. She went on to suggest altering some terminology in the publicity material: 'I used the term "institute" when talking to Miss Player and Miss Taylor, and some other people familiar with the American scene, but I do not think it has much meaning in Australia, or rather that it conveys the wrong meaning, so I would prefer very much not to use it. I think if we talk about it as an informal refresher course it would be much better.'[10]

In 1944 Parker was awarded a special fellowship by the Commonwealth Fund of New York to study psychiatric social work at the University of Chicago's School of Social Service Administration (the home of Charlotte Towle), and to visit other centres.[11] When she was granted a senior Fulbright award in 1951, the second year of the Fulbright scheme in Australia, she became the first Australian social worker to be awarded a Fulbright and had the distinction of being one of only two women among the thirty-three recipients. She combined this with a Smith-Mundt scholarship, another American government award.[12] On this, her third American visit, Parker studied social research methods at Chicago, returning via Britain, where she discussed general developments in social work education.[13] She became the hub for American social work visits to Australia, promoting diffusion of American social work educational ideas by ensuring that the visiting scholars were shared with the other states and reached a wide audience.

On returning from her 1944 visit to the US, Parker managed the seamless introduction of an American social work educator when she organised for Dorothy Sumner to join the staff of the University of Sydney in 1945 to lecture in social casework. Sumner had studied social work at the New York School of Social Work and had been a supervisor in the family casework division of the United Charities of

Chicago and at the School of Social Service Administration of the University of Chicago.[14] She became the third social worker with North American expertise to teach at the University of Sydney (the Canadian Elizabeth Govan being the first and Parker the second).

Through Parker, the University of Sydney was successful in adopting American social casework expertise far earlier than Melbourne, which struggled to find suitable teachers until the appointment of Len Tierney. In 1980 the New South Wales Government named the Norma Parker Correctional Centre for Women in her honour.

Lyra Taylor

Lyra Taylor OBE (1884–1979) was born in Taranaki, New Zealand, one of four children. Her English-born father was a farmer who died young, and she attended school in Wellington and then Victoria University College on scholarships, graduating as a lawyer in 1918 and becoming the first woman to be admitted to the bar in New Zealand.

After visiting juvenile courts in Baltimore, she became interested in social work, and enrolled at Johns Hopkins University, graduating with a Master of Arts degree in social economics and social work in 1927. She worked at the Johns Hopkins Hospital and the Baltimore Family Welfare Association (where Mary Richmond was still the head) between 1925 and 1929, for a further decade at the Montreal Family Welfare Association, and later at the YWCA. She also taught at McGill University in Montreal. In 1940 she became general secretary of the YWCA in Sydney, where she introduced 'more liberal policies, encouraged self-reliance, tolerated smoking and drinking (in moderation) and invited servicemen to the Y for "Open House"'.[15] After deciding not to renew her contract in 1942 because of disagreement with the YWCA board over her liberal approach, she returned to

Canada, where she was offered a job with Dupont (then manufacturing most of Canada's wartime munitions), doing the sort of work with munitions workers that Jean Robertson was doing in Melbourne.[16] In 1971 Taylor recalled:

> Here I was sitting in the company's office in Montreal on a day when it was snowing heavily and very, very cold and I received a telephone call from the Australian High Commissioner in Ottawa asking if I would be willing to return ... to Australia and set up a social work and research section in the Commonwealth Department of Social Services.[17]

When she accepted this position, Lyra Taylor not only started a new government-based field of professional social work in Australia, but also helped to build a national cohort of skilled social workers, through her detailed staff supervision on the lines she had learnt in America. Her staff were located in every Australian state, including Tasmania, Western Australia and Queensland – which did not yet have their own schools of social work. As she later recalled, during her training 'you had close and careful supervision. You had the famous Gordon Hamilton visiting from New York to conduct classes right in the agency.' One of 'Lyra's girls', as they were known, Barbara Sturmfels (née Gordon), recalled Taylor's supervision style when she was a new graduate in the Perth office in the 1940s: 'She had no difficulty in building up a sense of confidence in her (very green) appointees, and backed it up by going in to bat for them with their state seniors, by fairly frequent visits, and supplying and encouraging professional reading.' This young workforce played an important professional role:

> We were never in doubt about the relationships between the legal framework within which we worked, and our social work principles. Other staff were there to establish eligibility: but we could assist clients who could not easily do this, to demonstrate why they might fall within the rules. And we were there to provide a general social casework service to the Department's clients.[18]

Taylor's regular travel around Australia resulted in her taking on the role of a roving social work ambassador; in this capacity she had a strong influence on the founding of the social work course at the University of Queensland in 1954. When she died in 1979 she left her entire estate to the Victorian Branch of the AASW. Speaking at the Victorian Branch annual general meeting that year, Len Tierney captured the spirit of the woman:

> She had no patience with the footling and pretentious and over the years had developed a formidable wit which ruffled many a vanity. To the young she was kind and had a way of enlisting you to causes which was difficult to resist. As she disposed of a point of view with a few well aimed arrows she would reflect upon the unfortunate inanities of others and then would say 'But you and I Leonard ...'[19]

John Crisp, a social worker whose aunt Kathleen Crisp was Taylor's deputy and successor, was one of the handful of people who attended Lyra Taylor's funeral. For some reason she was buried in an unmarked grave in the Fawkner Cemetery in Melbourne's northern suburbs. This may have been a verbally expressed wish, but was not an instruction in her will. In 2020 the Victorian Branch of the AASW organised the erection of a headstone, but a full biography would be a more appropriate memorial.

Apart from their individual contributions to the establishment of social work in Australia, Norma Parker and Lyra Taylor were founders and supporters of Australia's national social work association, which is discussed in the next chapter.

I shall now turn to the Australian Red Cross Society and the Fulbright scheme, an Australian non-government organisation and an American government program, respectively, each of which played a vital role in strengthening the profession in Australia and in transferring American social work. It is worth examining both of these programs in some detail, as they illustrate cultural barriers to accessing American expertise, and show how connections were eventually established.

The Australian Red Cross Society

The Australian Red Cross Society, which was a major social work employer and which after World War II urgently needed staff to work with returning servicemen and women, took action on two fronts. As discussed in Chapter 5, in 1944, before the war had ended in the Pacific, Australian Red Cross sent three social workers – Margaret Grutzner, Mernie Yeomans and Helen Clarke – to London to train as psychiatric social workers by taking the LSE's American-style Mental Health Certificate, following up in 1946 with Margaret Whale from Sydney. It also started a recruitment drive to attract social workers from the US and Britain.

Dr John Newman-Morris wanted social workers to work in rehabilitation and psychiatric hospitals, particularly with former prisoners of war. The role of Red Cross social workers after the war was to work with doctors, psychologists (or psychiatrists) and vocational guidance officers, with the social worker's role being to re-integrate the patient into their community. Joan Tuxen recalled a social work role that would seem familiar today, apart from the fact that in 1944 she worked from a tent in an army camp in Parramatta (west of Sydney): 'I had to sit on my papers because the wind blew across the plains … and … had to put them under my bed at night time.' Her young clients were mostly amputees who were flown directly from New Guinea:

> I would work with them during the day, trying to prepare them for discharge. I would get somewhere – I used the Army Education Officer who was a psychologist for assessing their mental ability but a lot of them came from the remote Hunter Valley … They resisted having educational vocational tests, but then I found out that they were illiterate and they didn't want to admit it … I tried to work positively with them in the daytime but then on the weekend the members of the Limbless Soldiers Association came around to visit patients and their view was: don't do anything so that you can get a better pension! So everything I was doing in the week was undone by the Limbless Soldiers Association.[20]

When Tuxen moved back to Victoria the following year, to the main military hospital (now Austin Health) in the leafy Melbourne suburb of Heidelberg, she was in charge of a large staff of Red Cross social workers and welfare workers, both on site and also at Bonegilla (then a large military camp and hospital, near Albury on the New South Wales–Victoria border). She said:

> They [social workers] were responsible to commanding officers on medical matters. My role was liaison with the senior social

workers on matters of policy, and appointment of staff and any social problems. I worked also with community groups such as the RSL, AIF Women's Association and with the Widow's Guild and others so that we discussed mutual problems with nationalised services and unofficially became the beginning of the Victorian Council of Social Service.[21]

Australian Red Cross was particularly keen to recruit Americans, but ultimately recruited far more British social workers. For this endeavour it appointed two Australian women with high social prestige: Lady Sybil Lavarack in Washington and Lady Hilda Owen in London. Lady Sybil was the wife of Lieutenant General Sir John Lavarack, head of the Australian military mission in Washington. In her capacity as Australian Red Cross liaison officer in the US, Sybil Lavarack was asked in 1945 to head up a search for three suitable American senior social workers. She knew very little about social work, but took the advice of Norma Parker, who recommended Margaret Leal, associate director of the New York School of Social Work, to assess the candidates' qualifications.[22]

Recruiting American social workers to Australia proved difficult, as experienced social workers were also in demand in the US, Australian salaries were significantly lower than American salaries, and Lavarack had no social work networks in the US (the Americans were equally ignorant about Australia). Ultimately, the two social workers she did recruit were relatively recent graduates, not the experienced professionals that the Australian Red Cross Society and the University of Melbourne had wanted. In October 1945 Marion Duncan became the first American social worker to be recruited. She held a Bachelor of Science in social administration from Ohio State University (1936) and a Master of Social Work from Pennsylvania School of Social Work (1942). Her salary of £600 per annum, plus a living allowance of £200, was considerably more than that of the university's director of training (£500) or of the national director of social service in Australian Red Cross (£475).[23]

Although Lavarack's negotiations with a number of other promising candidates came close to success,[24] in the end only one other American was recruited. Elizabeth Ann Stringer, who held a bachelor's degree from Carleton College (1942) and a master's from the University of Chicago's School of Social Service Administration (1944), was posted to Sydney in 1946. She had only two years' experience, and was described as 'shy and lacking in life experience'.[25] Her appointment caused considerable ill-feeling between the local social workers and Red Cross because of the high salary; the archives of Australian Red Cross include acrimonious communications between the University of Sydney's Kate Ogilvie and Marion Urquhart at Red Cross in Melbourne.[26]

There were real cultural barriers for these Australians (which were well understood by Parker and Taylor), and the case of the failure to recruit Dr Anne Morrison in 1946 illustrates the problem. Lavarack was keen to recruit this impressively qualified older woman, who held a two-year certificate (1926) and a PhD (1932) from the prestigious women's college Bryn Mawr, the first American college to offer social work doctorates. Among her many appointments, Morrison had been acting assistant dean at Western Reserve University at Cleveland, Ohio, and had held senior posts in American Red Cross during the war.[27] In March 1946 Lavarack wrote to Marion Urquhart in Australia: 'Miss Morrison or Dr. as she is sometimes called – came to see me this morning. We had a long talk, she is a most charming and intelligent woman – no one could help being attracted by her personality.'[28]

But Urquhart, who was looking for caseworkers, may have been nervous of this experienced older woman.[29] Lavarack was understandably annoyed when Urquhart rejected her, saying she was 'disappointed that you felt that Miss Morrison had not sufficient experience in casework. American Red Cross ... said she was such a brilliant woman that she would not have any difficulty.'[30] But Urquhart, like Lavarack, would have been ignorant of American social work education and unaware of the import of Morrison's qualifications, particularly her doctorate.

In England, Lavarack's counterpart, Lady Hilda Owen, Australian Red Cross liaison officer in London, faced a far easier task recruiting ten British social workers.[31] Owen had been 'chairman' of the National Junior Red Cross Committee, and very active in New South Wales. She had volunteered to travel to Britain in 1944 as part of the Australian Red Cross mission to Britain. The mission is summed up in the advertisement that appeared in *The* (London) *Times*, *The Manchester Guardian*, the feminist publication *Time and Tide*, and in the publication of the Institute of Hospital Almoners:[32]

> Australian Red Cross Society invites applications from qualified social workers, including medical social workers and psychiatric social workers to take part in case-work programme for rehabilitation of medically unfit service men and women. Salary: Australian pounds, 350–450 pa according to qualification, minimum stay two years ... The Society is endeavouring to build up the standard of its casework service, and in common with all agencies in Australia finds that the supply of available social workers is very small ... the Society provides fieldwork placements for the Boards of Social Studies of New South Wales and

Victoria and for the Institutes of Hospital Almoners. Suitably qualified social workers assist with the supervision of students.[33]

These social workers formed another strand of dissemination of social work expertise, and also served as experienced field supervisors, who were so desperately needed by the University of Melbourne. They were not American, but the LSE's Mental Health Certificate was de facto an American qualification and, in addition, the almoners were among the more highly professionalised of the British social workers (normally having an additional year of training).

An atmosphere of intimacy can be seen in the English correspondence, not found in the increasingly terse communications about American social workers. In May 1946 Jean Robertson wrote to Urquhart: 'in fact I do see a very large number of social workers wishing to go to Australia who come to me for advice, and I saw a number of applicants for the Melbourne University post and also the Sydney post. I have hurriedly got in touch with some of the more suitable ones.'[34] Owen was closely supported by Robertson and by Helen Rees, a former director of the Victorian Institute of Hospital Almoners and founding head of the Sydney almoner course. Along with Mrs Jervis-Reid of the Emergency Help Committee[35], they formed a regular interview panel for applicants.[36] They understood what was required in Australia, and would have been able to answer applicants' questions knowledgeably, based on their personal experience.

Eight British social workers were recruited through this campaign: Elizabeth Hanby, Rowena Beatty, Joyce Cuthbertson, Elsie Thomas, Rosemary Cook, Joyce Taylor, Miss Jackson and Mary White,[37] with the addition of two others – the wife of Jim Cardno,[38] a British psychologist who was the new head of social work at the University of Sydney, and Jean Hepburn,[39] a connection of Helen Rees whose husband was in the British Navy stationed in Australia – making the tally ten in all. In June 1946 Alfred Brown, secretary general of Australian Red Cross, wrote to Owen, thanking her for her efforts and the 'endless trouble which Miss Rees and Miss Robertson have taken making recommendations about the eight social workers we have now appointed', indicating that Newman-Morris (whom they both knew well) hoped to see them to thank them personally. Brown went on to say: 'We feel that very much of the successful response has been due to your own efforts, and we are delighted with the applications and the speed with which the whole thing has been handled.'[40] In November 1946 Urquhart wrote to Margaret Whale, who was by then studying at the LSE on her Red Cross scholarship: 'Miss Beatty and Miss White arrived on 17th December … Joan Tuxen was having a beach party for the other English Almoners so Miss Beatty and Miss White were able to go too.'[41] The ease with which Australian Red Cross recruited British social workers was largely due to existing networks and personal friendships, although the unpleasantness of the war and Britain's harsh environment in its aftermath probably made the thought of beach parties in Australia attractive. On the other hand, the lack of cultural understanding and absence of networks made American recruitment a high hurdle.

The Fulbright program

From 1951 the Fulbright program provided a new wave of opportunities for the international transfer of social work knowledge.[42] The scheme had been established in the US after the war by J. William Fulbright, Democrat senator for Arkansas, former law professor, and Rhodes scholar. Its aim was to 'contribute to "mutual understanding" between people in the US and partner countries, and, thus, over the long term, to the maintenance of international peace'.[43] This educational and cultural exchange program commenced operation in Australia in 1949.[44] (Appendix 16 lists the American Fulbright scholars in Australia in this period.)

Until the mid-1960s, Australian Fulbright recipients received only travel costs and had to provide evidence of US dollar support from sources such as American philanthropic organisations or university scholarships.[45] Norma Parker, upon returning to Melbourne after her time as the first Australian social worker to be awarded a Fulbright scholarship (1951),[46] played a pivotal role in bringing American social workers to Australia on Fulbright scholarships.[47] By 1963 seven social workers had come to Sydney in this way (one of these was shared with Adelaide), one came to Melbourne to work with Lyra Taylor at the Commonwealth Department of Social Services, and in 1963 Ella Dye became the first social work Fulbright scholar at the University of Melbourne.

Georgia Travis and Margaret Thornhill were the first American social workers to come to the University of Sydney on Fulbright scholarships (1953–54). Travis's visit illustrates the calibre of these American visitors and demonstrates the broad teaching agenda of the Fulbright scholars. Travis was not the only American social worker to maintain contact with Australian social workers over decades: Alice Overton in particular maintained many long-term friendships and welcomed numerous Australians to America.

Georgia Travis, a Chicago graduate, was teaching at the University of Colorado and later became a professor in the school of social work at San Diego State College, California.[48] The Georgia Travis Center for Women and Children at San Jose is named in her honour.[49] While Travis was on staff at the University of Sydney, Norma Parker and the

Fulbright program generously enabled her to travel interstate to share her knowledge. Her report also records that:

> the University [of Sydney] believed the community to most need help in basic social work. It was felt that the greatest weakness in the training of students was in the practical or fieldwork the students secure in the social agencies, and therefore that my major focus should be on helping the social workers of the agencies to become more proficient.[50]

In addition to her teaching, Travis gave fourteen major speeches in Sydney, Newcastle and Brisbane.[51] In Melbourne she ran a workshop on 'Relationship in casework' for the AASW's Victorian Branch, resulting in an article in *Forum*,[52] and gave an address on 'The family doctor in America' at the AASW conference in Sydney. In the 1969 issue of the *Australian Journal of Social Work*, which honoured Norma Parker on her retirement, Travis's 'Notes on supervision' from her earlier visit were published.[53] The Victorian Branch of the AASW, often in collaboration with the university, saw that the Fulbright scholars had ample opportunities to teach in Melbourne. In addition to the workshop run by Travis in 1954, Margaret Thornhill addressed fifty members of the Victorian Branch about 'a survey which she had conducted with a group of social workers in Sydney into the needs of unwed mothers and their children'.[54] The 1956 AASW Victorian Branch annual report recounted:

> We began and ended the year with speakers from overseas, both Fulbright scholars from North America. Dr. R. Bram [not a social worker] brought to Australia by the New Education Fellowship

spoke on group dynamics. Mrs. Elton Brown [Dorothy Brown] a medical social worker who is attached to the Commonwealth Department of Social Service while in Australia gave some very pertinent and thought provoking observations about Social Work in Australia as she sees it.[55]

That same year, the AASW Victorian Branch hosted a seminar by Esther Twente in the Melbourne offices of the Commonwealth Department of Social Services, on 'The philosophy of social work', attracting twenty-eight registrations.[56] In September 1960 Alice Overton conducted a two-day institute in advanced social casework, on the topic 'Clarification as part of the casework process',[57] hailed as a great success.[58] Overton also consulted with the Brotherhood of St Laurence social workers, who were then working on a multi-problem family project with a clientele similar to that of the St Paul Project where Overton worked. This was the Family Service Project,[59] which the BSL had undertaken jointly with the Victorian Housing Commission to assist in the transfer to state government housing of families living at Camp Pell, a notorious former army camp on Royal Park (a large tract of parkland just outside Melbourne's central business district), which had provided accommodation to the poor during the post-war housing shortage.

As discussed in Chapter Six, it was not until 1963 that the University of Melbourne's BSS was successful in sponsoring a Fulbright scholar, Ella Dye. The Fulbright scholars made a major contribution, particularly in the development of social casework expertise in Victoria. A small number of Australians were also awarded scholarships: Norma Parker, Ray Brown, Alma Hartshorn and Marjorie Awburn. Of these, Parker had the strongest influence in Australia.

The LSE's Mental Health Certificate

Not all American influence on Australian social work came directly from America. A further hitherto unrecognised American influence was the London School of Economics and Political Sciences' Mental Health Certificate. This started in 1929 as a wholly American course grafted onto the LSE, funded and controlled for more than a decade by the American Commonwealth Fund.[60] Thus, while the Australians who undertook this qualification had the opportunity to make friendships with English social workers and to immerse themselves in the institutions of post-war Britain, the techniques they learnt were American, and they returned home steeped in American casework skills.[61]

Holders of the LSE Mental Health Certificate represented an important strand in the introduction of American casework to Australia (see Appendix 17 for details). They were dotted around the Melbourne social work agencies, in supervision and leadership roles, thus giving them an opportunity to teach staff and students in professional supervision. They appear to have had less influence in Sydney, where Fulbrighters had more influence.

Australian Red Cross, in addition to directly recruiting overseas social workers, specifically engaged the four social workers it had sent to the LSE to supervise and educate its own staff, thus disseminating American casework methods Australia-wide. Margaret Grutzner would have a long career at the University of Sydney, while in Melbourne Lorna Hay initially worked part-time teaching psychiatric social work at the university, and part-time first at the Royal Children's Hospital,[62] and then at the Royal Melbourne Hospital. Later she worked full-time at the university where, over several decades, she disseminated her LSE Mental Health Certificate knowledge to students. Helen Clarke (née Eggleston) was a strong influence on the profession in Victoria and gave occasional lectures in the social work course. Later, Una Riall and Hay also took on important roles in the professional social work association, each editing its journal, *Forum*, at different times.

As discussed previously, Patricia Holmes (later Duxbury), who was selected by the state government to strengthen psychiatric social work in Victoria, did not stay long in the Department of Mental Hygiene. However, her long subsequent career in the Department of Social Welfare placed her in a significant position to influence Victorian social work practice. In 1957, on her return from England, the Australian Joan Robertson, another ex-servicewoman (not to be confused with the Scottish academic Jean Robertson) was recruited to work in the social work department at the new Larundel Psychiatric Hospital, which had previously been a World War II army camp. Robertson was a local leader, responsible for building a modern psychiatric social work department in the new mental health service, which Dr Cunningham Dax was in the process of revolutionising. In Robertson's words, Dax 'was treating the patients as people and had unlocked the doors of the wards'.[63] Here an important part of the psychiatric social worker's role was assessing the family situation and helping the patient to return and remain home. The Fulbright scheme and the LSE Mental Health Certificate gave Australian social workers an opportunity to study American casework and student supervision, as well as abnormal psychology and psychopathology, topics that were later offered in Dr Alan Jeffrey's psychopathology course at the University of Melbourne and studied by most social work students in the 1960s.

A cultural Iron Curtain

Before Australia's post–World War II immigration program began, most non-Indigenous Australians were of British descent, and many still identified with Britain. But the stationing of American service personnel in Melbourne during the conflict did broaden some people's horizons. Australians became better informed about the world, and their previous focus on the British Empire widened to include the Pacific and the United States, among other places.[64]

The overriding international influence on the early years of Melbourne social work was American. After the war, Norma Parker and Dorothy Sumner brought a strong American social work sensibility to the University of Sydney course. Australia desperately wanted what the Americans were teaching, but were puzzled by Americans and their society. Cross-cultural understanding took time to develop, and was eventually achieved through a series of individual relationships and growing networks. The social workers who were based in Melbourne, however, including the head of the Australian Red Cross national social work service, Marion Urquhart, were slower than the Sydney social work group in coming to grips with the cultural and organisational differences. The inept way in which the University of Melbourne attempted to recruit American staff, especially the esteemed Florence Hollis as described earlier, and the misconceptions surrounding possible recruitment of Dr Ann Morrison, add to the picture.

Melburnians did harbour prejudices: 'Collective wartime memories confirm the stereotype that was familiar before the war, so the US forces are remembered as efficient, wealthy, handsome, well-dressed and glamorous, if simultaneously somewhat immoral, crass and naïve.'[65] The throw-away remark in a letter from Australian Nancy Vercoe, who had been working alongside American social workers in Europe for the United Nations Relief and Refugee Administration, is illustrative of Melbourne attitudes: 'My object in coming here [to New York] was to see if the Yank is as silly at home as he is abroad. So far I have not had to change my opinion.' Nevertheless, the rest of the letter makes her admiration for American social work apparent.[66]

The frank reports of some of the returning American Fulbright scholars emphasise the 'foreignness' of America of the 1950s to Australians. In her report to the Fulbright organisation in the US, Georgia Travis reported: 'one woman commented after a party to which some of her friends had been invited to meet me "They were thrilled. You have no idea what it means to meet a real American and find out first-hand how different you are from the people who are pictured in the movies".' Another Australian said 'We are apt to think of Americans in terms of Marilyn Miller [Monroe], with her bosom and her bottom. The worst Iron Curtain is the cultural Iron Curtain around America — nobody knows what she is really like.'[67] Then, in answer to the question on the report form, 'What aspects of the United States did you find people in your host country most interested in?' Travis responded: 'Household appliances, clothes and book-burnings or witch-hunts [a reference to McCarthyism]'.[68] It was only through individual exposure and the development of friendships that the Melbourne social workers were eventually able to understand and relate to the culture of their American colleagues.

The University of Sydney's path in this direction had been smoothed a decade earlier than Melbourne's by Parker and the North Americans who taught there. But this is not a simple story of transfer of American expertise to Melbourne. British social workers also played an important part, particularly for the first decade after the war. Because of familiarity, and the failure to successfully connect with American social workers,

Melbourne's early social work educators drew on British social workers' expertise. They relied on Britons to strengthen the local workforce with the supply of more experienced staff who could undertake field supervision. In addition, the University of Melbourne turned to Britain for educators to strengthen its teaching capacity in the 1940s. Three women who provided advice over decades were Edith Eckhard, Helen Rees and Jean Robertson, who were part of a loose, informal British network that existed over many years and whose support made it relatively straightforward for Melbourne to recruit social workers from the UK (see Appendix 19).

The support of Jean Robertson, Helen Rees and Bryn Jervis-Reid for Lady Owen's recruitment drive has been discussed.[69] But the same names keep appearing. In 1947 Jean Robertson was on the University of Melbourne's staff selection panel (discussed in Chapter 6), where the other panel member with a long relationship with Australia was Edith Eckhard. It was Eckhard who wrote enthusiastically to Boyce Gibson about the superior qualifications of Audrey Rennison. In 1948 Robertson was again on an interview panel in London, this time for a lecturer in personnel practice, along with Betty Sharpe, Janet Kydd (from the LSE) and Mr Rae Thomas.[70] Edith Eckhard, Helen Rees and Jean Robertson were linked to each other, to British social work, and later to international social work, but they were also linked individually and together to many Australian individuals and organisations, in such a way that 'web' seems a more appropriate description than 'network'.

As Hegar has pointed out, international influence can be bi-directional,[71] and there is some evidence that Rees and Robertson brought their Australian experience to bear in England and other countries, including Singapore, where they later worked. This would be an interesting avenue for further research.

The University of Melbourne's BSS adhered to the original 1934 advice of its founder, Jocelyn Hyslop, to follow the American style of social work education: to teach professional skills and not merely social science theory as in Britain. A little later, Norma Parker and Lyra Taylor's national leadership and facilitation of national networking, the travel of Australians overseas after World War II, and the contributions of Fulbright, Commonwealth Fund, Carnegie and Australian Red Cross Society, were all factors in the transfer of social work knowledge and the development of a local skill base grounded in American social casework and fieldwork methods, and a commitment to generic rather than fragmented education. But at the time when this book finishes, 1960, there was still a long way to go.

I was a student at that time (University of Melbourne, 1959–62), and I believe that the course was strong in teaching social work professional values such as self-determination, non-judgemental attitudes, confidentiality, and client advocacy skills. Students gained good assessment and interview skills, always seeing the client in the context of society. Attention was paid to what was called social action and to the value of research. In the first term, our extensive observational visits to agencies ranging from prisons to mental hospitals and retirement villages gave us an overview of the field. The six strongly supervised placements, the last being three months full-time after completion of all academic work, was the main way in which skills were taught. We were certainly socialised into the profession. But as for what to do with a client who might appear in the office with a curly problem – this was not well taught at the University of Melbourne at that time, and was something that somehow we picked up, if we were lucky, from good supervision during the course or after graduation. The skills of social casework eluded us. Len Tierney, who by then held a Master of Science in social work from the New York School of Social Work at Columbia University, regretted 'a strong misunderstanding about US social work by people who had not been there and ... those who had been abroad were overwhelmed by seeing competence'.[72] In 1960 Norma Parker summed up the state of play : 'There is a body of theory in each of the methods by this time ... I don't believe you can get it sufficiently well in Australia.'[73] The University of Melbourne founders had established a course which was strong academically and locally respected with its graduates in great demand and in turn playing their own part in building the profession. It had been a leader in founding social work as a profession in Australia. It was not until the appointment of Len Tierney freshly returned from the US in 1960 that a new chapter began which strengthened the teaching of social work skills at the University of Melbourne.

10

A United Australian Profession

Truth-telling, which sounds such a noble enterprise, is itself the most complex of acts.

Ann Oakley, 2014[1]

We have traced the story of social work education in Victoria from 1929: its commitment throughout to high teaching standards despite the vexing lack of local experts, its survival through the Great Depression and World War II, its good fortune in its outstanding local advocates and extraordinary first head, its dedicated search for elusive American expertise which trickled into Australia but which was not achieved until the 1960s, its survival after a political scandal, and its important national contribution in establishing a course which – as Jocelyn Hyslop had hoped in 1935 – would prepare its graduates to actually 'do' social work, not merely theorise. The course established in Melbourne in the 1930s was the foundation on which today's Australian social work education has been built.

However, in this story there is one other important contributor to the success of the Melbourne course: the nationwide synergy created between Australia's three first social work courses (in New South Wales, Victoria and South Australia). The generous cooperation between the small cohort of social workers in the field and the schools strengthened the three schools of social work and prepared the ground for the massive expansion of job opportunities and of new social work courses in the 1970s.

By the end of World War II it had become clear to Australia's social work leaders that a formal national professional organisation was urgently needed. Social workers needed a national body to negotiate with the reforming post-war federal Labor government,[2] and to provide a single Australian social work voice to negotiate with international bodies.[3] Negotiations with the Commonwealth Government during the war had been unduly complicated by the fact that they had to be undertaken by individual state branches.

At the time of the 1946 federal election, which re-elected the Labor government, a referendum was held. The public voted in favour of the Australian Commonwealth Government taking over much of the provision of social security and the funding of healthcare.[4] Important parts of the social work domain were now under national control.

A single national organisation would also make it easier for the profession to network and disseminate ideas. Communication in Australia was not easy; the population then was only 9 million (25 million today), and mainly dotted around the coast of a large continent. Most communication was by letter, telegram and long-distance telephone call. Travel between capital cities was by overnight train or boat, and was costly. There was no national newspaper (*The Australian*, still the only national paper, commencing in 1964), although there were two national women's magazines: *The Australian Women's Weekly* and *Woman's Day*. The social workers used local newspapers and radio extensively for mass-media communication. The situation was further complicated by the fact that social work was developing at different rates in the various states.

The establishment of the Australian Association of Social Workers (AASW) in Sydney on 14 December 1946 under Norma Parker's leadership answered this need. The first executive was made up of members from the three states where there were schools of social work, with Sydney taking the lead. The New South Wales members were Norma Parker as inaugural president, Kate Ogilvie and Dorothy Sumner as vice-presidents, Margaret Grutzner as honorary secretary, with Viva Murphy as 'assistance secretary'. From Victoria, Lyra Taylor was also a vice-president, as was South Australia's Amy Wheaton. Melbourne's Alison Player, who voted at this meeting, was to take over the presidency seven years later, with Parker becoming vice-president (see Appendix 20).

The new AASW had approximately 400 members.[5] By 1960 the Victorian Branch had become the largest in Australia, with 224 members.[6] The national association brought together under one umbrella the associations of social workers that had been established in all the states: the Social Workers' Association of New South Wales (founded 1934), the Victorian Association of Social Workers (founded 1935) and the South Australian Association of Social Workers (founded 1942), as well as the three states without professional education programs: Queensland, Western Australia and Tasmania, where social workers organised professionally a little later.[7] The AASW had no paid staff until 1949, and was a loose federation of state branches, which allowed for local variations and encouraged grassroots involvement. This differs from today's AASW, which has more than 17,000 members and a substantial paid staff, and is closely directed by a national board.

The early constitution listed the objects of the AASW:

1. to promote and develop professional Social Work throughout the Commonwealth
2. to act in a representative capacity for the Social Work profession in matters pertaining to the Commonwealth as a whole
3. to educate and inform public opinion as to the aims and objects of social work
4. to promote and maintain standards of professional training and practice
5. to promote professional status and ensure good conditions of employment
6. to co-ordinate the activities of Social Workers' Associations in the various States of the Commonwealth and to facilitate the exchange of information and ideas between them.[8]

Defining eligibility for membership

Establishing criteria for eligibility to become a member of the AASW was an important early achievement. In her report to the federal council of the AASW in December 1950, Norma Parker reported that 'Membership of the Association is now limited to persons holding a professional qualification in social work from an approved School of Social Work or equivalent training body.'[9] It still retains this function, despite challenges to minimum standards in the 1970s[10] and again in 2011 when Karen Healy (AASW president 2011–17) and her team had a resounding success in an AASW election fought over a proposal of the AASW board to drop entry standards from a minimum of a four-year undergraduate degree to a three-year undergraduate degree, which would have allowed lesser-trained welfare graduates to join.

National negotiation and advocacy

By 1950 the AASW had achieved high-level government support. In her annual report Parker referred to the 'enthusiastic interest and support of the Director General of Social Services, F.H. Rowe'; the 'keen interest' of the minister for health and social services, Senator McKenna; and these men's discussions and consultation with Lyra Taylor at the Commonwealth Department of Social Services. Parker noted the work of the AASW in relation to the (post-war) immigration program and the pleasure of the AASW with the appointment in 1948 of a social worker to organise a social welfare service in the Department of Immigration. Another initiative of note had been work undertaken with the Commonwealth Employment Service, and the establishment of a social work program in its 'physically handicapped' division.[11]

Participating in an international profession

The second important concern, although not one of the original 'objects' of the AASW constitution, was Australia's formal connection with social work colleagues internationally. Norma Parker recognised a need for a national body to advise the Australian Government on welfare representation at the United Nations.[12] A national association would also facilitate communication with international colleagues, particularly with the International Conference of Social Work.[13] Jean Robertson, who had returned to Britain, and later Amy Wheaton and Helen James, were able to represent Australia at International Federation of Social Workers meetings held in Brussels and Paris shortly after World War II.

The AASW also had ambitions closer to home: in her president's report for 1950 Norma Parker wrote of the interest of Australian social workers in welfare programs in South-East Asia, and expressed a hope that the AASW would be able to send 'a large contingent' to the next International Conference in India.[14] During the post-war period Lyra Taylor supported the Columbo Plan (founded 1950), an intergovernmental program designed to strengthen relations between Asia and the Pacific by enabling Asian students to study in Australia and other Commonwealth countries. As mentioned earlier, Melbourne's Arthur Livingstone went to Pakistan to work for the United Nations, inaugurating the first school of social work in the Punjab.

Three Australians – Alison Player, Lyra Taylor and Marion Urquhart – attended the Fourth American National Conference of Social Work, held in Atlantic City in 1948. This also served as an international conference: instead of a full Congress of the International Federation of Social Work, international sessions had been added to this American event.[15] Among its more than 200 delegates, thirty-four countries outside the US were represented. Player was at that time the directress of training of the VIHA.[16] Urquhart, who was a guest of American Red Cross, combined the trip with a three-month study tour.[17] Taylor was the Australian delegate to the conference. Norma Parker, president of the AASW, had been selected as the Australian delegate, but was prevented from attending because of 'dollar restrictions'.[18] Knowledge gained at this conference was disseminated in Australia in the usual ways: Alison Player gave an address on social work and welfare in the US to the Council of Social Service (reprinted in *Forum*),[19] and Lyra Taylor reprinted and circulated 'the most outstanding address given at the conference', by Arthur J. Altmeyer, commissioner for social security, Washington, DC.[20] This pattern of disseminating information from conferences through either *Forum* or public addresses continued in this period.[21]

In addition, the AASW actively encouraged members to study overseas. The 1951 edition of *Forum* included an article titled 'Overseas

Experience of Social Workers', which contained a detailed explanation of conditions under which Australians could work in the US, as well as correspondence with the British Federation of Social Workers on mutual recognition of credentials.[22] In 1954 *Forum* contained advice from Alison Player, by then national president of the AASW and recently returned from the US, that 'the Federal office-bearers of AASW are now exploring the possibility of obtaining Fulbright grants for fares [to the US]'.[23]

Some social workers studied in the United States on their own initiative. Alison Player had studied in Boston in 1940. Joan Tuxen received a Rotary Foundation research scholarship in 1953, allowing her to study in Chicago under Charlotte Towle, whose writing she admired.[24] Len Tierney's study in the US in 1952–53 has already been mentioned. Teresa Wardell travelled to the US more than once, giving an address to the 1955 annual meeting of the Victorian Branch of the AASW on 'Observing social welfare in the US and the UK',[25] and in May 1960 reporting to the BSS on her attendance at the White House Golden Anniversary Conference of Children and Youth.[26] Marjorie Awburn, for many years the head of social work at St Vincent's Hospital (Melbourne), observed social work at St Vincent's Hospital New York while on a Fulbright scholarship, and undertook classes at Columbia University and a summer school at Smith College in 1957.[27] She also travelled regularly to international conferences throughout her career.

Spending time working in London hospitals became a common element of the experience of young Australian social workers, as part of the trend for touring overseas after graduation, but according to one social worker this was usually incidental to European travel, rather than a deliberate search for work experience.[28]

National conference

The first national conference of the AASW, on the theme 'The place of social work in Australia today', was held in Sydney on 5–7 September 1947. It was attended by 200 delegates – approximately half the membership of the AASW.[29] It projected an image of a well-established profession, having as its patron the director-general of the Commonwealth Department of Social Services, Mr F.H. Rowe, to whom Lyra Taylor reported directly. As president, Norma Parker gave the opening address; Lyra Taylor spoke on 'Social work and the statutory agency'; Dorothy Sumner on 'Social work and the voluntary agency'; and the heads of the three university social work courses, Ruth Hoban, J.A. Cardno and Amy Wheaton, all talked on 'Professional education for social work'. There were a dozen discussion groups. The conference ended with 'Social work and the international scene', in which 'speakers [were] chosen from those who have recently returned from experience abroad and from those social workers from other countries now working in our midst'.[30]

From 1947 onwards, conferences were held biennially,[31] being run by state committees and in the early days rotating between Sydney, Melbourne and Adelaide (see Appendix 2). In a similar vein to the American National Conference of Charities and Correction in the nineteenth century, these were crucial in promoting discussion and the sharing of ideas across the continent's vast distances.

A national journal

The dearth of local professional writing was a perpetual problem. Australians continued to rely on overseas textbooks and journals, and to look to America for social work expertise, while maintaining an interest in British social sciences. During World War II, social work texts used in the universities 'were still almost entirely foreign and the casework books and articles were all American'.[32] An example of this trend is a memo listing material selected for the Australian Red Cross Society's library by Margaret Grutzner while studying in England.[33] It includes the White Papers, the Beveridge Report, and material on government provision for returning services personnel. But Grutzner added: 'We have fewer government publications from America than from England, but quite a large proportion of the technical books on order are American.' Many of these publications were issued by 'voluntary societies' (non-government organisations) involved in social work, such as the Family Welfare Association in New York. Journals to which Australian Red Cross subscribed were *Social Work* from England and *The Family* from America.[34]

In the first edition of *Forum* as a national journal (1951), Norma Parker's foreword bemoaned the 'almost complete absence of anything which might be called professional literature' in Australia.[35] Earlier (in 1943) Parker had supported the journal *Social Service*, published by the Council of Social Service (New South Wales), hoping that it would 'attract intelligent interest to social questions and services'.[36] *Forum* started out as a Victorian journal in 1947,[37] expanding to become a national publication in 1951. Along with the national conference, it played a crucial role in disseminating ideas Australia-wide. Until 1958, each year two issues were published jointly by the AASW and the Australian Association of Hospital Almoners. When the latter was disbanded, the publication continued from 1959 under a new name: *The Australian Journal of Social Work*.

During the period covered by this book, *Forum* was based in Melbourne, where its editors were closely connected to the university as well as to the Victorian Branch of the AASW. Thus, through its staff and graduates, the University of Melbourne continued to play an important role in promoting social work ideas. It was not until 1966 that the editorship moved to Sydney.[38] Three of the early editors have already been mentioned in other contexts: Arthur Livingstone, Lorna Hay and Una Riall, all of whom taught in the University of Melbourne course. The other two editors were Eve Morrison and Jean Norman (now Downing).[39]

In her foreword to the first national edition of *Forum*, Parker talked of the 'solid achievements' of social work in its first twenty years in Australia: 'any social worker looking round the Commonwealth to-day finds justification for feelings of pride and satisfaction regarding the status and scope of social work'. She went on to delineate the many fields and agencies where social workers were then employed. She expressed the hope that the journal's 'columns do give us the opportunity we have lacked to date of expressing ourselves on professional topics, or sharing ideas in social work matters, and of learning through experience how to arrive at an effective presentation of professional knowledge'. She called for 'a keen and critical body of readers, willing to participate in written discussions and to help the Editorial Committee with ideas'.[40]

In the period up to 1960, the professional journal did play an active role in promoting interstate and international networking, containing a wide range of articles, including information about innovative social work programs; discussions of social work practice in Australia and other countries; news on staff changes and the travels of individual social workers; and book reviews. It also kept Australian social workers in touch with international developments, publishing detailed reports by Australian social workers of conferences attended overseas, particularly the International Social Work Conference series.

Networking between schools of social work

Formal networking between Australia's schools of social work lapsed after World War II with the unfortunate demise of the Australian Council of Schools of Social Work, which had been established with such fanfare in 1938. Despite the lack of a formal association, towards the end of the war the three schools of general social work, the almoner courses and the two major national social work employers (Australian Red Cross and the director-general of the Commonwealth Department of Social Services) were all included in a significant meeting chaired by H.C. ('Nugget') Coombs, director-general of post-war reconstruction, in Melbourne on 9 August 1945, to discuss supply and demand for trained social workers. They concluded that 'there was obviously a need for expanding the training facilities ... to meet urgent community needs' and 'the most significant limiting factor' was the availability of qualified supervisory staff for fieldwork. It was noted that the needs of the Department of Social Services, which was responsible for all social security payments, seemed to be especially pressing, estimating that it required at least twenty social workers.[41] Thus we see that, at this point, the need for social work education in Australia had attracted the attention of one of Australia's most senior public servants.

In the absence of a formal organisation of schools of social work, the AASW conferences provided a venue for informal meetings, as indicated by a letter from Ruth Hoban to the University of Melbourne's vice-chancellor, George Paton, requesting permission for three staff to attend the first conference of the AASW, in Sydney in 1947.[42] Hoban argued in support of her request that 'There are very many matters regarding the general aims and detail of training which we should welcome the chance to discuss at a full staff meeting.'[43]

The national AASW and a handful of members of its Queensland Branch (initially seventeen members in all) worked hard to establish the first social work course at the University of Queensland,[44] which commenced in 1956, becoming the fourth school in Australia.[45] Lyra Taylor and Marion Urquhart had played an important role, offering support and advice, and lobbying the university.[46]

The schools began meeting at the time of the AASW biennial conference. Unfortunately, however, a formal body representing the schools of social work of the kind set up in 1938 was not re-established. During this period it was left to the AASW to provide an auspice for the schools of social work to communicate and develop a united approach to educational programs. Today, the AASW remains the body that decides the minimum standards of courses whose graduates have been assessed as holding 'eligibility for membership of the AASW'.

Despite the turbulent years of the Great Depression and World War II, in less than thirty years small interest groups set up in Sydney and Melbourne to establish education for the new profession of social work in Australia had achieved national unity of purpose between the schools of social work. Moreover, the establishment of the AASW consolidated these gains and provided a basis for consistent national development. This national cooperation was of immeasurable assistance to the University of Melbourne and the other founding schools of social work.

In 1960, at the point where this account finishes, the University of Melbourne course had brought together aspects of British and American social work, just as Jocelyn Hyslop had hoped. Whether, as she had predicted, it was 'better than either' is debatable, but it was certainly different from either, while still containing elements of both. It also had some uniquely Australian aspects. In 1960 the course leaders were still a little uncertain about the course's own identity, and dissatisfied with the way it was teaching social casework and fieldwork, but it had laid strong academic foundations. In the American style the course had put a premium on teaching its students how to actually 'do' social work, and had not fallen into the trap of splitting into numerous specialist courses, as had happened in Britain. The young Len Tierney, with his recent master's degree from the New York School of Social Work, had just been put in charge of the department, later going on to complete a doctorate at Columbia University and a career teaching social work at the University of Melbourne, which resulted in his mentoring a new generation of social work leaders.

Although Jocelyn Hyslop had been the undisputed national social work leader in the 1930s, by the end of World War II the University of Sydney's Norma Parker was emerging as the national leader. These two women had known each other from the start, and in fact the much younger Parker had been one of the guests at the Lyceum Club when Melbourne welcomed Jocelyn Hyslop in 1934. Parker's forty-year career, in which she nurtured the profession nationally from her base in Sydney, helped to lift Australian social work standards, and through her work in the national AASW she helped keep a unity of purpose among social workers.

In the rapid expansion of social work education in Victoria after 1970, the three new schools of social work that sprang up in Victoria (at La Trobe and Monash universities and the Preston Institute of Technology, which was later amalgamated with the RMIT University social work course) were able to start teaching in an environment where establishment battles had been fought and won and there was a ready market for their graduates. The University of Melbourne's social studies department, along with local social workers, had done an excellent job of preparing the ground for them. The selection of the American social work educational path in both Sydney and Melbourne had proved to be fortunate, so that by 1960 the building blocks for academically strong generic professional education were firmly in place in Australia. Today's more than thirty schools of social work and over 17,000-member AASW were built on firm foundations.

The three founding courses had each congratulated themselves on acceptance into their local university. They saw this as acknowledgement of their status and, at least in Melbourne and Adelaide, the incorporation solved most of their financial problems. The significance of this achievement can be seen when looking at a comparable female profession at the time, physiotherapy, which took five attempts (starting in 1907) before it was eventually admitted as a course at the University of Melbourne in 1991.[47] But the question must be asked: did the need to comply with university regulations, and the lack of sympathy for this female profession from the universities, inhibit the development of the profession? Certainly Martha Morrison Dore, writing at the time of the centenary of the Columbia University School of Social Work, argued that independence from a university in its formative stage had strengthened, not weakened, Columbia social work's efforts.[48] On the other hand, the milieu of a university, the ability to combine university subjects with specific social work subjects, or to combine a diploma with a bachelor's degree, did enrich the student experience. The guidance and support of leaders inside the university, such as Sandy Boyce Gibson and Georgina Sweet, was also important.

11

Changing Themes in Social Work

Before closing, I wish to remind the reader that this book is a study of the founding of professional social work education in Melbourne and Australia, not of the changing arenas in which social work has been practised. As stated in the introduction, social work's core values and philosophy have endured from the beginning. But social work is a flexible profession, and in subsequent decades it has responded to many new challenges and adapted its way of working as our society has changed. The present-day reader may be shocked by the omission from this book of themes that are integral to social work today but that did not emerge until the 1970s – or even later. By the 1950s, social problems arising from mass post-war immigration were just starting to appear, but women's issues were almost invisible until the second-wave women's movement started in the late 1960s. The broad recognition of the effects of dispossession on Aboriginal and Torres Strait Islander people occurred still later. Social workers are embedded in their society, and generally share the ignorance or blindness of that society. Although social workers may be found at the vanguard of change, or advocating reform in their workplace or in their private capacity, social work is not a radical profession. Its members will be found behind the scenes, supporting client groups in fighting for change, but such work is unlikely to be documented in the written historical record.

History must be viewed through the lens of the time. The period about which I have written was a different world, and today's understanding of some of these issues had yet to evolve. Here I shall touch on just two of the important themes that emerged in the second half of the twentieth and early twenty-first centuries: those of women and of Indigenous Australians. These are stories that are still emerging, and the situation is not static. Indeed, since I started writing this book, the international Me Too movement has emerged, and in 2021 shocking allegations of the rape of a young staffer in Australia's Parliament House once again raised questions on the issue of gender inequality in Australia.[1]

Feminism – on being a women's profession

Despite my commitment to the women's cause, I have not written this book from a particularly feminist perspective. The fact that social work has been predominantly a women's profession in Australia has been a problem for building the profession, but in the early days it was an advantage for many individuals. At a time when few women could pursue careers in the prestigious professions of law, engineering or medicine – even if they had managed to obtain qualifications and employment – social work was an attractive career, and was taken up by highly intelligent women. A series of case studies in *The Half-Open Door* by Melbourne historians Patricia Grimshaw and Lynne Strahan illustrates the barriers faced by women graduates.[2] Among the members of Melbourne's BSS, the zoologist Dr Georgina Sweet and medical practitioner Dr Vera Scantlebury Brown were examples of gifted women professionals whose careers were restricted solely because of their gender. At that time, women could make very good careers in the uncontested field of welfare. Examples in the post-war era include Lyra Taylor, who held a senior position in the Australian Public Service as the inaugural head of social work in the Commonwealth Social Services Department, and Joan Tuxen, who for decades led the development of the influential Victorian Society for Crippled Children.[3] But these early leaders did suffer from the routine discrimination of the time, being paid at a lower rate than men under the award, and after marriage being barred from permanent employment in the public service, and from superannuation.

This situation had still not changed by the 1970s. An article on discrimination against women in social work that I wrote for *The Australian Journal of Social Work* in 1973,[4] well after the period covered in this book, was largely ignored at the time.

Unfortunately, early attempts at building the profession were bedevilled by the regular loss of talented women to marriage and child-rearing. The second-wave women's movement has not made as much difference to this situation as might have been hoped, despite equal opportunity legislation, radical improvements in women's employment opportunities, and the provision of child care. My own experience suggests that some of the reasons for this include problems in accommodating part-time workers who need to prioritise child-rearing, the 'double shift' of employment and housework in traditional families, female expectations, and possibly covert prejudice and discrimination. Whatever the reasons, the result is that many talented women social workers make a far smaller contribution to their profession than they are capable of making.

Women as clients

Turning to the question of women as clients, it was not until the advent of second-wave feminism that the rights of women to personal achievement and personal safety in a male-dominated society started to be recognised and more actively pursued, with the resulting establishment of an entirely new range of services: from rape crisis centres, to women's refuges, to Commonwealth government pensions for single mothers, to state and national legislation for equal opportunity.

Indigenous Australians

By the same token, it is hard now to imagine that the alienation of the First Australians was virtually ignored in social work education in the years up to 1960, but such was indeed the case, both in the University of Melbourne's department of social studies and in society in general. In her autobiography, Fay Marles (née Pearce), who was a social work student between 1944 and 1948, mentions 'a series of lectures given by Caroline Kelly, an anthropologist who had lived with Aboriginal people whose lives, actions and values she described factually and with complete respect'.[5] These lectures probably resulted from an opportunistic invitation to Kelly, who was giving lectures in Sydney and Melbourne at the time;[6] there is no evidence of Aboriginal matters being a regular subject in the curriculum. Some individuals and small groups in society certainly worried that something was not right: in 1950 the Victorian Council of Social Service published a forty-seven page research report on Aboriginal residents of Melbourne;[7] at the Fourth Australian Conference of Social Work in 1953, Eleanor Williams presented a paper on behalf of the Western Australian Branch that raised detailed concerns about the treatment of Aboriginal people;[8] and from the 1950s University of Melbourne social work students were involved in Abschol, a scheme started by the National Union of Australian University Students to provide tertiary education scholarships for Aboriginal students.[9] At that point, no Indigenous Australians had had the opportunity to complete a university course. During this period, Australia viewed assimilation as the best way to deal with minority groups: migrants and Indigenous people just had to fit in. With massive post-war European immigration, this attitude gradually changed. But listening to the account of one 1962 Melbourne social work graduate, Reg Worthy,[10] of working with government departments managing Aboriginal affairs in the Northern Territory and in Victoria, though he was outraged at the miserable living conditions of Aboriginal people, today his solutions are seen as inappropriately assimilationist. I would like to think that a twenty-first century social worker would have consulted with local communities, listened to them, and respected the ways in which the Aboriginal people wanted to express their own identity and culture, rather than encouraging a sort of 'equality', which in fact meant conformity with non-Aboriginal society. Worthy was not alone in failing to understand Aboriginal culture.

It has taken decades of protests, dialogue, research, exposés, education by Indigenous people, and international awareness-raising about racism for Australia's non-Indigenous population to begin to reframe its own place in history, not as 'discoverers' but as invaders of sovereign territory, and for our society to begin to understand the strength and the continuity over millennia of Aboriginal and Torres Strait Islander cultures. This is still a matter of argument, unfortunately. The strong voice we hear today from Aboriginal parliamentarians, lawyers, bureaucrats, doctors, nurses, social workers and other professionals, as well as on television, the stage, cinema, opera, dance and the visual arts, was virtually non-existent at the moment this story ends. Then, as Sally Morgan wrote in her best-selling autobiography *My Place*,[11] denying Aboriginal heritage was a strategy for survival. Her own family successfully passed as Indian to avoid the threat of child removal. It was not until 1967, well after the end of this history, that a landmark national referendum fully included Aboriginal people in the Australian constitution and importantly, for the first time, counted them in the national census.

Nevertheless, much more needs to be done: despite the 2017 Uluru Statement from the Heart,[12] a First Nations voice has yet to be enshrined in the Australian constitution. Shamefully, on 14 October 2023 a national referendum to change the Australian constitution to allow an independent Indigenous voice to parliament was rejected nationally. Today, the social work course at the University of Melbourne has Aboriginal staff members and students, and includes Aboriginal content in its curriculum. The national board of the Australian Association of Social Workers has a dedicated position for an Aboriginal or Torres Strait Islander social worker, so that an Indigenous Australian voice is always heard at the organisation's highest level. Currently two of its nine directors, including president Linda Ford, a Bigambul woman from southern Queensland, and 348 members identify as Aboriginal or Torres Strait Islander. Exact numbers are not available, but there are also other Indigenous Australian social workers in Australia. For example, the organisation Indigenous Allied Health Australia (which offers free membership, as opposed to $725 per annum for the AASW) has approximately 706 Indigenous Australian members.[13]

Like the rest of Australia, social work is on a learning journey that has only just begun, and that will remain one of our challenges in the future. A recent article by Simon Gardiner, reflecting frankly on the way in which, early in his career, his lack of knowledge of the importance of family and community to Aboriginal people, and of the lasting scars suffered by the members of the stolen generations, hampered his best efforts to support an Aboriginal mother in her bid to reunite with her young children, is an important contribution to social work literature.[14] By working in a more culturally sensitive way, researching, listening and examining practice, the social work profession is gradually beginning to respond appropriately to this complex matter.

The arenas in which social work practices continue to change

What will be regarded as neglected arenas by social workers in another generation – the future equivalents of women and Indigenous Australians? Social workers are doing important work with survivors of bushfires and floods, events that are increasing in regularity and severity due to climate change. With the predicted rising of the oceans, the Pacific region will have climate refugees who will want to settle in Australia and New Zealand. What role will social work play here? And what role will the profession play as our continent dries, and food and water become more difficult to obtain? Will social workers involve themselves in the campaigns to prevent further warming of the planet? Will they be able to use their community-building skills to help Australians adapt to new ways of living, of growing food, and of using and sharing resources?

Areas for future research

Researching – and particularly documenting – examples of best practice in working with Indigenous Australians, both as individuals and in communities, should be a high priority for social work in the next decades. The law and systems must change too, but social workers have a contribution to make.

Questions arising from the gendered nature of the social work profession will provide an important area for research.[15] Comparisons with the development of the more masculinised profession of psychology, which works in a very similar domain, would be particularly interesting. Psychology at the University of Melbourne started some years later than social work, and after a slow beginning has professionalised very successfully.

Australian social work scholarship would benefit from further attention to social work histories. A detailed historical account of the origins of the University of Sydney's social work course is urgently needed. This would provide an interesting contrast with Melbourne, as the two schools had much in common, shared a commitment to American methods, were in touch with each other, yet had developed from different origins and evolved differently. And as John Lawrence pointed out in his obituary of Norma Parker, a history of her life, set in its time, would be a great contribution to knowledge, as it would span both the University of Sydney and the Australian Association of Social Workers.[16]

The history of the Australian Association of Social Workers itself is yet to be written. The founding of a national association in 1946 has been of great benefit to the development of the profession in Australia. It provided an early platform for national communication, and militated against fragmentation. The history of the development of fieldwork models, which is as much a problem in Australia today as it was in the 1930s, is of interest in part because the same arguments and possible solutions tend to recur.

There are individual stories to be investigated: the nationwide efforts of those Australian Red Cross Society social workers who worked with returned servicemen and women; the young Australian social workers, such as Nancy Vercoe, Nancy Fancourt and Betty Dow, who worked with international social workers in the United Nations Relief and Rehabilitation Association in Europe after the war;[17] and the early social workers in the Commonwealth Department of Social Services, who, as very young women in the 1940s and 1950s, traversed the remote areas of Australia. Their boss, Lyra Taylor, had a substantial legal career in New Zealand before becoming a social worker in the US, Canada, Sydney and Melbourne – a story still to be written.

The overlooked role of social work in early Australian social science also deserves to be reclaimed. The forgotten contribution of Sydney and Melbourne universities to the war effort through the development of industrial welfare training courses, and to post-war reconstruction, both only touched on in this book, needs to be told.

Ann Oakley's history *Women, Peace and Welfare* has uncovered networks of British and American social workers not previously documented.[18] The present volume touches on similar networks between British, Australian and American social workers; further exploration of Georgina Sweet and Stella May Allan's ('Vesta' of *The Argus*) connections through the Pan-Pacific Women's Association, which commenced in 1928, may well throw more light on these international women's networks. Georgia Travis, the first American social work Fulbright scholar in Australia, had already met English social work leaders Cherry Morris and Bryn Jervis-Reid in the US and visited them on her journey home from Australia in 1954.[19] These encounters hint at other networks of interest.

Finally, this book represents my own particular understanding of the story of the founding of social work at the University of Melbourne and of the Australian profession more broadly. As Oakley reminds us, there is no such thing as a single, unbiased historic truth. I will regard my endeavour as a success if it stimulates others to write about the history of social work in Australia, regardless of whether they agree with me or not. I have deliberately included extensive footnotes and appendices to provide an easier starting point for future researchers than I had. It is urgent that social workers write their history before too many memories are lost and personal archives destroyed.

Because of Australia's debt to American social work, it seems fitting to end this book as I began, with an American quotation. In the words of Ronald Feldman and Sheila Kamerman of Columbia University School of Social Work at the time of its centennial celebrations:

> *Social workers' understanding and appreciation of their profession's past will be the best guarantor of their future.*[20]

Appendices

Appendix 1:
Milestones in international social work

Date	Location	Milestone	Comment
1819	UK	Thomas Chalmers establishes District Visiting Scheme in Glasgow.	Chalmers was a clergyman; he divided parishes into districts with localised volunteer-friendly visitors. This was seen as one model for both the Charity Organisation Society (COS) and the Settlement movement.
1864	UK	Octavia Hill begins managing slum dwellings for John Ruskin.	Hill was an early COS educator; this move was a precursor to the settlement movement.
1869	UK	The Charity Organisation Society (COS) is founded.	COS led to a more scientific, rational approach to charitable giving. It attempted to distribute funds equitably.
1874	US	Forerunner of National Conference of Charities and Correction – Conference of Boards of Public Charities – held in New York City.	Became a national forum for philosophical and policy discussion. From 1875 to 1879 it was called Conference of Charities; 1880–81 Conference of Charities and Correction; 1882–1916 National Conference of Charities and Correction.
1877	US	First COS in the US is established, by Rev. S. Gurteen in Buffalo, New York.	Similar methodology to UK COS.

Appendices

Date	Location	Milestone	Comment
1882	US	Twenty-two COS now operate in the US. The COS philosophy is also adopted by other, existing organisations.	Rapid spread of COS and its 'scientific' approach.
1885	UK	Samuel and Henrietta Barnett establish Toynbee Hall.	Toynbee Hall was the first settlement house.
1889	US	Jane Addams starts Hull House in Chicago, with Ellen Starr.	Though not the first settlement house in the US, it is the best known. Addams was a successful activist and reformer.
c. 1890	UK	Octavia Hill and Margaret Sewell establish a one-year generalist training course in social work.	Forerunner of the COS school of social work.
1893	US	International Congress of Charities, Corrections and Philanthropy is held in Chicago.	Anna Dawes makes the first call in the US for social work training.
1894	UK	Mrs D. Gardner outlines the new COS training program.	
1895	UK	COS appoints the first almoner: Mary Stewart at Royal Free Hospital, London.	A separate strand of social work training is initiated; this was the start of what some saw as an elite part of the profession.
1895	US	Chicago School of Social Economics is established by Graham Taylor at Chicago Commons.	Many consider this the founding of modern social work in US; it became the Chicago School of Civics and Philanthropy in 1903.
1896	US	Graham Taylor starts Chicago journal *The Commons*.	An influential channel of communication.
1896	US	First appearance of settlement leaders at National Conference on Charities and Correction.	They spoke of various aspects of their work: research, social reform, club work, recreation, information, children.
1897	Canada/US	National Conference of Charities and Correction is held in Toronto	Mary Richmond presented her landmark paper on the need for training. Jane Addams stated at the conference: 'I have not the great fear of pauperizing people which many of you seem to have.'

Appendix 1: Milestones in international social work

Date	Location	Milestone	Comment
1898	US	New York COS Summer School of Philanthropy is held.	This three-month course was a precursor of the Columbia University School of Social Work, and is claimed as the first formal social work training course in the US.
1899	Netherlands	Amsterdam Institute for Social Work Training is established	The first full-time social work education worldwide. Had been in contact with Octavia Hill.
1899	US	Mary Richmond publishes *Friendly Visiting Among the Poor*.	Richmond's interest in social work education was given form in print.
1901	UK	COS takes over Octavia Hill and Margaret Sewell's training course.	
1903	UK	COS establishes the School of Sociology and Economics.	First full-time school of social work in the UK.
1903	US	The Chicago School of Social Economics is reorganised by Graham Taylor.	Established the first one-year program of social service education in the US.
1904	UK	University of Liverpool opens a school for social science, to train social workers.	The first university social work training in the UK.
1904	US	Harvard and Simmons universities create the Boston School for Social Workers.	Claimed to be the first university social work training in the US.
1904	US	New York School of Philanthropy conducts a one-year course in social work.	Forerunner of Columbia University School of Social Work.
1905	US	Dr Richard Cabot introduces medical social work at Massachusetts General Hospital and shortly thereafter appoints Ida M. Cannon as social worker.	The start of American medical social work, under a strong medical advocate and with a social worker of great vision and practical wisdom.
1906	UK	The first Guild of Help is established, at Bradford.	Though Guild of Help was not connected to the social work training movement, British social work historians today see it as an antecedent of social work.
1907	UK	Hospital Almoners Council is founded, and takes over almoner training from COS.	Almoner training became a top-up year after general training.

Date	Location	Milestone	Comment
1907	US	Psychiatric social work commences at Massachusetts General Hospital in Boston.	Edith Burleigh and Ida M. Cannon started psychiatric social work in the US.
1908	Germany	Alice Salomon School of Social Work is established	Alice Salomon was a founder and served as both president and secretary of the International Committee of Schools of Social Work (later International Association of Schools of Social Work).
1908	UK	Social work training commences at University of Birmingham.	Most British social work training was at the LSE, but it was gradually introduced elsewhere.
1908	US	Chicago School of Civics and Philanthropy establishes a two-year training course in social work.	The first two-year training course in the US.
1909	US	Mary Richmond leaves Philadelphia for New York and starts work at the Russell Sage Foundation.	Richmond was responsible for the development of technical assistance resources for charity agencies.
1910	US	Jane Addams, first woman president of the National Conference on Charities and Correction, gives a speech on 'Charity and social justice', which highlights the distinction between the COS and settlement houses.	Some writers claim there was a rift between settlement and COS philosophies, although this popular view is disputed by some historians. It is an oversimplification, as the situation varied in different parts of the country and at different times.
1912	UK	The London School of Economics and Political Science (LSE) takes over COS training.	COS was concerned that practical work would suffer under the academic approach of social scientists (and was eventually proved correct).
1912	US	Social work department at Massachusetts General Hospital works with the Boston School of Social Work to establish a one-year Master of Social Work course.	The beginning of medical social work training in an existing university social work department.

Appendix 1: Milestones in international social work

Date	Location	Milestone	Comment
1914	US	Mary Jarrett and Elmer E. Southard at Boston Psychopathic Hospital start a six-month training course in psychiatric social work.	Followed a decade of social workers practising as psychiatric social workers. The US was ahead of Britain in this field.
1915	US	National Conference of Charities and Correction is held at Baltimore, Maryland.	
		(i) Abraham Flexner of the New York Education Board, who had played a major role in reform of the medical profession, gives a paper titled 'Is social work a profession?', concluding that it was not.	(i) Flexner's paper damaged the emerging profession's view of itself, and still resonates in the US today.
		(ii) Mary Richmond's paper is titled 'Social Workers in a Changing World'.	(ii) Richmond defended casework, and deplored antagonism between caseworkers and reformers as 'socially mischievous'.
		(iii) Zilpha Smith and Edith Abbott emphasise educationally based field practice, with schools of social work in control.	(iii) Social work teachers staked a claim to be in control of student field placements.
1917	US	The National Conference on Charities and Correction changes its name to the National Conference of Social Work.	Emphasis shifted from broad social policy to administration and methods of practice.
1918	US	Smith College starts psychiatric social work training.	Other major universities, including those in New York, Chicago and Philadelphia, incorporated this into their curriculum.
1919	US	New York School of Philanthropy changes its name to New York School of Social Work.	Still closely tied to the COS, and less closely to Columbia University.
1919	UK	Edith Verena Eckhard is appointed as senior tutor in the social science department at LSE.	Eckhard had an important social work career and assisted establishment at the University of Melbourne.
1920	Brussels	Central School of Social Service is founded.	Pioneer school of social work in Belgium.

Date	Location	Milestone	Comment
1921	UK	Eckhard's book *The Mother and the Infant* is published.	The third book in the Social Service Library Series, edited by Clement Attlee. It provided both statistics on infant mortality and practical strategies to help the survival of the infants of the poor.
1921	US	American Association of Social Workers is formed.	The first social work professional association in the US (merged into the National Association of Social Workers in 1955).
1922	Yenching, China	University of Yenching is established, including a department of sociology and social work – the first social work education in Asia.	Closed with the arrival of communism.
1922	UK	The Almoners Council becomes the Institute of Hospital Almoners.	This was a step in the strengthening of almoner training, which developed its own strong identity and a reputation for expertise.
1923–25	US	The Milford Conference meets.	Defined social casework and provided a common base for it as a major division of social work practice that crossed fields.
1924	South Africa	University of Cape Town and Transvaal University College each commence three-year diplomas in social work.	Patterned on British social studies courses, with emphasis on social science.
1925	Santiago, Chile	School of Social Work of the Welfare Board is founded.	Founded by Dr Del Rio of Medical School of University of Chile in Santiago, after a chance meeting with Belgian Dr René Sand, secretary-general of the League of Red Cross Societies based in Paris.
1926	US	Gertrude Vaile is elected president of the National Conference on Social Work.	In her presidential address Vaile spoke of the decline of the kind of crusading social work leadership that had been so evident in the days of the progressive movement.

Appendix 1: Milestones in international social work

Date	Location	Milestone	Comment
1928	UK	The first child guidance clinic in Britain is established, in Islington, London.	Funded by the US Commonwealth Fund, it became a training ground for psychiatric social workers.
1928	France	First International Conference of Social Work is held in Paris.	Arose from suggestions by international delegates to the US National Conference on Social Work. Received major funding from American philanthropists. O. Morrice Williams from Australian Red Cross Society attended.
1929	UK	The Commonwealth Fund finances and guides the first British course in psychiatric social work, at LSE.	Demonstrated the direct American influence on the establishment of psychiatric social work. Initially the focus was child guidance. It strengthened professional social work in the UK; Noel Timms went as far as describing it as 'the first professional social work in Britain'.
1929	US	Porter Lee delivers his address 'Cause and function' to the National Conference on Social Work in San Francisco.	An important debate, responding to concern that, by professionalising, social work was losing its earlier reformist aspects (social workers being now limited by constraints imposed by employers).
1929	UK	Eileen Younghusband joins the staff of LSE as a part-time tutor.	Younghusband had two periods of employment at LSE: 1929–39 and 1944–58. She resigned after disputes over the departmental reorganisation following the 'Carnegie Experiment'.
1932	South Africa	First degree course in social work established, at University of Stellenbosch.	
1932	Germany	Second International Conference of Social Work is held in Frankfurt.	Dr John Newman-Morris was the only Australian attending.

Date	Location	Milestone	Comment
1936	India	Tata Institute commences a two-year diploma training in social work.	Founded by American missionary Clifford Manshardt with support of the Tata family. Like Australia, it looked to Britain for social sciences and to America for professional courses and social work practice. This became the Tata Institute of Social Sciences.
1936	UK	Third International Conference of Social Work is held in London.	S. Greig Smith was the only Australian attending; he published a report in COS journal *The Other Half*.
1939	UK	Association of Psychiatric Social Workers is formed in London.	New social work career opportunities were opening up in the UK.
1940	US	New York School of Social Work affiliates with Columbia University.	Retained the name New York School of Social Work.
1946	UK	COS in UK changes its name to the Family Welfare Association.	Renaming heralded a new role, emphasising psychodynamic work with individuals.
1948	US	Fourth International Conference of Social Work is held in Atlantic City.	Australians Alison Player, Lyra Taylor and Marion Urquhart attended.
1950	UK	Richard Titmuss is appointed to the chair of social administration at LSE.	A new era was beginning. Titmuss was more actively interested than his predecessors in managing the social work program.
1950	UK	Cherry Morris publishes *Social Casework in Great Britain*.	The first book on social casework by British social workers.
1951	US	The 'Hollis-Taylor report' is published as *Social Work Education* in the US.	Minimum standards for American social workers were agreed on.
1952	UK	Edith Eckhard retires from LSE and dies shortly afterwards (1953).	Eckhard had joined LSE staff in 1919. For three decades she was greatly respected and for many years was the head of social work education at LSE.

Appendix 1: Milestones in international social work

Date	Location	Milestone	Comment
1954–58	UK	Carnegie United Kingdom Trust–funded course in casework commences at LSE.	Established due to the work of Eileen Younghusband, taught by local staff and by the American Charlotte Towle on a Fulbright scholarship; first generic social work course in Britain.
1955	US	National Association of Social Workers is created through the merger of seven organisations.	Membership limited to members of the seven associations and to social workers with a master's degree from an accredited school of social work.
1956	US	National Conference on Social Work changes name to National Conference on Social Welfare.	This was a continuation of the nineteenth-century National Conference on Charities and Correction.
1959	UK	'Younghusband report' is published.	A contribution to professionalising and coordinating British social work.
1962	US	New York School of Social Work is renamed Columbia University School of Social Work.	The school had formally entered Columbia in 1959, but was then called the New York School of Social Work of Columbia University.
1963	UK	Standing Conference of Organisations of Social Work is established.	Brought together eight professional associations speaking for social workers.
1968	UK	The 'Seebohm report' (*Report of the Committee on Local Authority and Allied Personal Services*) is published.	Represented a lost opportunity to raise the standards of social work education in England and Wales.
1970	UK	British Association of Social Workers is formed, but probation officers refuse to join.	The new BASW brought together most of the small professional social work associations.
1972	UK	Central Council for Education and Training in Social Work is created by parliament.	Minimum qualification for social work was set at two years. Medical social workers felt betrayed, as this was a drop in qualifications from their previous level.

Date	Location	Milestone	Comment
1995	UK	LSE ceases teaching social work.	Main reason given was lack of research emanating from the department, though perhaps social work had never been a good fit at the LSE.

Appendix 2:
Milestones in Australian social work

Year	Location	Milestone	Comment
1887	Melbourne	A Charity Organisation Society (COS) is founded.	Founded by Professor E.E. Morris of the University of Melbourne following a scandal over the death of Mr Jackman, a labourer who died from peritonitis on the doorstep of the Melbourne Hospital after being refused admission due to a lack of beds.
1889	Melbourne	The COS publishes its first *Guide to Melbourne Charities*.	Written guides to charities remained a feature of Victoria's welfare environment, with a guide later being published by the Victorian Council of Social Service, discontinued in the 1980s. It was an essential reference for social workers during the period discussed in the present volume.
1890	Melbourne	Professor E.E. Morris gives a talk at the Town Hall, comparing British and American COS.	Morris argued that Melbourne, as a new city, had more in common with the US than with UK. This started an interest in the American COS.
1890 and 1891	Melbourne	COS initiates Australasian conferences on charity.	Morris had admired the American National Conference on Charities and Correction and sought to replicate the idea.
1893	Chicago	Catherine Spence is the only Australian attending the International Congress of Charities, Corrections and Philanthropy, held at Chicago World's Fair.	Spence represented Melbourne COS and several other charities. She was listed in the proceedings as an honorary vice-president.
1900	Melbourne	COS starts publication of *The Charity Review*.	Useful, small, quarterly newsletter on welfare matters – ceased publication in 1916.
1902	England	Professor Morris dies unexpectedly while on leave in England, aged fifty-nine.	The COS lost a visionary leader.

Year	Location	Milestone	Comment
1909	Melbourne	Stanley Greig Smith, newly arrived from Britain, becomes secretary of the COS.	A powerful influence on the development of professional social work in Victoria for forty-seven years.
1913	Melbourne	The COS Aesculapius Fund provides aids and appliances such as wheelchairs and prostheses to patients of Melbourne hospitals.	In the absence of government assistance the COS took on this role, which is now regarded as a government responsibility.
1913	Melbourne	Children's Welfare Association of Victoria is established. Greig Smith is a founding member.	This peak body became the Centre for Excellence in Child and Family Welfare in 2003.
1914	Melbourne	COS runs a conference for relieving agencies (those giving financial support to the poor) on the central registration of clients.	'Double-dipping' by clients attending several agencies was a constant concern for relieving agencies, and something that the COS wanted to guard against through better coordination and information exchange.
1916	Melbourne	S. Greig Smith gives a lecture for the Children's Welfare Association on 'Social work as a field for service'.	Before there were trained social workers in Victoria, Smith often lectured on social work.
1921	Melbourne	Melbourne Hospital Red Cross Auxiliary establishes a volunteer-run tea room for patients, and by 1924 has set up a social service bureau to help patients who are still unwell after leaving hospital.	Provided assistance that was later seen as the role of the almoners.
1924	Melbourne	Morris House, the new COS-owned headquarters, opens.	Provided a hub for local charities. Named after the first COS president, the late Professor E.E. Morris.
1926	Melbourne	The COS begins a weekly conference of welfare agencies to discuss common problems and exchange ideas.	Another COS effort to improve coordination of charity.
1926		COS commences publication of *The Other Half*.	Through this publication Greig Smith promoted American social work and social research, and advocated for social work training. It ceased publication in 1937.

Appendix 2: Milestones in Australian social work

Year	Location	Milestone	Comment
1927	Melbourne	R.J. Love, Victoria's inspector of charities, after visiting Britain and North America advocates the appointment of almoners.	Love was an important advocate for almoners, being well placed as a senior public servant.
1927	US	Lyra Taylor, already a lawyer, completes MA in social economics and social work at Johns Hopkins University in Baltimore.	Initially interested in the social implications of law, Taylor became a lifelong social work leader, helping to introduce American methods to Australia.
1928	Paris	O. Morrice Williams of Australian Red Cross Society is the only Australian to attend the First International Conference of Social Work.	He did not keep up contact with the International Conference.
1928	Perth	Monsignor J.T. McMahon chooses Norma Parker and Constance Moffitt for scholarships to attend the School of Social Science at the Catholic University in Washington, DC. Some years later the Church sends Eileen Davidson to the US.	It has not been widely recognised that Western Australia took such early initiative in social work training; nor has the role of the Catholic Church been fully acknowledged.
1929	Sydney	The New South Wales Board of Social Study and Training (BSST) is established.	The BSST offered the first generic social work education in Australia.
1929	Melbourne	Victorian Institute of Almoners (VIA) is established.	Changed name to Victorian Institute of Hospital Almoners (VIHA) in 1933, although both names were used for some time.
1929	Melbourne	Agnes McIntyre arrives in Melbourne from St Thomas's Hospital, London.	Melbourne's first almoner and director of almoner training at the Melbourne Hospital.
1930	Melbourne	Dr John Newman-Morris publishes *Social Work in Hospitals: Some American Investigations*.	An extensive report of Newman-Morris's tour of American hospitals and social work schools.
1930 (Nov)	Melbourne	Lynette Henderson and Mary Noall are the first almoners to complete training at the VIA / VIHA.	They were Victoria's first locally trained social workers.

Appendices

Year	Location	Milestone	Comment
1930	Melbourne	Greig Smith delivers lectures on social casework and social problems to Presbyterian deaconesses and YWCA trainees.	Though not a trained social worker, in the absence of training in Australia Smith educated himself and was in demand as a speaker on social work.
1931 (Jun)	Melbourne	Committee on Training for Social Work is established.	A precursor to the Victorian Council for Social Training (est. 1933), it aimed to establish general social work training.
1932	Sydney	Aileen Fitzpatrick is appointed New South Wales' first paid director of social work training.	Fitzpatrick had been appointed honorary director in 1929 and was later paid a salary. An arts graduate, she remained in the role until 1940, when the course entered the University of Sydney.
1931	Melbourne	Norma Parker returns from the US with a social work qualification from the Catholic University of America in Washington, DC.	This made Parker the first Australian-born qualified (generic) social worker. She was a significant pioneer and represented the American social work view.
1931	Sydney	Misses Davis and Carrothers are awarded Diplomas of Social Science by the Board of Social Studies and Training in New South Wales.	They were the first trained social workers in New South Wales. 'Social science' was the terminology used at the LSE for its social work course.
1931	Melbourne	Dr (later Sir John) Newman-Morris is elected president of the Victorian Institute of Almoners.	Remained president until the VIHA was dissolved in 1950.
1931	Melbourne	Greig Smith is made honorary secretary of the Victorian Institute of Almoners.	Provided great support to almoner training, despite his personal commitment to general social work training.
1931	Melbourne	Committee on Social Training is formed, to explore the building of general social work training in Victoria.	Occurred at a well-attended meeting held at Melbourne Town Hall.
1932	Frankfurt	Dr John Newman-Morris attends Second International Conference of Social Work.	Newman-Morris went out of his way to educate himself about the new profession of social work.

Appendix 2: Milestones in Australian social work

Year	Location	Milestone	Comment
1932	US, UK, Europe	Carnegie Corporation funds Aileen Fitzpatrick of the New South Wales social work course on a nine-month study tour.	Fitzpatrick returned to Australia confident of her knowledge of social work.
1932	Melbourne	Norma Parker is appointed as the first social worker at St Vincent's Hospital, Melbourne.	Originally from Western Australia, Parker trained in the US.
1932 (Jun)	Melbourne	Committee on Training for Social Work and a sub-committee of the University of Melbourne's professorial board agree to establish a board outside, but officially linked to, the university. This will be the Board of Social Studies (BSS).	The link with the University of Melbourne was important in the development of the course.
1933	Melbourne	Victorian Council for Social Training is formed.	Australia's second general social work training body.
1933 (Feb)	Melbourne	First meeting of the Board of Social Studies (BSS).	The BSS would have direct responsibility for supervising the course, and reported to the new Victorian Council for Social Training.
1933	Melbourne	Training of general social work students commences in what was then called the Diploma of Social Science (as at the LSE).	The first four general social work students – Frances Penington, Muriel Watt, Marjorie Goodison and Lois Lethlean – started their training at the beginning of the 1933 academic year. Penington was dissatisfied with the course and did not complete, but after experience in the US became an important reformer, particularly in the sphere of public housing.
1933	Melbourne	Helen Rees is the third consecutive English almoner appointed as directress of training at the Victorian Institute of Hospital Almoners.	Rees was involved in planning and supporting the first generic social work course in Melbourne. She went on to play an important role in Sydney and internationally.

Appendices

Year	Location	Milestone	Comment
1933	Melbourne	The Victorian Institute of Almoners changes its name to the Victorian Institute of Hospital Almoners.	The reason is unknown. It could have been the influence of its new director, Helen Rees, or a desire to make its role clearer as the new generic social work training institution was established. The names may have been used interchangeably before this.
1934	Melbourne	Australian Association of Almoners is formed.	Disbanded in 1959.
1934	Sydney	New South Wales Association of Social Workers is formed.	
1934 (Dec)	Melbourne	Jocelyn Hyslop arrives from England to take up the position of first director of training for the BSS.	The success of the Victorian social work course can be attributed in large part to Hyslop's drive and intellectual rigour.
1934	Melbourne	VIHA writes to BSS suggesting that its qualification be taken after two years of general BSS training.	This proved to be a significant contribution to generic education on the American model, as it ensured that the two courses did not compete.
1935	Australia	Frederick Keppel, head of Carnegie Corporation, visits Australia.	Visit marked the beginning of a long association between the Carnegie Corporation and Australian social work.
1934–35	US	Sydney's Aileen Fitzpatrick, again funded by Carnegie Corporation, takes a student tour of American social work centres.	Tour later caused controversy, as students were unhappy about some aspects of it.
1935	Melbourne	Dorothy Bethune is appointed as director of VIHA.	The first Australian-trained almoner to hold this position.
1935	Melbourne	Victorian Association of Social Workers is formed, with Jocelyn Hyslop as its first president.	This was the beginning of a long and close association between social work educators and the professional body, one that continued for the entire period covered by the present volume.
1935 (Sep)	Adelaide	Meeting held at Adelaide Town Hall to establish social work training; a Board of Social Service Training is created for South Australia.	The establishment of an organisation for training social workers in South Australia.

Appendix 2: Milestones in Australian social work

Year	Location	Milestone	Comment
1935	Melbourne	The Diploma of Social Science changes name to Diploma of Social Service.	Hyslop considered this important, to indicate that this was a profession that implemented services, not one that merely studied society.
1936	London	Greig Smith attends the Third International Conference of Social Work.	Valuable exposure to international social work. He shared information locally on return home.
1936	Adelaide	Amy Wheaton commences as inaugural head of social work education in South Australia. As in New South Wales and Victoria, the course started outside the local university but with its support.	Although not a qualified social worker, Wheaton was very highly educated, had studied at the LSE and done intensive in-servicing. She has been acknowledged as a remarkable leader.
1936	Sydney	New South Wales Institute of Hospital Almoners is established. Helen Rees returns from England to take up appointment as first directress of training (1936–41) and establishes almoner department at Sydney Hospital.	The institute was established largely because professionally qualified social workers in New South Wales vigorously opposed Aileen Fitzpatrick, whom they considered had insufficient knowledge of social work to train social workers, despite her confidence in her own ability.
1937	Sydney	Porter Lee, head of New York School of Social Work, visits Sydney at the request of Frederick Keppel, at Carnegie Corporation expense.	Illness prevented a visit to Melbourne, but Jocelyn Hyslop travelled to Sydney to consult with Lee.
1937	Adelaide	South Australia's Board of Social Service Training changes its name to the South Australian Board of Social Study and Training.	Possibly intended to achieve uniformity with New South Wales and Victoria.
1938	Melbourne	Gertrude Vaile from Minnesota visits Melbourne.	A leading and influential American social work educator.
1938 (May)	Sydney	Meeting of Australian schools of social work is held.	Attended by Gertrude Vaile and directors of training from Victoria, New South Wales and South Australia, although New South Wales' director of almoner training was excluded.

Appendices

Year	Location	Milestone	Comment
1938	Sydney	Australian Council of Schools of Social Work is formed.	Dr John Newman-Morris (Victoria) was president, Harvey Sutton (New South Wales) secretary, Amy Wheaton (South Australia) treasurer. Firmly based on an American model.
1939 (May)	Melbourne	Diploma of Social Service changes its name to Diploma in Social Studies of the Victorian Council for Social Training.	Reason for change is unknown, but possibly uniformity with other states. To continue to reflect the professional nature of training, diploma stated that it was a 'course of training for social work'.
1939 (May)	Melbourne	Highly qualified Scottish social worker Jean Robertson takes up post as fieldwork tutor for BSS.	Second staff member in the course, but quickly seconded to welfare work with the Commonwealth Department of Supply. Robertson supervised a team of social workers and welfare officers supporting female munitions workers.
1940 (Feb)	Sydney	New South Wales' social work course is taken on by University of Sydney, with Canadian Elizabeth Govan as first director.	Aileen Fitzpatrick was unacceptable to the university.
1940 (Dec)	Melbourne	Victoria's social work course is taken on by University of Melbourne. First meeting of BSS as part of the university is held on 19 December.	From the outset it had been a goal of the BSS to become part of the university. BSS believed that a university-standard education was needed for this profession. Inclusion in the university also solved some financial problems.
1941	Sydney	Norma Parker joins University of Sydney social work course.	Parker acted as director for lengthy periods. She left in 1965 to become associate professor and head of department of social work in the school of sociology at University of New South Wales, retiring in 1969. During her career she provided national leadership of the profession.

Appendix 2: Milestones in Australian social work

Year	Location	Milestone	Comment
1941 (Dec)	Melbourne	Ruth Hoban accepts position of fieldwork tutor.	Would later become head of department.
1942	Adelaide	The South Australian course enters University of Adelaide. University Board of Social Science is established, to supersede the Board of Social Study and Training. Amy Wheaton continues as director of the course.	The term 'social science' reflects Wheaton's more sociological interests and British orientation.
1942	Sydney	Norma Parker is appointed assistant to the director of the social work program at the University of Sydney.	
1944 (Feb)	Melbourne	Victorian Council for Social Training is wound up at a BSS meeting.	Once the course was part of the university, the Victorian Council for Social Training was no longer needed. The university's professorial board now oversaw the course.
1944 (Dec)	Melbourne	Jocelyn Hyslop resigns as director of training for BSS.	Resignation due to ill health. Professor Boyce Gibson gave a highly laudatory farewell speech.
1944	Sydney	Dorothy Sumner joins University of Sydney as a lecturer.	Sumner taught casework; she had worked at the New York School of Social Work. She made an important national contribution over several years.
1944	Chicago	Norma Parker receives a special fellowship from the Commonwealth Fund of New York to study psychiatric social work at University of Chicago.	Parker also visited various social work centres in the US.
1944	Melbourne	Lyra Taylor is invited to start a social work and social research department in the newly founded Commonwealth Department of Social Services.	Taylor was responsible for supervising Commonwealth Government social work staff located in the capital cities of all Australian states. This established a new social work domain in Australia. She acted as an ambassador for social work and was a founding member of the executive of AASW.

Appendices

Year	Location	Milestone	Comment
1944	Melbourne	Ruth Hoban becomes acting director of the department of social studies at the University of Melbourne, effectively as of December.	Hoban managed the department during a difficult period, when qualified academic staff were difficult to find and student numbers had to be restricted because of the lack of field teachers.
1945	Brisbane	General Association of Social Workers is formed in Queensland.	This group later played a crucial role, along with Lyra Taylor, in establishing social work education at the University of Queensland.
1945 (Aug)	Melbourne	Ruth Hoban is appointed director of department of social studies, University of Melbourne.	Appointed without advertisement, Hoban became the first Australian to direct the course at the University of Melbourne.
1945	Melbourne	BSS agrees in principle to extend the social studies course to three years, and to incorporate almoner training.	It was significant that the medical social work specialty was to be brought under the same umbrella as general training.
1945 (Dec)	Melbourne	Dr Georgina Sweet resigns from the BSS.	The BSS minute of appreciation for Sweet's fifteen years of support notes that, as national president of YWCA, she had been one of the six conveners of the 1931 Melbourne Town Hall meeting.
1946 (Jan)	Melbourne	Georgina Sweet dies, aged seventy-one. In May the BSS observes a minute's silence in her memory.	Sweet bequeathed money for a social work bursary that continues today.
1946	Perth	General Association of Social Workers commences in Western Australia.	
1946 (Aug)	Sydney	J.A. (Jim) Cardno is appointed head of social work at University of Sydney.	An advertisement for a head with social work qualifications had been unsuccessful, resulting in the appointment of this psychologist graduate of Aberdeen and Cambridge universities.

Appendix 2: Milestones in Australian social work

Year	Location	Milestone	Comment
1946	Sydney	Australian Association of Social Workers (AASW) is formed.	This resulted from meetings of the state associations, which became branches of the new national association. (Tasmania was not included, as it did not have an association.)
1946	Sydney	Inaugural executive of AASW is appointed, with Norma Parker elected inaugural president.	Parker continued in the role until 1953, when she became vice-president.
1947	Melbourne	*Forum*, the publication of the Victorian Association of Social Workers, begins.	A small newsletter/journal which was typed and reproduced cheaply on a Roneo machine. Jean Norman (McGregor/Downing) was its first editor.
1947 (Sep)	Sydney	The First Australian Conference of Social Work is held.	Conference theme was social work in statutory agencies, voluntary agencies and professional education for social work.
1947	Melbourne	The first year of three-year Diploma of Social Studies at the University of Melbourne commences.	The diploma was frequently combined with a Bachelor of Arts, and sometimes with a Bachelor of Commerce, together requiring four years of study.
1948	Melbourne	Professor Boyce Gibson steps down from chairmanship of the BSS.	In its minute of appreciation, the BSS noted that Gibson had an equal commitment to the establishment of social science and to social work education.
1948	Melbourne	Professor Max Crawford of history department, University of Melbourne, is appointed as chairman of BSS.	BSS did not flourish under Crawford's chairmanship.
1948	Sydney	Board of Social Study and Training opts for a three-year undergraduate diploma.	Some had hoped for a postgraduate diploma, but this did not eventuate.
1948	US	Fourth International Conference of Social Work is held in Atlantic City.	Alison Player, Lyra Taylor and Marion Urquhart attended.
1949 (Feb)	Sydney	Jim Cardno resigns as head of social work at University of Sydney.	Cardno taught part-time until the end of the year.

Appendices

Year	Location	Milestone	Comment
1949	Sydney	Norma Parker, senior lecturer, is appointed acting director of social work course.	Parker provided continuity in the department by remaining in this role until 1955.
1949 (Aug)	Melbourne	Second Australian Conference on Social Work is held.	Main topic was rehabilitation; there was an emphasis on discussion groups.
1951 (Aug)	Adelaide	Australian Association of Social Workers Third National Conference is held.	Included family casework, psychiatric social work, community organisation, group work.
1951–52	Sweden, US and UK	Ruth Hoban takes a sabbatical, on a Carnegie Corporation travelling fellowship.	Hoban was based at the LSE and Columbia University. Arthur Livingstone acted as director of social studies in her absence.
1951	Melbourne	*Forum* becomes national journal of the AASW.	The editorship remained in Melbourne. National communication had been achieved.
1951	Chicago	Norma Parker is granted a senior Fulbright award combined with a Smith-Mundt scholarship, to study social research methods at the University of Chicago.	This was the second year of the Fulbright program in Australia. Parker was one of two women out of thirty-three recipients, and the first Australian social worker to obtain a Fulbright award.
1952	Melbourne	Geoffrey Bryce Sharp is appointed to do a one-year study on children who have left institutions.	Sharp had previously been employed in the psychology department of the University of Melbourne.
1953	Melbourne	Alison Player of Victoria is elected second national president of AASW.	A local Victorian leader with almoner and general social work qualifications, and some American experience, Player was instrumental in integrating medical social work into the generic social work diploma in Melbourne.
1953	Sydney	Fourth Australian Conference of Social Work is held.	Emphasis was on the family: in Asian countries, basic wage determination, social service benefits, family doctor, 'unwed mothers'. There was still great stigma attached to being a single mother, or the child of a single mother.

Appendix 2: Milestones in Australian social work

Year	Location	Milestone	Comment
1955	Melbourne	Len Tierney is appointed as part-time lecturer in social work at the University of Melbourne.	Tierney held a Master of Science in Social Work from Columbia University.
1955	Melbourne	Master of Arts in Social Studies instituted.	First enrolment 1956. Higher education for social workers was a serious lack in Australia at the time.
1955	Sydney	Dr Morven Brown is appointed reader in social work course at University of Sydney.	Brown was not a social worker. Had been senior lecturer in education at University of Sydney since 1951.
1955	Sydney	Norma Parker is appointed assistant director of the University of Sydney's social work course – responsible for professional part of the course.	This formalised the role Norma Parker had played for years.
1955	Sydney	New postgraduate diploma commences at University of Sydney.	Unsuccessful: only seven enrolments in three years. Course discontinued in 1957.
1955 (Aug)	Melbourne	Fifth National Conference of the Australian Association of Social Workers is held.	Main topic: mental health.
1955	Australia	AASW is registered with Commonwealth Arbitration Court.	Acknowledgement of social work as a profession; assisted with improving remuneration of social workers in Commonwealth Public Service. Ceased 1974.
1950	Paris	Amy Wheaton leads Australian delegation to the Fifth International Conference of Social Work in Paris, and attends the meeting of the International Schools of Social Work that followed.	
1956	Brisbane	Social work course commences at University of Queensland: Diploma of Social Studies.	Hazel Smith was first lecturer in charge, appointed in 1955.
1956 (Sep)	Melbourne	Sir John Newman-Morris resigns from BSS.	Newman-Morris was a strong champion of social work for almost twenty years.

Appendices

Year	Location	Milestone	Comment
1957	Melbourne	First discussion in University of Melbourne BSS of degree to replace diploma.	This was finally implemented seventeen years later, in 1974.
1957	Melbourne	Ruth Hoban is promoted to associate professor at University of Melbourne.	Hoban became the first social worker at this level in an Australian university.
1957	South Africa	Jocelyn Hyslop enters community of Anglican nuns: the Community of the Resurrection of Our Lord, Grahamstown.	Hyslop had entirely lost contact with colleagues in Australia.
1957 (Aug)	Adelaide	Education for Social Work: The Sixth Biennial National Conference of the Australian Association of Social Workers.	Topics included integration of classroom and fieldwork; an American experience; assessing progress of students; establishing education for social work in communities lacking trained social workers; staff development.
1957		AASW adopts interim code of ethics.	
1957	Melbourne	Professor Max Crawford (history) resigns from chair of the BSS; Professor Richard Downing (economics) takes over the role.	
1957	Adelaide	Amy Wheaton compulsorily retires at age sixty.	Wheaton continued lecturing elsewhere in the university and overseas for another decade. With professorial status, she worked as an examiner of postgraduate students in the Punjab, West Pakistan, Dacca, and East Pakistan until 1962.
1958	Melbourne	Professor A. Boyce Gibson resigns from BSS.	Reason given: pressure of work.
1958	Sydney	New South Wales Institute of Hospital Almoners ceases almoner accreditation.	Medical social work is incorporated into general training at University of Sydney.
1958	Sydney	Morven Brown resigns and Tom Brennan is appointed head of social work at University of Sydney. Norma Parker serves as acting director until Brennan arrives in December.	Thomas Brennan (MA, Cambridge) was an urban sociologist. Once again, the course was not run by a social worker.

Appendix 2: Milestones in Australian social work

Year	Location	Milestone	Comment
1958 (Feb)	Melbourne	Ruth Hoban marries Professor Max Crawford, until 1957 chairman of BSS.	
1958–59	UK, US	Hoban takes sabbatical in UK and US with Crawford.	
1958–59	Melbourne	Geoff Sharp is acting director while Hoban is on leave.	Communication problems between staff and Hoban grew.
1959 (Jul)	Melbourne	University of Melbourne's department of social work moves off campus, to 75 Royal Parade, Parkville.	The department's former home, a professor's house on the main campus, was demolished for the construction of the North Building. Social work was one of the first departments to go off campus, with the staff's petitions to stay ignored.
1959 (Jul)	Melbourne	Greig Smith resigns from BSS.	Now of retirement age; two years previously had retired from CWS.
1959	Melbourne	*Forum* changes its name to *Australian Journal of Social Work*.	Quality improves to a printed format (rather than typed and reproduced cheaply on a Roneo machine).
1959	Australia	Biennial national conference not held. Seventh conference was held in 1961.	The social workers wanted to give maximum support to the first National Conference of Social Welfare, held in 1960.
1959	Melbourne/ Adelaide	Dr Raymond Brown resigns from the University of Melbourne to take up position as head of University of Adelaide social work course.	This left the small University of Melbourne course very short staffed, at a time when the head of department and another staff member were on extended leave.
1960	Melbourne	Len Tierney is appointed as supervisor of social work studies.	A difficult situation for the relatively young Tierney.
1960	Melbourne	Professor J. Benjamin Beyrer from University of Connecticut spends a six-month sabbatical here.	Beyrer was recommended by Professor Eveline Burns of Columbia University, whom Ruth Hoban admired.
1961	Melbourne	Associate Professor Hoban moves out of the social studies department and takes on a purely research role in a unit with Max Crawford, her husband.	This represented the end of Hoban's influence in the social studies department. She pursued her interests in social history.

Appendices

Year	Location	Milestone	Comment
1961	Sydney	Seventh National Conference of the Australian Association of Social Workers: The Association and Social Work.	Topics included the function of professional social work in Australian social administration; ethics; salaries, status and salary negotiation; roles of schools of social work and the association in the development of professional practice.
1963	Sydney	Norma Parker once again acting director of department of social work.	Covering director's study leave.
1965		AASW adopts code of ethics in full.	This was an important step in establishing the profession.
1965		Greig Smith is made an Honorary Life Member of the AASW.	Although holding no formal qualifications (as his involvement preceded the commencement of training in Australia), Smith had been a member of the AASW from the beginning. His contribution to the profession was recognised with this appointment.
1966	Sydney	Starts social work degree: Bachelor of Social Studies.	Despite spirited argument in favour of the American title 'Bachelor of Social Work', the English director preferred the English term 'social studies'.
1965	Sydney	Norma Parker becomes associate professor and head of department of social work in the school of sociology at the University of New South Wales.	Three-year appointment.
1968	Sydney	University of New South Wales department of social work becomes an independent school, with the first full chair of social work in Australia.	Achievement of full chair was due to Parker's leadership.
1969	Sydney	Norma Parker retires from University of New South Wales.	She continued part-time research. AASW honoured her by establishing the Norma Parker Lecture, to be given at each national AASW conference.

Appendix 2: Milestones in Australian social work

Year	Location	Milestone	Comment
1968–91	Sydney	Professor John (R.J.) Lawrence becomes the first Australian professor of social work at University of New South Wales.	In his long career Lawrence provided national and international social work leadership.
1973	Melbourne	Preston Institute of Technology starts a social work course.	Victoria's second school of social work: four-year course, with University of Melbourne graduate Frances Donovan as inaugural head. It was popular with local social workers, because of its strong emphasis on practice, its Australian flavour and its continuing professional education workshops.
1974	Melbourne	Monash University starts a school of social work.	Inaugural head is Peter Boss (from England).
1974	Melbourne	Bachelor of Social Work course commences at University of Melbourne.	A new model, with streams A and B. Not one integrated course.
1974	Melbourne	Professor Verl Lewis is appointed to University of Melbourne's first chair of social work.	Lewis had a distinguished career in the US; to an extent this was a retirement position for him. He died (1980) not long after his return to the US in 1977.
1975–76	Melbourne	La Trobe University starts a school of social work.	Inaugural head is the distinguished American Herbert Bisno.

Appendix 3:
The road to a unified profession in the US and the UK

Year	US	UK
1903		London COS establishes the first full-time social work course in England.
1904	COS establishes first full-time social work course, with its New York School of Philanthropy.	
1912	Mary Richmond successfully argues that social work cannot be taught by 'university men' but must be taught by practitioners.	LSE subsumes the COS's social work course, despite the COS's fears that the practical element will be lost (which happened).
1923–25	Milford Conference establishes an agreed definition of social casework.	Up to eight organisations evolve, representing various social work specialties and fields of practice. Continues until 1970.
1951	'Hollis-Taylor report' establishes principles for programs for social work education and prevents a split in the profession: Bachelor and Master of Social Work are qualifications established.	
1952	Council on Social Work Education is established.	
1954		'Carnegie Experiment': the first generic social work course in Britain, specialising in social casework, commences at the LSE.
1955	National Association of Social Workers is established.	
1959		'Younghusband report' proposes a teaching model to integrate theoretical and practical training.
1963		Standing Conference of Organisations of Social Work is established, bringing together eight social work professional associations.
1968		'Seebohm report': aimed at improving social work educational standards, but has the opposite effect.

Appendix 3: The road to a unified profession in the US and the UK

Year	US	UK
1970		British Association of Social Workers is established. (Probation officers choose not to join.)
1971		Central Council for Education and Training in Social Work is created by an Act of Parliament.
1972		Certificate of Qualification in Social Work is established, with a two-year minimum qualification.

Appendix 4:
Establishment of Australian social work education, 1929–1942

Year	New South Wales	Victoria	South Australia
1929	Board of Social Study and Training of New South Wales (BSST) is established – the first general social work training body in Australia.	Almoner Agnes Macintyre commences at Melbourne Hospital – the first qualified social worker employed in Australia.	
1929		Victorian Institute of Almoners is formed; starts training local students, with Macintyre as directress. From 1933 onwards it is known consistently as the Victorian Institute of Hospital Almoners.	
1931	Aileen Fitzpatrick is appointed director of training for BSST.		
1933		Board of Social Studies (BSS) is established, and starts training students, with Greig Smith and Dorothy Bethune (and later Helen Rees) as main teachers.	
1934		Jocelyn Hyslop arrives from England via the US to take up position of director of training, attending her first BSS meeting on 12 December.	
1936	Helen Rees opens almoner department at Sydney Hospital and becomes directress of training for the New South Wales Institute of Hospital Almoners.		Amy Wheaton is appointed director of the South Australian Board of Social Study and Training, and inaugurates the course.

Appendix 4: Establishment of Australian social work education

Year	New South Wales	Victoria	South Australia
1940	February: Senate of the University of Sydney agrees to establish a Board of Social Studies in the university. Fitzpatrick is not reappointed. Canadian tutor Elizabeth Govan becomes the university's first director of social studies.	December: social work education in Victoria is taken on by the University of Melbourne. The first meeting of BSS in the university is held. All BSS staff and students transfer to the University of Melbourne.	
1942			The University of Adelaide Board of Social Science is established, to supersede the South Australian Board of Social Study and Training. Amy Wheaton remains as director with a substantial pay increase. Social work achieves university status.

Appendix 5:
Georgina Sweet's letters regarding Town Hall meeting to establish general social work education, 25 April 1931

Letter 1 [copy][1]
National Young Women's Christian Association of Australia
6th Floor, T. & G. Building, 145 Collins St
Melbourne C1

Cliveden Mansions,
East Melbourne C2
25th April, 1931

Mrs. Norman Brookes,
President, Almoners' Institute,
Care the C.O.S.,
Exhibition Street, Melbourne C.1.

Dear Mrs. Brookes,

For some time past the Australian organisation of which I am President (viz. the National Y.W.C.A. of Australia) has been facing the great desirability of proper educational training for social workers, and some 3 years ago we were about to approach the University to this end, when we found that the Sydney University was about to institute such a course. On inquiry into the scope and mechanisms of that course we found considerable discrepancy as compared with our own ideas as to what such a course should be. We recognised, however, that that did not necessarily mean that we were right and they were wrong, and therefore decided to wait a little and watch the results of the arrangements made in Sydney. So far as we have been able to find out, they have not been as satisfactory as could be wished. We have, therefore, been contemplating making a move in that direction in Melbourne. Then we discovered that the Central Council of Benevolent Societies were proposing to approach the University to the same end, and on further inquiry that the Almoners' Institute (of which you are President) had approached the University, which has taken no steps though the matter is by no means finalised. Before, however, hearing of the latter fact, Mrs. G. G. Henderson (President of the Central Council of Benevolent Societies), Mr. Greig Smith (Secretary of the Charity Organisation Society and

Appendix 5: Georgina Sweet's letters regarding Town Hall meeting

acting-Secretary of the Almoners' Institute), Mr. M.P. Hansen (Director of Education) and I had agreed <u>in our personal capacities</u> to convene a meeting – over which we hope the Lord Mayor may preside, and that he may allow us the use of the reception room at the Town Hall for this purpose. At this meeting we hope we may be able to stimulate or increase the interest of members of the different branches of social work in the community, in which the trainees or diplomees of such a training in social work might find a vocation. We know quite well that only too often is a social worker appraised solely on kind-heartedness and some experience. The meeting, therefore, is intended to be of a general educational character – the date for which the Lord Mayor has asked is <u>Friday, June 5th at 3.30 p.m.</u>

I am writing to you now to ask whether you would be so good as to allow yourself to be one of the signatures to the letter convening such a meeting. I am enclosing herewith a copy of the draft which has been prepared, and which I am submitting to each of the other signatories by this same post, for their consideration, comment and approval. We shall all be so glad if you will give us your valuable co-operation in this matter. I am leaving for Adelaide and Perth on Monday next, though I will be returning within three weeks. I should be glad, however, if at as early a date as possible you will be good enough to send a reply to this letter, 145 Collins Street, C.1., enclosing your suggestions or otherwise approval of the enclosed draft letter. If there are any questions further that you would like to raise, I shall be glad if you will ring Miss Griffin (F.1228).

Yours very sincerely,

"GEORGINA SWEET" per (illegible signature)
NATIONAL PRESIDENT, Y.W.C.A. OF AUSTRALIA
(Dictated but not signed by Dr. Sweet)

Letter 2, undated (copy)

145 Collins St.
Melbourne C.1
(date)

Dear Sir or Madam,

The present crisis, increasing as it does the demands on the various Social agencies, both of a remedial and of a preventive nature in the city and Commonwealth, has brought once more into prominence a need felt by many societies – some of them for a great number of years – viz., the need for making available for those desiring to do Social Service, in all its branches, some effective training by means of University courses and for field work through some other accredited agencies.

Feeling this need acutely, the Council of Mental Hygiene and the Institute of Almoners have already approached the Melbourne University in this regard. It has been felt, however, that other organisations who are already conscious of this need, would appreciate coming together to discuss this matter, and to make joint representation to the University.

A meeting has therefore been called by the undersigned, as individuals, though with knowledge of their respective organisations, to be held (by the courtesy of the Lord Mayor) in the Town Hall reception room on Friday, June 5th at 3.30 p.m. It is hoped that the Lord Mayor himself will preside at this meeting.

We hope that you and your organisation also are interested in the matter and will send an accredited representative to this meeting. Will you also please invite anyone else interested who had not received an invitation to attend.

Most countries with similar problems to Australia – e.g., Canada, U.S.A., Great Britain – have already well-established courses of this nature in connection with Universities. The Sydney University has already made a start in Australia itself to put this important, and seemingly permanent, demand for Social Service in all its aspects into the hands of workers who will approach this difficult part of the world's work with the scientific attitude which is based on reliable knowledge gathered up out of the combined experience and experiments of social workers throughout the world.

Hoping for your presence at the meeting,

Signatories: Mrs. Norman Brookes, M.P. Hansen, Mrs. G.G. Henderson, S. Greig Smith, Sir Richard Stawell, Dr. Georgina Sweet

---

Mrs. Norman Brookes	is President of the Almoners' Institute
Mr. M.P. Hansen	is Director of Education
Mrs. G.G. Henderson	is President, Central Council of Benevolent Societies
Mr. Greig Smith	is Secretary of the Charity Organisation Society
Sir Richard Stawell	is President of the Council of Mental Hygiene
Dr. Georgina Sweet	is National President of the Y.W.C.A. of Australia

Appendix 6:
Guest list for official welcome to Jocelyn Hyslop, held at the Lyceum Club, Melbourne, 7 December 1934[2]

Members of the executive committee of the Victorian Council for Social Training

Dr John Newman-Morris and Mrs Eleanor Newman-Morris
Professor J.A. Gunn and Mrs Gunn
Mr S. Grey Smith
Sir Richard Stawell
Dr Guy Springthorpe
Dr R.S. Ellery
Dr John F. Williams
Dr K.S. Cunningham
Mrs G.G. Henderson
Mr Warren Kerr
Mr C. Fox
Miss N. Parker (Norma Parker, St Vincent's Hospital almoner)

Members of the Board of Social Studies

Associate Professor G.L. Wood
Professor G.W. Paton
Dr H.F. Maudsley
Dr Georgina Sweet
Miss M. Gutteridge
Mr G.W.W.B. Hughes
Miss L.M. Henderson (Lynette Henderson, almoner)

Substantial donors

Mr and Mrs Herbert Brookes
Mr G.R. Nicholas
Mr F. Laycock
Mr S. Ricketson

Others

Professor W. Osborne
Mr Mac-Mahon Ball
Mr H. Burton

Appendix 7:
Strengthening of Victoria's Board of Social Studies curriculum following commencement of Jocelyn Hyslop in 1934

	1933	1935
University Subjects	Economics part I, political philosophy, public administration, commercial and industrial organisation.	Economic history, organisation of education, economics part I, modern political institutions, educational seminar.
University Extension Subjects	N/A	Psychology of development, physiology, nutrition.
Lectures and Tutorials Provided by the Board of Social Studies	**Year One**: fifteen tutorials in the history of social work (Joan Brett and Greig Smith). **Year Two**: fifteen tutorials on social legislation and social services plus six additional tutorials provided by Constance Moffitt (child guidance clinic), Vera Scantlebury (maternal and child health) and Helen Rees (VIHA).	Introduction to the study of society (Jocelyn Hyslop and possibly Professor Henderson, member of the BSS), fieldwork discussion (Hyslop), casework (Greig Smith), social organisation (Henderson), mental hygiene (Maudsley and Williams), special institutions/advanced casework (Hyslop). An individual monthly tutorial provided for each student.
Practical Work/Fieldwork	**Year One**: two half-days per week in the COS during term, 300 hours full-time with the COS during long vacation. **Year Two**: two half-days per week, including directed visits to institutions (e.g. Sustenance Department, Children's Welfare Department, YWCA, kindergartens) depending on student's interest.	**Year One**: two full days weekly throughout the university term. First term: observation of constructive and preventive children's work, e.g. baby health centres, creches, day nurseries and state schools. Subsequently work done in the COS and other relief agencies. Four consecutive weeks after exams in November. **Year Two**: two full days weekly throughout the university term. Four consecutive weeks as a probationer in the field of the student's special interest after completing final exams. In the last two terms a student specialised in their special interest. Also visits of observation to public and private institutions such as homes and hospitals.

Appendix 7: Strengthening of Victoria's Board of Social Studies curriculum

This comparison illustrates how, following the commencement of Jocelyn Hyslop as director of Victoria's Board of Social Studies in December 1934, university teaching in Victoria was strengthened, casework introduced, and the amount of fieldwork (previously called practical work) increased.[3]

Appendix 8:
Snapshots of Victoria's Board of Social Studies over time, showing gradual change of composition

(Each member's occupation at the time of his or her appointment has been added where known.)

Membership of Victoria's first Board of Social Studies, 22 February 1933

The inaugural BSS[4] was chaired by Associate Professor G.L. (Gordon) Wood (economics) and comprised Professor John Alexander Gunn (adult education), Dr Georgina Sweet (retired zoologist, and philanthropist), Dr Henry Maudsley (psychiatrist), Miss Joan Brett (second director of training, Victorian Institute of Hospital Almoners), Miss Mary Gutteridge (former principal, Free Kindergarten Union and Kindergarten Training College, and pioneer of nursery schools),[5] Mr Stanley Greig Smith (secretary, COS), and Professor Leslie Wrigley (education – never actually attended a meeting, as he died in 1933).[6]

The BSS held its first meeting on 22 February 1933 at Morris House.[7] By July 1933 Dr John Newman-Morris (chief spokesman for the VIHA) was an ex-officio member.[8]

This small board met frequently and played an active role in day-to-day management of the course.

Membership of Victoria's last Board of Social Studies outside the University of Melbourne, 13 December 1940[9]

The final Board of Social Studies before joining the University of Melbourne was chaired by Professor Alexander (Sandy) Boyce Gibson and comprised Miss Dorothy Bethune (VIHA), Dr Georgina Sweet, Mr Colin Badger (director of the University Extension Board and involved with the Workers' Education Association),[10] Mr Menzies (identity unknown), Miss Kate Jacobs (social worker and tutor), Mr Greig Smith, Professor Max Crawford (history), Dr Vera Scantlebury Brown (director of the Maternal and Child Health Department; honorary lecturer), Mrs Eileen Edwards (psychologist, part-time lecturer at the Kindergarten Training College), Professor Peter MacCallum (pathology) and Miss Jocelyn Hyslop (director).

Those listed on the previous page were the ones present at the meeting. It was a slim and effective board, with most members directly concerned in teaching social work and in developing the profession.

Membership of Victoria's first Board of Social Studies inside the University of Melbourne, 19 December 1940[11]

Present: Miss Dorothy Bethune (social worker), Mr Greig Smith (COS), Miss Jocelyn Hyslop (director), Professor A. Boyce Gibson 'appointed Chair for the meeting', Mr James (identity unknown – possibly taught in the personnel course), Dr John Newman-Morris (president, VIHA), Associate Professor Gordon Wood.

Apologies: Mrs Eileen Kellaway (philanthropist and sister of Dr Vera Scantlebury Brown), Professor Roy Douglas ('Pansy') Wright (physiology).

At this meeting Professor George Paton (vice-chancellor) was elected chairman, on Gibson's motion.

At the next meeting, held on 20 February 1941, Paton was in the chair and in addition to those identified in the December meeting, Professor Peter MacCallum, Mrs Isabel Medley (wife of John Medley, registrar of the University of Melbourne), Mr Colin Badger, Mrs Norman Brookes (later Dame Mabel Brookes) and Dr Georgina Sweet are also listed as BSS members.[12]

Membership of Victoria's Board of Social Studies, May 1950[13]

Present: Professor Max Crawford (chair), Miss Ruth Hoban (director), Mrs Herbert (Ivy) Brookes (philanthropist), Dr Arthur Phillips (child psychiatrist and sessional lecturer), Miss Dorothy Bethune (medical social worker), Miss Audrey Rennison (lecturer in casework), Mr C.R. Thomas (lecturer in industrial welfare), Miss Alice Hyde (lecturer in group work), Professor Henderson, Professor Wilfred Prest (economics), Miss Marion Urquhart (social worker).

Apologies: Sir John Newman-Morris (VIHA), Dr Raynor C. Johnson (master of Queen's College, University of Melbourne), Reverend J.M. Murphy (rector of Newman College, University of Melbourne), Professor Ian Maxwell (English), Dr H.M.L. Murray (Commonwealth Department of Labour), Miss Lyra Taylor (Department of Social Services, social worker), Dr R. Kaye Scott (part-time lecturer in social studies and medical practitioner), Mr Greig Smith (secretary, COS), Professor Oscar A. Oeser (psychology), Professor Alexander (Sandy) Boyce Gibson (philosophy), Professor Gordon Wood (commerce), Mrs Laurie McBriar (Douglas/O'Brien) (lecturer in social history).

Most of those present taught in the course, either full-time or part-time. Many influential members absent from this particular meeting.

Membership of first meeting of Victoria's Board of Social Studies for the year 1960 (held in May)[14]

Present: Professor Charles Moorhouse (chairman, engineering), Associate Professor Ruth Hoban (director of social studies department), Professor Jackson (unidentified), Dr Elwyn A. Morey (psychology), Professor William Woodruff (commerce), Miss Marjorie Awburn (social worker, St Vincent's Hospital), Mrs Audrey Cahn (lecturer in dietetics, University of Melbourne), Miss Betty Dow (social worker, Royal Melbourne Hospital), Miss Lorna Hay (lecturer in psychiatric social work, social studies department), Miss Alice Hyde (lecturer in group work), Mrs Laurie O'Brien (lecturer in social history), Mr Geoffrey Sharp (lecturer in social organisation B – sociology), Mrs Beryl Thomas (social worker, Alfred Hospital), Mrs Cynthia Turner (née Green) (lecturer in social organisation B – sociology), Miss Teresa Wardell (social worker/field work), Mr Creighton Burns (lecturer, politics), Mrs Gwenneth M. Dow (lecturer, education), Mr Justice Barry* (judge, Supreme Court of Victoria), Mrs Herbert (Ivy) Brookes* (philanthropist), Miss Catherine Good* (social worker), Miss Nancy Hillas (social worker, Brotherhood of St Laurence), Father Eric Perkins* (social worker and Catholic priest), Miss Joyce Sambell* (social worker).

Apologies: Professor Eric Love (mathematician, dean of Faculty of Arts), Associate Professor Jean Polglaze (economics), Mr Stanley W. Johnston (lecturer, criminology), Dr Winston Rickards (child psychiatrist, part-time lecturer), Professor Maurice Ewing (surgery), Professor Wilfred Prest (commerce), Miss Dorothy Bethune* (social worker), Mr A.G. Cunningham* (unidentified), Dr Eric Cunningham Dax* (head of Victorian Mental Health Service), Dr Alec Whatmore* (head of Victoria's new Social Welfare Department).

In attendance: A.J. Glasson Williams (assistant registrar, University of Melbourne), and Mr H.G. Helms (unidentified).

Appendix 8: Snapshots of Victoria's Board of Social Studies over time

*Asterisk indicates that the person is one of ten 'additional members for 1960 following election'.[15]

With thirty-two members, the BSS had become unwieldy. Professor Moorhouse, a professor of engineering and not a trained social worker, represented the social work course at the university's professorial board. The large number of staff (which included many sessional teachers) meant that BSS meetings were becoming an occasion for staff to air their grievances. The BSS structure was by now clearly outdated.

Appendix 9:
Organisations represented on the Victorian Council for Social Training, 1937–1938[16]

Anzac House Children's Clinic
Association for Advancement of the Blind
Australian Council for Educational Research
Baptist Union of Victoria
British Medical Association
Catholic Social Service Bureau
Catholic Women's Social Guild
Central Council of Benevolent Societies
Charities Board
Charity Organisation Society
Children's Courts Office
Children's Welfare Association
Children's Welfare Department
Church of Christ
Church of England
Country Women's Association
Education Department
Emily McPherson College
Free Kindergarten Union of Victoria
Girls' Employment Movement
Headmasters' Association
Headmistresses' Association
Health Department
Hospitals in Melbourne: Alfred, Children's, Eye and Ear, Queen Victoria, Royal Melbourne, St Vincent's, Women's
Household Employment Committee
Janet Clarke Hall (a women's residential college at the University of Melbourne)
Melbourne City Mission
Mental Hygiene Department
Methodist Church Social Service Department
National Council of Women
Pensions Branch
Playgrounds Association of Victoria

Appendix 9: Organisations represented on the Victorian Council for Social Training

Presbyterian Church (Public Questions Committee)
Presbyterian Deaconesses' Training Institute
Probation Officers' Association
Salvation Army
Special Magistrates' Association
St Mary's Hall (a Catholic women's residential college at the University of Melbourne)
St Hilda's Church of England Training House
St Vincent de Paul Society
Toc H (part of an international welfare organisation established after World War I).
Travellers Aid Society
Victorian Association of Ladies' Benevolent Societies
Victorian Baby Health Centres' Association
Victorian Council for Mental Hygiene
Victorian Institute of Hospital Almoners
Victorian Society for Crippled Children
Victorian Vocational Guidance Centre
Victorian Women Citizens' Association
Victorian Women's Graduates' Association
YMCA Melbourne
YMCA National Organisation
YWCA Melbourne
YWCA National Organisation

Appendix 10:
Prospectus for the subject
'Modern political institutions',
University of Melbourne, c. 1938[17]

Second-year subject: Modern political institutions; university second-year subject

Two lectures weekly throughout the year.

The following is the full description of this subject contained in the above prospectus:

> A comparative study of the practice of modern government. A. The democracies. 1. A brief analysis of theory of modern democratic government. 2. A study of the working of govt in Britain France and the USA (a) the party system; (b) the electoral system; (c) the legislature; (d) the executive and civil service. B. Fascism in Italy. The theory and practice of the corporative state. C. National Socialism in Germany. The politics and government of Germany before 1918. The Weimar era, 1919–1933. The Third Reich. D. The soviet system in theory and practice. The constitution of the USSR. The organization and functions of the Communist party and the Third International. The technique of Soviet planning.

Comment: This subject caused the BSS considerable angst because of the high failure rate, yet its refusal to compromise is an example of its high standards. It was aware that students found this subject difficult, but considered it essential, given the state of the world in the late 1930s, and flatly refused to grant diplomas to students who could not pass it. An exception was Teresa Wardell, who managed to call the BSS's bluff. By 1934 she had completed all course requirements except this subject, but did not pass it. She was then employed by the Catholic Social Services Bureau in a social work role, where she was highly successful. In 1942, after MPI had been discontinued as a subject, the Victorian Council for Social Training agreed to allow Wardell to submit a 10,000-word thesis on child welfare and pay a fee of three guineas in order to qualify for the Diploma of Social Studies,[18] which was granted in 1944. Like many social work students, Wardell came from an influential Melbourne family, being the granddaughter of famous Melbourne architect William Wardell, who designed St Patrick's Cathedral, among numerous other landmarks.

Appendix 11:
Two-year Diploma of Social Studies, University of Melbourne, 1942[19]

First year	Second year
Economics part I	Political institutions A
Hygiene and nutrition	Hygiene and nutrition
Psychology	Mental hygiene
Social history	Social history
	Child study

Appendix 12:
Three-Year Diploma of Social Studies, University of Melbourne, 1947[20]

Specialty	First year	Second year	Third year
Medical social work	Social work Part I	Social work Part II	Social work Part III Medical problems
	Psychology Part I	Mental health	
	Economics Part I Social biology	Social organisation A Social history Political institutions A or Philosophy Part I	Social organisation B
Group work	Social work Part I	Social work Part II	Social work Part III Social psychology
	Psychology Part I Economics Part I or Political institutions A or Philosophy Part I	Child and adolescent psychology Social organisation A	Social organisation B
	Social biology	Social history Mental health	
Family casework	Social work Part I Social biology Psychology Part I Economics Part I	Social work Part II Social organisation A Mental health Social history	Social work Part III Child and adolescent psychology
Personnel practice	Social work Part I Psychology Part I Social biology Economic history Part I	Social work Part II Mental health Social organisation A (including industrial relations) Economics Part I Political institutions A or Philosophy Part I	Personnel practice Industrial psychology Social organisation B

Appendix 13:
Diploma of Social Studies Courses
A (Generic) and B (Personnel), 1960s

Course A: Generic

First year	Second year	Third year
Social work Part I	Social work Part II	Social work Part III
Psychology Part I	Psychology Part II A	Psychology III / Psychopathology
Social biology		Social organisation B or Australian history
Social organisation A	Social history	Social organisation B or Australian history

Course B: Personnel

Personnel course has diverged. Subjects could be taken in various year orders, and comprised Social psychology, Economics A, Economics B, Industrial administration, Industrial relations personnel practice, Psychology Part I, Social biology, Social work Part I, Social work Part II.

Appendix 14:
Ruth Hoban – Research, publications and sabbatical leave reports

The following is an overview of Ruth Hoban's contribution, not an exhaustive list.

Surveys[21]

Social Services Survey, Covering Social Services Available to Residents of the Municipality of South Melbourne, Victoria, Australia, 1943, Melbourne: City of South Melbourne, 1944.[22]
Report on Maternity and Pre School Services in the City of Prahran.[23]

Hoban was interested in social surveys; During her term as head of department the social studies department conducted a number of surveys, mainly on behalf of and funded by social agencies. A 1960 report gives a flavour of department research under Hoban's leadership: 'A survey of trainees undertaking selected voluntary youth leadership training courses conducted by the National Fitness Council in Victoria in 1956' (Alice Hyde); 'An investigation of the social organisation of the hospital in the Australian community and of professions related to large hospitals' (Geoffrey Sharp and Cynthia Turner); 'Conditions leading to family breakdown' (Kathleen E. Arthur); 'Effect of maternal employment on family life' (Geoffrey Sharp, Cynthia Turner, Margaret Kelso, Lois Hobson (later Bryson)); 'The financing of voluntary welfare activities' (Rosemary Otto); 'The history of voluntary social work in Victoria' (Laurie O'Brien), 'The medical and social consequences of accidents' (Ian McNicol Smith, Barbara Lethgren – Alfred Hospital).[24]

Writing

Article in the *Proceedings of the First Australian Conference of Social Work* (1947).
'A three-year training for social work', *Forum* (now *Australian Journal of Social Work*), vol. 4, no. 2, 1950, pp. 1–2.
'Assessing the progress of students', in *Proceedings of the Sixth Biennial National Conference of the Australian Association of Social Workers*, Adelaide, 1957, p. 66.[25]
The Future Development of Social Studies in the Australian Universities, University of Melbourne, 1963.[26]

University of Melbourne Department of Social Studies: Significant Changes in Social Economic and Political Life Which Have Had a Direct Bearing on Training for Social Work.[27]

Sabbatical leave 1951–52 (funded by the Carnegie Corporation)

Goal: 'To study developments in training for social work within universities'.

In North America

Most time spent at Columbia University in New York.

Also visited schools of social work in Pittsburgh, Cleveland, Chicago, Denver, Salt Lake City, San Francisco, Los Angeles, New Orleans, Philadelphia, Toronto, Ottawa and Montreal.

Visited Dr Helen Witmer at the Children's Bureau in Washington.

Conferences

Annual Conference of the American Association of Schools of Social Work, New York, 1952.

Bi-annual Conference of the International Committee of the Schools of Social Work, Stockholm, 1952.

In United Kingdom

Based at LSE department of social science and administration.

Visited Edinburgh, Liverpool, Manchester, Sheffield, Birmingham and Oxford.

In London visited the Family Welfare Association, Maudsley Hospital, Tavistock.

Sabbatical leave 1958–59

(Undertaken with her new husband, historian Professor Max Crawford, who had a Fulbright Scholarship)[28]

Purpose: 'To study developments in education for social work within universities and to learn of research in progress in the field of social welfare'.

In North America

Hoban spent five-and-a-half months in the US and Canada.

In the US she visited the School of Social Work, University of Wisconsin; School of Social Service and Administration, University of Chicago; School of

Social Work, University of North Carolina; and the New York School of Social Work, Columbia University. She visited Harvard to discuss with Professor David Owen his research into the history of philanthropy in nineteenth-century England.

She visited the US Federal Government Children's Bureau in Washington, again seeing Helen Witmer; University of Wisconsin's children's psychiatric clinic; Madison Diagnostic Center; Mendota State Mental Hospital; Madison General Hospital; and Wisconsin State Department for Children and Youth.

In Canada she visited the Toronto School of Social Work.

In Britain

She spent most of her five months at the LSE. She also visited the universities of Edinburgh, Oxford and Birmingham; the Institute of Almoners in London; and 'a number of social work agencies which had responsibility for supervising students' practical work'.[29]

Conferences

She attended the Annual Conference of the American Historical Association, in Washington, DC (December 1958), where she heard papers on the history of social welfare.

In Europe she attended the Regional Conference of the International Association of the Schools of Social Work, in Strasbourg (July 1959) and the preceding two-day meeting of the executive board of the International Association of the Schools of Social Work, as a newly appointed member.

She visited Greece and Italy

Later work

After stepping down from her position as head of social work, Hoban remained involved with the International Association of Schools of Social Work. In June 1964 Eileen Younghusband wrote her a friendly letter, regretting that Hoban would not be attending the international conference in Athens (1964).[30] Hoban was a member of the program committee for the thirteenth congress, held in Washington, DC, in 1966.[31] She commenced research into some historical aspects of social work. She was particularly interested in Selina Sutherland, a Presbyterian nurse and missionary known for her work with the children of the poor in the nineteenth century, to whom two archival boxes are dedicated.[32] Another box contains Hoban's research on the development of social conscience in Australia.[33]

Appendix 15:
Full-time staff of the social studies department, University of Melbourne, 1940–1960

Dates	Staff member	Qualifications
1934–45	Jocelyn Sophia Hyslop (Hyslop headed the original course outside the university from 1934, and shepherded it into the university in 1940.)	Cert Soc Science with Distinction Diploma of Sociology (LSE) BSc (Economics) 2nd Class Honours (LSE) Mental Health Certificate with Distinction (LSE)
1941 (8 months)	Kate Jacobs	VIHA Cert, Cert Social Science (Melbourne)
1941–63	Eileen Ruth Hoban (later Crawford)	BA (Melbourne) B Com (Melbourne) Dip Ed (Melbourne) Cert Soc Science and Admin (LSE).
1942–46	G. Vera Gaetjens	BA (Adelaide) Diploma in Industrial Psychology (University of London)
1944–52	Arthur Stanley Livingstone	BA (Hons) (Melbourne)
1946–64	Alice Hyde	Dip Soc Studs (Liverpool)
1947–89	Laurie Rose O'Brien	BA (Melb)
1947–60	(Grace) Audrey Rennison	MA (Cantab) Cert Soc Science and Admin (LSE)
1951–55	Alma Hartshorn	BA (Qld) Dip Soc Stud (Sydney)
1954–78	Geoffrey Bryce Sharp	MA (Melbourne)
1957–60	Raymond (Ray) George Brown	MSS (Bryn Mawr) BA, Dip Soc Stud (Melbourne) PhD (Birmingham)
1960–96	Leonard (Len) Tierney	BA, Dip Soc Stud (Melbourne) MSc (Columbia University, New York) PhD (Columbia University, New York)
1960–67	Lorna Hay (later Leckie)	BA Dip Soc Stud, Cert Mental Health (LSE)
1960–2007	Catherine James (née Brown, also Brockenshire and finally Bassett)	BA Dip Soc Stud (Melbourne) MSW Melbourne

Appendix 16:
American Fulbright social work scholars who visited Australia, 1953–1963[34]

Year	Scholar	From	Australian host
1953	Georgia Travis	Colorado University	University of Sydney
1953	Margaret Thornhill	Western Reserve University	University of Sydney
1956	Dorothy Brown	Beekman-Downtown Hospital, New York City	Commonwealth Social Services, Melbourne
1956	Esther Twente	University of Kansas	University of Sydney and University of Adelaide
1960	Alice Overton	St Paul, Minnesota: St Paul Project	University of Sydney
1960	Gayle B. Newcombe	Not known	University of Sydney
1961	Elizabeth Watson	Department of Child Welfare, California	University of Sydney
1961	Dorothy Gage	Oregon, delinquency control projects	University of Sydney
1963	Ella Dye	University of Connecticut	University of Melbourne

1953: Georgia Travis

Travis, the first American social work Fulbright scholar to visit Australia, is discussed fully in Chapter 8.

1953: Margaret Thornhill

A graduate of Western Reserve University, Thornhill came to the University of Sydney as a senior research scholar.[35] In addition to her teaching in Victoria and New South Wales, her report to Fulbright lists ten newspaper articles and four radio broadcasts, as well as two articles published in *Social Service*.[36]

1956: Dorothy Brown

Mrs Elton Brown (Dorothy Brown) was a medical social worker who was attached to the Commonwealth Department of Social Service while in Australia.[37] Brown was director of the social service department of Beekman-Downtown Hospital in New York City. She addressed the Fifth Biennial Conference of the AASW.

Appendix 16: American Fulbright social work scholars who visited Australia

1956: Esther Twente

Twente, from the University of Kansas, was attached to the universities of Sydney and Adelaide. She held a master's degree from the University of Chicago (1945) and founded the department of social work at the University of Kansas.[38]

1960: Alice Overton (MA)

Overton worked in St Paul, Minnesota, where she both led and had been responsible for the written material in the St Paul Project, which was designed for 'deprived and disadvantaged families whom local agencies had failed to reach and help'. Later, while teaching at the University of Southern California, she was a supporter of Martin Luther King; she and some of her students took part in the protest march from Selma to Washington, DC.[39] She was co-author with Katherine Tinker of *The Casework Notebook: Greater St Paul United Fund Councils, Family Centred Project*, which had been published in 1957 and reprinted in 1959. The *Australian Journal of Social Work* reported that Overton's experience had included 'periods as Director of an institution for delinquent girls, co-ordinator for a casework project (under the auspices of the New York City Youth Board and the Department of Welfare) for hard to reach families and project director of the Family Centered Project of St Paul'. Overton's obituary in *Australian Social Work* in 1988 emphasises lifelong friendships with Australian social workers, many of whom visited her in the US.[40]

1960: Gayle B. Newcombe (BA)

Newcombe was attached to the social work department at the University of Sydney at the same time as Overton. Her scholarship had been awarded 'for her interest in studying assimilation aspects of the Australian migration programme'. She planned to look at the Good Neighbour Council, and at both government and voluntary organisations.[41]

1961: Elizabeth Watson

Watson, from the Department of Child Welfare in California, gave a paper at the Seventh National Conference of the AASW, held in Sydney in 1961, in which she reported on research she had undertaken on government child welfare services during her stay in Sydney.[42]

1961: Dorothy Gage

Gage had worked in 'delinquency control programs' in Oregon.[43]

1963: Ella Dye (MSc, Columbia University)

Ella Dye was the first social work Fulbright scholar to be attached to the University of Melbourne's department of social studies. Her particular expertise was in fieldwork. She was one of many visitors from the University of Connecticut, a university with which the University of Melbourne social work academics still have a strong connection.

Appendix 17:
Australians holding the Mental Health Certificate from the London School of Economics and Political Science

Year	Name	Place
1933	Mary Noall	Melbourne
1935	Madeline Williams	England, but spent the second half of her life in Australia
1940	Una Riall	Melbourne
1945	Helen Clarke (later Eggleston)	Melbourne
1945	Margaret Grutzner	Melbourne and Sydney
1945	Mernie Yeomans (later Foley)	Melbourne
1947	Margaret Whale	Sydney
1948	Millie Mills	Sydney
1951	Patricia Holmes (later Duxbury)	Melbourne
1952	Joyce Grant	Melbourne
1955	Lorna Hay (later Leckie)	Melbourne
1955	Joan Robertson	Melbourne

Appendix 18:
George Paton, vice-chancellor of the University of Melbourne, memorandum to staff regarding Communist allegations, 1 May 1962[44]

THE UNIVERSITY OF MELBOURNE

I wish to say a few words about the position in Social Studies because some publicity has recently been given to allegations that were made last year by a weekly journal. It was alleged that there was, within the Department, a Communist conspiracy aimed at taking control of it – there was incidentally a long string of accusations of various types of misconduct by certain members of staff.

The University Council set up an advisory committee under the chairmanship of Mr. Justice Adam. This committee after an exhaustive enquiry lasting several months, reported to Council last year and a summary of that report was issued as a press release. The committee decided that there was no evidence of a 'Communist plot,' and no evidence of anything which could be described as 'misconduct' on the part of any member of staff. It is only fair to the members of staff concerned to emphasise that these findings were accepted by the Council of the University.

There are occasionally issues in any University which arouse controversy not only within the institution but outside. A University does not exist to stifle freedom of expression. But the University must feel concern at the repetition of unfounded allegations against members of its staff: the Council has dealt with these issues by a proper machinery, and the verdict of the umpire should be respected.

G.W. Paton
Vice-Chancellor   1st May 1962

Appendix 19:
Three influential British social workers

Edith Eckhard, Helen Rees and Jean Robertson formed the core of a British social work network that did a great deal to assist the early development of social work education in Melbourne (and Australia). Each had an international outlook and a commitment to generic social work education.

Edith Verena Eckhard (1885–1952)

Edith Eckhard worked at the LSE from 1919 to 1952, the year of her death. In his history of the LSE, Ralf Dahrendorf describes her as 'the heart and soul of the social science department and for many years its defacto head'.[45] She had been educated at St Leonards School in Scotland, and at Newnham College (Cambridge), where she studied economics.[46] Before joining the LSE staff she had been honorary secretary of the Manchester School for Mothers (1912–15), honorary secretary of the Manchester Babies Hospital (1914–16), secretary of the National Association of Infant Welfare and Maternity Centres (1916–17) and secretary of the Leeds Baby Welcome Association (1917–18). Her book *The Mother and The Infant* was published in 1921 as part of the Social Service Library, edited by Clement Attlee. She introduced psychiatric social work to the LSE, having been awarded a Commonwealth Fellowship,[47] and toured the US between January and April 1928,[48] visiting schools of social work, juvenile courts, COSs and family welfare societies, hospitals, Settlement houses, probation associations, psychiatric associations, and child guidance bureaux, in New York, Baltimore, Boston, Chicago, Washington and Philadelphia.

Helen Rees (1903–1989)

Helen Rees was the third British almoner to head the VIHA (Melbourne), arriving in Australia in 1933. She also taught in Victoria's general social work course before Jocelyn Hyslop's arrival. Grace Dedman wrote: 'Miss Helen Rees, Director of Training at the Institute of Almoners (UK) was one of those who worked tirelessly for the establishment of generic social work courses in universities.'[49] Rees had read English at Newnham College (Cambridge) and in 1928 undertook almoner training, following which she worked for five years at the Sheffield City Hospital. She returned to England from Melbourne in late 1935, but within a few months had come back to Australia to establish the Sydney

Hospital Almoner Department, becoming the inaugural training director of the New South Wales Institute of Hospital Almoners. In 1941 she returned to England 'to make a study of medical social work under wartime conditions and its role in post-war reconstruction',[50] later moving to the Radcliffe Infirmary, Oxford. She worked as director of studies at the Institute of Almoners in London until 1958. She then worked as a Colombo Plan adviser on establishing training for welfare staff in Malaya. Her last position was as the first county welfare officer in West Suffolk, where she managed health and welfare.[51]

In 1989, when she died aged eighty-six, *Australian Social Work* carried an obituary referring to her close friendships with Amy Wheaton, Jocelyn Hyslop, Norma Parker and Kate Ogilvie, all women who made 'an enormous contribution to social work development and education in Australia'.[52]

Jean Robertson, CBE (1908–1974)

Jean McDonald Robertson (MA, Dip Soc Sci, Glasgow) was the second staff member to be employed by Victoria's Board of Social Studies. Professor Boyce Gibson described her as 'intellectually brilliant'. Though she stayed in her position with the BSS for only fifteen months, she made an important contribution to social work in Australia during World War II through her role in developing industrial welfare work in the munitions factories for the Commonwealth Department of Labour.

On return to England Robertson became secretary to the British *Report on the Neglected Child and His Family* (1948).[53] She left Britain in 1949 for New Zealand, where she taught in its first social work course (at Victoria University, Wellington); by 1952 she was in Singapore, becoming the founding head of the University of Malaya's new social work course.[54] In 1950 Robertson visited Australia and spoke to the AASW Victorian Branch on 'Developing social work in a new community'.[55] In 1960 she accepted an appointment as assistant director of social studies at the University of Melbourne, but later withdrew her acceptance. In 1967 she left Singapore after fifteen years to take up the first chair of social work at Hong Kong University. She returned to Britain in 1972, dying two years later in a car accident in France.[56]

Appendix 20:
Founding executive of the
Australian Association of Social Workers

President: Norma Parker CBE

Norma Parker (1906–2004), Honorary Life Member of the AASW. See pp. 166–169.

Vice-president: Lyra Taylor OBE

Lyra Taylor (1894–1979), Honorary Life Member of the AASW. See pp. 169-172.

Vice-president: Katharine (Kate) Ogilvie MBE

Kate Ogilvie (1902–1983), a New South Wales social work pioneer, held a BA (Hons) in history from the University of Sydney (1924). In 1926 she was appointed secretary (equivalent of today's CEO) of the Rachel Forster Hospital for Women and Children. When she was selected for the Australian women's hockey team's overseas tour in 1930,[57] the Rachel Forster Hospital gave her a year's leave to study hospital administration in Britain and the US. The hospital sent her back to gain a certificate at the Institute of Almoners in London.[58] On returning to Sydney she founded the Rachel Forster Hospital's almoner department, going on to work as an almoner in several hospitals and becoming director of training of the New South Wales Institute of Hospital Almoners. In 1954 she was appointed as a lecturer in social work at the University of Sydney.

Among Ogilvie's many contributions, during World War II she was honorary director of the forerunner of Sydney's Family Welfare Bureau, which she established. The Rachel Forster Hospital named the Katharine Ogilvie Social Work Department in her honour, and in 1988 the University of Sydney established the Katharine Ogilvie Memorial Award for social workers undertaking postgraduate research.[59] John Lawrence describes her as a forceful woman who was a 'formidable champion of the many causes she espoused', while also being patient, perceptive and caring with clients. He adds: 'She made lasting friendships and her many serious endeavours were leavened by a great sense of humour.'[60]

Vice-president: Dorothy Sumner

Dorothy Sumner was an American colleague and friend of Norma Parker, who joined the staff of the University of Sydney in 1945 on Parker's return from her second period of study in the US. Originally graduating from the University of Syracuse, Sumner then qualified as a social worker at the New York School of Social Work (Columbia University). She had been a supervisor in the family casework division of the United Charities of Chicago and had worked at the School of Social Services Administration of Chicago University, where Parker had studied in 1944. At that time, developing expertise in social casework was a high priority for Australian social workers, making Sumner a very valuable addition to the field. While in Australia she also travelled interstate to teach social casework, and she presented a paper on social work in the voluntary agency at the first Australian conference on social work in 1947.[61]

Vice-president: Amy Wheaton MBE

Honorary Life Member of AASW.
Amy Wheaton (née Priest, 1898–1988), founder of the first social work course in South Australia, was highly regarded for her intellect, and much loved by the local social work profession. She gained her MA from the University of Adelaide in 1923 and BSc (Economics) from the LSE in 1931. In 1936, on invitation from the University of Adelaide, she returned from England to take on the role of (honorary) director of the South Australian Board of Social Study and Training, the first social work educational body in South Australia. She had a long and active professional career, which is discussed in Elaine Martin's PhD thesis.[62] Among her achievements, she was the only woman invited to the World Congress of Sociology in Zurich – the first congress of the newly formed International Sociological Association. She was involved in a wide range of organisations, local and international, including working for the welfare secretariat of the United Nations between 1948 and 1962. Nancy Bates concludes: 'She had a quirky sense of humour and delighted in debate and exchange of ideas, while the ash from her cigarette fell unheeded.'[63]

Honorary secretary: Margaret Grutzner

Honorary Life Member of AASW and ASWU.
Margaret Grutzner (1917–82) was the youngest of the founding AASW executive members. She grew up in Shepparton, Victoria, where her father was a doctor.

She held a BA and Diploma of Social Studies from the University of Melbourne and a Certificate (then taken as a third year after the Diploma of Social Studies) from the Victorian Institute of Hospital Almoners. She was one of the four young Australian social workers selected by the Australian Red Cross Society in 1944 to undertake the Mental Health Certificate at the LSE, thus becoming one of Australia's first specialist psychiatric social workers.

Grutzner's career spanned working for the Kindergarten Union in Victoria, the Australian Red Cross Society, and the Repatriation Department. In 1960 she was appointed to a lectureship at the University of Sydney, in a position jointly administered by the Faculty of Medicine's department of psychiatry and the social work department. Her obituary notes her 'flair for friendship which kept her in touch throughout her life with school and university contemporaries'.[64]

Assistance secretary: Viva Murphy

Viva Murphy (1904–97) graduated from the University of Melbourne with a BA in 1928; after a decade of school teaching she enrolled in the Victorian Institute of Hospital Almoners course. She worked in the Catholic Social Service Bureau in Melbourne, in St Vincent's Hospital Sydney, and in senior roles for the Australian Red Cross Society in Sydney and Brisbane. She was active in starting the Queensland Branch of the AASW, of which she was the first president. Among other posts she had several stints as an educator at the University of Sydney. Following a period of study in the US she was appointed to the Australian Legation in New York, eventually rising to the position of vice-consul of the Australian Consulate General in New York in the 1950s. Her activism continued in later years when she became a founding member of the Paddington Society, Australia's first resident activist organisation, which worked to preserve the historic inner-Sydney suburb of Paddington.[65]

Second national president: Alison Player

Alison Player (later Mathew) (1906–2005) grew up in Melbourne, matriculated at the age of fourteen, and after twelve years helping to care for her sick father (who was a local GP) at the age of twenty-six enrolled in the Melbourne Diploma of Social Studies followed by the Almoner course. After working at the Geelong and Alfred hospitals she became convinced that she would only grasp the key concepts of social work by studying in America, and spent several months in Boston in 1940 in a series of observational visits in hospitals, and then as a student at the Israel Hospital under Ethel Cohen. She said that here she learnt not only about casework but also administration and education for social work.[66]

Player's diverse career included being chief almoner at the Royal Melbourne Hospital and the last director of the Victorian Institute of Hospital Almoners.[67] She was responsible for overseeing the merging of Victoria's almoner training with the University of Melbourne's social work course, where she subsequently lectured on health social work. She was a Victorian pioneer whose career spanned almoner and general social work. In the 1950s she transferred her interests to family social work, after having been appointed to the position of deputy director of Turana Reception Centre (a state government children's institution), a post from which, because of the bar on married women being public servants, she had to resign when she married fellow social worker Hamish Mathew. She also made significant contributions while working at the Citizens Welfare Service and at Kildonnan Children's Home.

Player was president of the Australian Association of Almoners (1950–52) and took over from Norma Parker as national president of the AASW (1953–59).[68] She helped establish the social work profession, and grew with it. She was a life member of the Australian Association of Social Workers and of the Victorian Council of Social Service. As she said in 1979: 'Reflecting back I see clearly the progression from each phase to the next, related to personal as well as professional development. I could not imagine any profession which could be as rewarding.'[69]

Appendix 21:
Name changes of women mentioned

Unmarried name	Married name
Barbara Beatty	Barbara Spalding
Jessie Brookes	Jessie Clarke
Catherine Brown	Catherine Brockenshire, James, Bassett
Ivy Deakin	Mrs Herbert Brookes
Laurie Douglas	Laurie McBriar, O'Brien
Helen Eggleston	Helen Clarke
Barbara Gordon	Barbara Sturmfels
Cynthia Green	Cynthia Turner
Tania Harris	Tania Coppel
Lorna Hay	Lorna Leckie
Patricia Haynes	Patricia Goding
Eileen Ruth Hoban	Ruth Crawford
Lois Hobson	Lois Bryson
Patricia Holmes	Patricia Duxbury
Jean McGregor	Jean Norman, Downing
Alison Player	Alison Mathew
Vera Scantlebury	Vera Scantlebury Brown
Rosemary Scoullar	Rosemary Nairn
Edna Smale	Edna Mendelsohn
Elaine Wilson	Elaine Martin
Mernie Yeomans	Mernie Foley

Acknowledgements

When I retired after a career of fifty years in social work, I became interested in knowing more about Australian social work history. I was persuaded that if I were to be anything but a dilettante I should pursue this interest through the discipline of a doctorate. This book has been developed from that doctorate, which I undertook in the schools of social work and historical and philosophical studies at the University of Melbourne, and completed in 2015. I owe a debt of gratitude to my supervisors, Professor Marie Connolly and Professor Kate Darian-Smith, for the support and guidance that helped to shape a doctorate that spanned the two disciplines. A Melbourne Abroad Travelling Scholarship from the university assisted with my travel to the US and Britain in 2013. I owe particular thanks to several people who provided detailed advice during the writing of the thesis: John Lawrence, who invited me to stay with him and his wife, Trish, in Sydney and shared his personal archive with me; Bruce Lagay and Renate Howe, who gave wise counsel over many cups of coffee; and David Nichols, who has encouraged me over the years. Thanks also to Haydie Gooder, who was a patient and meticulous editor of the final document.

This book was a separate project. I feel honoured to be joining Monash University Publishing's list of scholarly publications and thank Julia Carlomagno and Kate Morgan for their wise and friendly editorial guidance. I am indebted to the Department of Social Work and the

Social Work Alumni Association of the University of Melbourne for their generous financial support which has made publication possible. Detailed comments on the manuscript were made by Rosemary Sheehan, who as one of the examiners of the thesis had encouraged me to seek a wider audience; Dorothy Scott, who reminded me to include examples of what these early social workers actually did in their daily work in order to make the text relevant for a present-day audience; while Michael Nichols identified areas that needed clarifying for a twenty-first century, non–social work audience. The present head of social work at the University of Melbourne, Louise Harms, both encouraged me and reminded me of the sensibilities of the current generation of social workers. Belinda Nemec, who edited my original manuscript, gave her usual excellent advice, helping me to transform what had been academic research into a book for the general public, hunting down clichés and generally bringing order to the manuscript.

Many other people shared their recollections. Barbara Sturmfels reflected on her adventurous early career, but unfortunately this book comes too late for three other people with whom I had long discussions – Geoff Sharp, Lydia Eady and Joan Robertson – to see it in its final form. Thea Mendelsohn and Bronwyn Daddo gave me papers that had belonged to their courageous mothers (Edna Smale and Lynette Henderson). Alice Garner generously shared her unpublished research on the Fulbright program. Peter Hollingworth used his international Anglican connections to link me to Sister Carol of the Community of the Resurrection of Our Lord in South Africa, who had vivid memories of Jocelyn Hyslop and provided copies of documents relating to Hyslop's life in that Anglican religious order. David Green shared memories of his own social work experience in the US in the 1960s.

Acknowledgements

I owe thanks to the British Social Work History Network, which invited me to attend one of its meetings in 2013, and also to Jane Lewis and Sonia Exley from the London School of Economics and Political Science. I acknowledge a particular debt of gratitude to Ann Oakley from the University of London, who gave me a generous amount of time discussing the research she was then undertaking for her book *Women, Peace and Welfare: A Suppressed History of Social Reform, 1880–1920* (Policy Press, 2019).

Because very little has been written about the history of Australian social work, I relied on archives in telling this story. The scaffolding of this book is derived from Archives and Special Collections at the University of Melbourne, where I owe Katie Wood particular thanks. Jane Beattie, Chen Chen, Sophie Garrett and Georgina Ward also gave invaluable assistance. The Baillieu and Brownless libraries at the university were also excellent resources. In addition, I drew heavily on the extensive Australian Red Cross Archives (then held by Red Cross in North Melbourne and since transferred to University of Melbourne Archives), where I was guided by Moira Drew, and lastly the archives of the Victorian Branch of the Australian Association of Social Workers: my thanks to Kerry Kustra. In addition, Cindy Smith, chief executive officer of the Australian Association of Social Workers, provided statistics on Aboriginal membership of the association and explained some of the barriers that prevented Aboriginal and Torres Strait Islander social workers from joining. John Lawrence's private records, now in University of New South Wales Archives, were invaluable. Vivian Papaleo from the Brotherhood of St Laurence was particularly helpful in providing photographs of social workers in the workplace. Both St Leonards School and Glenalmond College in Scotland kindly mailed me material relating to Jocelyn Hyslop and her father. In the

Acknowledgements

US thanks are due to Bethany Antos at the Rockefeller Archive Center for facilitating access to the Commonwealth Fund Archives, and at Columbia University to Jane Gorjevsky with the Carnegie Collection and the Rare Book and Manuscript Library, Butler Library. In the UK the archivists of the London School of Economics and Political Science mailed material to Melbourne and later gave me access to files on my visit there.

Many people have helped by discussion, including Mary Nash (New Zealand), Irwin Epstein (US), Karen Healy (Queensland) and in Melbourne Maggie Pinkney, Nicole Tokatlian, Yvonne Adami, Alice Barrese, Tamsin Nichols, Wendy Bunston, Liz Orr, Jenny Conrick, Kathy Sanders, Denise Brown, Janet Launder, Bill O'Reilly and John Langmore. I am grateful to all those who took time to share their opinions and experiences, and who encouraged me in this endeavour, not all of whom I have named here. The book has benefited from the advice of many people, but I am ultimately responsible for its contents.

Image Credits

1. Porter Raymond Lee papers, Rare Book & Manuscript Library, Columbia University, New York.
2. Author's collection.
3. Porter Raymond Lee papers, Rare Book & Manuscript Library, Columbia University, New York.
4. 'Merchants of Misfortune', *The Herald* (Melbourne), 15 October 1938, p. 33.
5. *The Other Half*, December, vol. 2, no. 2, 1929. Courtesy State Library of Victoria.
6. Handbill, Citizens Welfare Service, 1980.0087, unit 2, University of Melbourne Archives.
7. Wikimedia Commons.
8. Author's collection.
9. 'Opinions After 10 Years of Social Service', *The Argus* (Melbourne), 24 October 1944, p. 8.
10. Gift to the Nicholson Museum of Pottery Vase from the Island of Cyprus, 3 October 1952. Courtesy University of Sydney Archives.
11. Courtesy University of Sydney Archives, ref 0045850.
12. Photograph by Ken Bell. Courtesy University of Toronto Archives.
13. Women's Supplement, *The Sydney Morning Herald* (Sydney), 28 January 1941, p. 8.
14. Courtesy University of Tasmania Archives.
15. *The West Australian* (Perth), 1 July 1931, p. 16.
16. Marie Mansfield, Portrait of Norma Parker, Oil on linen, 46 x 36cm, 2023. Courtesy St Vincent's Hospital, Sydney.
17. Author's collection.
18. 'Let's Talk of Interesting People', *The Australian Women's Weekly* (Sydney), 30 January 1937, p. 1.
19. Author's collection.
20. Author's collection.
21. Author's collection.
22. Courtesy of University of Adelaide Library Special Collections.
23. Courtesy of the University of Queensland Archives, UQA S909 p. 916.
24. Author's collection.
25. 'A Woman's Letter', *The Bulletin* (Sydney), 3 April 1940, p. 32.
26. 'Visiting Delegates', *The Adelaide Advertiser*, 24 November 1945, p. 7.
27. Author's collection.
28. Author's collection.
29. Author's collection.
30. Author's collection.

Image Credits

31 National War Memorial, accession number 017486, 23 August 1944.
32 'Should Welcome D.P.s Here U.N.R.R.A. Worker Says', *The Sun* (Melbourne), 7 August 1947, p. 18.
33 'Returns from Overseas', *The Argus* (Melbourne), 23 July 1945.
34 'U.S. Think We're Truly Rural', *Launceston Examiner* (Tasmania), 17 December 1953, p. 110.
35 'Social Workers Urged to Study the Individual', *The Argus* (Melbourne), 29 August 1949, p. 6.
36 Courtesy of the National Archives of Australia, NAA: A1501, A647/5.
37 Author's collection.

Notes

Introduction: Social Work – A New Concept in 1929 Australia

1. Verl Lewis, 'Historical studies and social policy analysis', *Contemporary Social Work Education*, vol. 1, no. 2, 1977, p. 38. An American social worker and historian, Lewis was the first professor of social work at the University of Melbourne.
2. R.J. (John) Lawrence, *Professional Social Work in Australia*, Canberra: Australian National University Press, 1965.
3. Lawrence later published a book chapter ('Introduction: Australian social work in historical, international and social welfare context', in Phillip Boas and Jim Crawley (eds), *Social Work in Australia: Responses to a Changing Context*, Melbourne: Australian International Press in association with the Australian Association of Social Workers, 1976, pp. 1–27); and an autobiography (*Seeking Social Good: A Life Worth Living; An Autobiography in Six Volumes*, Sydney: R.J. (John) Lawrence, 2017); these works have added to this story.
4. Katherine Kendall, *Social Work Education: Its Origins in Europe*, Alexandria, Virginia: Council on Social Work Education, 2000, pp. 75–92.
5. The precursor to the University of Sydney course commenced in 1929; the Melbourne almoner course, later part of the university course, commenced in 1929 and the precursor to the university course in 1933. A smaller course commenced in Adelaide in 1936.
6. The population of Melbourne was 5,078,193 as at 30 June 2019 (Australian Bureau of Statistics, 'Regional population' (2018–19 financial year), published 25 March 2020, https://www.abs.gov.au/statistics/people/population/regional-population/2018-19).
7. Australian Broadcasting Corporation, 'Melbourne named world's most liveable city for the fourth year running, beating Adelaide, Sydney and Perth', *ABC News*, 19 August 2014, https://www.abc.net.au/news/2014-08-19/melbourne-worlds-most-liveable-city-for-the-fourth-year-running/5681014.
8. 'Alison Mathew (née Player) interviewed by Marjorie Glasson in the Australian Association of Social Workers Oral History Project [sound recording]', October 1972, p. 4, https://nla.gov.au/nla.obj-193570456/listen.
9. BSS minutes, October 1938, p. 152, University of Melbourne Archives (hereafter UMA).
10. Elizabeth Danto, *Historical Research*, New York: Oxford University Press, 2008, pp. 38–40.

11 Robert Fisher, 'Speaking for the contribution of history: Context and the origins of the social welfare history group', *Social Services Review*, vol. 73, no 2, 1999, p. 191.
12 Shurlee Swain, 'Writing social work history', *Australian Social Work*, vol. 61, no. 3, 2008, p. 193.
13 Swain, 'Writing social work history', p. 195.
14 Lawrence, *Professional Social Work in Australia*, pp. x, xi, 172; Paul Anderson, *The Greig Smith Social Work History Collection: A Bibliography and Guide*, Melbourne: The Citizens Welfare Service of Victoria, 1987, pp. 64, 68, 69.
15 Damian Gleeson, 'The professionalisation of Australian Catholic social welfare, 1920–1985', PhD thesis, Sydney: University of New South Wales, 2006.
16 Laurie O'Brien and Cynthia Turner, *Establishing Medical Social Work in Victoria: Discussion and Documents*, University of Melbourne, Department of Social Studies, 1979; Jean Snelling, 'Medical social work', in Cherry Morris (ed.), *Social Casework in Great Britain*, London: Faber & Faber, 1954, p. 86; Phyllis Willmott, '1895–1945: The first 50 years', in Joan Baraclough et al. (eds), *100 Years of Health-Related Social Work 1895–1995; Then–Now–Onwards*, Birmingham, UK: British Association of Social Workers Trading, 1996, p. 8.
17 Elspeth Browne, *Tradition and Change: Hospital Social Work in New South Wales*, Sydney: Australian Association of Social Workers, New South Wales Branch, 1996, p. 1; Michael Horsburgh, *Doing Good Well: Seventy Years of Social Work Education at the University of Sydney 1940–2010*, University of Sydney, Faculty of Education and Social Work, 2010, p. 12; Elaine Martin, 'Gender, demand and domain: The social work profession in South Australia 1935–1980', PhD thesis, University of Melbourne, 1990; Elaine Martin, 'The importance of the trained approach: Social work education in South Australia, 1935–1946', *Australian Social Work*, vol. 36, no. 1, 1983, pp. 11–22; Elaine Martin, 'Themes in the history of the social work profession', *International Social Work*, vol. 35, 1992, pp. 327–45; Marcia Foley, 'From social policy to social work: The antecedents and origins of mental health social work in Western Australia', PhD thesis, University of Western Australia, 2010; Frances Crawford and Sabina Leitman, 'The shaping of West Australian Social Work 1920–1970', *Australian Social Work*, vol. 54, no. 3, 2001, pp. 31–54; Helen Pavlin, *Social Work in the University of Queensland: The First Twenty-Five Years*, Brisbane: University of Queensland, Department of Social Work, 1981.
18 Richard Kennedy, 'Some origins of social casework in nineteenth-century Melbourne', *Australian Social Work*, vol. 26, no. 2, 1973, p. 5; Richard Kennedy, *Charity Warfare: The Charity Organisation Society in Colonial Melbourne*, Melbourne: Hyland House, 1985; Mark Peel, *Miss Cutler and the Case of the Resurrected Horse: Social Work and the Story of Poverty in America, Australia and Britain*, University of Chicago Press, 2012; Stephen Garton, *Out of Luck: Poor Australians and Social Welfare 1788–1988*, Sydney: Allen & Unwin, 1990.
19 Katie Wright, '"Help for wayward children": Child guidance in 1930s Australia', *History of Education Review*, vol. 41, no. 1, 2012, pp. 4–19; Allyson P. Holbrook, 'Models for vocational guidance in Australia 1920s–1930s: American

influence in conflict with British tradition', *The Vocational Aspect of Education*, vol. 41, no. 109, 1989, p. 44.

20   Anne Heywood, 'Clarke, Jessie Deakin (1914–2014)', in *The Australian Women's Register*, 2003, modified 2020, https://www.womenaustralia.info/biogs/AWE0623b.htm.

21   'Alison Mathew interviewed by Marjorie Glasson in the Australian Association of Social Workers Oral History Project [sound recording]', October 1972, p. 13, National Library of Australia, https://nla.gov.au/nla.obj-193570456/listen.

22   Katherine Kendall, *Social Work Education: Its Origins in Europe*, Alexandria, Virginia: Council on Social Work Education, 2000, pp. 75–92.

23   By then Sydney had a Canadian head of school, and from the early 1940s the American-trained Norma Parker taught in the school.

24   Jane Miller, 'Building a professional discipline', in Dorothy Scott and Jane Miller (eds), *A Love of Truth and a Love of Service: The Social Work Legacy of Leonard Tierney*, Faculty of Medicine, Dentistry and Health Sciences, University of Melbourne, 2019, pp. 31–59.

25   The New York School of Social Work became the Columbia University School of Social Work in 1962.

26   Ann Oakley, *Father and Daughter: Patriarchy, Gender and Social Science*, Bristol, UK: Policy Press, 2014, p. 239.

27   Margaret Macmillan, *The Uses and Abuses of History*, London: Profile Books, 2010, p. 37.

Chapter 1 – The Emergence of Social Work in Britain and the US

1   Anna Dawes, quoted in Leslie Leighninger, *Creating a New Profession: The Beginnings of Social Work Education in the United States*, Alexandria, Virginia: Council on Social Work Education, 2000, p. 1.

2   Helen Bosanquet, quoted in Mike Burt, 'Social work occupations in England, 1900–39: Changing the focus', *International Social Work*, vol. 51, no. 6, 2008, p. 752.

3   Kendall, *Social Work Education*, pp. 75–90.

4   Kendall, *Social Work Education*, pp. 75–90.

5   John Pierson, *Understanding Social Work: History and Context*, Glasgow: Open University Press, 2011.

6   Burt, 'Social work occupations in England', p. 760; David Burnham, 'Selective memory: A note on social work historiography', *British Journal of Social Work*, vol. 41, 2011, p. 11.

7   Burt, 'Social work occupations in England', pp. 752–3.

8   Helen Bosanquet's husband was the philosopher and political theorist Bernard Bosanquet. They met during the course of their philanthropic work.

9   Kendall, *Social Work Education*, p. 40.

10 ibid., p. 19.

11 These women had post-secondary education, though not necessarily in a university.

12 James Leiby, *A History of Social Welfare and Social Work in the United States*, New York: Columbia University Press, 1978, p. 129.
13 Jane Addams, *Twenty Years at Hull House* (1930), US: Signet Classic, 1961, p. xii.
14 The main ethnic groups were from Germany, Greece, Italy, French Canada, and European Jewish communities, many of whom did not speak English.
15 Harry Specht and Mark E. Courtney, *Unfaithful Angels: How Social Work Has Abandoned its Mission*, New York: The Free Press, 1994, p. 82.
16 Leiby, *A History of Social Welfare and Social Work*, p. 129.
17 ibid., p. 129.
18 ibid., pp. 131–5.
19 Jane Lewis, *The Voluntary Sector, the State and Social Work in Britain: The Charity Organisation Society/Family Welfare Association Since 1869*, Aldershot, UK: Edward Elgar Publishing, 1995, p. 28.
20 Kendall, *Social Work Education*, p. 26.
21 Clement Attlee, *The Social Worker*, London: G. Bell and Sons, 1920, pp. 73–6; Kendall, *Social Work Education*, pp. 34–5.
22 Kathleen Woodroofe, *From Charity to Social Work in England and the United States*, London: Routledge and Kegan Hall, 1962, p. 90.
23 Woodroofe, *From Charity to Social Work*, p. 91.
24 Barbara Levy Simon, 'In search of nuance in historical research about social work practice' (paper presented at the Third International Conference of Practice Research, Silberman School of Social Work at Hunter College, New York City, 9–11 June 2014), p. 3 (author's collection, Melbourne).
25 Kendall, *Social Work Education*, p. 43.
26 David M. Austin, *History of Social Work Education*, School of Social Work, University of Texas, 1986, p. 9.
27 Kendall, *Social Work Education*, p. 43. Research by Professor Marjorie Smith of Columbia University documents the way the London COS's training lectures were developed after 1895: Marjorie Smith, *Professional Education for Social Work in Britain: An Historical Account* (1953), London: George Allen & Unwin, 1965, p. 5.
28 Alfred Kahn, 'Themes for a history of the first hundred years', in Ronald A. Feldman and Sheila B. Kamerman (eds), *The Columbia University School of Social Work: A Centennial Celebration*, New York: Columbia University Press, 2011, p. 10.
29 Kahn, 'Themes for a history', p. 11.
30 Kendall, *Social Work Education*, p. 73; Pierson, *Understanding Social Work*, p. 43; Austin, *History of Social Work Education*, p. 2.
31 Joan S. Clarke, 'The break-up of the Poor Law', in Margaret Cole (ed.), *The Webbs and their Work*, London: Frederick Miller, 1949, p. 113, quoted in Kendall, *Social Work Education*, p. 57.
32 Kendall, *Social Work Education*, p. 90.
33 ibid., p. 72.
34 COS pamphlet, quoted in Kendall, *Social Work Education*, p. 72.

35 C.S. Loch, quoted in Smith, *Professional Education for Social Work in Britain*, p. 52.
36 Smith, *Professional Education for Social Work in Britain*, p. 58.
37 Ken Moffatt and Alan Irving, '"Living for the brethren": Idealism, social work's lost enlightenment strain', *British Journal of Social Work*, vol. 32, 2002, p. 421.
38 Kendall, *Social Work Education*, p. 72.
39 Moffatt and Irving, 'Living for the brethren', p. 421.
40 Kendall, *Social Work Education*, p. 106. Smith, *Professional Education for Social Work in Britain*, p. 64.
41 O'Brien and Turner, *Establishing Medical Social Work in Victoria*, p. 66.
42 Martha Morrison Dore, 'Clinical practice', in Feldman and Kamerman (eds), *The Columbia University School of Social Work*, p. 118. The New York School of Philanthropy was an earlier incarnation of Columbia University School of Social Work.
43 Austin, *History of Social Work Education*, p. 3.
44 NASW Foundation, 'Mary Ellen Richmond (1861–1928)', in *NASW Pioneers Biography Index*, Washington, DC: National Association of Social Workers Foundation, https://www.naswfoundation.org/Our-Work/NASW-Social-Work-Pioneers/NASW-Social-Workers-Pioneers-Bio-Index.
45 Austin, *History of Social Work Education*, p. 3.
46 Mary Richmond, *Social Diagnosis*, New York: Russell Sage Foundation, 1917, p. 3.
47 Austin, *History of Social Work Education*, p. 5.
48 Pierson, *Understanding Social Work*, p. 31.
49 Hazel Osborn, 'One door, many mansions: 1974–1995', in Baraclough et al. (eds), *100 Years of Health-Related Social Work*, p. 65.
50 Grace Dedman, '1946–1973: Reconstruction and integration: Social work in the National Health Service', in Baraclough et al. (eds), *100 Years of Health-Related Social Work*, p. 42.
51 Roy Lubove, *The Professional Altruist: The Emergence of Social Work as a Career 1880–1930*, New York: Athenaeum, 1969, p. 24.
52 Harriet Bartlett, 'Ida M. Cannon: Pioneer in medical social work', *Social Service Review*, vol. 49, no. 2, 1975, p. 228.
53 Lubove, *The Professional Altruist*, p. 34.
54 Georgia Travis, *Round Peg, Round Hole: A Life of Medical Social Work*, California: The author, 1993.
55 Lubove, *The Professional Altruist*, p. 34.
56 ibid., pp. 34, 92.
57 John Stewart, 'Psychiatric social work in inter-war Britain: Child guidance, American ideas, American philanthropy', *Michael*, vol. 3, 2006, p. 80.
58 Stewart, 'Psychiatric social work in inter-war Britain', p. 87.
59 'Edith Eckhard and Lucy E. Beach visit to the USA', series 16, box 23, folder 258, 'Mental Hygiene England', Commonwealth Fund Archives, Rockefeller Archive Center, New York.

60 Noel Timms, *Psychiatric Social Work in Great Britain: 1939–1962*, London: Routledge & Kegan Paul, 1964, p. 23.
61 Timms, *Psychiatric Social Work in Great Britain*, pp. 34–6, 23.
62 Austin, *History of Social Work Education*, p. 11. Lubove, *The Professional Altruist*, p. 83.
63 Lubove, *The Professional Altruist*, p. 98.
64 Edward D. Lynde, 'Community agencies and the clinic', in National Conference of Social Work Proceedings, 1924, pp. 418–21, quoted in Lubove, *The Professional Altruist*, p. 95.
65 Austin, *History of Social Work Education*, p. 10.
66 Timms, *Psychiatric Social Work in Great Britain*, pp. 17–18.
67 Woodroofe, *From Charity to Social Work*, p. 136.
68 ibid., p. 20.
69 Leslie Leighninger, *Social Work: Search for Identity*, Westport, Connecticut: Greenwood Press, 1987, p. 12.
70 Robert L. Barker, *Milestones in the Development of Social Work and Social Welfare*, Washington, DC: NASW Press, 1999, p. 13.
71 Leighninger, *Social Work: Search for Identity*, p. 126.
72 ibid., p. 140.
73 ibid., pp. 141–2.
74 ibid., pp. 141–2.
75 Barker, *Milestones in the Development of Social Work*, pp. 17–18.
76 Howard Karger, 'Lessons from American social work education: Caution ahead', *Australian Social Work*, vol. 65, no. 3, 2012, p. 1.
77 Elizabeth Macadam, *The Social Servant in the Making: A Review of the Provision of Training for the Social Services*, London: George Allen & Unwin, 1945, p. 32.
78 Macadam, *The Social Servant in the Making*, p. 24.
79 Malcolm Payne, *The Origins of Social Work: Continuity and Change*, Hampshire, UK: Palgrave Macmillan, 2005, pp. 232–3.
80 Cherry Morris (ed.), *Social Casework in Great Britain*, London: Faber & Faber, 1959, pp. 218–19.
81 Macadam, *The Social Servant in the Making*, p. 37.
82 Alma Hartshorn, *Milestone in Education for Social Work: The Carnegie Experiment, 1954–1958*, Dunfermline, Scotland: The Carnegie United Kingdom Trust, 1982, p. 86.
83 Hartshorn, *Milestone in Education for Social Work*, p. 93.
84 David Donnison (LSE), interview by Sonia Exley, 19 December 2012 (unpublished), p. 11, Private collection, London.
85 NASW Foundation, 'Charlotte Towle (1896–1966)', in *NASW Social Work Pioneers Biography Index*, Washington, DC: National Association of Social Work, https://www.naswfoundation.org/Our-Work/NASW-Social-Work-Pioneers/NASW-Social-Workers-Pioneers-Bio-Index.
86 Hartshorn, *Milestone in Education for Social Work*, p. 93
87 Oakley, *Father and Daughter*, p.123. Edith Eckhard was still nominally in charge.

88 Payne, *The Origins of Social Work*, p. 60.
89 Kendall, *Social Work Education*, p. 107.
90 Oakley, *Father and Daughter*, p. 116.
91 Ralf Dahrendorf, *LSE: A History of the London School of Economics and Political Science, 1895–1995*, Oxford University Press, 1995, p. 298.
92 Employment application, 14 January 1929, Eckhard, E.V. (Miss), staff file, LSE Archives.
93 Dahrendorf, *LSE: A History*, p. 299.
94 Kathleen Jones, *Eileen Younghusband: A Biography*, London: Bedford Square Press, 1984, pp. 67–8; Sue Donnelly, 'A life of social work and friends—Eileen Younghusband', blog entry, LSE, 27 February 2017, https://blogs.lse.ac.uk/lsehistory/2017/02/27/a-life-of-social-work-and-friends-eileen-younghusband/.
95 David Donnison, *Social Policy and Administration Revisited: Studies in the Development of Social Services at the Local Level*, London: George Allen and Unwin, 1975, p. 253.
96 Jones, *Eileen Younghusband: A Biography*.
97 Olive Stevenson, *Reflections On a Life in Social Work: A Personal and Professional Memoir*, Buckingham, UK: Hinton House, 2013, p. 58.
98 Gill Bridge (LSE), interview by Sonia Exley, 6 February 2013, p. 13 (transcript supplied by interviewer).
99 Hazel Osborn, 'One door, many mansions: 1974–1996', in Baraclough et al. (eds), *100 Years of Health Related Social Work*, p. 65.
100 Leiby, *A History of Social Welfare and Social Work*, pp. 99, 121.
101 E.E. Morris, *Charity Organisation Societies: In England & the United States; A Paper Read at a Meeting of the Council of the Melbourne Charity Organisation Society, Held at the Town Hall, on Wednesday, 26th March, 1890*, Melbourne: Massina & Co., 1890.
102 Leiby, *A History of Social Welfare and Social Work*, p. 120.
103 Dedman, '1946–1973: Reconstruction and Integration', p. 42.
104 Joan Baraclough and Reg Wright, 'Kay McDougall: As well as teaching social workers she founded their first magazine' (obituary), *The Guardian*, 29 July 1999, https://www.theguardian.com/news/1999/jul/29/guardianobituaries2.
105 Britain and Australia also benefited from some of these funds. The LSE was generously funded by both the Commonwealth Fund and the Carnegie United Kingdom Trust, while the Carnegie Corporation supported Australian social work in its early days.
106 James A. Smith, 'The evolving role of American foundations', in Charles T. Clotfelter and Thomas Ehrlich (eds), *Philanthropy and the Nonprofit Sector in a Changing America*, Indianapolis: Indiana University Press, 1999, p. 36.
107 Ruth Crocker, 'From gift to foundation: The philanthropic lives of Mrs. Russell Sage', in Lawrence J. Friedman and Mark D. McGarvie (eds), *Charity, Philanthropy, and Civility in American History*, New York: Cambridge University Press, pp. 199–215.

108 Jonathan Dickens, 'Social work in England at a watershed—as always: From the Seebohm Report to the Social Work Task Force', *British Journal of Social Work*, vol. 41, no. 1, 2011, p. 35.

Chapter 2 – Precursors of Social Work in Victoria

1. S. Greig Smith, in 'Social work: The need for training', *The Other Half*, December 1930, p. 69.
2. Edward Jenks, quoted in R.J.W. Selleck, *The Shop: The University of Melbourne, 1850–1939*, Melbourne University Press, 2003, p. 306.
3. From 1935 called the Royal Melbourne Hospital.
4. 'Inquest: Death at the hospital door', *The Argus*, 10 February 1887, p. 8.
5. Anderson, *The Greig Smith Social Work History Collection*, p. 3.
6. Professor Morris [E.E. Morris], 'A charity organisation society', *The Argus*, 19 March 1887, p. 5.
7. Until well into the twentieth century, public hospitals in Victoria were classed as charities. From 1924 they were managed by the Charities Board. At the point where this book ends, in 1960, they were overseen by the Hospitals and Charities Commission. They shared the concerns of other charities about eligibility for service, assessment of ability to pay, and fundraising from the general public. Wealthier people would have been treated either at home or in a private nursing home.
8. Lawrence, *Professional Social Work in Australia*, p. 20.
9. Introduced in 1910 and replacing the Victorian Government's age pension of 1900.
10. Australian Bureau of Statistics, 'History of pensions and other benefits in Australia', *1301.0 Year Book Australia*, 1988, updated June 2019, pp. 1–4, https://www.abs.gov.au/AUSSTATS/abs@.nsf/3d68c56307742d8fca257090002029cd/8e72c4526a94aaedca2569de00296978!OpenDocument.
11. Shurlee Swain, 'The Victorian charity network in the 1890s', PhD thesis, University of Melbourne, 1976, p. 29.
12. Shurlee Swain, 'Destitute and dependent: Case studies in poverty in Melbourne, 1890–1900', *Historical Studies*, vol. 19, 1980, pp. 98–107.
13. Swain, 'Destitute and dependent', pp. 98–107.
14. Swain, 'Destitute and dependent', p. 99.
15. 'Opinions after 10 years of social service', *The Argus*, 25 October 1944, p. 8. This patronising view was ascribed to social work by historians such as Richard Kennedy and Mark Peel (Kennedy, *Charity Warfare*; Peel, *Miss Cutler and the Case of the Resurrected Horse*).
16. Luke Henriques-Gomes, 'Billion-dollar robodebt settlement reveals massive scale of welfare crackdown disaster', *The Guardian*, 17 November 2020, https://www.theguardian.com/australia-news/2020/nov/17/billion-dollar-robodebt-settlement-reveals-massive-scale-of-welfare-crackdown-disaster.
17. Anderson, *The Greig Smith Social Work History Collection*, p. 9.
18. ibid., pp. 5, 3.

19 Olive Wykes, 'Morris, Edward Ellis (1843–1902)', in *Australian Dictionary of Biography*, vol. 5, Melbourne University Press, 1974, http://adb.anu.edu.au/biography/morris-edward-ellis-4251.
20 COS minutes, June 1887, p. 5, UMA.
21 Anderson, *The Greig Smith Social Work History Collection*, p. 5.
22 Swain, 'The Victorian charity network', pp. 98–9.
23 COS minutes, September 1887, p. 11, CWS, 1980/0087, UMA.
24 COS minutes, July 1891, p. 277, CWS, 1980/0087, UMA; COS minutes, February 1892, p. 340, CWS, 1980/0087, UMA; Anderson, *The Greig Smith Social Work History Collection*, p. 6.
25 COS minutes, January 1889, p. 4, CWS, 1980/0087, UMA.
26 Anderson, *The Greig Smith Social Work History Collection*, p. 6.
27 *Proceedings of the First Australasian Conference on Charity, Held in Melbourne, From 11th to 17th November, 1890, Convened by the Charity Organization Society of Melbourne*, Melbourne: R.S. Brain, Government Printer, 1891; *Proceedings of the Second Australasian Conference on Charity, Held in Melbourne, from 17th to 21st November, 1891, convened by the Charity Organization Society of Melbourne*, Melbourne: R.S. Brain, Government Printer, 1892.
28 COS minutes, July 1911, p. 75, UMA.
29 COS minutes, November 1887, p. 16, CWS, 1980/0087, UMA.
30 Dorothy Scott and Shurlee Swain, *Confronting Cruelty: Historical Perspectives on Child Protection in Australia*, Melbourne University Press, 2002, pp. 11–33.
31 COS minutes, 29 March 1892, p. 357, UMA. COS decided not to involve itself in the problem of baby farming, but became actively involved in winter distress planning.
32 Anderson, *The Greig Smith Social Work History Collection*, p. 5.
33 Morris, *Charity Organisation Societies*.
34 ibid., p. 11.
35 ibid., p. 9.
36 Kennedy, *Charity Warfare*, p. 212.
37 Selleck, *The Shop*, p. 360.
38 ibid., p. 360.
39 Anderson, *The Greig Smith Social Work History Collection*, p. 10.
40 Stanley was his first name, but he was always known by his second name, Greig. Smith was his surname.
41 Anderson, *The Greig Smith Social Work History Collection*, p. 10; Ruth Hoban, 'Stanley Greig Smith M.B.E., J.P., F.C.I.S.' (obituary), 1971, unit 16, 6, Hoban Archives, UMA.
42 Hoban, 'Stanley Greig Smith', p. 1.
43 ibid., p. 8.
44 ibid., p. 4.
45 ibid., p. 7.
46 COS minutes, 22 December 1913, p. 276; 22 February 1915, p. 376; 31 March 1924, p. 36; 14 June 1926, p. 462, UMA.
47 COS minutes, 1 July 1914, p. 310, UMA.

48 COS minutes, 21 July 1924, p. 172, UMA.
49 Anderson, *The Greig Smith Social Work History Collection*, p. 9.
50 ibid., p. 73. What is left of this library, which includes pamphlets and books, is held in Special Collections, Baillieu Library, University of Melbourne.
51 Anderson, *The Greig Smith Social Work History Collection*, p. 73.
52 S. Greig Smith, 'The great and the small,' *The Other Half*, September 1926, p. 2.
53 Jacob Riis, *How the Other Half Lives* (1890), Boston: Bedford St Martin's Press, 1996.
54 'International Charities Correction and Philanthropy, Chicago, 1893', p. 73, copy held in Greig Smith Social Work History Collection, Baillieu Library Special Collections, University of Melbourne.
55 This was O. Morrice Williams of the Australian Red Cross Society. Williams did not follow up his attendance in any way. Letters from organisers of the international social work conference series, including Dr René Sand of Belgium (March 1929) and Dorothy Kahn, president of the American Association of Social Workers (1936), requesting information and support, met with Williams' rejection.
56 'International conferences on social work', *The Other Half*, March 1936, p. 11.
57 S. Greig Smith, 'Social work under the microscope: Some notes on the Third International Conference', *The Other Half*, April 1937, pp. 17–20.
58 Anderson, *The Greig Smith Social Work History Collection*, p. 69.
59 '"Tommy the Growler": A review', *The Other Half*, December 1930, pp. 71–2.
60 COS minutes, 19 January 1892, p. 335, UMA.
61 Smith, quoted in Hoban, 'Stanley Greig Smith', p. 5.
62 COS minutes, 26 July 1916, p. 506, UMA.
63 S. Greig Smith, 'Fifteen years in retrospect: Social work achievements', *The Other Half*, April 1933, pp. 45–6.
64 'Social work: The need for training', *The Other Half*, December 1930, p. 71.
65 'Training for social work: An Australian experiment', *The Other Half*, March 1929, p. 7.
66 'Hospital social service: The work of the almoner', *The Other Half*, December 1929, p. 23.
67 'Training for social work', *The Other Half*, March 1930, p. 40; Agnes Macintyre, 'Equipment for welfare work: The value of training', *The Other Half*, September 1931, pp. 96–9.
68 'Social work: The need for training', p. 69.
69 COS minutes, June 1913, p. 228, UMA.
70 COS minutes, 6 July 1925, p. 282, UMA.
71 COS minutes, 20 February 1911, p. 49, UMA; COS minutes, 31 May 1926, p. 455, UMA.
72 COS minutes, 3 September 1923, p. 79, UMA.
73 'The hospital and the family', *The Other Half*, June 1929, p. 15.
74 BSS minutes, July 1933, p. 11, UMA.
75 Lydia Eady, interview by the author, 16 September 2010.

76 Owen W. Parnaby, *Angus Mitchell: Rotarian and Peace Maker*, Melbourne: The author, 1998, pp. 12–13.
77 Renate Howe, *A Century of Influence: The Australian Student Christian Movement, 1896–1996*, Sydney: University of New South Wales Press, 2009, p. 120.

Chapter 3 – Australia's First Social Work Courses

1   Lawrence, *Professional Social Work in Australia*, p. 45.
2   ibid., p. 33.
3   ibid., p. 34.
4   ibid., p. 45.
5   Horsburgh, *Doing Good Well*, p. 18. In 1951 a reconstituted Board of Studies in Social Work was established.
6   Lovell was later founding professor of the university's psychology department, and finally dean of the Faculty of Arts there.
7   W.M. O'Neil, 'Lovell, Henry Tasman (1878–1958)', in *Australian Dictionary of Biography*, vol. 10, Melbourne University Press, 1986, http://adb.anu.edu.au/biography/lovell-henry-tasman-7247.
8   D.R. Walker, 'Sutton, Harvey (1882–1963)', in *Australian Dictionary of Biography*, vol. 12, Melbourne University Press, 1990, http://adb.anu.edu.au/biography/sutton-harvey-8721.
9   Kerry Regan, 'Fitzpatrick, Aileen (1897–1974)', in *Australian Dictionary of Biography*, vol. 14, Melbourne University Press, 1966, http://adb.anu.edu.au/biography/fitzpatrick-aileen-10194.
10 Regan, 'Fitzpatrick, Aileen'.
11 Lawrence, *Professional Social Work in Australia*, p. 50.
12 ibid., p. 51.
13 Norma Parker, 'The beginnings of social work in New South Wales: A personal account', *Australian Social Work*, vol. 57, no. 3, 2004, p. 219. Parker (1906–2004) was an American-educated Australian social work pioneer, and first president of the Australian Association of Social Workers.
14 Lawrence, *Professional Social Work in Australia*, p. 50.
15 This claim is repeated, for instance, in Regan, 'Fitzpatrick, Aileen'.
16 Carnegie Corporation Grants, 'Lee, Porter, 1935–1940', box 201, folder 9, Rare Book and Manuscript Library, Butler Library, Columbia University, New York.
17 Parker, 'The beginnings of social work in New South Wales', p. 219.
18 R.J. (John) Lawrence, 'Researching Australian social work history', in R.J. (John) Lawrence 'Memoir', (unpublished manuscript, 2014–), p. 89, John Lawrence personal archive (now at University of New South Wales, Sydney).
19 Browne, *Tradition and Change*, p. 11.
20 Parker, 'The beginnings of social work in New South Wales', p. 222.
21 Lawrence, *Professional Social Work in Australia*, p. 51.
22 ibid., p. 110.

23 University of Sydney, *Sydney School of Education and Social Work*, https://sydney.edu.au/education_social_work/about/history/social_work.shtml, viewed 22 November 2020.
24 Horsburgh, *Doing Good Well*, p. 12.
25 ibid., p. 13.
26 Browne, *Tradition and Change*, pp. 38–9.
27 Horsburgh, *Doing Good Well*, p. 13.
28 Australian Red Cross Society annual reports, 1921–28: Report of Victorian Division, 1921–22, p. 43, Australian Red Cross Society (ARCS) Archives, UMA.
29 Red Cross Annual Report, 1923–24: Report of Victorian Division, p. 56, ARCS Archives, UMA.
30 O'Brien and Turner, *Establishing Medical Social Work in Victoria*, p. 30.
31 Lawrence, *Professional Social Work in Australia*, pp. 34–5.
32 ibid., p. 2.
33 R.J. Love, 'Excerpt from "Notes and recommendations by the Inspector of Charities (Victoria) as to hospitals and other philanthropic institutions and organisations"', Victorian Parliamentary Papers, vol. 11, no. 48, 1927, pp. 17–18, reprinted in O'Brien and Turner, *Establishing Medical Social Work in Victoria*, p. 66.
34 Love, 'Excerpt from "Notes and Recommendations"', p. 2.
35 Lawrence *Professional Social Work in Australia*, p. 47.
36 ibid., p. 48.
37 ibid., p. 5.
38 ibid., p. 49.
39 Victorian Institute of Hospital Almoners Executive Committee, *The Origin and Development of Medical Social Work in Victoria, With Special Reference to the Work of the Victorian Institute of Hospital Almoners*, Melbourne: J.S. McClelland, 1950, p. 4.
40 O'Brien and Turner, *Establishing Medical Social Work in Victoria*, p. 26.
41 The Victorian Society for Crippled Children and Adults was renamed as the Yooralla Society after amalgamation with Yooralla in 1977.
42 Joan Tuxen, in discussion with the author, 13 and 20 March 2004, p. 6.
43 Tuxen, in discussion with the author, p. 7.
44 O'Brien and Turner, *Establishing Medical Social Work in Victoria*, p. 23.
45 Gleeson, 'The professionalisation of Australian Catholic social welfare', p. 141.
46 Victorian Institute of Hospital Almoners, *The Origin and Development of Medical Social Work in Victoria*, p. 6.
47 BSS minutes, July 1933, p. 13, UMA.
48 Tuxen, in discussion with the author, p. 5.
49 Victorian Institute of Hospital Almoners, *The Origin and Development of Medical Social Work in Victoria*, p. 6. In 1950 the executive of the VIHA produced this booklet, outlining its history and key personnel and explaining its role in the establishment of general training. The anonymous author was probably Sir John Newman-Morris. The actual transfer of the course to the

university occurred in December 1940. The first year in which all staff were housed at the university was 1941.
50 'Alison Mathew interviewed by Marjorie Glasson in the Australian Association of Social Workers Oral History Project [sound recording]', October 1972, p. 5, National Library of Australia, https://nla.gov.au/nla.obj-193570456/listen.
51 Lawrence, *Professional Social Work in Australia*, p. 39.
52 ibid., p. 38; Parker, 'The beginnings of social work in New South Wales', p. 220.
53 Lawrence, *Professional Social Work in Australia*, p. 53.
54 Elaine Martin, 'Gender demand and domain: The social work profession in South Australia 1935–1980', PhD thesis, University of Melbourne, 1990, p. 62.
55 Martin, 'Gender demand and domain', p. 95.
56 Gleeson, 'The professionalisation of Australian Catholic social welfare', p. 93.
57 Frances Crawford and Sabina Leitman, 'The shaping of West Australian social work 1920–1970', *Australian Social Work*, vol. 54, no. 3, 2001, p. 45; Gleeson, 'The professionalisation of Australian Catholic social welfare', p. 117.
58 Damian Gleeson's research is important here; see for instance Gleeson, 'The professionalisation of Australian Catholic social welfare', p. 65.
59 Frances Crawford and Sabina Leitman have argued this; see Crawford and Leitman, 'The shaping of West Australian social work', p. 47.
60 Norma Parker, 'Early social work in retrospect', *Australian Social Work*, vol. 32, no. 4, 1979, p. 19.
61 Gleeson, 'The professionalisation of Australian Catholic social welfare', p. 117.
62 Browne, *Tradition and Change*, p. 15.
63 Lawrence, *Professional Social Work in Australia*, p. 38.
64 Pavlin, *Social Work in the University of Queensland*.
65 Len Tierney, correspondence to Queensland agent general, 1954, papers of Leonard James Tierney, 2008.0060, UMA.
66 Vaile was famous in America for a stirring speech about social work losing its mission to the poor, which she gave in 1926 when she was president of the National Conference of Social Work. NASW Foundation, 'Gertrude Vaile', in *NASW Pioneers Biography*, Washington, DC: National Association of Social Workers Foundation, https://www.naswfoundation.org/Our-Work/NASW-Social-Workers-Pioneers/NASW-Social-Workers-Pioneers-Listing.aspx?id=177.
67 BSS minutes, June 1938, pp. 134–6, UMA.
68 ibid., p. 135.
69 ibid., pp. 136.
70 ibid., p. 136, UMA.
71 BSS minutes, October 1938, p. 153, UMA.
72 BSS minutes, December 1938, p. 159, UMA.
73 'Social service training', *The Argus*, 21 July 1938, p. 7.
74 This was pointed out to me by John Lawrence (R.J. Lawrence, email to author, 3 November, 2013).
75 Lawrence, 'Introduction: Australian social work: In historical, international and social welfare context', in Boas and Crawley (eds), *Social Work in Australia*, p. 17.

Chapter 4 – Victoria's First General Social Work Course

1. Victorian Institute of Hospital Almoners, *The Origin and Development of Medical Social Work in Victoria*, p. 6.
2. Alexander Boyce Gibson, 'Board of Social Studies farewell to Miss J.S. Hyslop', 7 March 1945, Registrar's Correspondence, file 'Hyslop Miss J.S.', UMA312, 1945/426, UMA.
3. Georgina Sweet, letter to Mrs Norman Brookes, 25 April 1931, Australian Association of Social Workers, AA Hospital Almoners, unit 26, UMA (see Appendix 5, Letter 1, for full text). Mrs Norman Brookes (later Dame Mabel Brookes) was the sister-in-law of Mrs Herbert (Ivy) Brookes.
4. See Appendix 5, Letter 2, for full text of undated letter organised by Dr Sweet with the following signatories: Mr M.P. Hansen (Victorian director of education), Mrs G.G. Henderson (president, Central Council of Benevolent Societies, member of first executive committee of VIA and mother of Lynette Henderson, one of the first three almoners to qualify in Melbourne), Mr Greig Smith (Charity Organisation Society), Sir Richard Stawell (president of the Council of Mental Hygiene), Dr Georgina Sweet (national president of YWCA of Australia).
5. Selleck, *The Shop*, p. 646.
6. ibid., pp. 671–5.
7. 'Decline in Melbourne population', *The Canberra Times*, 25 January 1933, p. 1.
8. Selleck, *The Shop*, p. 649.
9. ibid., p. 650.
10. Professors Scott (chair), Osborne, Gunn, Agar, Bailey Marshall, and Allen, and Associate Professor Wood.
11. 'Training for social work', *The Other Half*, December 1932, pp. 33–4.
12. The Workers' Educational Association (commenced 1913), which was affiliated with the British WEA, provided well-organised courses of tutorials supported by academic staff from the University of Melbourne. The University Extension Program (commenced 1891) organised individual public lectures by specialists from the university in fields such as literature and science. The two programs clashed during the 1930s. See Gordon Dadswell, 'The Workers' Educational Association of Victoria and the University of Melbourne: A clash of purpose?', *Australian Journal of Adult Learning*, vol. 45, no. 3, November 2005, pp. 333–4.
13. 'Training for social work'.
14. Lawrence, *Professional Social Work in Australia*, p. 46.
15. ibid., p. 46.
16. BSS minutes, February 1933, p. 3, UMA.
17. ibid., p. 2, UMA.
18. BSS minutes, March 1933, p. 35, UMA.
19. 'Study of social science, director appointed, Miss Hyslop coming from Leeds', *The Argus*, 18 July 1934, p. 6.
20. BSS minutes, February–March 1933, pp. 3–5, UMA.
21. Later known as Professor W. McMahon Ball.
22. BSS minutes, April 1933, p. 7; June 1933, p. 10; UMA.

23 Later Vera Scantlebury Brown; the doctor who started the Victorian Government's Maternal and Child Health Service.
24 BSS minutes, October 1933, p. 21, UMA.
25 BSS minutes, November 1933, 24a, p. 33, UMA.
26 BSS minutes, 6 October 1933, p. 20, UMA.
27 ibid., p. 21, UMA.
28 Lesley Henderson, letter to Miss Onians (Newsboys Society), October 1934, box 7, Hoban Archives, UMA. The benefactors were Arthur William Coles (co-founder of Coles Variety Stores and lord mayor of Melbourne 1938–40), George Nicholas (founder of Aspro), Mr F. Laycock, Mr S. Ricketson, and Mr and Mrs Herbert Brookes (Herbert Brookes was a businessman and member of the University of Melbourne Council 1933–47; his wife was Ivy Brookes née Deakin, philanthropist, activist and supporter of equal pay for women, daughter of former Australian prime minister Sir Alfred Deakin).
29 BSS minutes, February 1934, p. 29, UMA.
30 BSS minutes, June 1933, p. 9; Honorary secretary of the BSS (Joan Brett), letter to E. Eckhard, 10 May 1933, item 26, box 20, file Australian Association of Social Workers 1990.0024, UMA.
31 This was Miss J. Macintyre, probably not Agnes Macintyre. She found the first applicant to be personally unsuitable. The second, Miss Kydd, was 'very suitable but unable to apply', and the third was Jocelyn Hyslop. Extract from letters from Miss Macintyre, 7 February to 6 April 1934, p. 261, box 20, file 'Australian Assoc of Social Workers/Almoners', UMA.
32 ibid.
33 BSS minutes, April 1934, p. 34, UMA.
34 'Director of social studies arrives: English and American methods discussed', *The Argus*, 8 December 1934, p. 13.
35 BSS minutes, 7 December 1934, p. 44, UMA.
36 'Afternoon parties and gaiety to-night in welcome to Miss Hyslop', *The Star* (Melbourne), 7 December 1934, p. 12, copy on Victorian Council for Social Training Publicity and Correspondence file, 'AASW/Assoc Hospital Almoners', UMA (see Appendix 6 for guest list).
37 BSS minutes, 20 December 1934, p. 46, UMA.
38 ibid., p. 46, UMA.
39 BSS minutes, February 1935, pp. 47, 47a, UMA.
40 Jocelyn Hyslop, circular letter, February 1942, file 'Vaile, Gertrude', Butler Library, Columbia University, New York.
41 An American psychologist, whose salary was funded by Melbourne philanthropist Annie Danks.
42 A Melbourne psychologist, who lectured at the Kindergarten Training College. Her daughter Katrina later became a social worker.
43 Psychiatrist at Sunbury Mental Hospital and the newly established Travancore Developmental Centre (run on the child guidance model).
44 BSS minutes, March 1938, p. 128, UMA.
45 BSS minutes, September 1938, p. 150, UMA.

46 BSS minutes, February 1940, p. 191, UMA.
47 BSS minutes, February 1941, UMA.
48 BSS minutes, May 1941, UMA.
49 'Alison Mathew interviewed by Marjorie Glasson in the Australian Association of Social Workers Oral History Project [sound recording]', October 1972, p. 9, National Library of Australia, https://nla.gov.au/nla.obj-193570456/listen.
50 Tuxen, in discussion with the author, 2004, p. 5.
51 ibid., p. 6.
52 ibid., p. 5.
53 Director's report, BSS minutes, June 1935, p. 57a, UMA.
54 BSS minutes, September 1937, p. 119; November 1937, p. 120; UMA.
55 BSS minutes, April 1937, p. 106, UMA.
56 BSS minutes, November 1937, p. 120, UMA.
57 BSS minutes, December 1937, p. 129, UMA.
58 BSS minutes, October 1938, p. 153, UMA.
59 BSS minutes, December 1938, p. 159, UMA.
60 BSS minutes, August 1940, p. 206, UMA.
61 'Jacobs, Kate, July 1940', Carnegie Corporation Grants, box 188, folder 6, Rare Book and Manuscript Library, Butler Library, Columbia University, New York.
62 Kate Jacobs, letter to registrar, 17 October 1941, Registrar's Correspondence, 1941/659, UMA.
63 Jocelyn Hyslop, letter to registrar, 21 October 1941, Registrar's Correspondence, 1941/659, UMA.
64 Jean Robertson, letter to registrar, 29 October 1941, Registrar's Correspondence, 1941/659, UMA.
65 BSS minutes, March 1940, p. 193, UMA.
66 BSS minutes, December 1941, p. 29, UMA.
67 Jane Miller and David Nichols, 'Moving among friends: The establishment of professional social work education at the University of Melbourne, 1929–1941', *Social Work in Health Care*, vol. 52, nos 2/3, 2013, pp. 115–17.
68 Miller and Nichols, 'Moving among friends', p. 115.
69 BSS minutes, March 1937, p. 100, UMA.
70 BSS minutes, April 1938, p. 118, UMA.
71 BSS minutes, February 1939, p. 190, UMA.
72 Miller and Nichols, 'Moving among friends', pp. 115–17.
73 J.S. Hyslop, letter to J.D.G. Medley (vice-chancellor), 11 June 1943, Registrar's Correspondence, file 'Hyslop, Miss J.S', UMA 312, 1945/426, UMA.
74 BSS minutes, November 1942, p. 49, UMA.
75 BSS minutes, May 1940, p. 199, UMA.
76 Director's report, BSS minutes, December 1939, p. 187, UMA.
77 BSS minutes, May 1940, p. 199, UMA.
78 Jocelyn Hyslop to Gertrude Vaile and others, circular letter, 1942, file 'Vaile, Gertrude', Butler Library, Columbia University, New York.
79 Jocelyn S. Hyslop and Jean M. Robertson, 'Overseas reception scheme in Victoria', *The Australian Quarterly*, vol. 13, no. 1, March 1941, p. 93.

80 Ellen Warne, Shurlee Swain, Patricia Grimshaw and John Lack, 'Women in conversation: A wartime social survey in Melbourne, Australia, 1941–1943', *Women's History Review*, vol. 12, no. 4, 2003, p. 531.
81 BSS minutes, October 1938, p. 152, UMA.
82 BSS minutes, October 1938, p. 152, UMA.
83 BSS minutes, 19 May 1941, UMA.
84 Gibson, 'Board of Social Studies farewell to Miss J.S. Hyslop'.
85 BSS minutes, September 1936, p. 95, UMA.
86 More details are contained in Miller and Nichols, 'Moving among friends'.
87 BSS minutes, August 1940, p. 196, UMA.
88 BSS minutes, October 1940, p. 208, UMA.
89 ibid., p. 208, UMA.
90 BSS minutes, August 1940, p. 196, UMA.
91 BSS minutes, October 1940, p. 213, UMA.
92 Selleck, *The Shop*, p. 655.
93 BSS minutes, 13 December 1940, p. 218, UMA.
94 ibid., , p. 218, UMA.
95 BSS minutes, 19 December 1940, p. 2, UMA.
96 BSS minutes, November 1940, p. 218, UMA.
97 BSS minutes, May 1939, p. 167, UMA.
98 BSS minutes, November 1942, p. 49, UMA.

Chapter 5 – International and National Opinion Leaders and Networks

1 *The Other Half*, vol. 4, no. 1, 1936, p. 11.
2 Fiona Paisley, *Glamour in the Pacific: Cultural Internationalism and Race Politics in the Women's Pan-Pacific*, Honolulu: University of Hawai'i Press, 2009, p. 18.
3 BSS minutes, 27 March 1935, p. 54, UMA.
4 'Corporation visitor to Southern Dominions', letter, 21 January 1937, box 21, folder 9, Carnegie Corporation Grants, Columbia University Archives.
5 BSS minutes, 20 and 27 March, 1 May 1935, pp. 54–8, UMA.
6 'Corporation Visitor to Southern Dominions'.
7 Kate Jacobs, letter to Charles Dollard, 1 July 1940, box 188, folder 6, Carnegie Corporation Grants File, Columbia University Archives.
8 Arthur Livingstone, 'Report on a period of observation and studies in the United States and Canada', March 1949 – June 1950, box 204, folder 5, Carnegie Corporation Grants File, Columbia University Archives.
9 Stephen Stackpole (Carnegie Corporation), letter to Ruth Hoban re $3,500 grant, 29 November 1950, box 2, Hoban Archives, UMA.
10 Porter Lee, letter to Frederick Keppel, 16 March 1937, box 201, folder 9, Carnegie Corporation Grants File, Columbia University Archives.
11 They discussed the BSS's origins, relationship with the university and the almoners, finances, and number of students.
12 BSS minutes, April 1937, p. 106, UMA.
13 BSS minutes, February 1936, p. 75, UMA. This was probably the M.L. Ferrard who wrote 'Notes on the psychiatric treatment of mental hospital patients:

Four paranoid schizophrenics', *British Journal of Psychiatric Social Work*, vol. 1, no. 1, 1947, pp. 45–56.
14   BSS minutes, inaugural meeting, 22 February 1933, p. 2, UMA.
15   Elizabeth J. Mellor, 'Gutteridge, Mary Valentine (1887–1962)', in *Australian Dictionary of Biography*, vol. 14, Melbourne University Press, 1996, https://adb.anu.edu.au/biography/gutteridge-mary-valentine-10383.
16   Due to his untimely death after a motor accident in 1933, Wrigley did not actually attend any meetings (Selleck, *The Shop*, p. 612).
17   BSS minutes, 22 February 1933, p. 1, UMA.
18   Newman-Morris took over from Mrs Norman Brookes.
19   BSS minutes, July 1933, p. 13, UMA.
20   BSS minutes, 15 May 1936, p. 79, UMA.
21   Scantlebury Brown's daughter, Catherine Brockenshire/James, later had a career as a social work lecturer in this department.
22   *Australian Dictionary of Biography*, published by the University of Melbourne from 1966, is now managed by the National Centre of Biography at the Australian National University in Canberra: see http://www.adb.anu.edu.au.
23   The Whitlam Labor government abandoned the British imperial honours system in 1975, replacing it with an Australian system.
24   Anderson, *The Greig Smith Social Work History Collection*, p. 12.
25   Hoban, 'Stanley Greig Smith'.
26   ibid.
27   Anderson, *The Greig Smith Social Work History Collection*, p. 11.
28   BSS minutes, 22 February 1933, p. 2, UMA.
29   Hoban, 'Stanley Greig Smith', p. 6.
30   ibid., p. 1.
31   When John Lawrence interviewed Gibson in the late 1950s, he said that Hyslop 'got on well with Smith – he took her well' (Alexander Boyce Gibson, interview with R.J. Lawrence, 1948–49, John Lawrence personal archive, UNSW).
32   Hoban, 'Stanley Greig Smith', p. 7.
33   Selleck, *The Shop*, p. 518.
34   BSS minutes, December 1946, p. 138; May 1946, p. 141; UMA.
35   Monica MacCallum, 'Sweet, Georgina (1875–1946)', in *Australian Dictionary of Biography*, vol. 12, Melbourne University Press, 1990, http://adb.anu.edu.au/biography/sweet-georgina-8728.
36   Georgina Sweet Bursary in Social Studies, Department of Social Work, Faculty of Medicine, Dentistry and Health Sciences, University of Melbourne, https://mdhs.unimelb.edu.au/study/scholarships/n/georgina-sweet-bursary.
37   Dr Renate Howe (historian), conversation with the author.
38   MacCallum, 'Sweet, Georgina'.
39   Howe, *A Century of Influence*.
40   Selleck, *The Shop*, p. 623. This was renamed University College when it became co-educational.
41   Selleck, *The Shop*, p. 650.

42 MacCallum, 'Sweet, Georgina'.
43 Paisley, *Glamour in the Pacific*, p. 1.
44 BSS minutes, 11 December 1942, p. 52, UMA.
45 The Australian Medical Association was not founded until 1962.
46 O'Brien and Turner, *Establishing Medical Social Work in Victoria*, p. 84.
47 John Newman-Morris, *Social Work in Hospitals: Some American Investigations*, Melbourne: Victorian Institute of Almoners, 1930.
48 Newman-Morris, *Social Work in Hospitals*, p. 2.
49 ibid., p. 3.
50 BSS minutes, 7 August 1935, p. 60, UMA.
51 Lawrence, *Professional Social Work in Australia*, p. 46.
52 Max Charlesworth, 'Gibson, Alexander Boyce (Sandy) (1900–1972)', in *Australian Dictionary of Biography*, vol. 14, Melbourne University Press, 1966, https://adb.anu.edu.au/biography/gibson-alexander-boyce-sandy-10295.
53 BSS minutes, May 1938, p. 133; August 1938, p. 137, UMA.
54 BSS minutes, 13 May 1938, p. 131, UMA.
55 Patricia Keep, 'Allan, Stella May (1871–1962)', in *Australian Dictionary of Biography*, vol. 7, Melbourne University Press, 1979, http://adb.anu.edu.au/biography/allan-stella-may-4998.
56 'Director of social studies arrives'; 'Opinions after 10 years of social service'.
57 BSS minutes, December 1933, p. 28b, UMA.
58 BSS minutes, August 1935, p. 59a, UMA.

Chapter 6 – Jocelyn Hyslop: A Public Intellectual

1 Gibson, 'Board of Social Studies farewell to Miss J.S. Hyslop'.
2 Kate Ogilvie, 'Interview with John Lawrence 1958/9', John Lawrence personal archive, UNSW.
3 'Director of social studies arrives'.
4 J.S. Hyslop, letter to John Medley (vice-chancellor), 21 September 1944, Registrar's Correspondence, 312, 1945/426, file 'Hyslop, Miss. J. S.', UMA.
5 John Medley (vice-chancellor), letter to J.S. Hyslop, 22 September 1944, Registrar's Correspondence, 312, 1945/426, file 'Hyslop, Miss J. S.', UMA.
6 Gibson, 'Board of Social Studies farewell to Miss J.S. Hyslop'.
7 'Director of social studies arrives'.
8 'Director of social studies arrives'.
9 'Director of social studies arrives'.
10 'Archibald Richard Frith Hyslop, warden of Glenalmond', *Glenalmond Chronicle*, vol. 164, December 1902, p. 1.
11 'In memoriam Archibald Richard Frith Hyslop, M.A.', *Glenalmond Chronicle*, vol. 283, December 1926, p. 1.
12 Elizabeth J. Morse, 'Lumsden, Dame Louisa Innes (1840–1935)', in *Oxford Dictionary of National Biography*, 23 September 2004, https://doi.org/10.1093/ref:odnb/48571.
13 Mary Campbell Brown (seniors secretary, St Leonards), letter to the author, 11 May 2010; also Morse, 'Lumsden, Dame Louisa Innes (1840–1935)'.

14 'Jocelyn S. Hyslop (born 1897) provided for Council re Staff Establishment Report', 1945/426, series 312, Registrar's Correspondence, file 'Hyslop, Miss J.S.', UMA.
15 'Student Christian Union', *Clare Market Review*, December 1919, p. 8; 'Student Christian Movement', *Clare Market Review*, March 1920, p. 30.
16 W.H.B. (Beveridge), director, LSE, 'Personal reference', 17 April 1928, Jocelyn Hyslop File, LSE Archives.
17 The Loch Exhibition 1918 and 1919, The Metcalf Scholarship for Women 1924 and 1926, Commonwealth Fund Scholarship 1931–32 (LSE/Central Filing Registry, p. 92, London School of Economics and Political Science, Archives and Rare Books, LSE Library, London (hereafter LSE Library).
18 J. Mair (secretary), letter to J. Hyslop, 2 June 1931, Jocelyn Hyslop student file, LSE Library.
19 David Shorney, *Teachers in Training: A History of Avery Hill College*, London: Thames Polytechnic, 1989, p. 129.
20 LSE/Central Filing Registry, p. 92, LSE Library.
21 ibid.
22 Timms, *Psychiatric Social Work in Great Britain*, pp. 17–18.
23 ibid., p. 21.
24 Secretary of LSE, letter to J. Hyslop, 4 November 1931, Jocelyn Hyslop student file, LSE Library.
25 'Director of social studies arrives'.
26 William Woodruff, *Beyond Nab End*, London: Abacus, 2009, p. 13. At one point in his career Woodruff, an economist, worked at the University of Melbourne and briefly chaired the BSS.
27 Mildred Scoville, letter to Miss Almena Dawley, 15 October 1934, Mental Hygiene—Eng, series 16, box 24, folder 279, Commonwealth Fund Archives, Rockefeller Archive Center, New York.
28 Mildred Scoville, letter to Miss Anna Belle Tracey, 19 October 1934, Mental Hygiene—Eng, series 16, box 24, folder 179, Commonwealth Fund Archives, Rockefeller Archive Center, New York.
29 Mildred Scoville, letter to Charlotte Towle, 26 October 1934, Mental Hygiene—Eng, series 16, box 24, folder 279, Commonwealth Fund Archives, Rockefeller Archive Center, New York.
30 Jocelyn Hyslop, letter to Frederick Keppel, 13 November 1934, Hyslop, Miss Jocelyn S, Carnegie Corporation Archive, Butler Library, Columbia University, New York.
31 The New York School of Social Work is now known as the Columbia University School of Social Work.
32 Hyslop, letter to Keppel, 13 November 1934.
33 Jocelyn Hyslop, 'A philosophy of social progress', *The Australian Quarterly*, vol. 10, no. 1, 1938, pp. 38–43.
34 Australia's national parliament had moved from Melbourne to Canberra, Australia's 'bush capital', eleven years previously, and the city was still being established.

35 Hyslop, 'A philosophy of social progress', p. 43.
36 Jocelyn S. Hyslop, 'Angles of social service: Training Council's director urges expert attack on problems' real causes, aid for re-adjustment in the families', *The Hospital Magazine* (Charities Board Victoria, Melbourne), August 1938, pp. 7–9.
37 Hyslop, 'Angles of social service', p. 7.
38 ibid., p. 7.
39 ibid., p. 8.
40 Jocelyn Hyslop, quoted in 'Reforms for children's courts', *The Argus*, 22 April 1936, p. 13.
41 Jocelyn Hyslop, quoted in 'Social work criticised', *The Argus*, 20 October 1938, p. 5.
42 BSS minutes, August 1935, p. 59a; 1936, p. 84, UMA.
43 Jocelyn Hyslop, quoted in 'Opinions after 10 years of social service'.
44 ibid.
45 Jane Carey, 'A transnational project? Women and gender in the social sciences in Australia, 1890–1945', *Women's History Review*, vol. 18, no. 1, 2009, p. 59.
46 Jocelyn Hyslop, letter to Edna Mendelsohn, 22 May 1936, author's collection, Melbourne.
47 Oakley, *Father and Daughter*, p. 148.
48 ibid., p. 219.
49 Alexander Boyce Gibson in discussion with John Lawrence, 1959–60, John Lawrence personal archive, UNSW.
50 Boyce Gibson in discussion with John Lawrence, 1959–60.
51 Pat Duxbury, interview with Carole Hamilton-Barwick (unpublished), 16 November 2010.
52 BSS minutes, November 1942, p. 49, UMA.
53 J.S. Hyslop, 'Plans for the future of the department of social studies', 15 September 1944, Registrar's Correspondence, UM312, 1945/426, UMA.
54 Owen was one of the inter-war followers of the tradition of the British sociological survey started by Booth, Rowntree and others (Hyslop, 'University of Melbourne, department of social studies', p. 2).
55 Hyslop, 'Plans for the future of the department of social studies'.
56 In May 1950 Greig Smith of the COS returned correspondence from the LSE with the advice that Hyslop had gone to South Africa and, he believed, from there to England (Secretary of CWS, letter to secretary of LSE, 31 May 1950, Jocelyn Hyslop File, LSE Archives).
57 The information held in the memorial book in the chapel of the Community of the Resurrection of Our Lord tells the rest of her story: Sister Jocelyn CR (Jocelyn Sophia Hyslop), Community of the Resurrection, Grahamstown, South Africa, extract from memorial book in chapel.
58 Alison Mathew, conversation with John Lawrence, 1959/60, John Lawrence personal archive, UNSW.
59 Amy Wheaton, conversation with John Lawrence, 1959/60, John Lawrence personal archive, UNSW.

60 The order's archive, now held at Grahamstown University, might throw light on this.

Chapter 7 – Consolidating the Course, 1945–1960

1. Ruth Hoban, letter to Stephen Stackpole, Carnegie Corporation, 26 November 1953, unit 2:1, Hoban Archive, UMA.
2. BSS minutes, April 1941, p. 8; May 1946, p. 146; UMA.
3. BSS minutes, December 1943, p. 84; February 1944, p. 88; May 1944, p. 98; UMA.
4. The name was changed from Diploma of Social Service to Diploma of Social Studies in 1939.
5. BSS minutes, April 1945, p. 130, UMA.
6. She too had personal exposure to American social work education and later succeeded Norma Parker, becoming the second president of the AASW.
7. 'Alison Mathew interviewed by Marjorie Glasson', p. 5.
8. 'Alison Mathew interviewed by Marjorie Glasson', p. 5.
9. BSS minutes, May 1954, p. 285, UMA.
10. Tuxen, in discussion with the author, 2004.
11. BSS minutes, June 1943, p. 71; August 1943, p. 76; UMA.
12. BSS minutes, October 1943, p. 78, UMA.
13. BSS Minutes, May 1950, p. 228 UMA.
14. Patricia Holmes (later Duxbury) held an honours degree in Arts (languages) from the University of Melbourne, and social work and almoner qualifications from the University of Sydney (Registrar Correspondence, Holmes, P., folder 1950/491, UMA; BSS minutes, May 1950, p. 228; September 1950, p. 30; UMA).
15. Jeffrey's model of practical teaching in his psychiatric clinic at the Royal Melbourne Hospital echoed the experience of the students of the LSE Mental Health Certificate in London (Margaret Whale, letter to Marion Urquhart, 16 December 1946, series 33, box 373, file '4P Scholarships Psychiatric', ARCS Archives, UMA).
16. *The Sun News Pictorial*, 2 April 1941 (reprint), box 13, Hoban Archive, UMA.
17. BSS minutes, December 1943, p. 84; February 1944, p. 88; May 1944, p. 98; March 1945, p. 130; UMA.
18. BSS minutes, December 1947, p. 192, UMA.
19. ibid., p. 192, UMA.
20. Lawrence, *Professional Social Work in Australia*, p. 118.
21. BSS minutes, February 1943, p. 59, UMA.
22. BSS minutes, October 1944, pp. 110–11, UMA.
23. BSS minutes, August 1945, p. 136; July 1946, p. 162; UMA.
24. BSS minutes, July 1974, p. 742, UMA.
25. Taylor was originally a New Zealander, but she spent most of her life in Australia.
26. Ruth Hoban, 'A three-year training for social work', *Forum*, vol. 4, no. 2, June 1950, pp. 1–2.

27 BSS minutes, April 1945, p. 130, UMA.
28 Dahrendorf, *LSE: A History*, p. 260.
29 BSS minutes, April 1945, p. 130, UMA.
30 BSS minutes, December 1945, p. 137, UMA. Elizabeth Wilmot later followed Vera Scantlebury Brown as head of Victoria's Maternal and Child Health Services.
31 Then known as Laurie Douglas, later McBriar and then O'Brien (BSS minutes, August 1945, p. 136; October 1947, p. 187; UMA).
32 Lawrence, 'Memoir', p. 115.
33 BSS minutes, June 1943, pp. 71–3, UMA.
34 BSS minutes, November 1943, p. 81, UMA.
35 BSS minutes, May 1951, p. 237, UMA.
36 BSS minutes, December 1949, p. 220, UMA.
37 Geoff Sharp, quoted in Lawrence, 'Memoir', p. 119.
38 I received one myself in 1959, and had friends who did transfer to psychology.
39 Carey, 'A transnational project?', pp. 58–9.
40 Ann Oakley, *Father and Daughter*, pp. 108–11.
41 BSS minutes, May 1948, p. 201, UMA.
42 Registrar Correspondence, folder 1952/953, UMA. After the death of her first husband, Arthur Howard Norman (of Norman Brothers, Pty Ltd, Melbourne printers and stationers) Jean Norman married professor of economics Richard Downing, becoming Jean Downing.
43 BSS minutes, August 1948, p. 204, UMA.
44 Ruth Hoban, 'Research report for the year ending 1960', box 9:1, Hoban Archive, UMA.
45 BSS minutes, February 1944, p. 94, UMA.
46 Theresa Wardell, box 6, Hoban Archive, UMA.
47 'Leonard Tierney, first and second year fieldwork reports', Student Folder, box 6, Hoban Archive, UMA. No third-year reports were found in the UMA holdings.
48 'Conference on supervision', 30 April 1946, box 14, Hoban Archive, UMA.
49 An idea suggested by Porter Lee a decade earlier.
50 Citizens Welfare Service Questionnaire, 1947, 1947/185, file 'CWS', pp. 5–7, Hoban Archive, UMA.
51 Fay Marles, *Aiming for the Skies: Leader in Social Welfare, Champion of Equal Opportunity*, Melbourne: Miegunyah Press, 2012, p. 37.
52 Marles, *Aiming for the Skies*, p. 37.
53 BSS minutes, May 1946, p. 146, UMA.
54 BSS minutes, May 1947, p. 183, UMA.
55 CWS minutes, August 1948, p. 148, Citizens Welfare Service Victoria, 1941–1960, 1980.0087, UMA.
56 Ruth Hoban, 'Notes AASW Vic Branch Meeting', 6 March 1958, box 30, Hoban Archive, UMA.
57 See Scott and Miller (eds), *A Love of Truth and a Love of Service*.

58 E.R. Hoban, 'Director's report (department of social studies)', BSS minutes, December 1959, pp. 138–43, UMA.
59 Joyce Grant and Len Tierney, 'An invitation to the introductory course on field work supervision', 4 September 1961, box 14, Hoban Archive, UMA.
60 Ella Dye, letter to Ruth Hoban, 10 July 1963, box 14, Hoban Archive, UMA.
61 Marles, *Aiming for the Skies*, p. 34.
62 BSS minutes, September 1955, p. 429; May 1956, p. 8; UMA.
63 Lois Hobson was later Lois Bryson; Barbara Beatty became Barbara Spalding.
64 Barbara Spalding (née Beatty), discussion with the author, February 2015.
65 Ruth Hoban, *The Future Development of Social Studies Courses in the Australian Universities*, University of Melbourne, 1963.
66 Horsburgh, *Doing Good Well*, p. 20.
67 BSS minutes, June 1943, p. 68, UMA.
68 BSS minutes, May 1944, p. 98, UMA.
69 Secretary general of Australian Red Cross Society (ARCS), letter to Lady Owen, 1 October 1945, series 33, box 326, ARCS Archives, UMA. Psychiatric social work included the four scholarships for the Mental Health Certificate at the LSE.
70 Secretary general, ARCS, letter to executive officer, Victorian Division, re Granting of scholarships, 8 May 1947, V61, box 19, 357, ARCS Archives, UMA.
71 Sir John Newman-Morris (national chair, ARCS), letter to Sir Robert Knox (Victorian chairman, ARCS), 18 July 1947, V61-347, file 'Social Service: General', 1944–1945, ARCS Archives, UMA. The travel grant was used to send Laurie O'Brien to London.
72 Hoban, letter to director-general, ARCS (Brown), 21 December 1945, series 33, box 321, file '4P Shortage Social Workers University Subsidies', ARCS Archives, UMA.
73 BSS minutes, May 1947, p. 185, UMA.
74 BSS minutes, May 1950, p. 227, UMA.
75 BSS minutes, July 1959, p. 117, UMA.
76 ibid., p. 123, UMA.
77 ibid., p. 123, UMA.
78 BSS minutes, May 1956, p. 5; December 1960, p. 169; UMA.
79 BSS minutes, May 1950, p. 224; December 1955, p. 432; UMA.
80 Hoban, *The Future Development of Social Studies Courses*, pp. 84–5.
81 BSS minutes, December 1960, p. 170, UMA.
82 Ray Brown (head of social work at the University of Adelaide), in Lawrence, 'Memoir', p. 136.
83 In Victoria alone, Monash University started a social work course in 1973, Preston Institute of Technology in 1974 (since subsumed by Royal Melbourne Institute of Technology, now RMIT University), and La Trobe University in 1975. New courses also sprang up in other states.

Chapter 8 – Winning and Losing: The Hoban Years

1. 'Record of interview', Ruth Hoban file 1950–1959, box 171, folder 2, Carnegie Corporation New York, Butler Library, Columbia University, New York.
2. Lawrence, 'Memoir', p. 121.
3. BSS minutes, September 1956, p. 10, UMA.
4. BSS minutes, July 1959, p. 117, UMA. Greig Smith retired from the Citizens Welfare Service in 1957 (Hoban, 'Stanley Greig Smith').
5. Boyce Gibson to John Lawrence, quoted in Lawrence, 'Memoir', p. 117.
6. Geoff Sharp, in conversation with John Lawrence, in Lawrence, 'Memoir', p. 115.
7. The universities of Adelaide and Sydney also had this anachronistic structure.
8. For example Miss Gaetjens, BA, from the YWCA, was appointed in 1942 (BSS minutes, December 1941, p. 29; February 1942, p. 34; UMA).
9. BSS minutes, July 1944, p. 107, UMA.
10. Livingstone, 'Personal record', box 204, folder 9, Columbia University Rare Books and Manuscript Library, Butler Library, Carnegie Corporation.
11. A.S. Livingstone, letter to Catherine Ford, 27 February 1956, p. 1, box 204, folder 9, 1–2, Carnegie Corporation, Butler Library, New York.
12. Livingstone, letter to Ford, p. 1.
13. 'From Dr. Merrick Jones small beginnings', *Newslink: The Annual Newsletter of the Institute for Development Policy and Management* (University of Manchester), no. 23, 2008–09, p. 5.
14. BSS minutes, December 1946, p. 178; May 1947, p. 183; UMA.
15. E.V. Eckhard, letter to W.B. Brander (Universities Bureau of the British Empire), 16 October 1946, Registrar's Correspondence, folder 1946/942, UMA.
16. Faculty Handbook, 1953, p. 5, Special Collections, UMA. BSS minutes, July 1946, p. 149; May 1947, p. 183; UMA.
17. 'Social studies appointments', in Professor Boyce Gibson, letter to the registrar, 15 November 1946, Registrar's Correspondence, folder 1946.942, UMA; Advice from Professor Gibson to John Lawrence, in Lawrence, 'Memoir', pp. 91, 115.
18. Player had been the last director of the VIHA before it was disbanded in 1950.
19. 'Social studies almoner and lecturer in medical social work, University of Melbourne', 3 December 1949, Registrar's Correspondence, 1949/941, UMA.
20. BSS minutes, July 1949, p. 214, UMA.
21. BSS minutes, December 1954, p. 404, UMA.
22. Alma Hartshorn, *Milestone in Education for Social Work: The Carnegie Experiment 1954–1958*, Dunfermline, Scotland: The Carnegie United Kingdom Trust, 1982.
23. Anne Heywood, 'Hartshorn, Alma Elizabeth (1913–2004)', in *Australian Women's Archives Project: The Australian Women's Register*, 2003, modified 2006, http://www.womenaustralia.info/biogs/AWE0528b.htm.
24. Ruth Hoban, letter to Florence Hollis, 24 December 1948, Social Studies Staff, Registrar's Correspondence 1948/1003, UMA.

25 Special Collections, Smith College Libraries, correspondence with the author, 27 April 2012.
26 Florence Hollis and Rosemary Ross Reynolds Papers, Sophia Smith Collection, Smith College Libraries, https://findingaids.smith.edu/repositories/2/resources/720/collection_organization.
27 Parker, 'Early social work in retrospect', p. 13.
28 John Medley, letter to Mary Hester, 25 January 1949; John Medley, letter to Mildred Kilinski, 1 March 1949; Social Studies Staff, Registrar's Correspondence, 1949/942, UMA.
29 Livingstone, 'Personal record'. Livingstone's itinerary took in Quebec, Montreal and Toronto in Canada, and in the US he visited Fritz Redl at Wayne University; Professor Grace Coyle at Western Reserve University; Paul Simon at Illinois State University; and Saul Bernstein at the Boston School of Social Work. He attended group work lectures at Boston George Brown University, and spent twelve months studying at Columbia University, including fieldwork at Hawthorne Cedar Knolls School, Manhattanville Center, and the Housing Research Division of the Community Service Society (A.S. Livingstone, lecturer, department of social studies, University of Melbourne), 'Report on a period of observation and studies in the United States and Canada, March 1949 – June 1960', p. 3, 1947–1957, 204.9, Carnegie Corporation Archive, Butler Library, Columbia University Archives, New York).
30 Livingstone, 'Report on a period of observation and studies in the United States and Canada', p. 3.
31 Arthur Livingstone, 'Group work', in *Australian Association of Social Workers Third National Conference, 24th–28th August, 1951*, Adelaide, n.d., item 7.
32 Scott and Miller (eds), *A Love of Truth and a Love of Service*.
33 'Len Tierney Social Work Travelling Award', Faculty of Medicine, Dentistry and Health Sciences, University of Melbourne, https://mdhs.unimelb.edu.au/study/scholarships/n/len-tierney-social-work-travelling-award.
34 L.J. Tierney, 'Letter to registrar, University of Melbourne, Application for readership in social studies', 31 July 1963, private collection of Michael Tierney (son).
35 Beyrer acted on the suggestion of Eveline Burns, with whom Hoban had established a friendship after her first sabbatical leave in 1951–52. Beyrer's qualifications were from Notre Dame and Indiana universities, with an MA from the School of Social Service Administration at the University of Chicago. He had connections with Columbia University School of Social Work and had worked for American Red Cross in Italy, in juvenile courts and public assistance, as well as having university teaching experience (BSS minutes, September 1960, p. 162, UMA).
36 'Fulbright lecturers and research scholars requested by the University of Melbourne for 1963: Associate Professor Ella Dye, University of Connecticut', file 'Fulbright, 1961/535', 'Nomination for Award' 1962/548, Registrar's Correspondence, UMA. Dye's referees included Beyrer, Harleigh Trecker and Gordon Hamilton.

37 'Personal', *The Argus*, 25 September 1920, p. 20; 'Dr. S.J. Hoban', *Brisbane Courier Mail*, 31 August 1931, p. 13. Nadine Slattery (client services consultant, Springvale Botanical Cemetery, Melbourne), email to author, 9 April 2014. Birth and death dates: Southern Metropolitan Cemeteries Trust, *Deceased Search*, https://smct.org.au/deceased-search.
38 Eileen Ruth Hoban/Crawford, Student record 260125, UMA.
39 Sue Donnelly (LSE archivist), email to the author, 16 April 2014.
40 She implies that the reason she received no marks at honours level was merely the lack of availability of honours courses in economics, whereas her university record shows that, in fact, she failed approximately one-third of her subjects on first sitting.
41 Ruth Hoban, letter to John Lawrence, 27 July 1958, John Lawrence personal archive, UNSW.
42 Ruth Hoban, *Social Services Survey, Covering Social Services Available to Residents of the Municipality of South Melbourne, Victoria, Australia, 1943*, Melbourne: City of South Melbourne, 1944.
43 Hoban, 'A three-year training for social work'.
44 Ruth Hoban, 'Report on sabbatical leave', p. 9, box 1, folder 4, 1981/0087, Hoban Archive, UMA.
45 Hoban, 'Report on sabbatical leave', p. 10.
46 ibid.
47 Hoban arrived in England in January 1952 and Edith Eckhard died on 9 August 1952. Eckhard had been due to retire aged sixty-five in June 1951 but her contract had been extended for an additional year. Hoban may not have had the opportunity to meet Eckhard.
48 Donnison, *Social Policy and Administration Revisited*, p. 255.
49 Richard Titmuss, in Smith, *Professional Education for Social Work in Britain*, p. 13.
50 Smith, *Professional Education for Social Work in Britain*, p. 53.
51 Hoban 'Report on sabbatical', p. 15.
52 ibid., pp. 14–18.
53 ibid., p. 14.
54 Hoban, letter to Stackpole, 26 November 1953, p. 2.
55 Ruth Hoban, 'Assessing the progress of students', box 14:2, Hoban Archive, UMA.
56 'No. 1. Director's report', BSS minutes, December 1959, pp. 138–43, UMA.
57 Austin, *History of Social Work Education*, p. 20.
58 Eileen Younghusband, *Report of the Working Party on Social Workers in the Local Authority Health and Welfare Services*, London: Ministry of Health, HMSO, 1959.
59 Eileen Younghusband, *Training for Social Work: Third International Survey*, New York: United Nations, 1958.
60 'No. 1. Director's report'.
61 Hoban, *The Future Development of Social Studies Courses*, p. 20.
62 ibid., p. 101.

Notes

63   ibid., p. 104.
64   ibid., pp. 2–4.
65   Austin, *History of Social Work Education*, pp. 29–31.
66   Eileen Ruth Hoban, handwritten notes for *Dictionary of International Biography*, 1991.0087, box 2, Hoban Archive, UMA.
67   Laurie McBriar (O'Brien), in R.J. (John) Lawrence, 'Memoir', vol. 2, p. 134.
68   Alison Player, quoted in Lawrence, 'Memoir', vol. 2, p. 145.
69   Beryl Thomas, quoted in Lawrence, 'Memoir', vol. 2, p. 139.
70   Len Tierney, quoted in Lawrence, 'Memoir', vol. 2, p. 141.
71   Kathleen Crisp (Lyra Taylor's deputy) quoted in Lawrence, 'Memoir', vol. 2, p. 143.
72   Marion Urquhart, quoted in Lawrence, 'Memoir', vol. 2, p. 144.
73   Audrey Rennison, quoted in Lawrence, 'Memoir', vol. 2, p. 106.
74   Kate Ogilvie, quoted in Lawrence, 'Memoir', vol. 2, p. 109.
75   Geoff Sharp, quoted in Lawrence, 'Memoir', vol. 2, p. 133.
76   Lawrence, 'Memoir', vol. 2, p. 178.
77   Lawrence, 'Memoir', vol. 2, pp. 153–4.
78   BSS minutes, September 1960, p. 162, UMA.
79   Fay Anderson, *An Historian's Life: Max Crawford and the Limits of Academic Freedom*, Melbourne University Press, 2005, p. 244.
80   G.B. Sharp in discussion with the author, 1 May 2014.
81   BSS minutes, December 1957, p. 72, UMA.
82   BSS minutes, December 1958, p. 87, UMA.
83   Sharp in discussion with the author.
84   BSS minutes, December 1958, p. 103, UMA.
85   BSS minutes, December 1958, pp. 90, 93, UMA.
86   They tried first for the library's space when the library function moved to the new Baillieu building, and then for other professors' houses on campus.
87   Sharp in discussion with the author.
88   Anderson, *An Historian's Life*, p. 329.
89   ibid., p. 329.
90   ibid., p. 330.
91   This inquiry had damaged the careers of a number of its witnesses, just as McCarthyism had done in the United States.
92   Anderson, *An Historian's Life*, p. 327.
93   ibid., p. 333.
94   ibid., p. 337.
95   G.W. Paton 'Memo: The University of Melbourne', 1 May 1962, box 2, Hoban Archive, UMA.
96   Anderson, *An Historian's Life*, p. 349.
97   ibid., p. 351. Crawford's philanthropy study was never completed, although boxes of notes and primary material on 'Development of a social conscience in Australia' remain in Hoban's archive at UMA.

98   Sir George Paton (vice-chancellor, University of Melbourne), letter to Ruth Hoban, 11 December 1961, box 2, Hoban Archive, UMA. Hoban was then located at 205 Royal Parade.
99   'Staffing in the department of social studies', box 2, Hoban Archive, UMA; BSS minutes, September 1960, p. 162, UMA. Robertson was concerned about leaving Singapore without a suitable replacement, but would have been aware of the troubles in the social studies department.
100 'Staffing in the department of social studies'.
101 Scott and Miller (eds), *A Love of Truth and a Love of Service*, pp. 33–4.
102 Life Membership Certificate, Victorian Council of Social Service, 1967, box 2, Hoban Archive, UMA.
103 Elizabeth Ozanne, memo to Alun Jackson and Dorothy Scott, 6 May 1996, supplied to author by Elizabeth Ozanne, author's collection, Melbourne.

Chapter 9 – The Post-war Search for Overseas Expertise

1   Georgia Travis, 'Fulbright scholar report', 1954, pp. 90–103, A1838 250/9/8/4/2 Part 2, file 'United States of America—Relations with Australia—United States Educational Foundation—General', National Archives of Australia.
2   Mildred C. Scoville (Commonwealth Fund, New York), letter to Miss Govan, 6 January 1944, in R.J. (John) Lawrence (ed.), *Norma Parker's Record of Service*, Sydney: AASW, Department of Social Work, University of Sydney, University of New South Wales, 1969, p. 63.
3   R.J. (John) Lawrence, 'In memoriam: A tribute to Norma Parker', *Australian Social Work*, vol. 57, no. 3, 2004, pp. 299–303.
4   Norma Parker's extensive contribution to Australian social work is covered in *Norma Parker's Record of Service*, a compilation of writings and extended curriculum vitae which was prepared by John Lawrence at the point of Parker's retirement in 1969.
5   Lawrence (ed.), *Norma Parker's Record of Service*, pp. 1–2.
6   Parker, 'Early social work in retrospect', p. 14.
7   Lawrence (ed.), *Norma Parker's Record of Service*, p. 4.
8   Norma Parker, 'Letter to AASW branch presidents', February 1954, AASW/Assoc of Hospital Almoners, 1990.0024, unit 16, UMA.
9   Rebecca Hegar, 'Transatlantic transfers in social work: Contributions of three pioneers', *British Journal of Social Work*, vol. 38, 2008, p. 723.
10 Norma Parker, letter to Hamish MacKenzie, 7 June 1949, p. 1, AASW/Assoc Hospital Almoners, 1990.0024, unit 18, UMA.
11 Lawrence (ed.), *Norma Parker's Record of Service*, p. 5.
12 Alice Garner and Diane Kirkby, *Academic Ambassadors, Pacific Allies: Australia, America and the Fulbright Program*, Manchester University Press, 2019, pp. 149, 154–5.
13 Lawrence (ed.), *Norma Parker's Record of Service*, p. 6.
14 'Social studies tutor Miss. D. Sumner arrives', *The Sydney Morning Herald*, 10 July 1945, p. 6.

15 Anthea Bundock, 'Taylor, Lyra Veronica Esmerelda (1894–1979)', in *Australian Dictionary of Biography*, vol. 16, Melbourne University Press, 2002, https://adb.anu.edu.au/biography/taylor-lyra-veronica-esmeralda-11831.
16 'Lyra Taylor interviewed by Marjorie Glasson in the Australian Association of Social Workers oral history project [sound recording]', 29 November 1971, transcript, pp. 4–6, National Library of Australia, https://nla.gov.au/nla.obj-193571266/listen.
17 'Lyra Taylor interviewed by Marjorie Glasson'.
18 Barbara Sturmfels, email to the author, 21 February 2017.
19 Len Tierney 'Tribute to the late Lyra Taylor', *Australian Social Work*, vol. 32, no 2, 1979, pp. 49–50.
20 Tuxen, in discussion with the author, 2004.
21 ibid.
22 'Report of chairman, National Social Service Committee to National Council Meeting', 18 December 1945, p. 2, series 33, box 326, file 'Red Cross 4P staff', ARCS Archives, UMA; 'Recommendation to National Executive', 16 October 1945, series 33, box 321, file '4P Shortage of Social Workers', ARCS Archives, UMA.
23 'Salaries 1945', ARCS, telegram to Lavarack, 17 October 1945, series 33, box 321, file 'Shortage of Social Workers—American Social Workers', ARCS Archives, UMA.
24 For example, Edith Newman and Miss Novogrod (secretary general), letter to Lavarack, 29 December 1945, series 3, box 393, file '4P Shortage of Social Workers'; Lavarack, letter to secretary general, ARCS, 30 July 1945, series 33, box 373, file '4P Shortage of Social Workers'; Lavarack, telegram to secretary general (Brown), 28 July 1946; Secretary general (Brown), letter to Lavarack, 3 November 1946, series 33, box 373, file 'Shortage of Social workers—American Social Workers', ARCS Archives, UMA.
25 Miss Elizabeth Anne Stringer, 'Reference from dean of students, University of Chicago', The School of Social Service Administration, 24 January 1946, series 33, box 373, file '4P Scholarships Psychiatric, 1946', ARCS Archives, UMA.
26 Marion Urquhart, File note of phone call from Kate Ogilvie, 26 March 1946, series 33, box 373, file '4P Shortage Social Workers—American Social Workers, 1946', ARCS Archives, UMA.
27 Miss Anne H. Morrison, 'Summary of educational background and work experience', copied 28 March 1946, series 33, box 373, 1946, file '4P Shortage Social Workers—American Social Workers, 1946', ARCS Archives, UMA.
28 Sybil Lavarack to director-general, 16 March 1946, series 33, box 373, 1946 file '4P Shortage Social Workers—American Social Workers, 1946', ARCS Archives, UMA.
29 Marion Urquhart, memo/letter to secretary general, ARCS, 29 March 1946, series 33, box 373, 1946, file '4P Shortage of Social Workers—American Social Workers, 1946', ARCS Archives, UMA.

30 Lavarack, letter to secretary general, ARCS, 15 April 1946, series 33, box 373, 1946, file 'Shortage Social Workers—American Social Workers 1946', ARCS Archives, UMA.
31 Secretary general, ARCS, letter to Lady Owen, 2 October 1945, MU:WS 4, series 33, box 326, file '4P Shortage of Social Workers—English Social Workers', ARCS Archives, UMA.
32 Hilda Owen, letter to secretary general, ARCS, 20 April 1946, Ref FL.304, ARCS 33/373, file '4P Shortage of Social Workers—English Social Workers', ARCS Archives, UMA.
33 Secretary general, ARCS, letter to Hilda Owen, 19 March 1946, 6, ARCS 33/370, file 'London Rep Correspondence Outward 1946', ARCS Archives, UMA.
34 Jean Robertson, letter to Marion Urquhart, 4 April 1946, ARCS 33/373, file '4P Shortage of Social Workers—English Social Workers', ARCS Archives, UMA.
35 Mrs Bryn Jervis-Reid (OBE), another British social worker with American links, offered hospitality to Georgia Travis in England in 1954 following her Fulbright year in Australia (Travis, *Round Peg, Round Hole*, p. 198).
36 Hilda Owen, letter to secretary general, ARCS, 4 June 1946, ref FL312 file 'Names of Selection Committee'; ARCS 33/373, file '4P Shortage of Social Workers—English Social Workers'; ARCS Archives, UMA.
37 Secretary general, ARCS, letter to Hilda Owen, 29 May 1946 (copy), FL309, Social Service Appointments, ARCS, 33/373, file '4P Shortage Social Workers—English Social Workers', ARCS Archives, UMA.
38 Secretary general, ARCS, letter to Hilda Owen, 29 October 1946, ARCS 33/373, file 'Shortage of Social Workers—English Social Workers', ARCS Archives, UMA.
39 Helen Rees, letter to National Red Cross, 27 March, 1945, ARCS 33/326, Red Cross Staff, file '4P, Mrs. Hepburn', ARCS Archives, UMA.
40 Secretary general, ARCS, letter to Hilda Owen, 19 June 1946, ARCS 33/373, file 'Shortage of Social Workers—English Social Workers', ARCS Archives, UMA.
41 Marion Urquhart, letter to Margaret Whale, 28 November 1946, ARCS 33/373, file '4P Scholarships Psychiatric 1946', ARCS Archives, UMA.
42 The basis of most of the following discussion is Dr Alice Garner's research on the American social workers who visited Australia, and her unpublished paper, 'Where Carnegie and Fulbright meet: Workshop—Melbourne University' (February 2010).
43 Garner, 'Where Carnegie and Fulbright meet', p. 5.
44 ibid., p. 4.
45 ibid., 12.
46 ibid., 12.
47 'Travis, Georgia Ball' (obituary published in *San Jose Mercury News* on 17 March 2002), https://www.legacy.com/obituaries/mercurynews/obituary.aspx?n=georgia-ball-travis&pid=259252&fhid=2112.

48 Georgia Travis, 'Notes on supervision', *Australian Journal of Social Work*, vol. 22, no. 2, 1969, p. 19.
49 'Travis, Georgia Ball' (obituary).
50 Travis, 'Fulbright scholar report'.
51 ibid.
52 Georgia Travis, 'On relationship', *Australian Journal of Social Work*, vol. 7, no. 1, 1954, pp. 20–31.
53 Travis, 'Notes on supervision'.
54 Australian Association of Social Workers, Victorian Branch, *Annual Report*, 1954, John Lawrence personal archive, UNSW.
55 Australian Association of Social Workers, Victorian Branch, *Annual Report*, 23 February 1956, John Lawrence personal archive, UNSW.
56 Australian Association of Social Workers, Victorian Branch, *Professional Education Committee Annual Report*, 1956, John Lawrence personal archive, UNSW.
57 'News from the field: Victoria', *Australian Journal of Social Work*, December 1960, p. 15.
58 BSS minutes, December 1960, p. 169, UMA.
59 This project is discussed in some detail in Scott and Miller (eds), *A Love of Truth and a Love of Service*, pp. 132–48.
60 Stewart, 'Psychiatric social work in inter-war Britain, p. 83.
61 Unfortunately, the LSE did not categorise its graduates by nationality, making it impossible to search its records specifically for Australians. Furthermore, as all the Mental Health Certificate holders were women, the problem of name changes arises. My list of Australians holding the LSE qualification (Appendix 17) is no doubt incomplete.
62 Until 1953 the 'Children's Hospital'. It received its royal designation almost twenty years after the Melbourne Hospital added royal to its name (Peter Yule, *The Royal Children's Hospital: Faith, Hope and Love*, Melbourne: Halstead Press, 1999, p. 375).
63 Joan Robertson in discussion with the author, 11 November 2010.
64 Kate Darian-Smith, *On the Homefront: Melbourne in Wartime, 1939–1945*, Melbourne University Press, 2009, p. 207.
65 Darian-Smith, *On the Homefront*, p. 233.
66 Nancy Vercoe, letter to Marion Urquhart, 18 December 1946, ARCS 33/373, file '4P Shortage of Social Workers—American Social Workers, 1946', ARCS Archives, UMA.
67 Georgia Travis, 'Fulbright scholar report', p. 11.
68 ibid., p. 13.
69 Lady Hilda Owen, letter to secretary general, ARCS, 13 November 1946; Urquhart, memo to secretary general, ARCS, 21 June 1946; series 33, box 373, 1946 Multiple Files, ARCS Archives, UMA.
70 BSS minutes, May 1948, p. 200, UMA.
71 Hegar, 'Transatlantic transfers in social work', p. 724.

72 Len Tierney, quoted in R.J. Lawrence, *Seeking Social Good: A Life Worth Living: An Autobiography in Six Volumes*, vol. 2, Sydney: The author, 2017, p. 141.
73 'Letter from Norma Parker, May 1960', in Lawrence, 'Memoir', p. 154.

Chapter 10 – A United Australian Profession

1 Oakley, *Father and Daughter*, p. 239.
2 Lawrence, *Professional Social Work in Australia*, p. 174.
3 The introduction of a national income security scheme gradually removed the role of social workers from direct provision of money and food vouchers, although it did continue until the 1960s in agencies such as the Brotherhood of St Laurence and the Citizens Welfare Service.
4 Management of health services was retained by the states.
5 *Second Annual Report of the Queensland Branch of the Australian Association of Social Workers*, Brisbane, 1947, John Lawrence personal archive, UNSW.
6 Hoban, *The Future Development of Social Studies Courses*, pp. 81–7.
7 Lawrence, *Professional Social Work in Australia*, pp. 79, 95, 172.
8 'Draft constitution of the Australian Association of Social Workers', John Lawrence personal archive, UNSW.
9 Norma Parker, 'Building the national professional association', in Lawrence (ed.), *Norma Parker's Record of Service*, pp. 140–3.
10 Lawrence, 'Introduction: Australian social work: In historical, international and social welfare context', p. 21.
11 Parker, 'Building the national professional association', p. 148.
12 Norma Parker 'Letter to Enid Lyons, acting president Social Workers' Association of New South Wales, 2 April 1946', in Lawrence (ed.), *Norma Parker's Record of Service*, p. 117.
13 Parker 'Letter to Enid Lyons', p. 117.
14 Parker, 'Building the national professional association', p. 148.
15 Lynne M. Healy, 'Introduction: A brief journey through the 80 year history of the International Association of Schools of Social Work', *Social Work and Society: International Online Journal*, vol. 6, no. 1, January 2008, pp. 115–27, https://ejournals.bib.uni-wuppertal.de/index.php/sws/article/view/98/160.
16 Social Service minutes, series 359/61, 1947, 2, ARCS Archives, UMA.
17 Conference into social workers, ARCS 392/33, Miss Urquhart, 1948, ARCS Archives, UMA.
18 'Report of Miss Marion Urquhart, national director of social service, on her visit to the USA', 33/392, file '4P Circulars, Conf International Conference Social Workers', ARCS Archives, UMA.
19 Alison Player, 'Miss Player's address to the Council of Social Service', *Forum*, vol. 3, no. 2, 1949, pp. 5–6.
20 F. Rowe (director-general, Commonwealth Social Services), letter to honorary secretary of the AASW, 23 July 1948, Victorian Branch, AASW/Assoc Hospital Almoners, 1990.0024, unit 14, UMA. Altmeyer was an advocate for the expansion of social security benefits in the US and had been involved in

drafting the original US *Social Security Act* in 1934 during the presidency of Franklin Delano Roosevelt.

21 H.M. James, 'The Sixth International Conference of Social Work, held at Madras, December 12–19, 1952', *Forum*, vol. 6, no. 5, 1953, pp. 31–50; Alison Player, 'Seventh International Conference of Social Work, University of Toronto, 27th June to 3rd July, 1954', *Forum*, vol. 2, 1954, pp. 27–8.
22 'Overseas experience of social workers', *Forum*, vol. 5, no. 2, 1951, pp. 6–8.
23 Alison Player, 'Possibility of employment overseas', *Forum*, vol. 1, 1954, p. 35.
24 Tuxen, in discussion with the author, 13 March 2004.
25 Teresa Wardell, 'Observing social welfare in the US and the UK', address to annual meeting of Victorian Branch of AASW, 24 February 1955, AASW/Assoc Hospital Almoners, 1990.9924, unit 16, UMA.
26 BSS minutes, May 1960, p. 149, UMA.
27 Leonor Flynn and Rosemary Flynn, 'In memory: Marjorie Awburn', *Entre Nous e News* (alumnae newsletter of Presentation College, Windsor, Melbourne), October 2011, pp. 8–11.
28 Kathy Sanders (née Adair, who worked in two London hospitals in the early 1960s), discussion with the author, 2020.
29 The conference committee was made up mainly of members of the AASW executive, who came from the three states where social work was being taught: Norma Parker, Katharine (Kate) Ogilvie, Dorothy Sumner, Amy Margaret Grutzner, Eric Troy and Viva Murphy from Sydney; Lyra Taylor from Melbourne; and Amy Wheaton from Adelaide.
30 Australian Association of Social Workers Conference Programme, 'The place of social work in Australia today', *First Australian Conference of Social Work, Sydney, September 5–7, 1947*, AASW/Assoc Hospital Almoners, Unit 18, 1990.0024, UMA.
31 With the exception of 1959 when, for unknown reasons, there was no conference. The tradition continues.
32 Lawrence, *Professional Social Work in Australia*, p. 121. A reading of the ARCS archives, BSS minutes and handbooks, and *Forum*, confirms Lawrence's assessment.
33 Marion Urquhart, memo to unknown recipient, 28 March 1945, Australian Red Cross Society National Headquarters Social Service, Library mu:mm (Marion Urquhart), series 33, box 327, ARCS Archives, UMA.
34 Urquhart, memo to unknown recipient, 28 March 1945.
35 Norma Parker, 'Foreword from the president of the Australian Association of Social Workers', *Australian Journal of Social Work* (formerly *Forum*), vol. 5, no. 1, 1951, pp. 1–2.
36 Lawrence (ed.), *Norma Parker's Record of Service*, p. 56.
37 Christine Bigby, 'Reflecting on 60 years of Australian social work', *Australian Social Work*, vol. 60, no. 4, 2007, p. 387. *Forum* started out as a modest publication produced inexpensively on an office Roneo machine. It was probably typed up by Jean Norman.
38 Bigby, 'Reflecting on 60 years of Australian social work', p. 387.

39 Jean Norman, formerly McGregor and later Downing, financially supported social work research at the University of Melbourne, and later made a substantial contribution to endowing the university's first chair of social work. She was awarded the university's prestigious Jocelyn Hyslop Medal in 2016.
40 Parker, 'Foreword from the president of the Australian Association of Social Workers'.
41 Director-general, Ministry of Post War Reconstruction, letter to secretary-general, Australian Red Cross, 27 August 1945, 33/373, file '4P Shortage of Social Workers General', ARCS Archives, UMA.
42 The titles, locations and dates of the national conferences are as follows: First National Conference of the AASW, Sydney, 1947; Second National Conference of the AASW, Melbourne, 1949 (followed by a refresher course in casework); AASW Third National Conference 'Social Work at Home and Abroad', Adelaide, 24–28 August 1951; Fourth National Conference of the AASW, Sydney, 2–6 October 1953 (followed by Refresher Course, 7–10 October); Fifth Australian Conference of Social Workers, Melbourne, 12–16 August 1955; Education for Social Work Sixth Biennial National Conference of the AASW, Adelaide, August 1957; no conference was held in 1959, to allow social workers to give maximum support to the first National Conference of Social Welfare; Seventh National Conference of the Australian Association of Social Workers, 'The Association and Social Work', Sydney, August 1961 (Lawrence, *Professional Social Work in Australia*, p. 188).
43 Ruth Hoban, letter to George Paton, UM 312, 1947/986, Hoban Archive, UMA.
44 Australian Association of Social Workers, Queensland Branch, *Third Annual Report*, Brisbane, 1948, p. 1, John Lawrence personal archive, UNSW.
45 Australian Association of Social Workers, Queensland Branch, *Second Annual Report*, Brisbane, 1947, p. 2, John Lawrence personal archive, UNSW.
46 Australian Association of Social Workers, Queensland Branch, *Sixth Annual Report for the Period Ending December 1951*, p. 1, John Lawrence personal archive, UNSW.
47 Joan M. McMeeken, *Science in Our Hands: Physiotherapy at the University of Melbourne, 1895–2010*, Faculty of Medicine, Dentistry and Health Sciences, University of Melbourne, 2018, pp. 185, 231.
48 Martha Morrison Dore, 'Clinical practice', in Feldman and Kamerman (eds), *The Columbia University School of Social Work*, p. 119.

Chapter 11 – Changing Themes in Social Work

1 Katharine Murphy, 'Brittany Higgins hospitalised and receiving support "after months of political pressure"', *The Guardian*, 4 June 2021, https://www.theguardian.com/australia-news/2021/jun/04/brittany-higgins-hospitalised-and-receiving-support-after-months-of-political-pressure.
2 Patricia Grimshaw and Lynne Strahan, *The Half-Open Door: Sixteen Modern Australian Women Look at Professional Life and Achievement*, Sydney: Hale and Iremonger, 1982.

3   Later the Victorian Society for Crippled Children and Adults, subsequently subsumed by the Yooralla Society.
4   Jane Nichols, 'The silent majority', *Australian Social Work*, vol. 26, no. 4, 1973, pp. 35–43.
5   Marles, *Aiming for the Skies*, p. 37. Years later, as Victoria's inaugural commissioner for equal opportunity (1977–87), Marles made an important contribution, employing Aboriginal staff to implement legislation against racial discrimination.
6   Heather Radi, 'Kelly, Emily Caroline (1899–1989)', in *Australian Dictionary of Biography*, Melbourne University Press, vol. 17, 2007, http://adb.anu.edu.au/biography/kelly-emily-caroline-carrie-12720.
7   University of Melbourne, *Dark People in Melbourne: A Study of Aborigines and Part-Aborigines in Melbourne*, Melbourne: Victorian Council of Social Service, 1950. This publication presented research carried out by the psychology and social studies departments at the University of Melbourne into the status of Aboriginal Victorians. It is further evidence that there was concern on the subject of Aboriginal welfare, but to a twenty-first century sensibility it provides a disturbing picture of prejudice and discrimination.
8   Eleanor Williams, 'Western Australia: A review of the welfare, progress and assimilation of Aborigines with particular reference to the position in Western Australia', *Proceedings of the Fourth Australian Conference of Social Work*, Sydney, 1953, p. 87.
9   Phillip Boas, Tania Harris (Coppel) and Rosemary Scoullar (Nairn) took turns as president of Abschol; Colin Benjamin, who was a little younger, played a leadership role later.
10 Reg Worthy and Barbara Erskine, 'Reg Worthy interviewed by Barbara Erskine in the Bringing them home oral history project (sound recording)', 1999, National Library of Australia, http://nla.gov.au/nla.obj-218237228.
11 Sally Morgan, *My Place*, Fremantle, WA: Fremantle Arts Centre Press, 1990.
12 *From the Heart*, https://fromtheheart.com.au/.
13 Cindy Smith (chief executive officer, AASW), personal correspondence, 11 and 12 October 2021.
14 Simon Gardiner, 'My brilliant career', *Children Australia*, vol. 45, no. 2, June 2020, pp. 74–9.
15 The doctorate of Elaine Martin (née Wilson), a history of social work at the University of Adelaide written from a feminist perspective, makes a contribution to this discussion (Martin, 'Gender, demand and domain').
16 Lawrence, 'In memoriam: A tribute to Norma Parker'.
17 'Should welcome D.P.s here U.N.R.R.A worker says', *The Sun* (Melbourne), 7 August 1947, p. 18; 'Celebrating our pioneers: A photographic record of Victorian social workers and others in the community services from the Depression years of the 1920s and 1930s until the end of the Second World War' (a project of the University of Melbourne, funded by the Lyra Taylor Fund of the Victorian Branch of the AASW, n.d.), author's collection, Melbourne.

18 Ann Oakley, *Women, Peace and Welfare: A Suppressed History of Social Reform, 1880–1920*, UK: Policy Press, University of Bristol, 2019.
19 Travis, *Round Peg, Round Hole*, pp. 198–201.
20 Feldman and Kamerman (eds), *The Columbia University School of Social Work*, p. 5.

Appendices

1 Georgina Sweet, letter to Mrs Norman Brookes, 25 April 1931, Australian Association of Social Workers, Association of Hospital Almoners, unit 26, UMA.
2 'Afternoon parties and gaiety to-night in welcome to Miss Hyslop', *The Star* (Melbourne), 7 December 1934, p. 12, copy on Victorian Council for Social Training Publicity and Correspondence file, AASW/Assoc Hospital Almoners, UMA.
3 Sources: BSS minutes, 22 February 1933, p. 2; September 1933, p. 18; February 1935, pp. 48, 49; UMA.
4 BSS minutes, inaugural meeting, 22 February, 1933, p. 2, UMA.
5 Mellor, 'Gutteridge, Mary Valentine (1887–1962)'.
6 Selleck, *The Shop*, p. 612.
7 BSS minutes, 22 February 1933, p. 1, UMA.
8 BSS minutes, July 1933, p. 13, UMA.
9 BSS minutes, 13 December 1940, p. 218, UMA.
10 Selleck, *The Shop*, p. 655.
11 BSS minutes, December 1940, p. 1, UMA.
12 ibid., pp. 1, 3, UMA.
13 BSS minutes, May 1950, p. 224, UMA.
14 BSS minutes, May 1960, p. 145, UMA.
15 ibid., p. 146, UMA.
16 Victorian Council for Social Training, *The Trained Social Worker*, Melbourne: E.J. Gay Print, 1937, p. 6 (copy on UM312, 1940/577, UMA).
17 Undated, but estimated as c. 1938 because of dates of other material in this folder. Copy of 'Prospectus', box 7, Hoban Archive, UMA.
18 Victorian Council for Social Training, correspondence with Teresa Wardell, 12 November 1942, box 3, Hoban Archive, UMA.
19 BSS minutes, October 1941, p. 24, UMA.
20 BSS minutes, August 1946, p. 166, UMA.
21 'Work submitted in connection with the recommendation for the promotion of Miss E. R. Hoban', n.d., box 2, Hoban Archive, UMA.
22 As a result of this survey, the municipality of South Melbourne appointed a social worker, Christina Thompson, who was a South Melbourne resident and by then a war widow.
23 Full details not known. Cited in 'Work submitted in connection with the recommendation for the promotion of Miss E.R. Hoban'.
24 'Research report for the year ending 1960', Box 7, Hoban Archive, UMA.

25 Ruth Hoban, 'Assessing the progress of students', box 14, 2, Hoban Archive, UMA.
26 Author's collection, Melbourne.
27 Box 6, 91/57, Hoban Archive, UMA.
28 'Director's report', BSS minutes, 17 December 1959, pp. 138–43, UMA.
29 'Director's report', BSS minutes, 17 December 1959, p. 143, UMA.
30 Eileen Younghusband, letter to Ruth Hoban, 25 June 1964, IASSW, Box 2, Hoban Archive, UMA.
31 Swithun Bowers, correspondence, 21 October 1965, IASSW, Box 6, Hoban Archive, UMA.
32 Hoban Archive, Boxes 4 and 10, UMA.
33 Hoban Archive, Box 2, UMA.
34 Details of these scholars have been obtained from Alice Garner's research records.
35 Lawrence (ed.), *Norma Parker's Record of Service*, p. 239.
36 Margaret Thornhill, 'Fulbright scholar report', 1954, pp. 179–87, A1838 250/9/8/4/2, Part 3, file 'United States of America—Relations with Australia—United States Educational Foundation—General', National Archives of Australia.
37 Australian Association of Social Workers, 'Victorian Branch Annual Report', 23 February 1956, John Lawrence personal archive, UNSW.
38 'Biography of Esther Twente', Personal Papers of Esther E. Twente 1937–1966, University of Kansas Libraries, Kenneth Spencer Research Library, https://archives.lib.ku.edu/repositories/3/resources/109.
39 Norma Parker, 'Obituary: Alice Overton', *Australian Social Work*, vol. 41, no. 2, 1988, p. 45.
40 Parker, 'Obituary: Alice Overton', p. 44.
41 'News from the field: New South Wales', *Australian Journal of Social Work*, vol. 13, no. 1, 1960, p. 20.
42 ibid., p. 12.
43 ibid., p. 12.
44 George Paton (vice-chancellor, University of Melbourne), Memo to university staff, 1 May 1962 (copy), box 2, Hoban Archives, UMA.
45 Dahrendorf, *LSE: A History*, p. 298.
46 '23 October 1952', Staff file 'Eckhard, E.V. (Miss)', LSE Archive.
47 Edith Verena Eckhard died on 9 August 1952 ('23 October 1952', Staff File 'Eckhard E.V. (Miss)', LSE Archive).
48 'Edith Eckhard and Lucy E. Beach visit to the USA', series 16, box 23, folder 258, 'Mental Hygiene England', Commonwealth Fund, Rockefeller Archive Center, New York.
49 Grace Dedman, '1946–1973: Reconstruction and integration: Social work in the National Health Service', in Baraclough et al. (eds), *100 Years of Health-Related Social Work*, pp. 21–47.
50 'Obituary', *Australian Social Work*, vol. 43, no. 11, 1989, p. 46.
51 ibid.

52 Lawrence, *Professional Social Work in Australia*, p. 116.
53 Ann Wee, 'Social work education in Singapore: Early beginnings', in Ngoh Tiong Tan and Kalyani K. Mehta (eds), *Extending Frontiers: Social Issues and Social Work in Singapore*, Singapore: Eastern Universities Press, 2002, p. 13.
54 Wee, 'Social work education in Singapore', p. 9.
55 Meeting of AASW Victorian Branch, November 1950, Unit 14, AASW/Assoc Hospital Almoners, UMA.
56 University of Glasgow, 'Jean Robertson', *The University of Glasgow Story*, updated 3 April 2013, https://universitystory.gla.ac.uk/biography/?id=WH3026&type=P&o=&start=0&max=20&l=.
57 Ruth Lee, 'Ogilvie, Katharine Florinda', in *The Encyclopedia of Women & Leadership in Twentieth-Century Australia*, Australian Women's Archives Project, 2014, http://www.womenaustralia.info/leaders/biogs/WLE0048b.htm.
58 Norma Parker, 'The early days: Beginnings of social work education in N.S.W.', in *Katharine Ogilvie, Social Work Educator, An Appreciation by Her Colleagues*, Department of Social Work, University of Sydney, 1965, p. 4.
59 Lee, 'Ogilvie, Katharine Florinda'.
60 R.J. (John) Lawrence, 'Ogilvie, Florinda Katharine (1902–1983)', in *Australian Dictionary of Biography*, vol. 18, Melbourne University Press, 2012, http://adb.anu.edu.au/biography/ogilvie-florinda-katharine-15399.
61 Jane Miller, 'The predominance of American influences on the establishment of social work education at the University of Melbourne, 1920–1980', PhD thesis, University of Melbourne, 2015, p. 287.
62 Martin, 'Gender, demand and domain'.
63 Nancy P. Bates, 'Wheaton, Amy Grace', in *Australian Dictionary of Biography*, vol. 18, Melbourne University Press, 2012, http://adb.anu.edu.au/biography/wheaton-amy-grace-15810.
64 'Obituary Margaret Elizabeth Grutzner 5.1.17 to 2.9.82', *Australian Social Work*, vol. 35, no. 4, 1982, p. 2.
65 Ruth Lee, 'Murphy, Violet Matilda Myrtle', in *The Encyclopedia of Women & Leadership in Twentieth-Century Australia*, Australian Women's Archives Project, 2014, http://www.womenaustralia.info/leaders/biogs/WLE0101b.htm.
66 'Alison Mathew interviewed by Marjorie Glasson', p. 5.
67 'Alison Mathew interviewed by Marjorie Glasson', p. 5; O'Brien and Turner, *Establishing Medical Social Work in Victoria*, p. 145.
68 Lawrence, *Professional Social Work in Australia*, p. 132.
69 Most of this information was derived from an address by Alison Mathew (née Player) entitled 'Recollections of professional practice', given at a seminar at the Royal Melbourne Hospital on 19 October 1979 (*Australian Social Work*, vol. 23, no. 4, 1979, pp. 21–2).

Bibliography

Archival and other primary sources

Author's collection, Melbourne

Includes personal photographs, records of interviews, some preliminary material from the University of Melbourne's 'Celebrating Our Pioneers' project, and personal and collected correspondence, including original letters from Jocelyn Hyslop to Edna Mendelsohn, 1944.

Columbia University Rare Book & Manuscript Library, Butler Library, New York

Collection: Carnegie Corporation Grants
Gibson, Alexander Boyce.
Hoban, Ruth.
Hyslop, Jocelyn.
Jacobs, Kate.
Lee, Porter (grant).
Lee, Porter (correspondence).
Livingstone, Arthur.
Prospectus/Correspondence with Victorian Council for Social Training.

Collection: Columbia University
Lee, Porter.
Vaile, Gertrude.

Community of the Resurrection, Grahamstown, South Africa

Memorial book in chapel.

John Lawrence personal archive (now at University of New South Wales, Sydney)

This collection is not formally catalogued. It includes original documents and records of interviews with social work leaders of the 1940s and 1950s, Lawrence's extensive personal correspondence, an unpublished personal memoir, and a range of rare and out-of-print journals and books.

London School of Economics and Political Science, Archives and Rare Books, LSE Library, London

Calendars: 1931–32, 1932–33.
Eckhard, Edith Verena, staff file.
Handbooks: 1952–60.
Hoban, Eileen Ruth, student record.
Hyslop, Jocelyn Sophia, student file.
LSE/Central Filing Registry, 1931–38 and 1942–46.

National Archives of Australia

Georgia Travis, 'Fulbright scholar report', 1954, A1838 250/9/8/4/2 Part 2, file 'United States of America—Relations with Australia—United States Educational Foundation—General'.
Margaret Thornhill, 'Fulbright scholar report', 1954, pp. 179–87, A1838 250/9/8/4/2, Part 3, file 'United States of America—Relations with Australia—United States Educational Foundation—General'.

Rockefeller Archive Center, Sleepy Hollow, New York

Commonwealth Fund Archives 1918–88: Series 16: English Mental Hygiene Program.

Royal Children's Hospital, Melbourne

Social Work Department Archives.

Smith College Libraries, Northampton, Massachusetts

Florence Hollis and Rosemary Ross Reynolds Papers, Sophia Smith Collection, https://findingaids.smith.edu/repositories/2/resources/720/collection_organization.

Michael Tierney (son of Len Tierney), private collection

Correspondence of Len Tierney.

University of Kansas Libraries, Kenneth Spencer Research Library

Personal Papers of Esther E. Twente 1937–1966, https://archives.lib.ku.edu/repositories/3/resources/109.

University of Melbourne Archives

Organisational records

Australian Association of Social Workers (AASW), 1981.0098; 1983.0080.
Australian Association of Social Workers (AASW)/Australian Association of Almoners, 1972.0026.
Australian Association of Social Workers (AASW) /Association of Hospital Almoners, 1990.0024.

Australian Red Cross Society (ARCS), Series 11, 12, 13, 14, 27, 33, covering minutes and correspondence 1920–61.
Board of Social Studies (BSS), minutes, 2000.0014.
Citizens Welfare Service Victoria, 1980.0087.
University of Melbourne, registrar's correspondence UM 312, 1940–1960.

Personal papers
Crawford, Raymond Maxwell, 1991.0113 and 2000.9936.
Gibson, Alexander Boyce, 1974.0017.
Hoban, Eileen Ruth, 1990.0087.
Tierney, Leonard James, 2008.0060.
Wardell, Theresa Mary, 1986.0123.

University of Melbourne, Baillieu Library, Special Collections

The Greig Smith Social Work History Collection.
University of Melbourne, Social Work Student Handbooks: 1952–60.

Records of interviews (unpublished)

Author's personal collection, Melbourne

Beatty/Spalding, Barbara, in discussion with author (notes), February 2015.
Eady, Lydia, in discussion with author (notes), 16 September and 29 November 2010.
Robertson, Joan, in discussion with author (notes), 11 November 2010.
Sharp, G.B., in discussion with author, 1 May 2014.
Tuxen, Joan, in discussion with author (transcript), 13 and 20 March 2004.

London School of Economics and Political Science

Bridge, Gill, in interview with Sonia Exley (transcript), 6 February 2013.
Donnison, David, in interview with Sonia Exley (transcript), 19 December 2012.

National Library of Australia

Mathew, Alison (née Player): 'Alison Mathew interviewed by Marjorie Glasson in the Australian Association of Social Workers Oral History Project [sound recording]', October 1972, https://nla.gov.au/nla.obj-193570456/listen.
Taylor, Lyra: 'Lyra Taylor interviewed by Marjorie Glasson in the Australian Association of Social Workers oral history project [sound recording]', 29 November 1971, transcript, https://nla.gov.au/nla.obj-193571266/listen.
Worthy, Reg, and Barbara Erskine, 'Reg Worthy interviewed by Barbara Erskine in the Bringing them home oral history project (sound recording)', 1999, National Library of Australia, http://nla.gov.au/nla.obj-218237228.

Private collection, London

Donnison, David (LSE), interview by Sonia Exley, 19 December 2012.

Newspapers, journals and magazines

The Advertiser (Adelaide)
The Age (Melbourne)
The Argus (Melbourne)
The Australian Women's Weekly
The Canberra Times
The Courier Mail (Brisbane)
The Examiner (Tasmania)
The Guardian (Australia edition)
The Herald (Melbourne)
The Mercury News (San Jose)
The Star (Melbourne)
The Sun (Melbourne)
The Sydney Morning Herald
The West Australian

Published sources

All websites were viewed in March 2021.

Addams, Jane, *Twenty Years at Hull House* (1930), US: Signet Classic, 1961.
Anderson, Fay, *An Historian's Life: Max Crawford and the Limits of Academic Freedom*, Melbourne University Press, 2005.
Anderson, Paul, *The Greig Smith Social Work History Collection: A Bibliography and Guide*, Melbourne: The Citizens Welfare Service of Victoria, 1987.
'Archibald Richard Frith Hyslop, warden of Glenalmond', *Glenalmond Chronicle*, vol. 164, December 1902, p. 1.
Attlee, Clement, *The Social Worker*, London: G. Bell and Sons, 1920.
Austin, David M., *History of Social Work Education*, Social School of Social Work, University of Texas, 1986.
Australian Broadcasting Corporation, 'Melbourne named world's most liveable city for the fourth year running, beating Adelaide, Sydney and Perth', *ABC News*, 19 August 2014, https://www.abc.net.au/news/2014-08-19/melbourne-worlds-most-liveable-city-for-the-fourth-year-running/5681014.
Australian Bureau of Statistics, 'History of pensions and other benefits in Australia', *1301.0 Year Book Australia*, 1988, updated June 2019, pp. 1–4, https://www.abs.gov.au/AUSSTATS/abs@.nsf/3d68c56307742d8fca257090002029cd/8e72c4526a94aaedca2569de00296978!OpenDocument.
——, 'Regional population' (2018–19 financial year), published 25 March 2020, https://www.abs.gov.au/statistics/people/population/regional-population/2018-19.
Australian Dictionary of Biography, University of Melbourne Press, 1966–, now managed by the National Centre of Biography, Australian National University, Canberra; see http://www.adb.anu.edu.au.
Baker, Ron, 'In praise of social work practice', *Australian Social Work*, vol. 31, no. 2, 1978, pp. 5–13.

Bibliography

Baraclough, Joan, et al. (eds), *100 Years of Health-Related Social Work, 1895–1995; Then–Now–Onwards*, Birmingham, UK: British Association of Social Workers Trading, 1996.

Barker, Robert L., *Milestones in the Development of Social Work and Social Welfare*, Washington, DC: NASW Press, 1999.

Bartlett, Harriet, 'Ida M. Cannon: Pioneer in medical social work', *Social Service Review*, vol. 49, no. 2, 1975, pp. 208–298.

Bates, Nancy P., 'Wheaton, Amy Grace', in *Australian Dictionary of Biography*, vol. 18, Melbourne University Press, 2012, http://adb.anu.edu.au/biography/wheaton-amy-grace-15810.

Bigby, Christine, 'Reflecting on 60 years of Australian social work', *Australian Social Work*, vol. 60, no. 4, 2007, pp. 387–90.

Boas, Phillip, and Jim Crawley (eds), *Social Work in Australia: Responses to a Changing Context*, Melbourne: Australian International Press in association with the Australian Association of Social Workers, 1976.

Braithwaite, Rose Mary, 'Foreword', in Alma Hartshorn, *Milestone in Education for Social Work: The Carnegie Experiment, 1954–1958*, Dunfermline, Scotland: The Carnegie United Kingdom Trust, 1982, pp. vii–x.

British Life and Thought: An Illustrated Survey, London: British Council, Longmans and Green, 1940.

Browne, Elspeth, *Tradition and Change: Hospital Social Work in New South Wales*, Sydney: Australian Association of Social Workers, New South Wales Branch, 1996.

Bulmer, Martin, 'The development of sociology and of empirical social research in Britain', in Martin Bulmer (ed.), *Essays on the History of British Sociological Research*, Cambridge University Press, 1985, pp. 1–31.

Bulmer, Martin, (ed.), *Essays on the History of British Sociological Research*, Cambridge University Press, 1985.

Bundock, Anthea, 'Taylor, Lyra Veronica Esmerelda (1894–1979)', in *Australian Dictionary of Biography*, vol. 16, Melbourne University Press, 2002, https://adb.anu.edu.au/biography/taylor-lyra-veronica-esmeralda-11831.

Burnham, David, 'Selective memory: A note on social work historiography', *British Journal of Social Work*, vol. 41, 2011, pp. 5–21.

——, *The Social Worker Speaks: A History of Social Workers Through the Twentieth Century*, Surrey, England: Ashgate, 2012.

Burt, Mike, 'Social work occupations in England, 1900–39: Changing the focus', *International Social Work*, vol. 51, no. 6, 2008, pp. 749–62.

Carey, Jane, 'A transnational project? Women and gender in the social sciences in Australia, 1890–1945', *Women's History Review*, vol. 18, no. 1, 2009, pp. 45–69.

Charlesworth, Max, 'Gibson, Alexander Boyce (Sandy) (1900–1972)', in *Australian Dictionary of Biography*, vol. 14, Melbourne University Press, 1966, https://adb.anu.edu.au/biography/gibson-alexander-boyce-sandy-10295.

Clotfelter, Charles T., and Thomas Ehrlich (eds), *Philanthropy and the Nonprofit Sector in a Changing America*, Indianapolis: Indiana University Press, 1999.

Cole, Margaret (ed.), *The Webbs and their Work*, London: Frederick Miller, 1949.

Crawford, Frances, and Sabina Leitman, 'The shaping of West Australian social work 1920–1970', *Australian Social Work*, vol. 54, no. 3, 2001, pp. 31–54.
Cree, Viviene E., *From Public Streets to Private Lives*, England: Avebury, 1995.
——, 'Introduction: Reading social work', in Vivienne E. Cree (ed.), *Social Work: A Reader*, Oxon: Routledge, 2011, pp. 1–8.
Cree, Viviene E. (ed.), *Social Work: A Reader*, Oxon: Routledge, 2011.
Cree, Viviene E., and Steve Myers (eds), *Social Work: Making a Difference*, Bristol: Policy Press, 2008.
Crocker, Ruth, 'From gift to foundation: The philanthropic lives of Mrs. Russell Sage', in Lawrence J. Friedman and Mark D. McGarvie (eds), *Charity, Philanthropy, and Civility in American History*, New York: Cambridge University Press, pp. 199–215.
——, *Mrs. Russell Sage: Women's Activism and Philanthropy in Gilded Age and Progressive America*, Bloomington: Indiana University Press, 2006.
Dadswell, Gordon, 'The Workers' Educational Association of Victoria and the University of Melbourne: A clash of purpose?', *Australian Journal of Adult Learning*, vol. 45, no. 3, November 2005, pp. 331–51.
Dahrendorf, Ralf, *LSE: A History of the London School of Economics and Political Science, 1895–1995*, Oxford University Press, 1995.
Danto, Elizabeth, *Historical Research*, New York: Oxford University Press, 2008.
Darian-Smith, Kate, *On the Homefront: Melbourne in Wartime, 1939–1945*, Melbourne University Press, 2009.
Davis, Fiona, Nell Musgrove and Judith Smart (eds), *Founders, Firsts and Feminists: Women Leaders in Twentieth Century Australia*, eScholarship Research Centre, University of Melbourne, 2011, http://www.womenaustralia.info/leaders/fff/about.html.
Dedman, Grace, '1946–1973: Reconstruction and integration: Social work in the National Health Service', in Joan Baraclough et al. (eds), *100 Years of Health-Related Social Work 1895–1995; Then–Now–Onwards*, Birmingham, UK: British Association of Social Workers Trading, 1996, pp. 21–47.
Dickens, Jonathan, 'Social work in England at a watershed—as always: From the Seebohm report to the Social Work Task Force', *British Journal of Social Work*, vol. 41, no. 1, 2011, pp. 22–39.
Donnelly, Sue, 'A life of social work and friends—Eileen Younghusband', blog entry, LSE, 27 February 2017, https://blogs.lse.ac.uk/lsehistory/2017/02/27/a-life-of-social-work-and-friends-eileen-younghusband/.
Donnison, David, *Social Policy and Administration Revisited: Studies in the Development of Social Services at the Local Level*, London: George Allen and Unwin, 1975.
Dore, Martha Morrison, 'Clinical practice', in Ronald A. Feldman and Sheila B. Kamerman (eds), *The Columbia University School of Social Work: A Centennial Celebration*, New York: Columbia University Press, 2011, pp. 117–45.
Eckard, Edith, *The Mother and the Infant*, London: Bell and Sons, 1921.
Ehrenreich, John H., *The Altruistic Imagination: A History of Social Work and Social Policy in the United States*, Ithaca and London: Cornell University Press, 1985.
Feldman, Ronald A., and Sheila B. Kamerman (eds), *The Columbia University School of Social Work: A Centennial Celebration*, New York: Columbia University Press, 2011.

Ferrard, M.L., 'Notes on the psychiatric treatment of mental hospital patients: Four paranoid schizophrenics', *British Journal of Psychiatric Social Work*, vol. 1, no. 1, 1947, pp. 45–56.

First International Conference of Social Work, Paris, July 8th–13th, 1928, Paris: Imp. union, 1929.

Fisher, Robert, 'Speaking for the contribution of history: Context and the origins of the social welfare history group', *Social Services Review*, vol. 73, no. 2, 1999, pp. 191–217.

Flexner, Abraham, *'Is Social Work a Profession?', Paper Presented at the National Conference on Charities and Correction, 1915*, New York School of Philanthropy, 1915.

Flynn, Leonor, and Rosemary Flynn, 'In memory: Marjorie Awburn', *Entre Nous e News* (alumnae newsletter of Presentation College, Windsor, Melbourne), October 2011, pp. 8–11.

Foley, Marcia, 'From social policy to social work: The antecedents and origins of mental health social work in Western Australia', PhD thesis, University of Western Australia, 2010.

Fook, Jan, Martin Ryan, and Linette Hawkins, *Professional Expertise: Practice, Theory and Education for Working in Uncertainty*, England: Whiting and Birch, 2000.

Friedman, Lawrence J., and Mark D. McGarvie (eds), *Charity, Philanthropy, and Civility in American History*, New York: Cambridge University Press, 2003.

'From Dr. Merrick Jones small beginnings', *Newslink: The Annual Newsletter of the Institute for Development Policy and Management* (University of Manchester), no. 23, 2008–09, p. 5.

From the Heart, https://fromtheheart.com.au/.

Gardiner, Simon, 'My brilliant career', *Children Australia*, vol. 45, no. 2, June 2020, pp. 74–9.

Garner, Alice, and Diane Kirkby, *Academic Ambassadors, Pacific Allies: Australia, America and the Fulbright Program*, Manchester University Press, 2019.

——, 'Where Carnegie and Fulbright meet: Workshop—Melbourne University', unpublished paper presented at *Philanthropy and Public Culture: The Influence and Legacies of the Carnegie Corporation of New York in Australia*, a workshop of the Academy of the Social Sciences in Australia held at the University of Melbourne in February 2010.

Garton, Stephen, *Out of Luck: Poor Australians and Social Welfare 1788–1988*, Sydney: Allen & Unwin, 1990.

Georgina Sweet Bursary in Social Studies, Department of Social Work, Faculty of Medicine, Dentistry and Health Sciences, University of Melbourne, https://mdhs.unimelb.edu.au/study/scholarships/n/georgina-sweet-bursary.

Gleeson, Damian, 'The professionalisation of Australian Catholic social welfare, 1920–1985', PhD thesis, Sydney: University of New South Wales, 2006.

——, 'Some new perspectives on early Australian social work', *Australian Social Work*, vol. 61, no. 3, 2008, pp. 207–25.

Greenwood, Ernest, 'Attributes of a profession', *Social Work*, vol. 1, no. 3, 1957, p. 54.

Grimshaw, Patricia, and Lynne Strahan, *The Half Open Door: Sixteen Modern Australian Women Look at Professional Life and Achievement*, Sydney: Hale and Iremonger, 1982.

Harris, John S., 'State social work: Constructing the present from moments in the past', *British Journal of Social Work*, vol. 38, 2008, pp. 662–79.

Hartshorn, Alma, *Milestone in Education for Social Work: The Carnegie Experiment, 1954–1958*, Dunfermline, Scotland: The Carnegie United Kingdom Trust, 1982.

Healy, Lynne M., 'Introduction: A brief journey through the 80 year history of the International Association of Schools of Social Work', *Social Work and Society: International Online Journal*, vol. 6, no. 1, January 2008, pp. 115–27, https://ejournals.bib.uni-wuppertal.de/index.php/sws/article/view/98/160.

Hegar, Rebecca, 'Transatlantic transfers in social work: Contributions of three pioneers', *British Journal of Social Work*, vol. 38, 2008, pp. 716–33.

Heywood, Anne, 'Clarke, Jessie Deakin (1914–2014)', in *The Australian Women's Register*, 2003, modified 2020, https://www.womenaustralia.info/biogs/AWE0623b.htm.

——, 'Hartshorn, Alma Elizabeth (1913–2004)', in *Australian Women's Archives Project: The Australian Women's Register*, 2003, modified 2006, http://www.womenaustralia.info/biogs/AWE0528b.htm.

Hoban, Ruth, *The Future Development of Social Studies Courses in the Australian Universities*, University of Melbourne, 1963.

——, *Social Services Survey, Covering Social Services Available to Residents of the Municipality of South Melbourne, Victoria, Australia, 1943*, Melbourne: City of South Melbourne, 1944.

——, 'A three-year training for social work', *Forum*, vol. 4, no. 2, June 1950, pp. 1–2.

Holbrook, Allyson P., 'Models for vocational guidance in Australia 1920s–1930s: American influence in conflict with British tradition', *The Vocational Aspect of Education*, vol. 41, no. 109, 1989, pp. 43–52.

Horsburgh, Michael, *Doing Good Well: Seventy Years of Social Work Education at the University of Sydney 1940–2010*, University of Sydney, Faculty of Education and Social Work, 2010.

'The hospital and the family', *The Other Half*, June 1929, pp. 14–16.

'Hospital social service: The work of the almoner', *The Other Half*, December 1929, p. 23.

Howe, Renate, *A Century of Influence: The Australian Student Christian Movement, 1896–1996*, Sydney: University of New South Wales Press, 2009.

Hugman, Richard, 'But is it social work?: Some reflections on mistaken identities', *British Journal of Social Work*, vol. 39, 2009, pp. 1138–53.

Hyslop, Jocelyn S., 'Angles of social service: Training Council's director urges expert attack on problems' real causes, aid for re-adjustment in the families', *The Hospital Magazine* (Charities Board Victoria, Melbourne), August 1938, pp. 7–9.

——, 'A philosophy of social progress', *The Australian Quarterly*, vol. 10, no. 1, 1938, pp. 38–43.

Hyslop, Jocelyn S., and Jean M. Robertson, 'Overseas reception scheme in Victoria', *The Australian Quarterly*, vol. 13, no. 1, March 1941, pp. 89–93.

'In memoriam Archibald Richard Frith Hyslop, M.A.', *Glenalmond Chronicle*, vol. 283, December 1926, p. 1.

'International conferences on social work', *The Other Half*, March 1936, pp. 10–11.

International Federation of Social Workers, 'Global definition of social work' (approved July 2014), https://www.ifsw.org/what-is-social-work/global-definition-of-social-work/.

James, H.M., 'The Sixth International Conference of Social Work, held at Madras, December 12–19, 1952', *Forum*, vol. 6, no. 5, 1953, pp. 31–50.

Jones, Kathleen, *Eileen Younghusband: A Biography*, London: Bedford Square Press, 1984.

Kahn, Alfred, 'Themes for a history of the first hundred years', in Ronald A. Feldman and Sheila B. Kamerman (eds), *The Columbia University School of Social Work: A Centennial Celebration*, New York: Columbia University Press, 2011, pp. 7–63.

Karger, Howard, 'Lessons from American social work education: Caution ahead', *Australian Social Work*, vol. 65, no. 3, 2012, pp. 1–15.

——, *The Sentinels of Order: A Study of Social Control and the Minneapolis Settlement House Movement, 1915–1950*, Lanham, Maryland: University Press of America, 1987.

Katharine Ogilvie, Social Work Educator, An Appreciation by Her Colleagues, Department of Social Work, University of Sydney, 1965.

Keep, Patricia, 'Allan, Stella May (1871–1962)', in *Australian Dictionary of Biography*, vol. 7, Melbourne University Press, 1979, http://adb.anu.edu.au/biography/allan-stella-may-4998.

Kendall, Katherine, *Social Work Education: Its Origins in Europe*, Alexandria, Virginia: Council on Social Work Education, 2000.

Kennedy, Richard, *Charity Warfare: The Charity Organisation Society in Colonial Melbourne*, Melbourne: Hyland House, 1985.

——, 'Some origins of social casework in nineteenth-century Melbourne', *Australian Social Work*, vol. 26, no. 2, 1973, pp. 5–7.

Kent, Raymond, 'The emergence of the sociological survey, 1887–1939', in Martin Bulmer (ed.), *Essays on the History of British Sociological Research*, Cambridge University Press, 1985, pp. 53–67.

Lawrence, R.J. (John), *Argument for Action, Ethics and Professional Conduct*, England: Ashgate, 1999.

——, 'In memoriam: A tribute to Norma Parker', *Australian Social Work*, vol. 57, no. 3, 2004, pp. 299–303.

——, 'Introduction: Australian social work in historical, international and social welfare context', in Phillip Boas and Jim Crawley (eds), *Social Work in Australia: Response to a Changing Context*, Melbourne: Australian International Press in association with the Australian Association of Social Workers, 1976, pp. 1–27.

——, 'Ogilvie, Florinda Katharine (1902–1983)', in *Australian Dictionary of Biography*, vol. 18, Melbourne University Press, 2012, http://adb.anu.edu.au/biography/ogilvie-florinda-katharine-15399.

——, *Professional Social Work in Australia*, Canberra: Australian National University Press, 1965. Page references in the present volume are to this original 1965 printed edition, although a differently paginated version is available online at https://press.anu.edu.au/publications/professional-social-work-australia.

——, *Seeking Social Good: A Life Worth Living; An Autobiography in Six Volumes*, Sydney: The author, 2017, https://www.rjohnlawrence.com/seeking-social-good.

Lawrence, R.J. (John) (ed.), *Norma Parker's Record of Service*, Sydney: AASW, Department of Social Work, University of Sydney, University of New South Wales, 1969.

Lee, Ruth, 'Murphy, Violet Matilda Myrtle', in *The Encyclopedia of Women & Leadership in Twentieth-Century Australia*, Australian Women's Archives Project, 2014, http://www.womenaustralia.info/leaders/biogs/WLE0101b.htm.

——, 'Ogilvie, Katharine Florinda', in *The Encyclopedia of Women & Leadership in Twentieth-Century Australia*, Australian Women's Archives Project, 2014, http://www.womenaustralia.info/leaders/biogs/WLE0048b.htm.

Leiby, James, *A History of Social Welfare and Social Work in the United States*, New York: Columbia University Press, 1978.

Leighninger, Leslie, *Creating a New Profession: The Beginnings of Social Work Education in the United States*, Alexandria, Virginia: Council on Social Work Education, 2000.

——, *Social Work: Search for Identity*, Westport, Connecticut: Greenwood Press, 1987.

'Len Tierney Social Work Travelling Award', Faculty of Medicine, Dentistry and Health Sciences, University of Melbourne, https://mdhs.unimelb.edu.au/study/scholarships/n/len-tierney-social-work-travelling-award.

Lewis, Jane, *The Voluntary Sector, the State and Social Work in Britain: The Charity Organisation Society/Family Welfare Association Since 1869*, Aldershot, UK: Edward Elgar Publishing, 1995.

Lewis, Verl, 'Historical studies and social policy analysis', *Contemporary Social Work Education*, vol. 1, no. 2, 1977, pp. 36–42.

——, 'Stephen Humphreys Gurteen and the American origins of charity organization', *Social Service Review*, vol. 40, no. 2, 1966, pp. 190–201.

Livingstone, Arthur, 'Group work', in *Australian Association of Social Workers Third National Conference, 24th–28th August, 1951*, Adelaide, n.d.

Love, R.J., 'Excerpt from "Notes and recommendations by the Inspector of Charities (Victoria) as to hospitals and other philanthropic institutions and organisations"', *V.P.P.*, vol. 11, no. 48, 1927, pp. 17–18, reprinted in Laurie O'Brien and Cynthia Turner, *Establishing Medical Social Work in Victoria: Discussion and Documents*, University of Melbourne, Department of Social Studies, 1979, pp. 65–6.

Lubove, Roy, *The Professional Altruist: The Emergence of Social Work as a Career 1880–1930*, New York: Athenaeum, 1969.

Macadam, Elizabeth, *The Social Servant in the Making: A Review of the Provision of Training for the Social Services*, London: George Allen & Unwin, 1945.

MacCallum, Monica, 'Sweet, Georgina (1875–1946)', in *Australian Dictionary of Biography*, vol. 12, Melbourne University Press, 1990, http://adb.anu.edu.au/biography/sweet-georgina-8728.

Macintyre, Agnes, 'Equipment for welfare work: The value of training', *The Other Half*, September 1931, pp. 96–9.

Macmillan, Margaret, *The Uses and Abuses of History*, London: Profile Books, 2010.

Marles, Fay, *Aiming for the Skies: Leader in Social Welfare, Champion of Equal Opportunity*, Melbourne: Miegunyah Press, 2012.

Martin, Elaine, 'Gender, demand and domain: The social work profession in South Australia 1935–1980', PhD thesis, University of Melbourne, 1990.

——, 'The importance of the trained approach: Social work education in South Australia, 1935–1946', *Australian Social Work*, vol. 36, no. 1, 1983, pp. 11–22.

——, 'Themes in the history of the social work profession', *International Social Work*, vol. 35, 1992, pp. 327–45.

Mathew, Alison, 'Recollections of professional practice' (paper given at a seminar at the Royal Melbourne Hospital on 19 October 1979), *Australian Social Work*, vol. 23, no. 4, 1979, pp. 21–2.

McMahon, Anthony, 'Redefining the beginnings of social work in Australia', paper presented at AASWE conference, Perth, 29 September – 2 October 2002 (a revised version was published in *Advances in Social Work and Welfare Education*, vol. 5, no. 1, 2003, pp. 86–94).

McMeeken, Joan M., *Science in Our Hands: Physiotherapy at the University of Melbourne, 1895–2010*, Faculty of Medicine, Dentistry and Health Sciences, University of Melbourne, 2018.

Mellor, Elizabeth J., 'Gutteridge, Mary Valentine (1887–1962)', in *Australian Dictionary of Biography*, vol. 14, Melbourne University Press, 1996, http//adb.anu.du.au/biography/gutteridge-mary-valentine10383.

Mendes, Phillip, 'The history of social work in Australia: A critical literature review', *Australian Social Work*, vol. 58, no. 2, 2005, pp. 121–31.

Miller, Jane, 'Building a professional discipline', in Dorothy Scott and Jane Miller (eds), *A Love of Truth and a Love of Service: The Social Work Legacy of Leonard Tierney*, Faculty of Medicine, Dentistry and Health Sciences, University of Melbourne, 2019, pp. 31–59.

——, 'The predominance of American influences on the establishment of social work education at the University of Melbourne, 1920–1980', PhD thesis, University of Melbourne, 2015.

——, (as Jane Nichols), 'The silent majority', *Australian Social Work*, vol. 26, no. 4, 1973, pp. 35–43.

Miller, Jane, and David Nichols, 'Establishing a twentieth-century women's profession in Australia: Jocelyn Hyslop, the little known story of the founding director of social work at the University of Melbourne', *Lilith, A Feminist History Journal*, vol. 20, 2014, pp. 21–33.

——, 'Moving among friends: The establishment of professional social work education at the University of Melbourne, 1929–1941', *Social Work in Health Care*, vol. 52, nos 2/3, 2013, pp. 110–24.

Moffatt, Ken, and Alan Irving, '"Living for the brethren": Idealism, social work's lost enlightenment strain', *British Journal of Social Work*, vol. 32, 2002, pp. 415–27.

Morgan, Sally, *My Place*, Fremantle, WA: Fremantle Arts Centre Press, 1990.

Morris, Cherry (ed.), *Social Casework in Great Britain*, London: Faber & Faber, 1959.

Morris, E.E., *Charity Organisation Societies: In England & the United States; A Paper Read at a Meeting of the Council of the Melbourne Charity Organisation Society, Held at the Town Hall, on Wednesday, 26th March, 1890*, Melbourne: Massina & Co., 1890.

Morris, Robert, Bess Dana, Paul Glasser, Rachel Marks, Martin Rein, Paul Schreiber, and Beatrice Saunders, *Encyclopedia of Social Work, Sixteenth Issue, Volumes 1 and 2*, New York: National Association of Social Workers, 1971.

Morse, Elizabeth J., 'Lumsden, Dame Louisa Innes (1840–1935)', in *Oxford Dictionary of National Biography*, 23 September 2004, https://doi.org/10.1093/ref:odnb/48571.

Musgrove, Nell, 'Teresa Wardell: Gender, Catholicism and social welfare in Melbourne', in Fiona Davis, Nell Musgrove and Judith Smart (eds), *Founders, Firsts and Feminists: Women Leaders in Twentieth Century Australia*, eScholarship Research Centre, University of Melbourne, 2011, pp. 130–48, http://www.womenaustralia.info/leaders/fff/about.html.

NASW Foundation, 'Charlotte Towle (1896–1966)', in *NASW Social Work Pioneers Biography Index*, Washington, DC: National Association of Social Work, https://www.naswfoundation.org/Our-Work/NASW-Social-Work-Pioneers/NASW-Social-Workers-Pioneers-Bio-Index.

——, 'Eveline Burns (1900–1985)', in *NASW Pioneers Biography Index*, Washington, DC: National Association of Social Workers Foundation, https://www.naswfoundation.org/Our-Work/NASW-Social-Workers-Pioneers/NASW-Social-Workers-Pioneers-Listing.aspx?id=137.

——, 'Gertrude Vaile', in *NASW Pioneers Biography*, Washington, DC: National Association of Social Workers Foundation, https://www.naswfoundation.org/Our-Work/NASW-Social-Workers-Pioneers/NASW-Social-Workers-Pioneers-Listing.aspx?id=177.

——, 'Mary Ellen Richmond (1861–1928)', in *NASW Pioneers Biography Index*, Washington, DC: National Association of Social Workers Foundation, http://www.naswfoundation pioneers/r/richmond.html.

Newman-Morris, John, *Social Work in Hospitals: Some American Investigations*, Melbourne: Victorian Institute of Almoners, 1930.

'News from the field: New South Wales', *Australian Journal of Social Work*, vol. 13, no. 1, 1960, pp. 12–20.

'News from the field: Victoria', *Australian Journal of Social Work*, December 1960, p. 15.

Nichols, Jane, 'The silent majority', *Australian Social Work*, vol. 26, no. 4, 1973, pp. 35–43.

Oakley, Ann, *Father and Daughter: Patriarchy, Gender and Social Science*, Bristol, UK: Policy Press, 2014.

——, *Women, Peace and Welfare: A Suppressed History of Social Reform, 1880–1920*, UK: Policy Press, University of Bristol, 2019.

'Obituary', *Australian Social Work*, vol. 43, no. 11, 1989, p. 46.

'Obituary Margaret Elizabeth Grutzner 5.1.17 to 2.9.82', *Australian Social Work*, vol. 35, no. 4, 1982, p. 2.

O'Brien, Laurie, and Cynthia Turner, *Establishing Medical Social Work in Victoria: Discussion and Documents*, University of Melbourne, Department of Social Studies, 1979.

O'Neil, W.M., 'Lovell, Henry Tasman (1878–1958)', in *Australian Dictionary of Biography*, vol. 10, Melbourne University Press, 1986, http://adb.anu.edu.au/biography/lovell-henry-tasman-7247.

Osborn, Hazel, 'One door, many mansions: 1974–1995', in Joan Baraclough et al. (eds), *100 Years of Health-Related Social Work 1895–1995; Then–Now–Onwards*, Birmingham, UK: British Association of Social Workers Trading, 1996, pp. 57–89.

The Other Half, vol. 2, no. 3, December 1929, front cover.
The Other Half, vol. 4, no. 1, 1936, p. 11.
'Overseas experience of social workers', *Forum*, vol. 5, no. 2, 1951, pp. 6–8.
Owen, Arthur D.K., 'British social services', in *British Life and Thought: An Illustrated Survey*, London: British Council, Longmans and Green, 1940, p. 173.
——, 'The social consequences of industrial transference', *The Sociological Review*, no. 29, 1937, pp. 331–54.
Paisley, Fiona, *Glamour in the Pacific: Cultural Internationalism and Race Politics in the Women's Pan-Pacific*, Honolulu: University of Hawai'i Press, 2009.
Parker, Norma, 'The beginnings of social work in New South Wales: A personal account', *Australian Social Work*, vol. 57, no. 3, 2004, pp. 217–22.
——, 'Building the national professional association', in R.J. (John) Lawrence (ed.), *Norma Parker's Record of Service*, Sydney: AASW, Department of Social Work, University of Sydney, University of New South Wales, 1969, pp. 140–3.
——, 'The early days: Beginnings of social work education in N.S.W.', in *Katharine Ogilvie, Social Work Educator, An Appreciation by Her Colleagues*, Department of Social Work, University of Sydney, 1965, p. 4.
——, 'Early social work in retrospect', *Australian Social Work*, vol. 32, no. 4, 1979, pp. 13–20.
——, 'Foreword from the president of the Australian Association of Social Workers', *Australian Journal of Social Work* (formerly *Forum*), vol. 5, no. 1, 1951, pp. 1–2.
——, 'Obituary: Alice Overton', *Australian Social Work*, vol. 41, no. 2, 1988, pp. 44–5.
Parnaby, Owen W., *Angus Mitchell: Rotarian and Peace Maker*, Melbourne: The author, 1998.
Pavlin, Helen, *Social Work in the University of Queensland: The First Twenty-Five Years, 1956–1981*, Brisbane: University of Queensland, Department of Social Work, 1981.
Payne, Malcolm, *The Origins of Social Work: Continuity and Change*, Hampshire, UK: Palgrave Macmillan, 2005.
Peel, Mark, *Miss Cutler and the Case of the Resurrected Horse: Social Work and the Story of Poverty in America, Australia and Britain*, University of Chicago Press, 2012.
Pierson, John, *Understanding Social Work: History and Context*, Glasgow: Open University Press, 2011.
Player, Alison, 'Miss Player's address to the Council of Social Service', *Forum*, vol. 3, no. 2, 1949, pp. 5–6.
——, 'Possibility of employment overseas', *Forum*, vol. 1, 1954, p. 35.
——, 'Seventh International Conference of Social Work, University of Toronto, 27th June to 3rd July, 1954', *Forum*, vol. 2, 1954, pp. 27–34.
Proceedings of the First Australasian Conference on Charity, Held in Melbourne, From 11th to 17th November, 1890, Convened by the Charity Organization Society of Melbourne, Melbourne: R.S. Brain, Government Printer, 1891.
Proceedings of the Second Australasian Conference on Charity, Held in Melbourne, from 17th to 21st November, 1891, convened by the Charity Organization Society of Melbourne, Melbourne: R.S. Brain, Government Printer, 1892.

Radi, Heather, 'Kelly, Emily Caroline (1899–1989)', in *Australian Dictionary of Biography*, Melbourne University Press, vol. 17, 2007, http://adb.anu.edu.au/biography/kelly-emily-caroline-carrie-12720.

Regan, Kerry, 'Fitzpatrick, Aileen (1897–1974)', in *Australian Dictionary of Biography*, vol. 14, Melbourne University Press, 1966, http://adb.anu.edu.au/biography/fitzpatrick-aileen-10194.

Reisch, Michael, and Janice Andrews, *The Road Not Taken: A History of Radical Social Work in the United States*, Philadelphia: Brunner-Routledge, 2001.

Richmond, Mary, *Social Diagnosis*, New York: Russell Sage Foundation, 1917.

Riis, Jacob, *How the Other Half Lives* (1890), Boston: Bedford St Martin's Press, 1996.

Rogers, Everett M., *Diffusion of Innovations* (5th edn), New York: Free Press, 2003.

Scott, Dorothy, and Jane Miller (eds), *A Love of Truth and a Love of Service: The Social Work Legacy of Leonard Tierney*, Faculty of Medicine, Dentistry and Health Sciences, University of Melbourne, 2019.

Scott, Dorothy, and Shurlee Swain, *Confronting Cruelty: Historical Perspectives on Child Protection in Australia*, Melbourne University Press, 2002.

Sealander, Judith, '"Curing evils at their source": The arrival of scientific giving', in Lawrence J. Friedman and Mark D. McGarvie (eds), *Charity, Philanthropy, and Civility in American History*, New York: Cambridge University Press, 2003, pp. 217–39.

Seed, Philip, *The Expansion of Social Work in Britain*, London and Boston: Routledge and Kegan Paul, 1973.

Selleck, R.J.W., *The Shop: The University of Melbourne, 1850–1939*, Melbourne University Press, 2003.

Shorney, David, *Teachers in Training: A History of Avery Hill College*, London: Thames Polytechnic, 1989.

Siddiqui, Ulrike, 'Brief history of PPSEAWA', PPSEAWA International: Pan-Pacific & Southeast Asia Women's Association, www.ppseawa.org/about-ppseawa/history.

Skehill, Caroline, 'Editorial', *British Journal of Social Work*, vol. 38, 2008, pp. 619–24.

Smith, James A., 'The evolving role of American foundations', in Charles T. Clotfelter and Thomas Ehrlich (eds), *Philanthropy and the Nonprofit Sector in a Changing America*, Indianapolis: Indiana University Press, 1999, pp. 34–51.

Smith, Marjorie, *Professional Education for Social Work in Britain: An Historical Account* (1953), London: George Allen & Unwin, 1965.

Smith, S. Greig, 'Fifteen years in retrospect: Social work achievements', *The Other Half*, April 1933, pp. 45–6.

——, 'The great and the small,' *The Other Half*, September 1926, p. 2.

——, 'Social work: The need for training', *The Other Half*, December 1930, p. 69.

——, 'Social work under the microscope: Some notes on the Third International Conference', *The Other Half*, April 1937, pp. 17–20.

Snelling, Jean, 'Medical social work', in Cherry Morris (ed.), *Social Casework in Great Britain*, London: Faber & Faber, 1954, pp. 81–103.

Social Service Department, National Headquarters, Australian Red Cross Society, *The Voluntary Society and Social Service*, Melbourne: Australian Red Cross Society, 1947.

'Social work: The need for training', *The Other Half*, December 1930, pp. 69–71.
Southern Metropolitan Cemeteries Trust, *Deceased Search*, https://smct.org.au/deceased-search.
Specht, Harry, and Mark E. Courtney, *Unfaithful Angels: How Social Work Has Abandoned its Mission*, New York: The Free Press, 1994.
Stevenson, Olive, *Reflections On a Life in Social Work: A Personal and Professional Memoir*, Buckingham, UK: Hinton House, 2013.
Stewart, John, 'Psychiatric social work in inter-war Britain: Child guidance, American ideas, American philanthropy', *Michael*, vol. 3, 2006, pp. 78–91.
'Student Christian Movement', *Clare Market Review*, March 1920, p. 30.
'Student Christian Union', *Clare Market Review*, December 1919, p. 8.
Swain, Shurlee, 'Destitute and dependent: Case studies in poverty in Melbourne, 1890–1900', *Historical Studies*, vol. 19, 1980, pp. 98–107.
——, 'The Victorian charity network in the 1890s', PhD thesis, University of Melbourne, 1976.
——, 'Writing social work history', *Australian Social Work*, vol. 61, no. 3, 2008, pp. 193–6.
Tan, Ngoh Tiong, and Kalyani K. Mehta (eds), *Extending Frontiers: Social Issues and Social Work in Singapore*, Singapore: Eastern Universities Press, 2002.
Tierney, Len, 'Tribute to the late Lyra Taylor', *Australian Social Work*, vol. 32, no. 2, 1979, pp. 49–50.
Timms, Noel, *Psychiatric Social Work in Great Britain, 1939–1962*, London: Routledge and Kegan Paul, 1964.
Titmuss, Richard, 'Introduction', in Marjorie Smith, *Professional Education for Social Work in Britain: An Historical Account*, London: George Allen and Unwin, 1965, pp. 11–13.
'"Tommy the Growler": A review', *The Other Half*, December 1930, pp. 71–2.
Toren, Nina, *Social Work: The Case of a Semi-Profession*, Beverly Hills, US: Sage, 1972.
'Training for social work', *The Other Half*, March 1930, p. 40.
'Training for social work', *The Other Half*, December 1932, pp. 33–4.
'Training for social work: An Australian experiment', *The Other Half*, March 1929, pp. 7–8.
Travis, Georgia, 'Notes on supervision', *Australian Journal of Social Work*, vol. 22, no. 2, 1969, p. 19.
——, 'On relationship', *Australian Journal of Social Work*, vol. 7, no. 1, 1954, pp. 20–31.
——, *Round Peg, Round Hole: A Life of Medical Social Work*, California: The author, 1993.
Trevithick, Pamela, 'Integrating theory and practice in social work: The development of a knowledge and skills practice framework', PhD thesis, University of Bristol, 2009.
University of Glasgow, 'Jean Robertson', *The University of Glasgow Story*, updated 3 April 2013, https://universitystory.gla.ac.uk/biography/?id=WH3026&type=P&o=&start=0&max=20&d=.
University of Melbourne, *Dark People in Melbourne: A Study of Aborigines and Part-Aborigines in Melbourne*, Melbourne: Victorian Council of Social Service, 1950.

University of Sydney, *Sydney School of Education and Social Work*, https://sydney.edu.au/education_social_work/about/history/social_work.shtml.

Victorian Council for Social Training, *The Trained Social Worker*, Melbourne: E.J. Gay Print, 1937.

Victorian Institute of Hospital Almoners Executive Committee, *The Origin and Development of Medical Social Work in Victoria, With Special Reference to the Work of the Victorian Institute of Hospital Almoners*, Melbourne: J.S. McClelland, 1950.

Walker, D.R., 'Sutton, Harvey (1882–1963)', in *Australian Dictionary of Biography*, vol. 12, Melbourne University Press, 1990, http://adb.anu.edu.au/biography/sutton-harvey-8721.

Warne, Ellen, Shurlee Swain, Patricia Grimshaw, and John Lack, 'Women in conversation: A wartime social survey in Melbourne, Australia, 1941–1943', *Women's History Review*, vol. 12, no. 4, 2003, pp. 527–45.

'We introduce ourselves,' *The Other Half*, June 1926, p. 2.

Wee, Ann, 'Social work education in Singapore: Early beginnings', in Ngoh Tiong Tan and Kalyani K. Mehta (eds), *Extending Frontiers: Social Issues and Social Work in Singapore*, Singapore: Eastern Universities Press, 2002, pp. 6–19.

Williams, Eleanor, 'Western Australia: A review of the welfare, progress and assimilation of Aborigines with particular reference to the position in Western Australia', *Proceedings of the Fourth Australian Conference of Social Work*, Sydney, 1953, p. 87.

Willmott, Phyllis, '1895–1945: The first 50 years', in Joan Baraclough et al. (eds), *100 Years of Health-Related Social Work, 1895–1995; Then–Now–Onwards*, Birmingham, UK: British Association of Social Workers Trading, pp. 1–11.

Woodroofe, Kathleen, *From Charity to Social Work in England and the United States*, London: Routledge and Kegan Hall, 1962.

Woodruff, William, *Beyond Nab End*, London: Abacus, 2009.

Wright, Katie, '"Help for wayward children": Child guidance in 1930s Australia', *History of Education Review*, vol. 41, no. 1, 2012, pp. 4–19.

Wykes, Olive, 'Morris, Edward Ellis (1843–1902)', in *Australian Dictionary of Biography*, vol. 5, Melbourne University Press, 1974, http://adb.anu.edu.au/biography/morris-edward-ellis-4251.

Younghusband, Eileen, *Report of the Working Party on Social Workers in the Local Authority Health and Welfare Services*, London: Ministry of Health, HMSO, 1959.

——, *Training for Social Work: Third International Survey*, New York: United Nations, 1958.

Yule, Peter, *The Royal Children's Hospital: Faith, Hope and Love*, Melbourne: Halstead Press, 1999.

Index

A

AASW *see* Australian Association of Social Workers
Abbott, Edith 24
Aboriginal and Torres Strait Islander people 203, 206–209
Abschol 207
academic standards 13, 88–89, 122
Addams, Jane vii, 12, 18–19, 94
Aesculapius Fund 54
age pensions 40
Alfred Hospital 39, 54, 62
Allan, Stella May (Vesta) 104, 211
almoner training 9, 23, 57, 126
almoners 2, 52, 53–54, 56, 60–66
    in London hospitals 25
    training 25, 60, 63–64
    See also medical social workers; Victorian Institute of Almoners; Victorian Institute of Hospital Almoners
Almoners' Institute 73, 74
almoning 25, 68
Altmeyer, Arthur J. 194
America, Americans *see* United States
American Association of Hospital Social Workers 102
American Association of Social Workers 30
American National Conference of Social Work 194
amputation, amputees 64, 173
anatomy 132
Anderson, Jean 56
Anglicans 121–122
ARCS *see* Australian Red Cross Society
Argus, The 39, 47, 104–105

Asian students in Australia 194
ASIO *see* Australian Security Intelligence Organisation
assimilation policy 207
Association of Schools of Social Work (US) 70
Association of Training Schools for Professional Social Work (US) 130, 153
Audley, H.F. 77
Australasian Conference on Charity 45
Australia 2, 3, 12, 93
Australian Association of Hospital Almoners 197
Australian Association of Social Workers (AASW) ix, x, 31, 37, 54, 80, 180–181, 191–196, 200–202
    conferences 196, 199, *plate 35*
    history yet to be written 210
    national journal 196–198
    participation in international profession 193–195
Australian Broadcasting Commission (ABC) 105
Australian Council for Social Studies 71–72
Australian Council of Schools of Social Work 70–71, 72, 199
Australian Dictionary of Biography 97
Australian Journal of Social Work, The 197–198
Australian Quarterly, The 88
Australian Red Cross Society (ARCS) viii, ix, 9, 56, 136, 137, 148, 172–179, 182
    Newman-Morris as chairman 101–103
    and psychiatric social work 126
    research required 210

Index

Australian Security Intelligence Organisation (ASIO) 161, 162
Australian Universities Commission 155
Australian Women's Weekly, The 105, 190
Awburn, Marjorie 181, 195

B

baby farming 45
Bachelor of Arts/Diploma of Social Work 61, 130
Bachelor of Social Work
    United States 30
    University of Melbourne 130, 132, 139, 163
Badger, Colin 90
Baptists 119
Barber, Alice 146
Barnett, Oswald 96
Barnett, Samuel 18
Basri, Mr *plate 36*
Beatty, Barbara 139
Beatty, Rowena 177
begging 41, 42, 45
benefits 40
    See also pensions
Benevolent Asylum (North Melbourne) 40
Bethune, Dorothy 63, 65, 70, 90
Better Times 51
Beveridge Report 197
Beyrer, Associate Professor J. Benjamin 149
Black Friday bushfires 82–83
Board of Social Service and Training (Adelaide) 67
Board of Social Studies (BSS) 10
    applied to Carnegie Corporation for a grant 95
    approached by ARCS 140
    budget problems 86–87
    changing role of 144–145
    conditions for students 86
    course commenced 65
    course renamed 79, 90
    course to University of Melbourne 65–66, 74, 75–76, 94
    establishment of 75–76
    financial viability of course 89
    funding issues for course 89
    lack of strategy for meeting demand 142
    looking to America for advice 78
    media/publicity 104–105
    members of 77
    opinion leaders 96–97
    promotion and fundraising 77
    reliance on donations 86
    research 87–89
    right to reject unsuitable students 89
    short-staffed 160
    staff became university employees 90
    staff expansion 145–146
    standards for course 24
    supervision problem 140
    university entry for course 89–92
Board of Social Study and Training (BSST) 53, 58, 61, 70
Boehm, Werner 155
Bonegilla 173
Bosanquet, Helen 15, 17, 21
Boston Psychopathic Hospital 26
Boston School of Social Work 26
brain drain from Australia to the UK 3
Brett, Joan 9, 63, 77, 96
Britain, development of social work in 15–16
British Association of Social Workers 26, 35
British colonies (before Federation) 40
British Federation of Social Workers 195
British Journal of Social Work 36
British Medical Association 102
Britton, Clare *see* Winnicott, Clare
Brookes, Ivy (née Ivy Deakin) 6
Brookes, Jessie (later Jessie Clarke) 6
Brookes, Mrs Norman (later Dame Mabel Brookes) 62–63
Brotherhood of St Laurence 87, 128, 158, 181
Brown, Dorothy 181
Brown, Dr Morven 61

Brown, Dr Vera Scantlebury 77, 81, 90, 96, 104, 205
Brown, Ray 147, 160, 181
BSS *see* Board of Social Studies
BSST *see* Board of Social Study and Training
Bulletin of Child Welfare League of America 51
Bulletin, The 161–162
bursary bequeathed by Georgina Sweet 99
Butler, Nicolas Murray 19

C

Cabot, Dr Richard 8, 26, 102, *plate 2*
Camp Pell 181
Cancer Institute 141
Cannon, Ida 26, 67, *plate 2*
Canon, Antoinette (New York School of Social Work) 102
Cardno, J.A. (psychologist) 61, 196, *plate 14*
Cardno, Mrs 177
careers for women graduates 6
Carlton (Melbourne) 39
Carlton Central and Local Repatriation Committee 49
Carnegie Corporation 30, 59, 78, 95, 152, 164–165
Carnegie Experiment 32, 33
Carnegie United Kingdom Trust 32
Carnegie, Andrew 36–37
Carrum Downs rehousing settlement 87
Case Conference (ed. Kay McDougall) 36
case studies, training of students in 136
casework 29, 70–71, 182
Catholic Church 58, 68, 104, 166
Catholic orphanages 40
Catholic University of America 166
Catholics 44, 64, 68, 104
Central Council of Benevolent Societies 65, 74
Centrelink 42–43
Charitable Institutions, Royal Commission on 46
charities 40, 41–42, 46–47, 50
Charities and the Commons 36
Charities Review (New York COS) 36
charity distinguished from social work 118
Charity Organisation Quarterly 51
Charity Organisation Societies (London) 17, 19–20, 22
Charity Organisation Societies (United States) 20, 46
Charity Organisation Society (COS) viii, 2, 8, 74
    adopting American COS methods and programs 47
    Aesculapius Fund 54
    aims 42–44
    coordinating services 41, 45
    developed policy 41
    employment register 45
    establishment of 39–40
    friendly visitors 41
    guide to charities 45
    in hospitals 54
    inquiry officers 41
    library 51
    link to Melbourne establishment 44
    lobbying 49–50
    paved the way for social work education 52, 56, 65
    providing social work service 62
    relationship with Alfred Hospital 54
    role in broad social issues 45–46
    and social work 52–54
    sought out best practice 54
    supported almoner training 63
    unemployment and work schemes 45
Charity Review, The 51
charity worker, untrained 5
Chicago World's Fair 17, 52
child abuse x
child care 205
    See also baby farming
Child Endowment, Royal Commission on 49
Child Guidance Development Centre, Travancore 83–84

child guidance movement 27, 37
  clinics 68
child labour 19
child welfare
  deinstitutionalisation x
  state responsibility for 40
Child Welfare Advisory Council, New South Wales 58
Children's Welfare Association of Victoria 49, 53
Children's Court 87, 117
  Clinic 136
Children's Welfare Act 49
Chile, social work in 16
China 16, 22
Christians *see* Baptists; Catholics; Methodists; Presbyterians; Protestants; Student Christian Union; Young Women's Christian Association
Citizens Welfare Service viii, 43, 136, 137, 149
City Newsboys Society 52
Clark, Manning 138
Clarke, Helen 127, 172, 182–183
Clarke, Jessie (formerly Jessie Brookes) 6
clients, social work 42, 187
climate refugees 209
Cold War 144, 161
College Settlement (New York) 18
Columbo Plan 194
commercial and industrial organisation in coursework 76
Committee for Social Training 94
Committee of Inquiry into Feeblemindedness 49
Committee on Social Education, London COS 20
Committee on Training for Social Work 75
Common Human Needs (Charlotte Towle) 32–33
Commons, The (Chicago) 36
Commonwealth Department of Social Services 130, 158, 170, 179, 181, 193, 196, 211

Commonwealth Employment Service 45, 193
Commonwealth Fund 27, 78, 182
  of New York 164–165, 168
  Standard Oil 37
Commonwealth Government
  funding social security and healthcare 190
Commonwealth Nutrition Enquiry 118
Commonwealth of Australia 40
communication between states 190
Communism 7, 21–22, 162–163
Communist Party 161
community centres 55, 137
conferences
  Australian 47, 50, 52, 196, 199
  Pan-Pacific 100
  See also specific conferences by name
Cook, Rosemary 177
Coombs, H.C. ('Nugget') 199
corruption, municipal 18
COS *see* Charity Organisation Society
Council for Training in Social Work 32
Council of Mental Hygiene 74
Council of Social Service, New South Wales 58
Council of Social Work Education (Australian) 70
Council on Social Work Education (US) 30
Covid-19 pandemic 42
Crawford, Max (professor of history) 90, 144, 159–160, 161–162
Crippled Children's Society, 136
Crisp, Kathleen 158
Cummins, Anne 26, *plate 8*
Cuthbertson, Joyce 177
CWS *see* Citizens Welfare Service

D

Dandenongs bushfires 83
Darling, Dr James 55
Davidson, Eileen 68, 69
Davies, Stella 60

Index

Davis, M.C. 70
Dawes, Anna 15, 17, 20
Dax, Dr Eric Cunningham (psychiatrist) 141, 183
Deakin, Alfred 6
Deakin, Ivy (later Mrs Herbert Brookes) 6
deinstitutionalisation of child welfare x
del Rio, Dr Alejandro 16
Department of Immigration 193
Department of Labour and National Service 140
Department of Mental Hygiene 183
Department of Social Services (Commonwealth) ix, 130, 158, 170, 179, 181, 193, 199
Department of Social Studies 134
Department of Social Welfare 183
dependency, permanent 41
depression (in 1890s) 45, 47
   See also Great Depression
destitute people 40, 41
Devine, Edward 23
Dickens, Charles 17
Dickens, Jonathan 37
Diploma in Social Studies 90
Diploma of Social Science (Adelaide) 68
Diploma of Social Service 125–126
Diploma of Social Studies (University of Melbourne) viii, 65, 75
disadvantaged people, institutional housing for 40
dole 4
'bludgers' and 'cheats' 43
Donnison, David 34
Douglas, Laurie 132
Dow, Betty *plate 31*
Downing, Professor Richard 160
drugs, lack of training on x
Duncan, Marion 174–175
Dunstan, Albert (premier of Victoria) 87
Duxbury, Alan 127
Duxbury, Patricia (née Holmes) 120
Dye, Professor Ella 137, 149, 179

E

Eady, Lydia 55
Eakins, Aimee 68
Eckhard, Edith 9, 10, 27, 33, 78, 120, 153, 186, *plate 7*
ecology, students introduced to 132
economics (in courses) viii, 76
Edinburgh, psychiatric social work courses in 27
Edwards, Eileen 81, 90, 146
Emergency Help Committee 177
Estonia 21–22
Evatt, Evatt, Dr H.V. *plate 22*
Exhibition Youth Centre 137
exploitation of women 100, 120

F

Fabian Socialists 21
factories, women working in 85
family casework, training for 125
Family Service Project 181
family social work, importance of 126
family violence, lack of training on x
Family, The (journal) 51, 197
Fancourt, Nancy *plate 32*
Federal Department of Social Services *see* Commonwealth Department of Social Services
Federal Select Committee on Social Security 49
Federation 21, 40
Feeblemindedness, Committee of Inquiry into 49
female professions 202
female workforce, attrition in 142
feminism 119–121, 204–205
Fidler, Isabel 58
field training 24, 55
fieldwork 134–138
   assessment of 135
   supervision 81
   training for viii, 24, 79
   tutor, appointment of 85
First Nations *see* Aboriginal and Torres Strait Islander people

Index

Fisher, Robert 4–5
Fishermen's Bend Community Centre 137
Fitzpatrick, Aileen 58–60, 70, 166, *plate 10*
Forum 131, 180, 183, 194, 195, 197, 198
  renamed *The Australian Journal of Social Work* 197
foster homes for refugee children 87, 134
Fox, Mrs A. *plate 35*
Free Kindergarten Union 96
Freudian ideas and theory 68, 128
Fulbright award/program 9, 26, 168, 178–181
Fulbright, J. William 178

G

gambling, problematic x
Gardiner, Simon 208–209
Gardner, Mrs Dunn 21
generalist training 12
generic social work, British/Australian and American usage 12
Gibson, Alexander Boyce (professor of philosophy) 56, 73, 76, 88–90, 103–104, 106, 144
Gibson, William Ralph Boyce (professor of philosophy) 103
gold rush, Victorian 38
Goodison, Marjorie 77
Govan, Elizabeth 60–61, *plate 12*
Grant, Joyce 137
Great Depression viii, 2–3, 7, 68, 75
Grey, William 44
group work 12, 66, 125, 128–129, 137, 145, 146, 167
Grutzner, Margaret 127, 172, 182, 191, 197, plate 33
Gunn, Professor John A. 77, 96
Gutteridge, Mary 96

H

Hanby, Elizabeth 177
Harkness family 10
Harkness, Stephen 37

Hartshorn, Alma 34, 147, 181, *plate 27*, *plate 35*
Hay, Lorna 128, 147, 182–183, 198
healthcare funding and responsibility 40, 190
Henderson, Lynette 63
Henry, Alice 52
Hepburn, Jean 178
Higinbotham, George 43
Hill, Octavia 18, 20
historians 4–5
HIV/AIDS epidemic x
Hoban, Eileen Ruth 143–163, *plate 9*, *plate 26*
  background and education 150–151
  study of social studies courses 141–142
  survey research 88, 136
  teaching 81, 86, 126
  views on supervision 136, 137
Hoban, S.J. 150
Hobson, Lois 139
Hodge, Isabel ix, *plate 20*, *plate 21*
Hollis-Taylor inquiry 30
Hollis, Ernest V. 30
Hollis, Florence 148
Holmes, Patricia 127, 183
home visiting, difficulties with 82–84
hospital admissions, disorganised 39
Hospital Social Service 51
Hospitals and Charities Act 49
Hospitals and Charities Commission 141
Household Living Conditions, Melbourne Social Survey of 88
housing 40, 181
Housing Conditions of the People, Royal Commission on the 49
Hughes, Constance 62
Hull House, Chicago 18
human behaviour as course title 131–132
human relationships skills 28
Hyde, Alice 146
Hyslop, Alice Sophie 110
Hyslop, Canon Archibald 110

Hyslop, Jocelyn vii–viii, 6, 106–123,
    plate 9
    achievements 12, 91–92
    adoption of American curriculum 8–9
    advice on future directions 121
    advocated American approach for
        teaching 66, 79
    background and education 110–113
    commitment to research 87–88
    philosophy of the individual in
        society 114–120
    on psychiatric social work training 126
    rejected charitable approach 42

I

illness, social and psychological effects of
    101
immigration 184, 193, 207
income support 42
India, social work courses in 16
Indigenous Allied Health Australia 208
Indigenous Australians *see* Aboriginal
    and Torres Strait Islander people
industrial organisation in coursework 76
Industrial Revolution 17
industrial welfare ix, 85, 129–130
infantile paralysis epidemic ix, 84, 102
inquiry officers, policing and detective
    work of 42
Institute for Development Policy and
    Management, University of Melbourne
    146
Institute of Hospital Almoners, New
    South Wales 60
institutions for disadvantaged people 40,
    76, 116
intelligence tests 133
International Association of Schools of
    Social Work 32
International Committee of Schools of
    Social Work 71
International Conference of Charities,
    Correction and Philanthropy 52
International Conference of Social Work
    16, 52, 93, 94, *plate 1*

International Congress of Charities,
    Corrections and Philanthropy 17
International Refugees Council 150
International Social Service ix
international social work profession
    94–96
international transfer of ideas 94–96
International Youth Conference
    (London) 148
invalid pensions 40, 49
Iron Curtain, cultural 184–188

J

Jackman, John 39
Jackson, Miss 177
Jacobs, Kate (Kit) 85, 90, 95
Jarrett, Mary 26
Jeffrey, Dr Alan 127–128
Jenks, Professor Edward 39
Jewish Charity 36
Jika Reformatory 44
JobKeeper and JobSeeker programs 42
Jones, Kathleen 34
journals of social work
    national ix, 8, 53, 196–198
    United States 35–36, 51
    See also Forum; Other Half, The
juvenile delinquency 27

K

Kelly, Caroline (anthropologist) 206
Kelso, Margaret 146
Kendall, Katherine 15, 18, 22–23, 33
Keppel, Frederick 59–60, 95
Kildonnan Presbyterian children's home
    126
Kindergarten Training College 96
kindergartens 56
Kydd, Janet 186

L

La Trobe University, new school of
    social work 201
Labor government, postwar 190
labour colony established by COS 45

Ladies' Benevolent Societies 40–41, 44, 84, 104
Larundel Psychiatric Hospital, 183
laundries, as training school for women 46
Lavarack, Lady Sybil 174
Lawrence, John 1, 67, 142, 159
Lee, Porter 28, 59–60, 84, 95–96, *plate 1*, *plate 3*
Leeds Babies' Welcome Society 111
Legal Women's Association 117
Leiby, James 18, 19
Leigh, Virginia *plate 29*
Len Tierney Social Work Travelling Award 149
Lend-A-Hand (journal) 36
Lethlean, Lois 77
Lewis, Kate 34
Lewis, Verl 1, 2
library of Australian Red Cross Society 197
living conditions, shocking to trainees 6
Livingstone, Arthur 10, 95, 145–146, 148–149, 159, 198
local authorities (UK) 25, 155
Loch, C.S. 22, 25, 47
Loch, Lady 44
Loch, Sir Henry Brougham 44
London County Council 111
London poor, desperate living conditions of 17
London School of Economics and Political Science (LSE) 21–23, 32–34
   debate on core education for social work 153
   Hyslop studied at 110–111
   injustices of gender 120
   Mental Health Certificate scholarships 127
London School of Sociology and Social Economics 21
London slums 18
Lord Mayor's Metropolitan Hospital Fund 49
Love, R.J. (inspector of charities) 62, 63
Lovell, Professor Tasman 58
LSE *see* London School of Economics and Political Science
Lyceum Club 78
Lynde, Edward D. 28

M

Macadam, Elizabeth 31
Macintyre, Agnes S. 9, 53, 56, 62, 63, 65, *plate 19*
MacKay, Dr Kate 146
Mackley, T.C. 48
Macmillan, Margaret 11
malnutrition 116
Manchester psychiatric social work courses 27
Marles, Fay 136, 138–139
Massachusetts General Hospital 26, 67
Master of Arts in Social Studies, University of Melbourne 139
Master of Social Work in the US 30
maternity allowance 40
Mathew, Alison 143
   See also Player, Alison
Maudsley, Sir Dr Henry Carr 96
McCallum, Peter 90
McCarthyism 185
McDougall, Kaye 34
McKenna, Senator 193
McKenzie, Hamish 146, 147
McMahon, Monsignor J.T. 68
media (BSS publicity) 104–105
medical care, free 25
medical social work 8, 25–29, 65, 125, 130
   See also almoning
medical social workers 26, 157–158
   See also almoners
Melbourne 3, 38–39
   See also University of Melbourne
Melbourne Church of England Grammar School 43
Melbourne Hospital 39, 53, 62
Melbourne Social Survey of Household Living Conditions 88

Mendelssohn, Edna 118
Mental Health Certificate (LSE) 9, 27, 28, 67, 96, 111, 182–183
Mental Health Certificate scholarships at LSE 127
mental health in social work curricula viii, 12, 27, 80
Mental Hygiene Authority 141
Mentally Defective Children, Travancore Residential Centre for 84
Methodist Central Mission 150
Methodists 99, 100, 150
Milestone in Education for Social Work (Alma Hartshorn) 34
Milford Conference 29
Miller, Jane 187
Mitchell, Angus 55
Moffitt, Constance 68, 69
Monash University school of social work 201
Morgan, Sally 207
Morris House 47, 50, *plate 6*
Morris, Cherry 26, 31
Morris, Professor Edward Ellis 8, 31, 36, 39–40, 43–48, 52
Morrison, Dr Anne 175–176
Morrison, Eve 198
Morrison, Martha 23
Mount Macedon bushfires 83
Muhl, Dr Anita 81
Murphy, Viva 191

N

National Association of Schools of Social Administration (US) 30
National Association of Social Workers (US) 30, 35
National Catholic School of Social Services (Washington) 68
National Committee for Mental Hygiene (American) 27
National Conference of Charities and Correction 8, 21, 24, 35–36
National Conference of the AASW 149, 199
national conferences, lack of in Britain 36
National Council of Women 58, 59
national curriculum 70–72
National Fitness Council 87
National Insurance, Royal Commission on 49
National Union of Australian University Students 207
Neglected Children's Department 40
networking between schools of social work 199–202
New South Wales Child Welfare Advisory Council 58
New South Wales Council of Social Service 58
New South Wales Institute of Hospital Almoners 60
New South Wales' Board of Social Study and Training (BSST) 53, 58, 61
New Statesman, The 34
New York School of Philanthropy 23
New York School of Social Work viii, 8, 9, 113, 148–149, 188
Newman-Morris, Dr John (later Sir John) 8, 16, 52, 56, 63, 71, 87, 94, 96, 101–103, 126–127, 140, *plate 17*
newspaper boys 49, 52
newspapers 190
Night Shelters 40
Noall, Mary 63
Nobel Peace Prize 19
Norma Parker Correctional Centre for Women 168
Norma Parker Lecture 166
Norman, Jean 134, 198
North American Council of Schools of Social Work 155
nutrition viii, 131, 132
Nutrition Enquiry, Commonwealth 118

O

Oakley, Ann (sociologist) 11, 33, 34, 119, 134, 189
Oeser, Oscar A. (professor of psychology) 133

Ogilvie, Kate 60, 158–159, 175, 191, *plate 11*
Oliver Twist (Dickens) 17
Onians, Edith 52
opinion leaders in Board of Social Studies 96–104
orphanages 40
Other Half, The (journal) 8, 36, 51, 52, 53, 97, 98, 105, *plate 5*
overalls (almoners' uniforms) 64
Overton, Alice 179, 181
Owen, Lady Hilda 174, 176

P

Pan-Pacific Women's Association 8
Pan-Pacific Women's Conference (1930) 94
Parker, Norma ix, 12, 60, 61, 68, 69, 165–169, 179, 181, 185, 188, 191, 193, 194, 196, 197–198, *plate 15, plate 16*
    background and career 166–167
    at the University of Sydney 144, 184
part-time staff 146, 147
patients in hospital, means testing of 63, 64
Paton, Mrs *plate 35*
Paton, Professor George (later Sir George) 79, 161, 162
Patriotic Fund, World War I 49
pauperism 41
Penington, Frances 77
pensions 40, 42
Pearce, Miss D. *plate 35*
Perlman, Helen Harris x–xi
person in environment 114
personnel work 129–130
Petrov Inquiry 161
Philadelphia Child Guidance Clinic 112
philanthropy
    American 35, 36, 164–165
    Victorian 162
Philanthropy, New York School of 23
Phillips, Dr Arthur 81, 126, 127, 146

philosophy
    of the individual in society 114–120
    of social work 181
    in social work courses 76, 133
physiology 76, 116, 131, 132
physiotherapy 202
Pines, Stella 66–67, 68, 69
Player, Alison x, 4, 6, 82, 126, 135–136, 146, 147, 191, 194, 195, *plate 26, plate 36*
Playgrounds Association 118, 137
polio 84, 102, ix, *plate 20*
political institutions in courses viii, 77
Poor Laws and Relief of Distress, Royal Commission on the 21
poor people, attitudes towards 41
Port Melbourne settlement 55
Portus, Dr G.V. (Jerry) *plate 22*
post-war reconstruction 129
postgraduate education, lack of 139
poverty viii, 17, 42, 47
practical work in courses 65, 70, 76, 77, 132, 135, 155
    See also fieldwork
practice and theory, integration of 72
prerequisites for social work students 81
Presbyterian children's home 126
Presbyterians 53, 126
preschools 118–119
Prest, Wilfred (economist) 88
Preston (Victoria), bushfires 82–83
Preston Institute of Technology 201
prisoners of war, former 172
probation officers, correspondence course for 31
Protestant orphanages 40
Protestants 64
psychiatric clinic, Royal Melbourne Hospital 128
psychiatric social work 25–29, 127–128, 183
    training for 125, 126
psychiatric social workers
    after World War II ix
    lack of 126–127

psychology viii, 28, 76, 132–133, 209–210
psychology department, University of Melbourne 132–133
psychosis 128
public administration, in proposed social work course 76
publicity for social work education 104–105

Q
Queen Victoria Hospital for Women and Children 62
Queen's Memorial Infectious Diseases Hospital 102

R
radio, used by social workers 190
rape crisis centres 206
recruitment of social workers 174, 176–178
Red Cross *see* Australian Red Cross Society
Red Cross Auxiliary, Melbourne Hospital 62
Rees, Helen 9, 10, 60, 63, 66, 70, 77, 177–178, 186, *plate 13*
Rees, Stuart (professor of social work) 61
referendum (1946) 190
refugees ix, 87, 209
relationships skills or therapy 28
Rennison, Audrey 9, 146, 158, 159, 186
research
    areas for future work 209–212
    by BSS 87–89
    role in social work course 133–134
    into social problems 55
Riall, Una 183, 198
Richmond, Mary vii, 12, 21, 23, 24, 28, 29, 79
Riis, Jacob 51
RMIT University 201
Roberts, Prof S.H. *plate 10*
Robertson, Jean 9, 85, 86, 88, 159, 163, 186, *plate 24*
Robertson, Joan 183

robodebt scandal 43
Rockefeller, John D. 37
Rorschach tests 133
Ross House 50–51
Rotary, support for settlement movement 55
Rowe, F.H. (director-general of the Commonwealth Department of Social Services) 193, 196
Royal Children's Hospital ix
Royal Commission on Charitable Institutions 46
Royal Commission on Child Endowment 49
Royal Commission on National Insurance 49
Royal Commission on the Housing Conditions of the People 49
Royal Commission on the Poor Laws and Relief of Distress 21
Royal Melbourne Hospital 64, 136, 137
    psychiatric clinic 128
Royal Park Psychiatric Hospital 126
Royal Perth Hospital social service department 68
Ruskin, John 18
Russell Sage Foundation 23, 37

S
Sage, Olivia 23, 37
Sage, Russell 37
salaries 175, 205
Salvation Army 41
Sambell, Joyce 137
Sand, René, Dr 16
sanitation 18–19
Sargeant, Delys 146
Scantlebury, Dr Vera 77, 81, 90, 96, 104, 205
scholarships 99, 111, 140, 141, 179, 181, 207
School of Social Service Administration, University of Chicago 24
school visitors 44
Scott, David 158

Scott, Emeritus Professor Dorothy xi
Scoville, Mildred 112–113
Scoville, Muriel 27, 165
Seebohm inquiry 25–26, 36
self-help 18, 50
settlement movement 17–19
   Australian 55–56
   British 18, 111
   connections with social work 2, 20, 32, 128
   relationship with Charity Organisation Society 20
'settlement' term not suitable for Australia 55
Sewell, Margaret 20
sexism *see* feminism; social work as women's profession; women
sexual assault, lack of training on x
Sharp, Geoff 147, 160, 161
Sharpe, Betty 186
Simmons College 26
Singleton Clinic 84
Sixteenth National Conference of Charities and Correction 46
Slum Abolition Board 49
Slum Abolition League 118
slums 17, 18, 82, 96, 99, 108, 111–112
Smith College school for psychiatric social work 26
Smith-Mundt scholarship 168
Smith, Barry 27
Smith, Hazel 69, *plate 23*
Smith, Marjorie 22–23, 153–154
Smith, Stanley Greig 48–52, 97–99, *plate 4*
   attended Third International Conference of Social Work 94
   BSS member 90, 96
   editor of *The Other Half* 8, 36, 51, 52
   honorary secretary of the VIA 63
   leader of COS 43
   teaching social work students 38, 53–54, 65, 77, 81
Smith, Zilpha Drew 24
social biology 131–132
social conditions, desperate (in the US) 26
Social Diagnosis (Mary Richmond) 23, 24
social dysfunction, causes of 114
social historians, interests of 5
social history viii, 132
social legislation, in proposed social work course 76
social philosophy 81
Social Policy and Administration Revisited (David Donnison) 34
social reformers in United States 18–19
social research in American Settlement movement 19
social sciences viii, 22, 37, 107, 133–134, 196
Social Security, Federal Select Committee on 49
social security, provision of 190
Social Service (journal) 197
social service rather than social science 79
Social Services Department, Commonwealth 136
social studies, applied (LSE course) 32
social theory in British social work education 16
Social Welfare Department, Victorian Government 141
Social Work (journal) 197
Social Work in Great Britain (ed. Cherry Morris) 31
Social Work Today 36
social workers
   as agents of social control 2
   cooperating between states 189–190
   demand for 139–142
   as distinct from untrained charity workers 5
   lack of academic pathways 138–139
   lack of, for fieldwork training of students 82
   middle class 3
   political leanings of 6–7
   where employed, in 1953 141–142

Social Workers' Association of New South Wales 191
sociological approach to social work 68
South Africa, social work courses in 16
South America, social work courses in 16
South Australia, establishment of social work course 66–68
South Australian Association of Social Workers 191
South Melbourne survey (Hoban) 151
South-East Asia welfare programs 193
Southard, Elmer E. 26
specialist fields of social work practice 125–130
Spence, Catherine 51–52
Spencer, Baldwin, Professor 100
St Paul Project 181
St Thomas' Hospital 62
St Vincent de Paul Society 41
Stackpole, Stephen 143
staffing 145–147, 205
Standard Oil's Commonwealth Fund 37
standards, academic 4, 13, 37, 70, 88–89
Starr, Ellen Gates 18
Stevenson, Olive 34
Stoneman, Ethel 68
Stringer, Elizabeth Ann 175
Student Christian Union 100, 111
substance abuse, lack of training on x
succession planning, lack of 139
Sumner, Dorothy 168–169, 191
Survey, The (journal) 36, 37, 51
sustenance' (unemployment benefit) 4
Sutton, Harvey (professor of medicine) 58, 71
Swain, Shurlee 5
sweated labour 116
Sweet, Dr Georgina (zoologist and philanthropist) 8, 55, 65, 73, 77, 94, 96, 99–101, 144, 204, *plate 18*
Sweet, George (Dr Sweet's father) 99

T

Taylor, Alice 30
Taylor, Graham 55
Taylor, Joyce 177
Taylor, Lyra ix, 136, 146, 158, 165, 191, 193, 194, 196, 200, *plate 25*
  career 169–172, 205
terminology, American/Australian/British 131–132
theory and practice, integration of 72
theory *versus* practical social work 22
Thomas, Beryl 146, 157–158
Thomas, Dr Lena 132, 146
Thomas, Elsie 177
Thomas, Rae 186
Thornhill, Margaret 179, 180
Tierney Social Work Travelling Award 149
Tierney, Leonard 9, 69, 137, 146, 147, 149, 163, 187–188, 201
Titmuss, Richard 33–34, 119, 153
Towle, Charlotte 32–33, 113, 195
Toynbee Hall 18
Travancore 83–84, 126, 136
Travis, Georgia 26, 179–180, *plate 34*
truancy 116
truth-telling 11, 189
Turana (children's home) 126
Turner, Cynthia 146
Tuxen, Joan 64, 82–83, 126, 173, 195, 205, *plate 30*
Twente, Esther 181

U

Uluru Statement from the Heart 208
unemployment 4, 45, 47, 48
United Kingdom *see* Britain; British
United Nations Relief and Refugee Administration 185
United Nations Relief and Rehabilitation Association 210
United Nations' Social Commission 32
United States
  Australian social workers seeking training 148

Australian views of 184–185
development of social work 15–16, 29
ideas transferred to Australia 93
Melbourne philanthropists' links with 47
models for Victorian social work education 8–9
search for direct transfer of expertise from 148–150
service personnel 184–185
social workers 174
University Extension Board 76
University Extension Movement 52
University of Adelaide 67–68
University of Connecticut 149–150
University of Melbourne
in the 1930s 75
adoption of British social sciences 9–10
attempt to recruit American staff 184
attracting Americans to work there 9
BSS course 65–66, 74, 89–92, 94, 160–161
lack of resources for social work course 80
role in the war effort 129
women students 75
University of Queensland 171, 200
University of Sydney 168–169
adopted American expertise 169, 184, 185
degree in social work 139, 210
role in the war effort 129, 211
settlement 56, 58
social work course viii, 1, 2, 7, 8, 57, 58, 60–61, 74, 129, 180
two-year diploma 139
University of Western Australia 69
University Women's Settlement 20
Urquhart, Marion 158, 175–177, 194, 200
Urwick, E.J. 22
US *see* United States
Uses and Abuses of History, The (Macmillan) 11

V

Vaile, Gertrude 70, 81, 85, 95
Vercoe, Nancy 184–185
Vesta *see* Allan, Stella May
VIA *see* Victorian Institute of Almoners
Victorian Association of Social Workers 191
Victorian Charities Board 102
Victorian Council for Crippled Children 102
Victorian Council for Mental Hygiene 65
Victorian Council for Social Training 90, 94, 102
Victorian Council of Social Service 206
Victorian Council of Social Services 163
Victorian Education Department 65, 74
Victorian Housing Commission 150, 181
Victorian Institute of Almoners (VIA) 62, 63, 64, 65
Victorian Institute of Hospital Almoners (VIHA) 52, 56, 65–66, 73, 76, 101, 125–126
Victorian Society for Crippled Children and Adults 64, 134
Victorian Society for the Prevention of Cruelty to Children 50
VIHA *see* Victorian Institute of Hospital Almoners
Visiting Committee for Industrial Schools 44

W

war effort 85, 129, 211
Wardell, Teresa 146, 195
wartime refugee children, foster homes for 87
Watt, Muriel 77
Webb, Sydney and Beatrice 21
welfare recipients, treatment of 42–43
Wesley Church 150
Whale, Margaret 127, 172, *plate 35*
Whatmore, A.R. (Alec) 141
Wheaton, Amy 67–68, 70, 71, 191, 196, *plate 22*

White House Golden Anniversary
    Conference of Children and Youth 195
White, Mary 177
Williams, Eleanor 206
Wilmot, Dr Elizabeth 132, 146
Winnicott, Clare 34
Witmer, Dr Helen 153
women
    exploitation of 120
    issues almost invisible 203
    paid less than men 205
    refuges for 206
    social work as profession for
        204–205, 209–210
    as social work clients 206
    status in universities 33
Women in Marital Conflict (Hollis) 148
wood yards for men requesting relief
    45, 46
Wood, Associate Professor Gordon L.
    76, 77, 96
Workers' Educational Association 76, 103
world view of the author 10–11
World War II ix, 3, 72, 85, 129,
    139–140, 184
    demise of Australian Council of
        Schools of Social Work 199
    impetus to social work 124–125
    post-war reconstruction 199
Wright, Roy Douglas (professor of
    physiology) 131
Wrigley, Professor Leslie (educationist)
    96

Y
Yeomans, Mernie 127, 172, *plate 28*
You Yangs bushfires 83
Young Women's Christian Association
    (YWCA) 8, 65, 74
Younghusband report 32
Younghusband Sir Francis 32
Younghusband, Dame Eileen 32, 33, 34,
    120, 153, 154, 155
youth work 27, 128
YWCA *see* Young Women's Christian
    Association

Z
Zilinskas, Dana *plate 27*

About the Author

Jane Miller is a retired social worker and life member of the Australian Association of Social Workers. She is the author of several books, including *Leading Social Work: 75 Years at the University of Melbourne* (2016), and co-editor (with Dorothy Scott) of *A Love of Truth and a Love of Service: The Social Work Legacy of Leonard Tierney* (2019). Her work appears in a range of print and online publications, including on the London School of Economics and Politics website. Jane contributed to the Royal Children's Hospital history *150 Years of Caring* (2021) and the Spoken Memories Project of the Australian Association of Social Workers, and worked with the University of Melbourne Social Work Alumni on a series of oral histories, 'Reflecting on Social Work Careers' (2021).